THE AMERICAN NON-DILEMMA

THE AMERICAN NON-DILEMMA

RACIAL INEQUALITY WITHOUT RACISM

Nancy DiTomaso

Russell Sage Foundation • New York

The Russell Sage Foundation

The Russell Sage Foundation, one of the oldest of America's general purpose foundations, was established in 1907 by Mrs. Margaret Olivia Sage for "the improvement of social and living conditions in the United States." The Foundation seeks to fulfill this mandate by fostering the development and dissemination of knowledge about the country's political, social, and economic problems. While the Foundation endeavors to assure the accuracy and objectivity of each book it publishes, the conclusions and interpretations in Russell Sage Foundation publications are those of the authors and not of the Foundation, its Trustees, or its staff. Publication by Russell Sage, therefore, does not imply Foundation endorsement.

Library of Congress Cataloging-in-Publication Data

DiTomaso, Nancy.
The American non-dilemma : racial inequality without racism / Nancy DiTomaso.
pages cm
Includes bibliographical references and index.
ISBN 978-0-87154-080-5 (pb : alk. paper)—ISBN 978-1-61044-789-8 (ebook)
1. African Americans—Civil rights. 2. African Americans—Economic conditions. 3. Equality—United States. 4. United States—Race relations. 5. Racism—United States. I. Title.
E185.61.D58 2013
305.896′073—dc23 2012048799

The paper used in this publication meets the minimum requirements of American National Standard for Information Sciences-Permanence of Paper for Printed Library Materials. ANSI Z39.48-1992.

Text design by Genna Patacsil.

RUSSELL SAGE FOUNDATION
112 East 64th Street, New York, New York 10065
10 9 8 7 6 5 4 3 2 1

Contents

Tables and Figures

About the Author

Nancy DiTomaso is vice dean for faculty and research and professor in the Department of Management and Global Business at Rutgers Business School–Newark and New Brunswick.

Acknowledgments

I want to thank many people for their help and support in the many years that this study has been in the making. I especially want to thank Eric Wanner and the Russell Sage Foundation for both financial support and encouragement in the development of this research, as well as for forbearance while I expanded the project. I am also extremely grateful for the wonderful year as a visiting scholar at the foundation.

The people who have read drafts of the proposal and various papers along the way are numerous, and I fear listing them because I will undoubtedly forget many who were generous with their time and insight. Rochelle Parks-Yancy and Corinne Post both provided invaluable assistance in the development and coding of the data, and Ann Smith worked on transcription, coding, and many other aspects of the data preparation and analysis. Their contributions are greatly appreciated. I also want to thank Robert Alford for guiding me through the development of the proposal in its many iterations and for helping me develop the original argument of the book. Unfortunately, Bob did not live to see the fruition of his mentoring, but I will always think of him as a dear friend and colleague.

I was fortunate to have an opportunity early on to talk about my research purpose with Michele Lamont, who shared with me the methodology that she used in several studies of race and class differences.[1] Her insights and encouragement were invaluable in the design of this study and in my thinking about how to collect meaningful data and work through its interpretation. Similarly, Jennifer Hochschild provided advice on the development of the study and talked with me about issues of methodology and data collection strategies. Both continued to be supportive as the project evolved. I am very grateful for their time and wise advice. In the process of completing the book, I was also fortunate to have two excellent anonymous reviewers who provided very detailed and helpful advice about revisions. The care with which they treated the assignment of reviewing and their very insightful suggestions were greatly appreciated. I was delighted to subsequently learn that the reviewers were Don Tomaskovic-Devey and Chris Tilly. I cannot thank them enough for providing just the direction I needed.

I also want to thank the following for their feedback and encouragement at various points along the way: Howard Aldrich, Barbara Bergmann, Marilynn Brewer, Emilio Castilla, Dalton Conley, Paul DiMaggio, John Dovidio, Anna Duran, Michael Emerson, Joe Feagin, Charles Gallagher, John Green, Patricia Gurin, Leonie Huddy, James Jackson, Heather Beth Johnson, Walton Johnson, James Kluegel, Karyn Lacy, Annette Lareau, Rhonda Levine, Frank Linnehan, Hazel Markus, Harvey Molotch, Christena Nippert-Eng, Fred Pincus, Jill Quadagno, Barbara Reskin, Tom Shapiro, Jim Sidanius, Christian Smith, Ryan Smith, Linda Brewster Stearns, Claude Steele, Stephen Steinberg, Marlie Wasserman, Rhys Williams, and Julia Wrigley.

I am grateful to Vanderbilt University, which allowed me to serve as a visiting scholar and provided me with access and space to do interviewing at the university during my time in Nashville. While there, I prevailed upon a longtime friend, Sharon Moss, who graciously allowed me to stay at her home while I was collecting data. She not only provided me with a place to stay but went out of her way to accommodate every need I had to further my research. During my stay in Ohio to do the interviews, personnel at both Malone College and Stark State College of Technology provided space and accommodations for me to do interviews. While in Ohio, I stayed with my parents, Betty and Cecil Claugus. They also gave me a great deal of assistance, including excusing me from a number of family gatherings, so that I could complete as many interviews as possible during the limited time I had to spend there. Unfortunately, both my mother and father died before they could see the finished product of my efforts with this book.

I also want to thank my family, who put up with many years of inconvenience while I was collecting data for and trying to write this book. My husband, Tom, and my children, Jessica and Alisa, made sacrifices so that I could work. Tom was left home alone and the kids were sent away to camp during the two summers I was away to do interviews. All were left alone during the year I spent as a visiting scholar at the Russell Sage Foundation. Fortunately, it seems we all got through it. I hope they feel that the outcome was worth the efforts to help.

My most sincere thanks, however, go to the people in New Jersey, Ohio, and Tennessee who agreed to be interviewed for this study, who welcomed me into their homes or met me at nearby universities or restaurants, and who shared with me the intimate details of their life histories and spent precious time with me away from their families and from work that they undoubtedly needed to be doing. The interviewees were gracious and thoughtful. They were cooperative and interested in the project that I was undertaking. Many said that they enjoyed the experience of thinking through their lives, and many clearly wanted to contribute to the book I was writing so that the views of people like them would be known and heard. While I am solely responsible for the way I have structured their stories and the interpretations that I have given to the views that they expressed to me, I hope that I am being faithful and honest to the stories they told me. My intent has been to be respectful of their lives and to present the interviewees with sympathy and understanding, even though I am addressing one of the most sensitive and easily misunderstood issues in American political culture. In the United States, rarely does one talk openly about racial issues, and few make their true feelings known to others or even, many times, to themselves. There is a strong incentive in American life to see ourselves as fair and decent people, and I hope to show that the interviewees who shared their stories with me, in fact, are fair and decent.

It is also the goal of this study, however, to try to understand how racial inequality gets reproduced, how people come to terms with those issues in their day-to-day experiences, and how they fit into the contemporary political landscape in which racial inequality has been in the background and yet is always relevant. To do so, I have needed to go beyond what people in my interviews told me and pay attention to what they actually said. I hope that I have done so respectfully and with gratitude in this book.

Prologue

GROWING up in a white, working-class family in the 1950s Midwest, I gave very little thought to and was rarely confronted with issues of racial inequality. Instead, I was interested in issues of class inequality and the future effects of economic changes on blue-collar workers. I have vague memories from high school of knowing that race was important, but probably like many others then and now, I thought that it did not have much to do with me. I watched with fear and concern as the civil rights movement unfolded on TV, and I noticed a strange sense of discomfort regarding the one or two African American kids who attended my large high school. Although I barely knew their names and never interacted with them, I was aware of a sense that somehow they were different when they walked down the hall, but I did not give it much thought. My concerns were about jobs, the economy, and, for myself, how to get a college education.

My parents, neither of whom had graduated from high school, were lucky members of the working class because they both had steelworker jobs and together they could make a decent living. In the 1950s, however, steelworkers were subject to periodic strikes, and I remember my parents' noticeable apprehension during those times and the focused look on my mother's face as she counted the dimes in the booklets she had been collecting for a rainy day when she would need them to make ends meet. I also remember knowing how different my life was from the lives of my relatives who did not make it into jobs in the steel factory. Some lived in abject poverty, sometimes in rural areas without running water, and almost always without steady jobs. It was quite clear to me even as a child that my life was different from the lives of my poorer relatives primarily because my parents belonged to a very strong union that made the company they worked for pay them decent wages. Interestingly, my parents did not necessarily see it that way. They had very little good to say about the union and a surprising degree of loyalty and gratitude to the company. They seemed to believe that the company was magnanimous and the union was corrupt, but they did follow closely and intently when negotiations were under way, and they knew to the penny what their jobs paid.

When I graduated from high school, my parents were proud that I was able to get a job as a secretary in the same steel company where they worked. They took it as a personal commendation of their good work records. Their highest aspirations for my brother and for other males in the family were for them to obtain jobs at this company, and my brother did so. He, however, went one step further and entered an apprenticeship in a skilled trade; my parents held only semiskilled jobs. At one time my mother, my father, my uncle, my brother, several cousins, and my brother-in-law all worked at the same company. After two years in my secretarial job at the company, during which time I attended college part-time in the evenings, I left to attend college full-time. My parents thought this was a foolish decision on my part. They insisted that I get documentation from the company indicating that I could return to my secretarial job at some point in the future if I wished to do so, since this company, like others that were the subject of bidding wages up during World War II, had developed a policy that once you left the company, you could never come back. Because there were few working-class jobs that paid such good wages and offered such good benefits, this policy was a significant threat to anyone who took the company for granted.

It was only after I left home to go to college full-time that I was confronted with civil rights as a social movement. I gradually learned more about racial inequality from my college classes. Then, of course, I got on board with others and became a strong proponent of civil rights and of redistributive policies to help the poor. As I took these ideas home, however, I confronted the resistance of my family, especially of my parents' generation, to such "highfalutin" ideas. In response, I heard of their dissatisfaction with "their" company hiring blacks into jobs like theirs, and I inevitably heard about how these blacks did not deserve such jobs or that they did not work hard enough. Race was not a usual topic of conversation in my family, but when raised as an issue, it was reacted to with dismay.

Such a response was doubly surprising, because when we moved to the "dream home" my parents were having built in 1964 (my last year in high school), it turned out that both the family next door and the one across the street were black. My parents were not pleased, but neither did they make an issue of it. Further, both my brother and my younger sister became best friends with the black kids who lived next door to us. My parents did not object, nor really have anything much to say about it, and they never objected when the kids were at or in our house. For years after, the family next door was welcomed at our family parties, and my relatives were very appreciative that, even though both we and they had moved away, members of this family attended the funerals of both of my parents.

Once I finished my undergraduate degree and went to graduate school, I moved into the world of the professional and managerial class, a world I found as alien to me as the issue of race had been in my family. I incurred many "identity crises," as I went between college and home and felt that I did not belong in either place. One of the most troubling issues in my graduate school experience was hearing my social science colleagues, on the one hand, making disparaging remarks about the racism of the white working class and, on the other, holding up the working class as the source of hope for progressive change. I felt that both issues were seriously misunderstood. Regarding the racism of the working class, I wished only that these students could understand the precariousness of unionized white workers' hold on stable lifestyles and the serious consequences for them of losing out on jobs like those at the steel company where my parents worked. Regarding the idea of the working class as progressives waiting in the wings for a social movement to mobilize them, I simply thought of my colleagues as exceedingly naive and disconnected from the working class that I knew, which was basically apolitical and mostly concerned with trying to move into and adopt a middle-class lifestyle. In more recent years, the working class members of my family, especially those in the generation after me, have been trying to maintain and hold on to middle-class status despite the disappearance of factory jobs like the ones my parents had held.

During graduate school, I was even more certain that my social science colleagues would not understand the extent to which I thought of their liberalism as a product of the good fortune of their class positions. From my view, they could afford to be generous because they did not directly compete with blacks for either housing or jobs. Although I had become deeply committed to the progressive policies of civil rights, equality, and justice, I did not see the working class that I knew as leading this movement. Indeed, most of the working-class people I knew rarely thought about, talked about, or involved themselves in politics, at least not beyond the local level. Doing so would have been very difficult at any rate. Most were working odd hours in factories that ran around the clock. Some were working more than one job, and many used the skills they had developed in the factory in an endless array of maintenance and home improvement jobs for themselves, their friends, or other family members, and some tried to use these skills to make additional money on the side. For everyone, time was precious and often in short supply. Although there were a lot of family get-togethers, there were few occasions that I can remember when my parents or family members involved themselves in community or civic affairs. In my environment, the only outside activities that were prevalent were the inevitable participation in church or sports and attendance at an occasional union meeting during contract talks when a strike was threatened. Family and work were the primary foci of the life I experienced in the working class.

In contrast to my family, however, I had been very involved in church and various evangelical religious groups, and this was the second reason I felt separated from my social science colleagues in graduate school. Church and faith had been essential parts of my core identity, and I continued to participate in church and religious groups into graduate school and beyond. My sense of justice and fairness was grounded in my religious beliefs, but few of those I knew to be involved in the social movements of the 1960s were churchgoers. While I strove to find a connection between my faith and my politics, I became increasingly uncomfortable in the kinds of churches where I had grown up, especially as these churches became increasingly politicized, but in a conservative, right-wing direction. As I became politically more liberal, two essential components of my background—religious evangelicals and the white working class—became increasingly conservative. Over time I found myself even more distanced from the life I had known, but I regularly returned home to visit my family, who always had been and remained very close—this was not a part of myself that I could leave behind. Hence, trying to understand these distinctions and how to bridge them became important intellectual and political goals.

In my professional life, I did research on inequality in several studies, including the influence of the working class in government ("theories of the state"); the role of unions in the public sector; and race, ethnic, and gender inequality in the Chicago labor force. As I moved from a sociology department to a business school in 1983, I took my interest in politics and inequality with me and fortuitously intersected with the growing interest among corporations in diversity in the labor force. This seemed like a perfect fit for my interests and new academic location. I began to do research and to teach courses on diversity in the labor force to master of business administration (MBA) students, and later to undergraduates, and I had the opportunity to be involved in groups that were trying to develop the field of diversity both in business school education and in corporate training.

For someone with a background in sociology, I found myself dissatisfied with the content of the training provided by diversity experts, both in the university and in corporations. Both groups tended to organize their discussion of diversity around the need to eliminate stereotypes and prejudice—that is, to combat racism. I found this approach to be wrongheaded. I thought the problem had more to do with the structures of inequality (such as access to jobs that pay a living wage) than with the personal prejudices of people in the workforce. In contrast to the typical approach used in business schools, I organized my courses on diversity around social science research on inequality in jobs, income, and education, rather than around prejudice and racism (or sexism). I found, however, that I had no more success (and possibly less) than those who talked about prejudice and stereotypes. In general I found, as others did, that corporate interest in and talk about race and diversity either puzzled whites who were forced to attend diversity training programs or, alternatively, assured them because they did not believe themselves to be prejudiced or to be someone who engaged in the use of stereotypes. But I also found that diversity training frequently made them mad and, not infrequently, resistant to the overall message regarding the value and benefits of diversity.

Such reactions emerged in a context that was puzzling to me but, on reflection, not unlike the images I had of my family growing up. I found that for my mostly white students (or corporate participants), race was not an especially salient issue. It was not something they thought about very often. If they did, they assumed it was about other people and not about them. And perhaps most importantly, I found that most students believed themselves to be part of the solution to racial inequality, not part of the problem. Most of the students in my classes fit a typical profile: everyone was nice, no one discriminated, everyone believed in equal opportunity and supported civil rights, but most everyone got irritated, if not mad, when the issue of affirmative action was raised. Hence, I asked myself a fundamental question, namely: *if there are no racists and no racism, then why is there still a problem with racial inequality?* It was through these observations and reflections on my own history that I came to conceptualize and develop this study. I specifically wanted to know how people like my students and my parents learned about and came to make sense of racial inequality; how they thought about their own life experiences with regard to it; and importantly, how they tapped into and used social resources that reproduced and reinforced the advantages they enjoyed as whites. Knowing how important access to jobs that paid a living wage was to my family, I knew that jobs would be a key theme in my interviews. And as I gained a broader perspective on the issues of racial inequality, I wanted specifically to understand why racial inequality was not more salient among white Americans, and specifically why it did not seem to create the kind of moral dilemma that Myrdal believed would lead to dramatic social change. Thus, I also wanted to understand how whites thought about racial inequality and their political engagement and commitments with regard to the politics of inequality.

To answer these important questions, I wanted to draw on research from sociology, political science, psychology, and history, because clearly dynamics from all of these fields come together in the lives of real people who develop ideas about how the world works, make decisions about what they want out of their lives, make choices from the array of social resources available to them, and out of their life experiences undertake political or social commitments that support or oppose change to existing social relations.

Some may object to my focusing on whites in this study, but in doing so, my framing is consistent with what Gunnar Myrdal said about his own study, namely:

> Although the Negro problem is a moral issue both to Negroes and to whites in America, we shall in this book have to give primary attention to what goes on in the minds of white Americans.… It became increasingly evident that little, if anything, could be scientifically explained in terms of the Negroes themselves.…
>
> All our attempts to reach scientific explanations of why the Negroes are what they are and why they live as they do have regularly led to determinants on the white side of the race line. (Myrdal 1944, lxxxiii)

Despite this keen insight, in *The American Dilemma* Myrdal focused instead on the lives and conditions of "Negroes" and not on what was happening with white Americans, as he said was required. With the assistance of a large staff of scholars, Myrdal's massive work outlined every aspect of life in the United States among American blacks, while giving very little attention to the "white side of the race line." In contrast, I do focus in this book on (non-Hispanic) whites, not only on their attitudes toward blacks (and other minorities) but also on their embeddedness within the social structure and the ways in which they use their social positions to access advantages for themselves and their families and friends. That is, I endeavor to explain how whites use social structure to gain and maintain racial advantage and how they construct meaning both about racial inequality and about themselves as whites in a world where whites, on average, are advantaged.

Some may also object to the primary focus in this book on the white-black divide. That is partly purposeful and partly pragmatic. Given the contrast I wanted to raise with Myrdal's book, it makes sense to concentrate primarily on white views of blacks rather than on minorities in general. Further, as was the case when Myrdal was writing, there is a special relevance to the relationship of whites to blacks, given the history of slavery and the civil rights movement.

According to Donald Kinder and Lynn Sanders (1996), no other issue divides Americans more. I do address issues with regard to Latinos and Asians in my discussions about immigration, but in the responses to various questions in the interview, it was clear that whites have a much more formed view of blacks than they do of Latinos or Asians. In addition to the substantive reasons for interviewing only non-Hispanic whites in this study, there are also practical reasons. Because I collected data through semistructured interviews and wanted a good representation in each region, each additional dimension to the interview base would have doubled the number of interviews needed. It was not possible to add that many more interviews to this study.

To get at the broad issues I want to address in this study, I undertook in-depth interviews that traced the life histories of the interviewees and asked specifically about education and jobs. In addition, I asked the interviewees how they thought about their lives and what factors led them to their current life outcomes. I also asked about their views on public policy issues and about their general outlook on issues regarding inequality. Given my background as someone who came from a white working-class family, who got involved in evangelical churches, and who then became upwardly mobile into a professional position and lived in an upper-middle-class suburb, I was familiar with the concerns addressed by the interviewees as I began to hear their life stories. Nearly everyone I talked to had access to some kind of social resources when looking for jobs. They used them readily, and they experienced life outcomes that were directly related to the kind of assistance they could derive from their social networks and their embeddedness in various kinds of communities.

Although the social resources available to some of the interviewees were so sparse that they were not able to provide much help, this was not the typical story, even among the working-class interviewees. Further, although some interviewees failed to avail themselves of the social resources at hand, or sometimes were not competent to use the social resources available to them, most of the interviewees had people within their social environments who could provide assistance, even when it was not sought, and sometimes even when it was actively resisted. Thus, the life outcomes of the white interviewees in my study were substantially improved because of their access to social resources from family, neighborhoods, schools, churches, and other social institutions with which they were engaged. This insight contributed to an important realization: almost all of the social science literature on race is organized around a framework of discrimination—cast, that is, in terms of the negative things that are done to blacks and other minorities—when it appears that much of the "action" in reproducing racial inequality comes in the form of advantages, that is, in the positive things that whites do for each other.

This insight resonates with my own life experiences. For example, in the process of writing this book, I became aware of how much effort, as a white, middle-class mother, I have had to make to keep my children on track (especially given how much time I had to spend away from them). Gaining advantage and having access to favor and to social resources that can provide advantages often take place in the context of natural tendencies for slacking, self-doubt, or immediate gratification, and advantages often accrue even against resistance and following the consequences of poor choices. When these kinds of behaviors are evident among blacks, we call them "oppositional culture," or even more bizarrely, we talk about the "fear of acting white," yet based on my observations of upper-middle-class white teenagers, acting white may well include episodes of irresponsibility, inattention, and screwing up. In this context, access to social resources can make up for many injudicious decisions made by white teenagers, often with a great deal of worry and effort on the part of parents who themselves got beyond similar periods in their own youth because of the social resources on which they could draw from family and neighborhoods (Ogbu 1978; Fordham 1996).[1] Growing up in America takes different pathways for white versus black youths (or others) because the greater social resources available to whites make it easier to provide second chances, extra options, and the means to recover from unfortunate decisions. White teenagers are more likely to get the benefit of the doubt and to experience officials in various institutions looking the other way when they transgress, and many can count on rescue when things do not go well. Black teenagers are often unable to count on this kind of protection and direction. I find in this study that such accommodations and special privileges from family, friends, and acquaintances continue into adulthood for whites in the United States—and indeed, throughout their careers.

Although access to social resources and the use of advantage for getting ahead were evident for almost all of the interviewees in this study, not all whites have access to the same kinds of advantages, nor do they all have the same outcomes when attempting to use social resources. Hence, when the interviewees in this study talked about their life experiences and their views of public policies that address issues of inequality and fairness, they did not sound similar. Instead, several distinct groups among the interviewees stood out that seemed to reflect differences in how well they were doing economically, their political views, and their interest in, engagement with, and concern about inequality. Thus, it was evident that to answer the questions I had posed about how whites come to understand racial inequality and about the relative advantages that whites enjoy, I had to understand the relationship of these various groups of interviewees to each other, and I had to place them in the contemporary political landscape of post–civil rights politics. I explain in the introduction how I categorized the different groups that emerged among the interviewees. Because they reflect the shifting political landscape in the United States, delving into their thinking about race and class inequality presents an opportunity for insight regarding current political changes in the country. The views expressed by the interviewees in this study are relevant, despite changes both nationally and internationally since the original interviews, because political attitudes in the population have remained fairly consistent over several decades across most major political issues (Kohut 2009), even as party identification has shifted and even though the political dynamics among leaders in the two major political parties have become increasingly hostile.

Despite the continued and extensive attention to issues regarding racial inequality in this country, I believe that our existing theoretical frameworks have often obscured rather than enlightened our understanding and that they have contributed to the contradictions represented by racial inequality in the contemporary United States: the primary focus on discrimination as an explanation for racial inequality rather than attention to the favoritism that takes place among whites through opportunity hoarding and the use of social capital; the dueling empirical evidence offered about whether the country is primarily conservative or liberal or neither; and the confused understanding of the role of race, class, and culture in these trends. I believe that the analysis in this study can explain why we have made less progress than all of us had hoped when the civil rights movement finally brought formal protection against discrimination, but not substantive protection against the advantages that accrue to whites.

My interpretation of the political landscape and my understanding of the main themes that need to be addressed to understand racial inequality have had to evolve as history has outrun the original context of my research. I believe, however, that the issues that I am addressing are fundamental in the structure of U.S. politics and culture and thus have not changed, despite the changing political environment of the last several years. We still frame racial inequality through a lens of discrimination rather than advantage. We still misunderstand and are surprised by our own politics. And we still misunderstand, I believe, the role of various groups of whites in post–civil rights politics. Understanding these issues and their continued importance are the main goals for this book.

Chapter 1

Introduction: Racial Inequality Without Racism

> The . . . great wars of this country have been fought for the ideals of liberty and equality. . . . [Now] the protection of the two oceans is gone forever . . . there is no way back. America is irredeemably in world politics. . . . [But] the treatment of the Negro is America's greatest and most conspicuous scandal. . . . America feels itself to be humanity in miniature. When in this crucial time the international leadership passes to America, the great reason for hope is that this country has a national experience of uniting racial and cultural diversities and a national theory, if not a consistent practice, of freedom and equality. . . .
>
> People want to be rational, and they want to feel that they are good and righteous. They want to have the society they live in, and their behavior in this society, explained and justified to their conscience.
>
> —Gunnar Myrdal, *An American Dilemma* (1944, 997, 1018–19, 20, 21, 1003)

WHEN Gunnar Myrdal wrote those words in the early 1940s, the United States was in the midst of World War II and the outcome was not yet known.[1] One of the central themes of Myrdal's famous book *An American Dilemma* (1944) was that if the United States emerged successfully from the war, it would not be able to assume a credible leadership position in world politics if it did not resolve the problem posed by American racial inequality. Myrdal argued that racial inequality caused "trouble" for white Americans, because it was "something difficult to settle and equally difficult to leave alone," despite the efforts of most whites to remove themselves from it or to suppress attention to it (Myrdal 1944, lxxvii). In Myrdal's analysis, racial inequality caused a moral dilemma for white Americans because the American creed of "liberty, equality, justice, and fair opportunity" for all was incompatible with the reality of racial inequality (lxxx). As such, he argued, it was becoming increasingly difficult for whites to avoid the issue, both because the circumstances that were emerging during World War II (and would intensify in its aftermath) made it politically costly on the international stage for the United States to allow such stark racial oppression at home and because political activists were advocating for change and bringing the issue to the fore on the domestic front (1004–10, 15–21). Myrdal argued that whites were conflicted within themselves about racial inequality and that this internal conflict, combined with the broader social and political conflict wrought by national and international circumstances, would ultimately lead to dramatic social change as a result of "political decision and public regulation," which he called "social engineering" (1022–24). He did not, however, think this would occur automatically or easily.

Although *An American Dilemma* was published in 1944, the introduction and conclusion to Myrdal's book sound amazingly contemporary and prescient. Now, as was true then, few subjects generate as much conflict in the U.S. political environment as race relations. Despite all that has transpired since the book was published, we still do not have a good understanding of racial inequality in the United States. As Myrdal (1944, 27) said:

> Wandering around the stacks of a good American library, one is amazed at the huge amount of printed material on the Negro problem. A really complete bibliography would run up to several hundred thousand titles. Nobody has ever mastered this material exhaustively, and probably nobody ever will. The intellectual energy spent on the Negro problem in America should, if concentrated in a single direction, have moved mountains.[2]

Depending on how one looks at the civil rights movement, one might claim that mountains *have* been moved. Racial inequality still exists, however, and it remains a troubling issue in the American psyche and political landscape. I believe that to make progress in understanding the reasons why and explain why the American dilemma that Myrdal identified did not lead to the social change that he envisioned, one has to look in a new way at race relations and racial inequality. I hope to do that in this book by explaining what I call the "American non-dilemma": why do white Americans not seem to experience ongoing racial inequality as the kind of moral dilemma that Myrdal anticipated? Troubled though they may be by issues of race, most white Americans are not riven by moral guilt about racial inequality. As Jennifer Hochschild (1995, 55–71) notes, most whites do not "understand what the fuss is about." This book explains why white Americans do not view racial inequality as a moral dilemma—indeed, why whites never think much about race at all.

Racial issues come into play for many whites, however, when they try to protect themselves from the uncertainties of the job market. In their efforts to hoard opportunities and to draw on social resources to get an inside edge in obtaining good jobs, whites have often confronted the tension between labor rights (broadly defined) and civil rights. I am using the term "labor rights" here to refer to the efforts by whites to protect themselves from the competition of the labor market—for example, by taking wages out of competition and hoarding job opportunities through the exchange of social capital. Such labor rights often conflict with the goals of the civil rights agenda to open up to blacks and other minorities those jobs that had been previously available primarily to whites. As such, most whites do not see their interests as being aligned with those of blacks (or other minorities), and there is often conflict among groups of whites who are in different economic circumstances and on different sides of the political spectrum about policies intended to open up job opportunities to blacks and other minorities. By design, civil rights policies are intended to affect the distribution of opportunities available to whites and blacks. Thus, as the majority among voters, whites are primary players in the conflict over such civil rights policies.

Racial Inequality Without Racism

One of the main arguments of this book is that we have been framing racial issues in ways that keep us from understanding what creates and reproduces racial inequality. Specifically, racial inequality is most often assumed to be the result of racism or discrimination, and providing equal opportunity within a context of individual effort and achievement has been offered as the primary solution to racial problems. I argue, instead, that framing racial issues through a lens of racism, equal opportunity, and individualism contributes to the inability of most whites to see the nature of their own participation in the creation and reproduction of racial inequality. Whites assume that other people are racists, but not them. They assume that equal opportunity embodies fairness, but they live lives of advantage—that is, of unequal opportunity. And their commitment to individualist explanations for inequality ignores the group-based nature of their search for advantage and the extent of their efforts to use social resources, including economic, social, and cultural capital, to gain advantage. Table 1.1 summarizes the dynamics that enable racial inequality to be reproduced without racism.

Another main objective of the book is to go beyond the issue of white racial attitudes to address Myrdal's contention that white engagement in political action could ameliorate the condition of blacks and create greater racial equality. Because I argue that there is an American non-dilemma and that whites do not feel especially guilty about or responsi-

Table 1.1 The Three-Part Process by Which Racial Inequality Is Reproduced Without Racism

White Explanations for Racial Inequality	Whites' Views of Themselves	Hidden Dynamics Behind the Reproduction of Racial Inequality
Prejudiced (racist) people	Committed to color-blindness	Segregated neighborhoods, schools, and workplaces
Discrimination (by racist people)	Committed to equal opportunity	Lives of unequal opportunity or advantage
Lack of effort, responsibility, or hope among blacks	Belief in their own individual effort, hard work, and talent	Group basis of social, cultural, and financial resources that provide unearned advantages

Bottom line: The search for "racists" provides legitimacy or "cover" for the dynamics of power and makes possible the opportunity hoarding that enables whites to receive advantages or privileges without being racists.

Source: Author's compilation.

ble for racial inequality, the nature of their political engagement is likely to be quite different from what Myrdal had hoped and anticipated. Racial issues have pervaded U.S. politics, even though, as Myrdal argued, many have tried to ignore them or suppress attention to them. Whites, however, were important participants in the civil rights movement, and they have continued to be important participants in post–civil rights politics. There is a gap, however, between principle and policy with regard to racial issues, and this gap contributes to an ongoing contest for white support in post–civil rights political campaigns. Each political party has endeavored to mobilize various groups of white voters, sometimes by using racially coded appeals in the guise of nonracial issues and sometimes by trying to change the subject so that the contest over race is not evident. Neither political party in the post–civil rights period has been successful in using explicitly racist appeals. Understanding these dynamics, and especially the interconnection between white racial attitudes and the role of various groups of whites in post–civil rights politics, should also help us understand the American non-dilemma.

The tension between what I am calling labor rights and civil rights can be seen in the well-documented gap between white acceptance of equal opportunity in principle but opposition to race-targeted policies, such as affirmative action, busing, and welfare, that are intended to enhance opportunities (Bobo et al. 2012). Although only a small percentage of whites now give prejudiced responses to survey questions, there continues to be a much larger percentage of whites who are opposed to the public policies that were enacted as part of the civil rights movement to bring about greater equality between blacks and whites. Lawrence Bobo and his colleagues (2009) trace the profile of racial attitudes over time and find that, from the 1950s on, whites became more accepting of integration in principle and that, as early as 1972, support for integration on several dimensions was normative among whites. They also document, however, that there has never been strong white support for race-targeted policies such as affirmative action and there has been limited acceptance of government action to enact other policies on behalf of blacks. Howard Schuman and his colleagues (1997) call this the "principle-implementation gap," others the "principle-policy gap" (see, for example, Jackman and Muha 1984; Jackman 1994; Sears 1988b; Sears, Sidanius, and Bobo 2000).

Racism and Discrimination Versus Opportunity Hoarding and Social Capital

There are three widely discussed explanations for the principle-policy gap: (1) that whites are "really" racists, despite their nonprejudiced responses on surveys, but that racism has taken a new, more symbolic form; (2) that whites give lip service to equality but defend group dominance; or (3) that when whites reject policies such as affirmative action, they are simply reflecting the American political values of hard work and effort.[3] Theories of "symbolic racism" (also called "new racism," "modern racism," or "racial resentment") assume that whites' true attitudes are reflected in their opposition to actually doing something to end racial inequality rather than in their survey responses about prejudice. "Aversive racism," "everyday racism," "laissez-faire racism," and "colorblind racism" are similar concepts (Blumer 1958; Bobo 1999). All of these conceptions argue similarly that despite the attitudes that whites express on surveys about prejudice, they really hold racist views but either will not admit it, do not know it, or perhaps are fooling themselves.[4]

The social dominance explanation for white racial attitudes gives less attention to attitudinal or cognitive origins of antiblack views and instead argues that the structural relationships between whites and blacks (and other racial-ethnic minorities) are the source of racial inequality. Bobo, for example, argues that whites simply believe that they should hold positions of dominance in relationship to blacks (Blumer 1958; Bobo 1999). Sidanius and his colleagues argue that there is an attitudinal component, which they call a "social dominance orientation," associated with the structural relationships among groups (Pratto et al. 1994; Sidanius and Pratto 1999). In contrast to the new racism and social dominance explanations for the principle-policy gap, Paul Sniderman and his colleagues argue that it is not racism that is the source of opposition to race-targeted policies, but rather whites' belief that blacks violate key principles of American values about the appropriate role of government and the requirements for responsibility and effort on the part of individuals (Sniderman and Carmines 1996, 1997).

In contrast to each of these explanations for white racial attitudes, I argue that one of the most important privileges of being white in the United States is not having to be racist in order to enjoy racial advantage. Rather than racism or discrimination being the primary mechanisms by which racial inequality is reproduced, I argue that it is the acts of favoritism that whites show to each other (through opportunity hoarding and the exchange of social capital) that contribute most to continued racial inequality. Indeed, racial inequality in the post–civil rights period requires that whites not see themselves as racists. As Mary Jackman notes, long-term inequality between groups must be legitimated, and doing so requires that overt conflict be suppressed or hidden. In fact, Jackman argues, whites are able to gain privileges "without active participation" and "hidden from their view" (Jackman 1994, 137). In this conception, it is not in the interests of whites either cognitively or politically to call attention to the privileges they may receive. Whites therefore cannot be openly hostile toward blacks, nor call attention to the political, economic, or status privileges that whites enjoy, without raising questions that might undermine the legitimacy of the stratification system and, indeed, cause the type of moral dilemma that Myrdal assumed.

Thus, it is in the interests of whites not to have a clear picture of the degree of racial inequality and even to misunderstand or misrepresent the extent to which whites, as a group, are privileged. In other words, the basis of racial inequality is cognitively hidden even from whites themselves. Interestingly, Myrdal raised similar issues in the 1940s. He argued that the "remarkable lack of correct information about the Negroes and their living conditions" among whites allowed whites what he termed the "convenience of ignorance" (Myrdal 1944, 40). Charles Mills (1997) argues that the "racial contract" creates for whites an "epistemology of ignorance" that makes it difficult for them to understand their participation in the reproduction of racial inequality.

I argue in this book that it is the focus on racism itself that enables whites to remove themselves from the conversation about race. That is, the emphasis given to racism in popular culture, public policy, and the academic literature enables whites to believe that race is not about them. The nature of white privilege, however, is that most of the time whites do not have to succumb to personal prejudice or engage in negative actions toward racial minorities in order to enjoy the privileges of being white. Because whites have access to valuable community resources and get both preference and the benefit of the doubt in many areas of their lives, they can count on racial privilege without having to fight for it or even defend it much of the time. These privileges are partly built into social institutions, but they also infuse whites' everyday interactions. These privileges not only constitute an invisible knapsack that whites carry around, filled with institutional social resources to use whenever necessary (McIntosh 1988), but also provide a cognitive experience of goodwill and affective preference that allows whites to feel confident, secure, and capable as they make decisions and encounter choices throughout their lives (Berger, Cohen, and Zelditch 1972; Brewer 1998; Hogg 2001; Jost and Elsbach 2001; Pettigrew 1979; Ridgeway 2001).

Whites thus attribute the problems of racial inequality to "those racists" (often defined in terms of prejudiced people who are still holding on to hostility toward blacks or other nonwhites). Most whites, however, believe themselves to be committed to color-blindness (that is, to the view that skin color does not or should not matter). They do not see themselves as racists or as prejudiced people. Thus, when problems of racial inequality are framed in terms of racism (whether new, old, or refashioned), whites can ignore the fact that most whites exchange favors with each other that provide an inside edge within the context of segregated communities, segregated schools and churches, and often segregated workplaces. Because racial inequality is defined in terms of racism (which most often is thought of in terms of intentional and personal prejudice), most whites can absolve themselves of any moral guilt about race.

Most whites conceive of racism as people who harbor ill will toward nonwhites doing bad things to them. As Linda Hamilton Krieger (1998) argues, this conception of discrimination is embedded in the way the civil rights laws have been written, and it is inherent in the meaning given to "racism" when we are told that whites at some fundamental level are "really" racist:

> The standard discrimination schema might be encapsulated as follows: discrimination occurs when a sexist, racist, or otherwise bigoted person makes decisions about members of a targeted group. Because of his negative feelings towards or beliefs about members of the disfavored group, the discriminator purposefully treats them unfairly. His negative feelings are likely to be expressed in racist or sexist comments. Even if the discriminator does not express these negative feelings, he knows of them and would admit them were he being honest. The kind of prejudice that leads to discrimination functions like a personality trait: it is something that exists inside the discriminator. It is relatively stable and expresses itself consistently over time and across different situations. (Krieger 1998, 1311)

To whites, "those racists" means others, not themselves. Using a framework of discrimination, most whites can examine their day-to-day experiences and feel confident that they have done nothing specifically harmful to blacks (or other nonwhites). As long as whites can attribute the problems of race to "those racists" and exclude themselves from that category, then they can easily hold on to this conception of themselves and think of racial issues as something that is about others but not about them. Given this, there is no moral crisis that moves whites toward political action to change the status quo. Instead, whites in the United States in the post–civil rights period feel morally comfortable and justified with regard to racial issues. Myrdal (1944, 37) observed even in the 1940s that there was racial inequality without racism:

> When talking about the Negro problem, everybody—not only intellectual liberals—is thus anxious to locate race prejudice outside of himself. The impersonal "public opinion" or "community feelings" are held responsible. The whites practically never discuss the issue in terms of "I" or "we" but always in terms of "they.". . . One can go around for weeks talking to white people in all walks of life and constantly hear about [racism] . . . yet seldom meeting a person who actually identifies himself with it.

Myrdal (1944, 1010) also believed that there was a principle-policy gap: "The social paradox in the North is exactly this, that almost everyone is against discrimination in general, but at the same time, almost everybody practices discrimination in his own personal affairs." Rather than framing this gap in terms of discrimination, however, I would rephrase Myrdal's statement in terms of the advantages that whites share with each other: "The social paradox in the United States is exactly this, that almost everyone says they support equal opportunity, but at the same time, almost everybody instead seeks unequal opportunity (that is, advantage) and relies on special favors for getting ahead—and almost everybody thinks they got ahead through individual effort." I argue that it is not discrimination that everyone practices in the post–civil rights period, but rather the hoarding of opportunities through the use of social capital and other social resources that whites share with each other (Tilly 1998). Whites seek out—and many of them find—ways to protect themselves from the increasing volatility of markets. They can do so, most of the time, without actively doing bad things to racial minorities. Instead, they do good things for each other, and the net result is the perpetuation of white privilege in an environment of racial liberalism. Because whites are better positioned as a group to avail themselves of social resources, they are able to benefit from racial inequality, even without racism. Further, because the processes by which whites help other whites are invisible or hidden from their view, whites feel no moral dilemma regarding their actions and fail to see how they might have contributed to the reproduction of racial inequality.

Equal Opportunity Versus Advantage

I also argue that the principle-policy gap is accompanied by a gap between a belief in equal opportunity as the primary solution to racial inequality and the lives of unequal opportunity enjoyed by most whites in the United States. That is, while most whites wholeheartedly affirm equal opportunity as a principle, they live lives of unequal opportunity—of advantage—to the extent that they can do so. Whites engage in both opportunity hoarding (passing along access to good jobs to their friends and family members) and the exchange of social, cultural, and financial capital among those in the family or community. Advantage might take the form of financial help from families and communities (for example, paying for college tuition or getting help with the purchase of a house), but it often takes the form of social capital such as help from networks of family, friends, and acquaintances in getting a job that pays a family wage (for example, vouching for someone, recommending a person for a job, providing valuable "inside" information about how to take tests or present oneself for the job, and, sometimes, actually hiring someone from one's network).

This does not, of course, mean that whites' actions and efforts are unnecessary because such privileges will always be available, no matter what. Indeed, for most people, including whites, there is a level of uncertainty about life outcomes that inherently requires them to strive to achieve and make their best effort. This is more the case for some than for others, and the gap between the lives of those with ready financial and social resources and those who live in resource-scarce environments is part of what makes some whites more determined than others to protect the boundaries of white privilege through conservative and increasingly hostile political behavior. But for most whites in the United States, there is usually a floor to their downward mobility and a number of paths they can take toward social stability and a "decent" life that will enable them to settle into a middle-class lifestyle by their midtwenties.

A paradox here—that nobody makes it on their own, but nobody makes it without their own effort either—provides a convenient explanation that makes it easy to forget the help one has received. As this paradox works itself out cognitively in the lives of people for whom social resources are available (for example, when they make the attribution error of attributing their success to their own efforts and talents rather than to the social context or circumstances in which they live), it results in self-esteem, self-confidence, and self-justification. What is surprising about this dynamic is not how many people rely on the use of social resources to "get ahead" in their lives, but how few of them recognize that social resources were their route to their success.

In my analysis, it is important to recognize that social resources are group-based, not individually based. There are ties that develop within communities, within residential neighborhoods, within school districts, through churches, among friends, and through other social connections, but because of the segregation of our communities and our places of employment, most social resources are passed from one person to another, within homogeneous groups, to people who are in a very real sense "like me." Importantly, advantage in this context is unearned. It does not accrue to those who demonstrate merit—many people gain access to advantages before they do so—but instead is the outcome of unequal opportunities that have been reserved for family members, friends, or acquaintances. These opportunities are passed along whether deserved or not and are often expropriated from companies that tout their commitment to being an "equal opportunity employer." This happens in all types of organizations, whether civil service, public-sector or private-sector, small or large. Opportunity hoarding and access to social capital provide their beneficiaries with an inside edge—the edge of whiteness.

Further, the social and financial resources upon which the whites in this study could draw came primarily from the accumulated resources of the generations before them. Because their parents, uncles or aunts, and friends and neighbors were able to protect themselves from the market through unionization, licensing, or tenure, these relatives and friends were able to accumulate wealth and pass it along to their children and friends (Conley 1999; Keister and Moller 2000; Oliver and Shapiro 1995). Most of the interviewees, however, thought of family resources as the result of their own hard work, effort, and motivation, not as the result of opportunity hoarding, insider access to jobs, and the consequent ability to accumulate family wealth. Previous generations of these interviewees' families had had access to jobs in unionized workplaces, in the public sector, or in small companies or large corporations that kept blacks out; to schools that excluded blacks; and to neighborhoods where blacks could not purchase homes. Nevertheless, whites in the study translated the privileges of exclusion manifested in the present as more a matter of personal character and morality than as the outcome of structural advantage.

It is certainly possible that whites would offer information, influence, or opportunity to blacks and other minorities, but most whites do not interact with minorities, attend school with them, work with them in similar kinds of jobs, or think of them when social exchanges take place. Nonwhites may endeavor to hoard opportunities or to exchange social capital among themselves, but their relatively less favorable structural positions in the economy make them less effective in doing so or make the effects of their efforts less stable. The social resources available to nonwhites are often less advantageous than those available to whites, the effects of using them are more likely to be interrupted or reversed, and once interrupted these resources are harder to recapture (Falcon and Melendez 2001). Although ethnic enclaves may be thought to provide the same sorts of advantages for members of minority groups, it is illustrative of the larger point that these "enclaves" must be set apart in order for ethnic minorities to gain preference; moreover, many of the relationships within ethnic enclaves are more like exploitation than privilege (Portes 1998; Portes and Landolt 1996; Portes and Rumbaut 1996). These are often captured workforces with limited and far fewer options outside of such enclaves than the privileged workforces that gain benefits while keeping others out.

So, while everyone might do it if they could, whites in the United States have been able to maintain structural advantages and reproduce racial inequality in their favor by hoarding opportunities, exchanging social resources within their own communities and neighborhoods, and maintaining a legitimating myth of individualism and self-determination to describe these efforts that they themselves know to be at best only part of the story (Falcon and Melendez 2001; Kluegel and Smith 1986; Sidanius and Pratto 1999). Further, when whites provide social resources by helping people in their neighborhoods or their communities—that is, people who are like them—they do not think of these positive actions toward other whites as contributing to racial inequality. Instead, they simply think of themselves as good citizens. And they believe themselves to be committed to equal opportunity as the standard of fairness. Whites say that "everyone deserves a chance," that "no one should be discriminated against," and that "what's fair is that everyone has an equal opportunity to be hired," but that is not how they live their lives. Indeed, the majority of the respondents in this study had obtained the majority of the jobs they had held in their lives by having an inside edge. Whether it made a lot of difference or only a little, it is quite likely that they were given the benefit of the doubt or offered a chance to "get in the door" and then to prove themselves, or perhaps they were extended second or third chances despite errors or misdirection. These whites did not, however, recognize the extent to which they had sought unequal opportunity by hoarding opportunities and using advantages.

Individualism Versus Group-Based Advantage

Despite the networks of influence that provide whites with access to social resources, there is a strong emphasis on individualism in U.S. culture that is quite real among whites and nonwhites alike. Whites hold to an atomistic view of the world that sees outcomes as the result of the decisions of individual people. The ideology of individualism in U.S. culture hides from whites the group-based nature of their advantage or privilege. When recounting their life stories, the interviewees thought about how hard they had worked, how uncertain had been the outcomes, and how necessary it had been to make a constant and persistent effort to stay "ahead." Almost all portrayed themselves as good workers, good neighbors, and responsible family members. Given the strong emphasis on individualism in U.S. culture, it is not surprising that many Americans are not especially egalitarian in their views. They believe that effort should be rewarded, even if that leads to substantial inequality. Indeed, a number of respondents in this study were quite suspicious of the idea of economic equality.

There is another paradox embodied in the views held by whites, namely, that they have to both know and not know how privilege works. Although the group-based nature of whites' advantages is invisible to them and hidden from their view, whites have to know how to access and use advantages, and they have to teach those skills to their children. Hence, they have to be sufficiently aware of how advantage works to use it successfully in daily interactions, but they have to keep that knowledge below the surface of their active consciousness and leave it unacknowledged. Otherwise, whites would have to confront issues of conflict about race—that is, the moral dilemma for which Myrdal had hoped. This contradiction is evident when we teach our kids about the importance of knowing the right people, but then tell them that their efforts and talents are all that count. Career guidance manuals tout the importance of networking, and professional organizations and even school systems teach people how to develop, foster, use, and rely on social networks. But when we explain achievement to others, the role played by networking often fades into the background as we highlight effort, talent, and credentials instead. Thus, when whites in our study recounted their life histories, they emphasized their personal effort and talent (or sometimes their flexibility or persistence when talent was not so evident), but they did not emphasize and barely mentioned the structural advantages or the social resources that provided them with unearned privileges and the means for getting ahead—meaning, literally, doing better than others. Even the small proportion of interviewees who adopted a more structuralist interpretation of poverty and inequality drew on social capital to improve their job situations but also attributed their success, as others did, to their individual capabilities and motivation. All of the groups in this study, therefore, sought access to social capital and engaged in opportunity hoarding as the means to achieve their life goals.

Since whites apply individualist explanations to their own lives, it obviously makes sense that they would apply it to the lives of blacks as well; hence, whites explain racial inequality, not in terms of their own racism or privilege, but as the failure of blacks as individuals to try hard enough, to be persistent, and to have "hope." Whites believe that what blacks themselves do, not what whites do to them, is the main source of racial inequality. And for many whites, this view of blacks itself takes on a moral dimension, because many whites feel that blacks either do not share the moral principles by which whites live their lives or that they violate those principles. In this regard, the explanation of white views outlined by Sniderman and his colleagues is consistent with how some whites view racial issues (Sniderman and Carmines 1997; Sniderman and Piazza 1993).

Thus, the search for racists, the reliance on equal opportunity as the standard of fairness, and the firm belief in the rewards of individual effort and talent all come together to assure whites that they deserve what they have achieved in their lives and that blacks could have the same outcomes if they would just "do it the way I did." From this view, there is no moral dilemma regarding egalitarian values and racial inequality because there is an assumption that people are responsible for their own life outcomes and can achieve anything they want if they just put their minds to it, make the necessary effort, and do not give up. That whites do not always do this themselves to get to where they are in their lives does not constitute hypocrisy as such, because the dynamics undergirding their own life outcomes are invisible to them. Most do not see the structures of segregation, the processes by which unequal opportunity is hoarded and passed along to friends and family, or the group-based nature of the advantages that whites pass along to other whites.

On the contrary, most whites in the post–civil rights United States see themselves as part of the solution rather than part of the problem. They believe themselves to be fair and decent people who reject prejudice and who do not discriminate. They are dismayed that some "stupid" people are still holding on to old prejudices. And they believe that opportunity exists for anyone who tries hard enough. They claim that the "best people" should get into schools, get jobs, and get rewarded, and often they are truly perplexed and confused that so many years after the active days of the civil rights movement there are still so many people who believe that race serves as a barrier in the United States. As Hochschild (1995) says, they do not understand the "fuss."

The Role of Whites in Racial Politics

Although the country as a whole moved toward consensus in support of civil rights in principle, it did not move toward consensus regarding the implementation of civil rights policies (Bobo et al. 2009). Perhaps it is precisely because support for civil rights in principle became normative in the country that civil rights policies, like the New Deal, have been a continual target of political movements to undermine or turn back the gains won by the civil rights movement. Civil rights policies, from school desegregation, busing, and welfare to affirmative action, have been constant sources of political conflict and legal challenge. Understanding these dynamics is also central to my argument. Myrdal's analysis of the American dilemma was a political argument that admonished whites, especially in the North, to support political change. Thus, to understand why racial inequality in the United States does not create a moral dilemma for whites, we have to understand the political role of whites in the post–civil rights period, especially with regard to inequality, the role of government in providing resources and regulation to encourage racial equality, and the response to policies closely aligned with racial politics like affirmative action.

The conflict over such policies has contributed to a transformation of the political parties in the United States and to a continued unsettledness about what civil rights should mean, what policies should be provided, who should provide them, and to whom policies should be targeted. The competition for the white vote has been closely tied up with the struggle over civil rights, and the Democratic Party has increasingly become the party of civil rights and the Republican Party the party of anti–civil rights. Party differences have often been especially sharp with regard to civil rights and antipoverty policies. Although there clearly has been improvement on a number of fronts for blacks in the United States, there has also been ambiguity about the extent, shape, and implications of the changes that have occurred. For example, the civil rights movement contributed to a growing black middle class—there are now substantially more blacks in managerial and professional jobs than in the past—but blacks have continued to be underrepresented in almost all such jobs, especially in the private sector. Further, the growth of a black middle class has been coincident with a growing level of unemployment among blacks who have no more than a high school degree, the expansion of welfare, and the incarceration of young black men (Braddock and McPartland 1987; Collins 1989; Conley 1999; Cose 1993; Cotton 1988; DiTomaso and Smith 1996; Farley 1984, 1999; Hacker 1992; Hochschild 1995; Holzer 1994; Jaynes and Williams 1989; Jencks 1992; Kirschenman and Neckerman 1991a; Kluegel 1985; Kozol 1991; Steinberg 1995; Thernstrom and Thernstrom 1997; Waldinger 1996; Wilson 1996). The gains that blacks made as a result of the civil rights movement have been counterbalanced by resistance from various groups to government implementation of civil rights legislation. In this context, the two major political parties have competed for the support of various groups of white voters in their efforts to form a winning coalition and, even more importantly, to gain a permanent majority.

Race, however, usually plays in the background, often implicitly framing political issues but rarely being used explicitly and openly, even in the 2008 election when Barack Obama was running for president. Tali Mendelberg (2001), for example, argues that political campaigns have frequently used race to frame differences between the parties and to prime racial resentment in white voters, but she finds that such race-baiting has been successful only as long as the racial dimension of the framing remains implicit rather than explicit. In other words, as long as white voters do not recognize the racial component of the message, racially coded appeals can have a powerful effect on eliciting voter support (Gaertner and Dovidio 1986), but once the racial dimension is made explicit, then whites are more likely to conform to the norm of racial equality and resist responding on the basis of the racial coding. Thus, in a sense there is a "new race relations" in the United States, if not a "new racism," and this new race relations has reshaped politics, but in a way that is hidden from view and often masked by the more explicit framing given to political issues.

Racial issues underlie much of the political dynamics in the United States even though racial issues are not especially salient for whites, even though support for civil rights in principle has become normative among whites, and even though explicit racial appeals in U.S. politics are increasingly unacceptable. Whites' continued opposition to government action to implement civil rights policies allows such policies to serve as wedge issues in the competition between the political parties for white votes. Although often masked in the guise of other issues, racial politics still drives white political attitudes and behavior, especially if whites believe that civil rights policies will affect their ability to hoard opportunities or to exchange the social capital that helps them protect themselves from market competition.

The two major political parties have competed especially for four groups of white voters: religious conservatives, who have become the base of the Republican Party; the white working class, especially that segment of the class who angrily believe that liberal social policies have undermined their access to good jobs; professionals, who by class should be aligned with the Republican Party but who have reacted negatively to the prominence of religious conservatives in the party and so have moved to the Democratic Party; and "independents," who are often thought of as swing voters because of their weaker attachment to either party. These groups are all represented in various ways by the interviewees in this study. Thus, in my analysis I explore the political views of the various groups of interviewees with regard to inequality, the role of government, and policies associated with racial politics, including taxes, welfare, and affirmative action.

Myrdal believed that the American dilemma would lead whites to support political change; I show why the American non-dilemma makes whites uncertain allies in the fight against racial inequality. Indeed, in many cases, white voters are mobilized against government policies that would affect the opportunities available to whites and blacks. I argue that the structural position of the interviewees with regard to how the civil rights movement affected their ability to hoard opportunities and draw on social capital influences their political views and their racial attitudes, both implicitly and explicitly.

To put my analysis in context, I discuss two major changes that have occurred in U.S. politics in the post–civil rights period: the transformation of racial politics into religious politics, and the transformation of the Democratic South to the Republican South. These two changes are interrelated, but each is significant in its own way. As early as the 1950s, the growing and widespread acceptance of civil rights normatively made it difficult for politicians even in the South to win elections with explicitly antiblack or prosegregation policies (Black 1971; Mendelberg 2001). Once it was no longer legitimate to use explicitly racist appeals, Republican political activists began to use an alternative framing of moral decline on the part of blacks (evoking, for example, irresponsibility, lack of discipline, laziness, wastefulness) that defined the basis for opposition to government policies to help blacks in particular and the poor more generally. As such, images of the inner city and black lifestyles became heated political issues (Katz 1989; Murray 1984). Further, blacks and the poor were conflated, even though the original formulation of the "war on poverty" under the Johnson administration included whites in Appalachia and those in rural areas as well as blacks in the inner city.

From Racial Politics to Religious Politics

Because of the need to make racial appeals implicit rather than explicit in the post–civil rights period, I argue that racial politics was transformed into religious politics, but that in both origin and background religious politics is still substantially about racial issues. This transformation began with the efforts to desegregate schools in the South. Resistance to school desegregation led to the creation of private "Christian" academies, in lieu of public schools, and over time resources, both public and private, have gradually been transferred to these schools. In developing the rationale for creating "Christian" academies, proponents argued that increasingly public schools lacked discipline and had become unsafe (Andrews 2002). Of course, these were coded ways to indicate that schools were desegregated. Although schools in the South were prominent in this transformation, moral rhetoric was used more generally to cast public institutions in a negative light and to promote privatization of public services and galvanize opposition to government spending for public services. Schools were attacked for lacking discipline, for teaching promiscuity and encouraging homosexuality, for promoting disrespect for traditional values, and for banning school prayer (Wilson 2003). Welfare was attacked for creating dependency and irresponsibility (Mead 1992). And the government was charged with being profligate with taxpayers' money, with funding immoral behaviors (like abortions and sex education), and with funding programs that undermined the moral fabric of the country and contributed to the deterioration and decline of life in the inner cities of large urban areas (D'Souza 1995; Murray 1984). These messages began to take hold in the common wisdom propagated through the new conservative media and became more frequently heard views expressed in the mainstream media as well. Efforts of the newly energized conservative movement began to pay off as more and more people began to see government not only as wasteful and inefficient but as immoral.

By appealing to voters on the basis of religious values, Republicans created a difficult situation for the Democratic Party. The ostensibly religious dimension of these changes has allowed the Republican Party to claim that it is the party that best represents traditional American values. Because the Democratic Party has tried, of necessity, to be more inclusive of different constituents, it has had more difficulty appealing to voters on the basis of values, leaving Democratic candidates open to attack on issues of morality and culture. Indeed, John Green (2000) finds that, among whites, those with traditional religious beliefs are more likely to identify with the Republican Party.

The "culture war" that emerged from these various social movement efforts has been fostered from the top down with the support of a group of wealthy men and women originally on the far right wing of the Republican Party who set out to create an institutional framework for turning the country back from the liberalism that emerged during the social movements of the 1960s (Weyrich 2003; Massey 2005). This group, which came to be known as the New Right, sponsored the emergence of the Religious Right. After initially trying to mobilize support for a third party, this right-wing movement actively sought to take over control of the Republican Party—and generally succeeded in doing so—with the goal of stoking the fires of a new conservatism in the country (Jorstad 1981; Viguerie 1979). Given the shift in both party identification and voting behavior, their efforts were largely successful through the second term of George W. Bush, but they failed to create a majority party. Instead, the Republican Party has reached approximate parity with the Democratic Party in terms of electoral votes for the presidential election, contributing to the very animated conflict between the two parties and the intense competition especially for the white vote. Despite these changes, the coalitions for both parties are unstable, and the competition between the Republicans and the Democrats to create an electoral majority continues unabated.

Competition for the white vote is highly contested, in part, because minority voters are assumed to have a strong preference for the Democratic Party. Both parties face dilemmas in their electoral efforts, however, as I discuss later in the book. The more the Republican Party has been associated with religious conservatives and the more the party has appealed to working-class whites using anti-intellectual themes, the more it has lost the support of more-educated voters, especially among professionals. Some evidence suggests that the growing political influence of religious conservatives in the Republican Party has led professionals to shift to the Democratic Party and contributed as well to the growth of independents, many of whom are former Republicans (Bolce and De Maio 1999a, 1999b; Hout and Fischer 2002). At the same time, the Democratic Party faces a long-standing tension in its electoral strategy: the more attention it gives to civil rights and especially black issues, the more likely it is to lose white votes (Frymer 1999). This tension has played out especially in the transformation of the white vote in the South.

The Transformation of the Democratic South into the Republican South

As racial issues began to drive a wedge between constituents of the Democratic coalition, the Republican Party opportunistically began to appeal to disaffected whites in the South (known as the "Southern strategy") and to working-class voters in the North. Goldwater's decision to oppose civil rights legislation as part of his 1964 campaign (although he had previously voted for civil rights legislation) was just one step in the gradual transformation of the Republican Party into the anti–civil rights party. Although Goldwater's efforts were disastrous in the 1964 election results, the path on which he embarked was in fact increasingly successful over time for the Republican Party, which has now almost fully captured white voters in the previously Democratic South. It is this shift or realignment that has enabled the Republican Party to gain parity with the Democratic Party in presidential elections. The Republican Party has been able to maintain its competitiveness, however, only by appealing consistently to white working-class voters who had been reliable constituents of the Democratic Party. According to Larry Bartels (2008b), its success with white working-class voters has been primarily in the South. At the same time, white working-class voters have become less reliable members of the Democratic coalition, and many of them have either not voted or have crossed over to third parties or to the Republicans.

Because the white working class was such an essential component of the New Deal coalition and has been necessary for the Democratic Party to win elections, a number of people have criticized the party for "forgetting" the white working class or for offending them (Teixeira and Rogers 2000). Thomas Frank (2004) lays the blame on liberalism for becoming irrelevant to the lives of middle-class (that is, white working-class)

Americans by embracing out-of-the-mainstream culture and putting class issues in the background in order to gain the support of corporations and workers in the new economy. Ruy Teixeira and Joel Rogers (2000) argue that the Democratic Party's failure to provide solutions to the economic decline faced by "America's forgotten majority" led to a distrust of government and resistance to the kind of governmental activism that was the hallmark of the 1960s and before that of the New Deal. Although these authors recognize that racial issues could be a factor in the disaffection of the white working class from the Democratic Party, they argue that it is not the main factor.

Thomas Edsall and Mary Edsall (1992), in contrast, argue that conflict over race and class undermined the support of the white working class for the Democratic Party. They describe the impact of antiwar and civil rights groups taking over the Democratic Party by pushing aside the party regulars who had encompassed and represented the white working class. In a statement during the Republican ascendancy of the 1980s, Gordon MacInnes (1996, 104–5) was even more emphatic in his charge that liberals in the Democratic Party drove the white working class away on the basis of race, and with them any chance for electoral success:

> Since the late 1960s, liberal Democrats have been hurt in presidential politics by their silence in the face of radically alien ideas on racial issues. Afraid to argue with either the Left or blacks, liberals ended up supporting or, at least, abetting crazy ideas. The collapse of the liberal discourse on issues of family stability, welfare dependency, and illegitimacy, and the abandonment of the concept of personal responsibility for crime and riots, left no position for liberals other than as apologists for extreme black views. . . .
>
> Thus the public agendas of the black and white elites were conveniently joined in the Democratic party. . . . The result was an electoral slaughter of historic proportions in 1972, the alienation of working-class Democrats, and the takeover of the national party machinery by ideologues and zealots determined to shut out the party's elected leaders in Congress and state capitals.

These issues have not been resolved within the Democratic Party and are likely to continue to be problematic for Democrats into the future. The party is criticized for not giving enough attention to racial inequality or for giving too much. It is criticized for ignoring the white working class or for allowing them to move the party back to an outmoded appeal to class warfare. It is criticized for giving too much attention to liberal social issues or for selling out to the forces of conservatism. The Democratic Party has not received a majority of white votes since 1964 (including in 2008, when Obama received only 43 percent of the white vote). Thus, the Democratic Party still needs to mobilize enough support among whites to win elections, and to do so requires gaining the support of both the white working class and white middle-class professionals—such as the members of both groups among our interviewees, who, as we will see, often saw each other as the main source of the misdirection with regard to government policies. At the same time, the Republican Party can mobilize a majority, especially at the presidential level, only with the support of religious conservatives and through a right-wing populism intended to appeal to the white working class, but both strategies cause negative reactions from white professionals. Thus, among white voters, there is instability of political support, and much of that instability turns on race and civil rights, albeit often in other guises.

Civil Rights Policies: Race, Rights, and Taxes[5]

Although I did not predefine the groups of interviewees in this study, as the interviews progressed it became clear that the interviewees fell into several distinct groups that mapped to the groups of white voters over which the two major political parties are in competition, as I later realized. In reporting the interview responses for these various groups, I endeavor to get at the substance of the principle-policy gap among white voters and thus to understand why whites do or do not support policies that address racial inequality. In addition to asking about inequality and equal opportunity in general, I specifically describe the responses to questions about welfare, taxes, affirmative action, and immigration. Here I provide only a brief overview.

What was immediately evident in the interviews was that the respondents knew very little about the contours of government programs. Without being cued with specific program names, respondents often could not fill in the details regarding major government policies. They had opinions about the role of government, but they did not know what government policies actually exist, what they entail, or how they function. Interviewees made many claims about who gets what from government programs that were sometimes far off the mark, and in doing so they often attributed a largesse to government programs or made claims about benefits to various groups that had no basis in fact.

In general, people in the United States do not live in a world of politics (Alvarez and Brehm 2002; Zaller 1992). Instead, they go about their everyday lives and worry most about getting through their day, paying their bills, and attending to the needs of family and friends. When posed with questions about political issues, the respondents could formulate and express an opinion, but their views did not necessarily reflect either long-standing or well-considered views. Even questions as seemingly straightforward as a request for their view of government received ambiguous answers. For example, most of the interviewees thought of government services as only for people who could not support themselves, and many of them said, when asked, that they neither got nor wanted anything from the government. In other words, very few of the respondents thought about the school systems where they or their children were educated, the roads they traveled, the safe water they drank, or the police and fire protection they enjoyed when asked what the government did for them. Instead, they thought automatically about welfare and other transfer payments. In that regard, most of the interviewees had a very limited view of what government should do, and many had images of government as wasteful, inefficient, and ineffective, if not corrupt.

Thus, the views expressed by the interviewees underlined a lack of trust in government, reinforcing other studies that have found a precipitous decline since the 1960s in overall trust in government and in the belief that government will generally do the right thing (Teixeira and Rogers 2000). Teixeira and Rogers (2000), for example, found that whereas in 1964, 80 percent of the population believed that "the government in Washington" would do the right thing most of the time, by the 1994 to 1996 period, only 20 to 30 percent of the population trusted the government in this way. Recent data suggest a moderation of this mistrust, but a majority still believe that government-run programs are likely to be inefficient and wasteful. In general, Democrats are less cynical about government than Republicans and independents (Kohut 2009). Yet mistrust or suspicion of government were evident in the responses of my interviewees; only a small proportion of interviewees identified themselves as politically liberal (23 percent of the total sample) and expressed more positive views of government. The liberal interviewees were more likely than the others to express support for government efforts to help the poor and to address issues of racial inequality, but the majority of the interviewees were either skeptical of government competence or indifferent to the issue.

Clearly something happened politically in the country in the post–civil rights period that has contributed to the remarkable shift in attitudes toward the government. Undoubtedly the disillusionment with government that arose with the opposition to the Vietnam War, the scandal of Watergate and consequent resignation of Richard Nixon, and other such events had an effect on views of government during the volatile politics of the post–civil rights period. But surely the government's actions and the public's reactions to public policies regarding civil rights also played a part in the decline of trust in government. After the violence against civil rights activists in the South was televised across the country in the 1960s, support for the civil rights movement grew, but there was an equally strong reaction against the racial riots that subsequently spread across the country. Perhaps sentiments with regard to

Figure 1.1 The Emergence of a Culture War As an Effort to Resist Civil Rights and Withdraw from Public Institutions

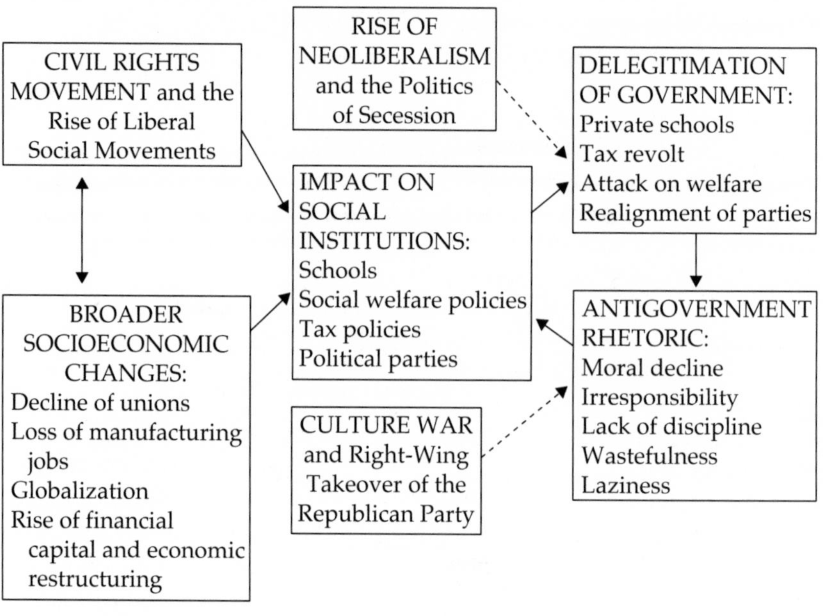

Source: Author's compilation.

civil rights policy also changed when civil rights activism moved beyond the South to the North. As blacks began to claim the citizenship rights that they had been denied prior to the passage of the Civil Rights Act of 1964, the Voting Rights Act of 1965, and similar legislation, a backlash emerged that was clearly linked to the efforts to implement the principles of civil rights in specific programs and policies (Edsall and Edsall 1992). And the funds that have poured into the effort to create a new conservatism have had remarkable effects as well. Figure 1.1 provides a framework for understanding these dynamics.

I argue that the combination of the civil rights movement (and other liberal social movements) and the socioeconomic changes in the country (including the decline of manufacturing jobs and unionization, the advent of globalization, and the financialization of the economy) at the time led to the creation of programs and policies that affected the social institutions of which whites were a part, including schools, political parties, and government programs at the local and state levels. As whites' ability to hoard opportunities and freely use social resources to get ahead were impeded by the implementation of civil rights policies, whites began to undertake what Robert Reich (1991) called the "politics of secession." Their efforts in this regard were part of a newly emerging right-wing effort to promote neoliberalism in contradistinction to the politics of social welfare. As such, whites began to withdraw from or deny resources to the public institutions that were likely to benefit blacks. Of course, the withdrawal from public schools in the South was notable in this regard. Similarly, as the Democratic Party became the party of civil rights, whites began leaving the party, especially across the South, and their exodus led eventually to a realignment of party identification and voting behavior. Further, as welfare became increasingly associated with "giveaways" to blacks, whites intensified their opposition to welfare policies (Gilens 1999). The growing disaffection with and rejection of government programs to help the poor, and especially poor blacks, contributed as well to tax revolts and to support for starving the government and reducing taxes, even at the expense of public services (Ladd and Bowman 1998; Teixeira and Rogers 2000). Because acceptance of civil rights became normative across the country as part of the liberal social movement, it was no longer possible to organize on racist appeals. Instead, a new religious politics supplanted racial politics, but with the same goal of maintaining white control of social institutions and privileges.

White voters became the primary target of the Republican Party in the wake of fears after 1964 that the Democratic Party could create a permanent majority, perhaps without needing a coalition with the South. Indeed, conservative fears were well founded, because the reconfiguration of the two parties made it increasingly possible (even if not probable) for the Democratic Party to win presidential elections without the South. Following Lyndon Johnson's election and the social movements surrounding his administration, well-connected political staff members of conservative Southern politicians embarked on plans to create a conservative movement to challenge the country's enthusiasm for liberalism (Weyrich 2003). Thus, unlike Teixeira and Rogers (2000), who argue that the success of the conservative movement reflected the response of working-class voters to the failure of the federal government to address the economic problems that emerged after 1973, I believe that the politics of secession and what turned into the "culture war" were largely about the responses to the movement for civil rights and what the civil rights revolution portended for the ascendancy of liberal politics in the United States. The civil rights movement also sparked the antiwar movement and the women's movement and contributed to an emerging politics of liberalism. The fear that these movements would permanently change the politics of the country was central to the rise of the New Right, then the Christian Right, and the subsequent revival of the various branches of the conservative movement (Diamond 1995, 1998). The emergence of neoliberalism was part of the same revival.

The respondents' views on these various policies were a mix of politics, social psychology, and the structural position of people like themselves in the stratification order (Kluegel and Smith 1986). Which of these influences was most powerful in the development of their views depended on whether they perceived themselves to be affected by the policy or by what the policy symbolized for people like themselves. For example, there were few respondents among my interviewees who claimed that they themselves had been harmed by affirmative action policies, but there were many interviewees who objected to affirmative action as unfair or harmful to whites (Bergmann 1996; Reskin 1998). In their discussion of these issues, it was clear that they had set up guidelines or rules for what was fair in employment practices that they did not apply to themselves. That is, their politics, social position (or position in the social structure), and social psychology all came together in their responses regarding various government policies.

Thus, when asked what they thought about changes in access to education and jobs for women, minorities, or immigrants, many argued that the person with the highest test score should be admitted to colleges and universities or that the "best person" should get the job. Yet none of the interviewees described themselves as having had the highest test score or having obtained their own job by these criteria. Instead, they talked about having capabilities even if they were not good students or good test-takers, or about proving themselves after they got the job, not before. Further, even though the interviewees espoused a commitment to equal opportunity and civil rights, they balked at the idea of affirmative action because, they said, there "must be another way." Yet few could offer any alternatives that would have the same result of providing access to jobs and education for minorities and women, and many retreated when asked about these issues with the declaration, "Life's not fair."

The interviewees in this study had mixed views about immigration. Given the efforts by some politicians to limit immigrants' access to public services, I had expected to hear more anti-immigrant rhetoric than I did. Instead, the comments about immigrants were surprisingly soft, with many of the interviewees saying things like, "We were all immigrants." Although often noting the hard work of immigrants, a number of interviewees also believed that immigrants needed to adapt to U.S. culture rather than expecting U.S. culture to adapt to them. They felt that immigrants should learn English and speak it while in the United States, and they strongly opposed immigrants being able to enter the country illegally or to receive public services without paying taxes. There was also some resentment expressed about immigrants who came to the United States and somehow expected to bring the culture of their home countries with them, as well as about immigrants earning money in the United States and then sending it or taking it home with them. The majority of the interviewees were not favorable about immigration, but few expressed strong views, and surprisingly, at least some interviewees welcomed immigrants and their contributions to the country.

A mix of politics, structure, and social psychology was also evident in attitudes toward welfare policies. Most of the interviewees argued that people should be self-sufficient, take responsibility for their own lives, work hard no matter how difficult or unpleasant it might be to do so, be persistent and flexible, and never give up hope. Yet many of the interviewees themselves relied on help from family and friends or neighbors, including getting special favors, receiving low- or no-cost loans, and having doors opened for them that were not open to others. Further, a few of the interviewees had themselves been on welfare or had received unemployment insurance, student loans, or some other kind of public benefit. They insisted, however, that they had taken such help only on a temporary basis; they felt that they had deserved that help because they had paid into the system or that, for them, it was only a "hand-up," not a "hand-out." Even as some interviewees described having passed up jobs themselves that they considered too degrading or dangerous, they insisted that welfare recipients, or the "lazy people" who "sit on their butts," should take whatever jobs are available and not depend on the government. That is, when they thought about welfare recipients, they did not think of people like themselves who might occasionally need support from government programs and who had access to advantages from family and friends; instead, they created the image of a moral "other"—someone who did not share their values of hard work, responsibility, and humility.

On the issue of taxes, however, I did not find strong support for the conservative rhetoric that I had expected, given that the theme of tax cuts has been so prevalent in many political campaigns during the last several years. Few of the interviewees in New Jersey or Ohio indicated much concern about the taxes they paid, and they often said that it would not affect them much if people made fewer demands on the government. Although some interviewees indicated that they would prefer to pay less, there was little talk about the government spending "their" money and little concern about second-guessing the government—except in the area of civil rights and welfare. The views expressed by these interviewees were consistent with research by Martin Gilens (1995): a majority of his respondents said that the government spends either too little money or about the right amount of money in a range of policy areas (see also Teixeira and Rogers 2000). Only on issues such as welfare, aid to inner cities, and foreign aid did Gilens find that a majority said the government spends too much—that is, too much on those policies that are thought to benefit blacks and other nonwhites.

The interviewees in my study from Tennessee, however, did express opposition to the amount of taxes they were paying, and many complained about the government spending "their" money. These concerns were presumably contextual, however, because a major political fight about increasing state taxes had just occurred at the time I did the interviews. Of course, the views of the Tennessee interviewees may also reflect a special sensitivity of people in the South to the role of government in funding the welfare state. Many of the Tennessee interviewees' comments about taxes included images of lazy and shiftless people who did not deserve the resources they were receiving, and for the most part it was clear that the interviewees had blacks in mind.

Neoliberalism, Good Jobs, and Racial Politics

Although this book focuses on racial inequality and the impact of the politics of race on the competition for the white vote, I want to acknowledge that racial politics has often been a vehicle for, rather than a driver of, the larger political narrative. The political project of wealthy elites to prevent the United States from becoming a liberal or social democratic nation has been driven by a corporate-led, anti-state, anti-union, anti-regulation agenda that uses racial politics to accomplish their goals. Well-funded political strategists have used race, albeit often implicitly, to motivate the white working and middle classes to embrace the neoliberal revolution, that is, the belief that markets and the private sector should dominate and government should "stay out of the way." Adopting neoliberalism, however, has worked against the interests of the white working and middle classes in the United States. Rather than seeing an overemphasis on markets as the source of their problems, the white working class has more often blamed either government support for blacks or the liberal "elites" who support government policies that the working class thinks go against their interests. Previously the white working class tried to gain access to good jobs by protecting themselves from market competition and trying to hoard good jobs for their family and friends, but their support for neoliberal politics has now opened them up to greater market competition in the labor market. Ironically, at the individual level whites tried to protect themselves from market competition via strategies of social closure and politically through opposition to the implementation of civil rights policies, but their support for such politics has led to increased precariousness in the labor market and worse opportunities for themselves over time (Kalleberg 2011). The white working class and even the middle class have ended up losers as government regulation has been eroded, union strength undermined, and capitalism left unconstrained. In other words, increasing numbers of white workers have been left to operate in the kind of labor market conditions that blacks were confined to in the pre–civil rights era.

A new conservative movement has emerged not only in reaction to the civil rights and other social movements of the 1960s but also from the consequences of globalization, changes in technology, and changes in geopolitics (such as the Arab oil embargo of 1973) that led to economic booms and busts in the United States, the end of wage improvements for those without college degrees, and a decline in good jobs and an increase in bad ones. The shift, for example, from manufacturing to financial services has dramatically improved wages for the few, but for many others wages have stagnated, working conditions have worsened, protections have been weakened, and job security has been eroded. These deteriorating economic conditions have undoubtedly influenced the political responses of people like my interviewees.

An important insight from the interviews in this study is that even "good jobs" are constantly under assault by employers trying to increase market competition by undermining the income and benefits received by workers. Through mergers and acquisitions, plant closings, offshoring, and outsourcing, many good jobs in the United States have disappeared over the last several decades, and along with these jobs the ability of workers to protect themselves from market competition. The primary mechanisms for providing job security and limiting market competition in the past were seniority, state licensing, unionization, and tenure (DiTomaso 2001; Weeden 2000). Workers have used each of these mechanisms to protect themselves from competition and from downward wage pressure, while employers and their political allies have adopted policies that try to force workers back into market competition. Seniority has been undermined by efforts to hire younger (and cheaper) workers, or it becomes a moot protection when jobs undermine health as workers age. State licensing often gets captured by the licensees, but there are always efforts by new groups to gain state recognition for skills that overlap the domain of the work being done by those already licensed. Unions have been undermined or threatened and membership in unions has declined dramatically in recent years, especially in the private sector. More recently, concerted efforts have been mounted by the right to break or shrink public-sector unions as well. Finally, tenure has been constantly under assault, and it has been undermined in principle by universities that hire the majority of faculty on non-tenure-track lines.

Because the civil rights movement endeavored to open up access to the "good jobs" that had been hoarded in the past by whites, it represented a threat to whites' primary mechanisms for protecting themselves from market competition. But support for neoliberal, antigovernment policies hardly provides a solution for white workers. Neoliberal policies make it more difficult for any workers—white or black—to protect themselves from the market. When workers compete with each other, wages are bid down. To prevent this outcome, workers have tried to take wages out of competition and capture higher wages. They have done so by trying to keep the supply of available workers artificially low, by drawing boundaries around who is allowed to do the work or to get trained for it, and by trying to prevent substitutes for their labor being made available.

The "rent" gained by workers who are able to protect themselves from market competition comes, theoretically, from employers, who then have to pay higher wages in order to hire sufficient workers. In such circumstances, the competition over rent becomes the major dynamic within the labor force, with workers attempting to limit competition for their labor in order to increase their wages and employers attempting to increase competition among workers in order to decrease wages. Employers do so by trying to find new sources of labor, using technological substitutes for labor, or finding ways to destroy the rent claims of workers by undermining seniority, breaking unions, weakening the protections of licensing or tenure, and otherwise endeavoring to break the hold of some labor groups on the availability of workers in a given occupation or industry. In general, a "competitive wage" is a low wage, and a job that is subject to market competition generally is not a "good" job. It is important to note the context when considering the efforts of white workers to hoard opportunities and protect themselves from market competition. There was growing inequality in household income in the United States from 1979 to 2007, with those in the lower part of the income distribution in 1975 seeing very little growth in income over this period, those in the middle seeing modest gains, and those at the very top of the income distribution seeing substantial increases (Congressional Budget Office 2011). Rent can increase from opportunity hoarding and from being protected from market competition, but neither mechanism protects workers in a period of declining opportunity overall and the kind of stagnation in wages that resulted from the neoliberal assault on the post–World War II labor-capital accord.

One of the primary ways in which workers have been able to limit competition and protect their access to good jobs has been by trying to enforce boundaries that define who is or is not considered an acceptable worker in a given occupation. Race, gender, citizenship, and other categorizations have been ways for white workers to try to keep good jobs for people like themselves and to limit the access of "outsiders" to "their" jobs, thus limiting the market competition (Glenn 2002; Tilly 1998). Such categorization provides easy markers for who is or is not part of the protected group, and by identifying some groups as "other," it contributes to the development of legitimating myths about competency and merit that support the institutionalization of opportunity hoarding by some groups seeking to limit the access of those other groups (Ridgeway 1986; Sidanius and Pratto 1999; Tilly 1998). Thus, capturing rents in labor markets is categorical. The type of inside edge that provides access to good jobs is limited to those with whom one identifies, to insiders in social networks, and to those who are believed to be trustworthy enough to return favors within the community without violating group norms.

One purpose of the civil rights movement, of course, was to open up labor markets that had previously been reserved for whites. Thus, the civil rights movement was about gaining for African Americans access to jobs that whites had passed among themselves, on the assumption that once blacks were given access to those jobs, they would retain the characteristics of the good jobs that had been available only to whites—high wages, good benefits, and protection from exploitation. Expanding the supply of labor for jobs that paid well but did not require much education, however, contributed to the erosion of the quality of those jobs, and ultimately to their disappearance. Whether intended or not, civil rights became a direct challenge to labor rights, such that the jobs that had been protected from the market for whites became less protected from market competition for everyone. Following the civil rights movement, and contrary to what was intended, many African Americans, rather than gaining access to the good jobs that had been the purview of whites only, could find only jobs paying "market wages"; unwilling to accept such wages, they were subsequently excluded from the labor market (frequently because employers preferred immigrants, who would work for much lower wages).

Thus, an important tension that has existed since the advent of the civil rights movement has been an ongoing effort to keep some jobs protected from the market in the context of a larger labor pool and new sources of labor continually available as immigration, globalization, changes in gender roles, and civil rights enforcement for racial and ethnic minorities open up these new sources. The response to the civil rights movement is therefore more complicated than being simply for it or against it. In the post–civil rights period, almost everyone endorses the concept of civil rights, but those who depend on access to jobs that are protected from labor market competition in order to have the possibility of a middle-class lifestyle are much less sanguine about the implementation of civil rights policies if doing so loosens their hold on good jobs or on their ability to pass along good jobs to their children, family, or friends. And the response has been especially hostile from those who do not have marketable skills to compete for jobs that pay middle-class wages if they are unable to gain access to jobs that are protected from the market. In other words, those who have few options to obtain other "good" jobs if their hold on unionized blue-collar jobs declines or their protection from seniority or tenure (and sometimes state licensing) erodes are much more ambivalent about the civil rights movement than those who have skills that might serve them well if they are forced into competing in the market for a decent job that will support themselves and their families.

In summary, a decent life depends on being protected from the market. Those jobs with the characteristics that make a middle-class life—that is, a decent life—possible, especially for those without a college education or valuable skills, are constantly expropriated from employers by current employees to pass along to family, friends, and acquaintances who share networks and social identity. Workers use social closure, opportunity hoarding, and social capital in what is otherwise thought of as a labor "market." In this context, employers used the opportunity of the civil rights movement to expand the labor supply and access to training, to undermine protections such as seniority, to break work rules, and ultimately to substitute technology for labor or to move jobs abroad. Thus, the civil rights movement did not just provide more opportunity to blacks while leaving everything else constant. The civil rights movement contributed to a multitude of changes that have made the labor market more competitive and left many white workers less protected and more vulnerable than before. As Sørensen (2000, 1553) argued, "Nothing guarantees that a competitive wage moves a worker above the poverty line . . . nothing guarantees that efficient labor markets create good lives." Thus, white workers' support for neoliberalism in its opposition to government civil rights policies has backfired by making them more, rather than less, vulnerable.

The Study Design

The data for this study consist of 246 semistructured interviews with randomly selected, white, non-Hispanic respondents between the ages of twenty-five and fifty-five, from three areas of the country: New Jersey, Ohio, and Tennessee.[6] These areas were chosen for both theoretical and practical reasons. I wanted one area that was diverse by race and ethnicity and one that was less diverse. New Jersey has one of the most diverse populations in the country. Ohio is a midwestern state with a less diverse population, especially in the areas where I did interviews. Then it also seemed prudent to include a southern state, because of the importance of the South to racial politics in the United States. These areas both fit my criteria and were areas to which I had access. Doing such a large number of interviews in each location required that I stay in the area for extended periods of time, so it helped to have family and friends with whom I could stay. Tables 1.2 and 1.3 provide the demographic breakdown of the interview sample and information on the locations where the interviews were done.

I adapted my methodology from that used by Michele Lamont (1992,

Table 1.2 Demographic Characteristics of the Interview Sample

Region	Women	Men	Total
New Jersey			
Working-class	16	20	36
Middle-class	28	29	57
Ohio			
Working-class[a]	25	27	52
Middle-class	19	20	39
Tennessee			
Working-class[a]	12	15	27
Middle-class	18	17	35
Total	118	128	246

Source: Author's compilation.
[a]Canton, Ohio, and the surrounding area have always been a predominantly working-class, manufacturing economy, with relatively well-paid blue-collar and unionized workers. Perhaps for this reason, there is a higher proportion of working-class interviewees in the Ohio sample. In contrast, Nashville, Tennessee, is a college and government town, as well as the "country music capital." Perhaps for this reason, and also perhaps because of the greater difficulty in Nashville of getting potential interviewees to agree to be interviewed, the proportion of working-class respondents in the Tennessee sample is smaller.

2000). I chose the twenty-five- to fifty-five-year-old age range because I wanted to talk with people who had come of age during or after the civil rights movement and were still of working age, although I did not restrict the sample to those still in the labor force.[7] Using demographic information on the proportion of white residents, income levels, education levels, and occupations, I identified zip code areas in each geographical area as predominantly middle-class or working-class. I then sent letters to potential respondents explaining that I was writing a book about how people develop their goals in life and how they go about trying to achieve them. I also told potential respondents that they would be asked about their views on public policy issues in order to understand how Americans think about their current economic situation. I followed up the letters with phone calls to determine the eligibility of the potential respondents.

Initially I defined "class" by whether or not the respondent had a four-year college degree (McCall 2001).This criterion seemed insufficient in some cases, however, because class is a family characteristic, not an individual one. Further, because most of the interviews were done in the respondents' homes, it was possible to supplement the educational information about the respondent with information on the respondent's apparent lifestyle.[8] The interview included detailed questions about the interviewee's educational and life history, starting with high school and

Table 1.3 Demographic Characteristics of Interview Areas, 2000

	New Jersey	Ohio[a]	Tennessee
Median family income			
Middle-class area 1	$105,056	$56,677	$69,446
Middle-class area 2	93,785	50,316	70,861
Working-class area 1	59,482	33,384	43,222
Working-class area 2	52,571	40,283	63,789
White non-Hispanic			
Middle-class area 1	87%	94%	95%
Middle-class area 2	81	96	96
Working-class area 1	85	94	85
Working-class area 2	93	93	93
Nonmanagerial jobs			
Middle-class area 1	44%	51%	36%
Middle-class area 2	41	57	38
Working-class area 1	69	81	64
Working-class area 2	62	82	58
Bachelor's degree or higher			
Middle-class area 1	52%	40%	70%
Middle-class area 2	62	34	58
Working-class area 1	16	6	28
Working-class area 2	28	8	36

Source: Data included here are illustrative of the zip codes from which respondents were drawn in each state. The data come from American FactFinder using Zip Code Tabulation Areas, U.S. Census Bureau: Profile of General Demographic Characteristics: 2000, Census 2000 Summary File 1 (SF 1) 100-Percent Data; Profile of Selected Social Characteristics: 2000, Census 2000 Summary File 3 (SF 3)—Sample Data; and Profile of Selected Economic Characteristics: 2000, Census 2000 Summary File 3 (SF 3)—Sample Data.

[a]The demographics of the areas of Ohio where the interviews were conducted document the working-class and manufacturing nature of this economy. Although the income and educational levels are higher in what I designated as middle-class areas, the overall level of education is much lower in this part of Ohio than in the other two interview areas, and the proportion of nonmanagerial jobs is higher in both the middle-class and the working-class areas in Ohio compared to New Jersey and Tennessee. These demographics also suggest that there is more mixture in the neighborhoods in this region of the country, with working-class and middle-class people more likely to live in the same neighborhoods in Ohio than is true in the areas in either New Jersey or Tennessee.

going through the date of the interview; socioeconomic information on their parents, siblings, children, and spouses; their conceptions of the factors that had most contributed to their current life circumstances; how they viewed themselves and others; and their views of various public policies. In addition to conducting qualitative interviews, I also asked respondents to fill out a short survey with questions taken from the American National Election Studies (ANES) so that I could compare this sample with a national sample.

I was especially interested in understanding the pathways or trajecto-

Table 1.4 Comparison of DiTomaso Study Interview Sample and American National Election Studies Sample

	DiTomaso	ANES	Statistically Significant
Education (3 = more than high school; 4 = some college; 5 = college degree)[a]	4.27	3.75	Yes
Income (2 = $31,000 to $50,000; 3 = $51,000 to $75,000)	2.85	2.41	Yes
Working-class	47%	43%	No
South	25%	37%	Yes
Egalitarianism (six items, three-point scale)[b]	2.20	2.18	No
Individualism (three items, three-point scale)[b]	2.28	2.22	No
Racial resentment (three items, three-point scale)[b]	1.95	2.32	Yes

Source: Author's compilation based on ANES surveys from 1986, 1994, 1996, 1998, and 2000.

[a]Because I wanted a sufficient number of middle-class and working-class interviewees in my sample, I did not endeavor to have a sample that was representative of the educational distribution in the U.S. white population. Thus, there is a larger proportion of college graduates in my sample, and also a higher average level of income.

[b]For each scale, the higher the number, the more the respondent holds these views; for example, a 3 represents the most egalitarian, the most individualist, and the most racially resentful.

ries by which the respondents moved through their careers and the circumstances surrounding each transition from one job to another. To have greater access to the data, I created a quantitative database to summarize some of the qualitative information provided in the interviews, including information about each job held; the kind of help or assistance, if any, used in obtaining the job; and other support provided to the interviewees at different stages of their lives. I also added information on religious and political identity to the survey data provided by the respondents, making it possible to compare the groups to each other both quantitatively and qualitatively. Using responses from the American National Election Studies, I was able to create measures of frequently used scales, including individualism, racial resentment, and egalitarianism, divided into two scales based on the work of David Sears, P. J. Henry, and Rick Kosterman (2000).[9] The survey also includes demographic information on respondents' age, education, income, family background, and employment status.

Table 1.4 provides information comparing my sample with that from the ANES. As can be seen from the table, the interviewees in my sample were less likely than those in a national sample to be from the South, and they had higher average levels of education and income. Because I wanted to have both middle- and working-class interviewees from each region, my sample included a higher proportion of those with a college education than would be likely in a strictly representative sample. The interviewees in my sample were also apparently less racially resentful than those in the national sample.[10] As part of the data collection, I gave the interviewees lists, taken from the work of Kluegel and Smith (1986), of the reasons why people might be rich or poor and why there is racial inequality. They were asked to choose two from each list and to explain why these were the reasons that made the most sense to them.

All of the interviews were tape-recorded and transcribed verbatim. They were then coded using software to analyze qualitative data.[11] Each interview took an average of two hours (with the shortest taking about an hour and a half and the longest four and a half hours). The interview transcripts varied from twenty-five to sixty-five single-spaced pages. In addition to coding the responses for each interview question, I also developed a set of topics or themes that emerged from the interview responses and coded these as well.

Sociopolitical Groups Among the Interviewees

As the interviews progressed, it became apparent that there were distinct groups of interviewees with similar opinions within the larger group. These groups turned out to parallel the groups among white voters who have been the target of the Democratic and Republican Parties: religious conservatives, working-class whites (especially those who are most animated about racial issues), professionals, and independents. Although there were also a few smaller groups that did not fit easily into these four categories, I give the most attention in my discussion to these four groups. Understanding the political views of each of these groups should help us understand how the American non-dilemma affects white support and opposition to policies that might ameliorate racial inequality.

Sorting the interviewees into these distinct groups required some decision rules. I defined the groups by the way they talked about the issues I asked them to address, not strictly by their demographics. Thus, I defined the groups, not by variables as such, but as they represented the intersection of relevant life events and personal attributes that made sense within respondents' lives. I would argue that these groups sounded different when they talked about the issues addressed in this study because their life experiences had created different, but coherent, social locations and identities, as evidenced by the fact that the groups tend to represent the most politically salient groups of whites who are of interest to the two major political parties. The groups I have created therefore reflect the differences among the interviewees in how they represented their views especially on public policy issues. The groups are mutually exclusive, and I categorized each interviewee into one group according to the following procedure:

Protestant evangelicals clearly seemed to be a distinctive group, so I started with them. I included within this category all respondents who talked in the interview about the importance of their faith, their belief in God or Jesus, being born again, or their active involvement in church or who made other such statements suggesting that religious identity was especially salient to them. I excluded from this group anyone who indicated that he or she was Catholic, Jewish, or secular and anyone who did not speak about religion at all. Based on these criteria, fifty-seven people were included in the Protestant evangelical category (23 percent of the sample). Table 1.5 confirms that the interviewees I identified as Protestant evangelicals were much more likely than any other category of interviewee to talk about religion. The Protestant evangelical group includes both middle- and working-class interviewees, but it is disproportionately middle-class (70 percent in my sample). The vast majority of the Protestant evangelicals—81 percent—identified themselves as politically conservative, and another 18 percent said they were moderate; only one person in this category indicated having liberal politics. Throughout the book, I distinguish those I define as "religious conservatives" (Protestant evangelicals who identified their politics as conservative) from those I define as "religious nonconservatives" (Protestant evangelicals who identified their politics as moderate or liberal). There were forty-six religious conservatives (19 percent of the sample) and eleven religious nonconservatives (4.5 percent of the sample).

I labeled another group of interviewees "working-class 'racists'." I identified these interviewees both by their class position and by their explicitly antiblack statements. I put thirty people (12 percent of the sample) in this category. For example, an insurance adjuster in New Jersey (D011 NJ M WC),[12] when asked about the changes that have occurred for African Americans with regard to jobs and education, said, "You walk into any government agency, it's 90 percent African Americans. . . . It means that America's lowering their standards and giving these people jobs and stuff." Similarly, a surveyor from Ohio (B008 OH M WC) said: "A lot of people I don't want to be around. I'm not going to sit here and say I want a whole bunch of black people coming to my house, because I don't. I don't want Asians coming here either."

There were eleven interviewees (4.5 percent of the sample) with four-year college degrees whose views were similar to those of the working-class "racists," although they did not necessarily use explicitly antiblack statements to the same degree. These interviewees I called "middle-class conservatives." For example, a small-business owner in New Jersey (D030 NJ M MC), when asked about the changes for African Americans,

Table 1.5 Average Number of Comments About Religion During Interview and Typical Religious Comment

Religious Category	Average Number of Comments	Typical Comment
Religious conservative	4.88	(B001 OH M MC) "I think religion has a lot to do with it. Church is probably the center of our social life. . . . My faith has also been probably more important in all."
Religious nonconservative	2.64	(C014 NJ F UMC) "I identify more as being a family that likes to be with other families, who have similar family values. We are Methodist, but we are very open. We're going to a Catholic church now."
Other religious	1.97	(B022 OH M WC) "I'm not that religious. I believe in God. I go to church. I don't go around preaching."
Catholics	1.76	(E315 OH M UC) "White, middle-class Catholics. We go to church, I guess."
Jews	1.75	(D051 NJ M MC) "I started as a Roosevelt Democrat. The Jewish population tends to be Democrat. I am a social liberal and a financial conservative."
Nonreligious or secular (among those who made some comment)	1.45	(D009 NJ M WC) "I'm Methodist, Protestant, and never really, after confirmation, I can't say I've been back more than five times."

Source: Author's compilation.

replied: "A lot of times they are not qualified. . . . I think it causes more friction . . . because sometimes you know this person got in because he may not have been qualified, but he was black or African American and he's there and somebody else was better qualified and didn't get in."

In contrast to these politically more conservative groups, those in the "rich white liberal" category were distinctive because of both their liberal politics and their relative affluence compared to the other interviewees. A total of forty-two interviewees (17 percent) were included in this category. These interviewees generally made statements supportive of welfare state–type programs for both racial minorities and the poor. These interviewees were also more likely than the others to use structural explanations for inequality rather than individualistic explanations. Thus, they were likely to talk about poverty and unemployment and about the need for the government to support better schools or job training. They expressed concern about inequality and a desire that something be done about it. And they implied that they were willing to be taxed more to support such programs. For example, a New Jersey man (D038 NJ M MC) who was unemployed at the time of the interview but who had worked as a salesman said with regard to whether it is right for some people to expect help from the government: "Because if somebody needs, if somebody is starting out at a lower station, I think it is only fair that the more well-to-do does reach down and help the less well-to-do. I think just because you're born to a certain situation doesn't mean that that is how you have to live the rest of your life."

I drew the label of "rich white liberal" from an upper-middle-class insurance executive from New Jersey (D047 NJ M MC) who defined himself as a "rich, white liberal, the easy kind." In making this statement, he was in fact revealing something very profound. For the most part, those for whom it was easy to be politically supportive of the civil rights movement and the expansion of the welfare state were those whose lives were least affected by such policies. In this regard, they were like my graduate school colleagues whose liberalism seemed to reflect the privileges of class and who often seemed far removed from the social issues that most concerned them.

There were another fourteen working-class interviewees (6 percent) who espoused similarly liberal views. These I called "working-class liberals." For example, an Ohio construction contractor (E368 OH M WC), when asked whether it was fair for those who have less to expect the government to help them, said:

> I don't think it's fair for people to expect anything. . . . You're entitled to what you work for, and I do believe that, but that being said, I think we as a society and we as a group of people have an absolute . . . that we have to also push a little over in the direction to help the people who don't . . . aren't quite as fortunate, or didn't have the advantages we have.

Finally, there were ninety-two interviewees (37 percent) whom I defined as the "apolitical majority." They were distinctive, in part, because they did not fit into any of the other categories. Most important, however, was that they did not have specific or consistent views on any of the political issues addressed, and by their own admission, they had never given much thought to such issues. For example, a New Jersey accountant (D028 NJ F MC) described her politics as "oh, nonexistent. . . . I don't even remember if I voted last time." Like the religious conservative group, the apolitical majority includes both working-class and middle-class people. The majority of the apolitical majority interviewees defined their politics as moderate, while 17 percent of this group said that they were liberal and 22 percent said that they were conservative.

Table 1.6 Sample Comments from Interviewees in Different Political Categories

Political Category	Sample Comment
Religious conservative (N = 46; 19 percent of sample)	(B002 OH M MC) "Well, we're taxed too high. I mean, you know our government . . . if you become successful . . . by your own means . . . they'll find a way to try to take some of that from you and redistribute it to people who maybe got involved . . . made poor life decisions, got involved in drugs, fried half their brain, now they're too stupid to make a decent living . . . I don't know, I think as far as the Christian community, I think they're pretty maligned a lot . . . and I think more the Christian community . . . they realize the moral decay in our country . . . and how it's not getting any better and by getting worse, it only leads to worse things. It's not going to make things any better."
Working-class "racist" (N = 30; 12 percent of sample)	(E360 OH M WC) "I don't agree with the 'African American.' . . . They're not from Africa . . . but now we're treating them differently than the Irish American, the Italian American. . . . Why should they have special treatment? I had nothing to do with the selling of their people as slaves. . . . Everybody, even employers are afraid to fire them because they're black. . . . You can't reprimand them. . . . And I think today there's a huge reverse discrimination going on, and we haven't seen the tip of the iceberg with it yet."
Middle-class conservative (N = 11; 4.5 percent of sample)	(B013 OH F MC) "The whole issue of welfare and all that, I have a problem with . . . I don't want to label it as a black community kind of thing, but I think some of the leadership in the black community isn't doing them any justice at all either. I think their leadership, the people that are speaking for them, sometimes are just way off base. . . . I just hate the scare tactics they use with the older people and with the black community and the Hispanic community and whatever, all the minorities."
Apolitical majority (N = 92; 37 percent of sample)	(C011 NJ F WC) "Do I vote? No. I should because it's a right that I have and you know . . . I don't know. I can't sit in front of the TV and listen and watch the news . . . you know what I'm saying. Right now that doesn't interest me at all."
Religious nonconservative (N = 11; 4.5 percent of sample)	(F007 TN F MC) "Most people, I guess . . . I think there are people that grow up in horrible, horrible situations, and to think that they can sort through all of that themselves, I'm not so sure. . . . I think it's hard for some people, much harder than it is for others."
Working-class liberal (N = 14; 6 percent of sample)	(B005) OH F WC) "Well, sure, I believe everybody deserves help. I mean everybody, at some point in life, I don't think there's one person on the face of this earth that can say at some point in their life they hadn't wished there was someone there to give them something."
Rich white liberal (N = 42; 17 percent of sample)	(C009 NJ M MC) "Yes, I'm not sure that's the solution, but I think it's fair to ask . . . the kind of help that it's just unconscionable not to supply, like a safety net for the truly needy . . . definitely that kind of help has to exist, and I'm always afraid that it's being eroded by insensitivity."

Source: Author's compilation.

Hence, there was some variation within this group, but the main marker of the apolitical majority was their lack of political engagement. Table 1.6 provides examples of comments made by each type of interviewee.

Understanding the differences among these groups of interviewees and placing them within the context of post–civil rights politics should provide insight into the principle-policy gap. Although each group was distinctive in terms of its politics, I show in my analysis that they were similar to each other in terms of hoarding opportunities and drawing on social resources. The apparent political differences among these groups seemed to depend on how the civil rights movement had affected their ability to use opportunity hoarding and to access social resources to claim the privileges of whiteness. Those whose opportunity hoarding had become impeded because of civil rights legislation were more likely to express antigovernment and anti–welfare state views. Those who had felt less of a personal impact from the civil rights movement were more supportive of government efforts to ameliorate inequality.

Among the interviewees, the religious conservatives, the working-class "racists," and the middle-class conservatives expressed opposition to government policies, and many of them had developed antigovernment views, although they differed in the types of issues that seemed of most concern to them. In contrast, the rich white liberals, the working-class liberals, and sometimes the religious nonconservatives were less likely to express antigovernment views, but these groups also differed in their views on civil rights, as I discuss at various points in the analysis. As reflected in the label, the apolitical majority did not have clear political views about either the civil rights movement or post–civil rights politics. My discussion gives greater attention to religious conservatives, working-class "racists," rich white liberals, and the apolitical majority not only because these are the larger groups but also because these are the groups over which there is the most competition between the two political parties.

The political identifications among my interviewees were similar to those in the country as a whole. For example, in exit polls for the 2008 election, 34 percent of voters indicated that they were conservative, 44 percent that they were moderate, and only 22 percent that they were liberal.[13] My sample includes 36 percent who described their politics as conservative (with the religious conservatives representing 60 percent of that total and working-class "racists" another one-third), 40 percent who either called themselves moderate or did not have clear political views, and 23 percent who described their politics as liberal (the rich white liberals representing 75 percent of that total and the working-class liberals only 25 percent).

Ideological perspectives in the country have not changed much from the time I did the interviews for this study. A 2009 report by the Pew Research Center concluded, "The political values and core attitudes that the Pew Research Center has monitored since 1987 show little overall ideological movement" (Kohut 2009, 1). The views expressed by the apolitical majority, although often inconsistent or unclear, were closer in content and tone to the conservative interviewees than they were to the liberal interviewees. Thus, liberal political views were distinctive among these white interviewees, whereas moderate and conservative views were more blurred and harder to distinguish from each other.

Myrdal believed that whites would face a moral dilemma and thus would be motivated to act politically to support change when confronted with the incompatibility between racial inequality and the tenets of the American creed. I provide an explanation for why most white Americans do not face the kind of moral dilemma that Myrdal anticipated and instead feel removed from racial issues. Even so, the two major political parties compete to gain white support for policies that either reinforce or undermine the substance of the civil rights movement. Post–civil rights politics has been especially hotly contested, and therefore understanding the political landscape of the interviewees is an important part of our story. I endeavor in my analysis to explain the interviewees' views about inequality, civil rights, and government.

The Plan of the Book

The data from this study are brought to bear to address specific issues in each chapter. Chapter 2 explores what is at stake for those looking for jobs—in other words, the context of opportunity hoarding and the use of social capital. A key point of this chapter is that even "good jobs" are under constant threat from the actions of employers intended to erode the protections that workers create for themselves. Finding jobs that are removed from market competition and protecting these jobs from employers' continual efforts to force them back into market competition create tensions when programs such as those associated with the civil rights movement try to open up access to the jobs that whites have tried to keep for themselves. In this chapter, I first explore the images that the interviewees use to describe what is fair for people to expect out of life, because this defines for them the outcomes they want to achieve. I then explain how opportunity hoarding addresses the problem of vulnerability in the labor market and why opportunity hoarding is about privilege rather than merit. I also discuss the interface between opportunity hoarding and racial politics.

In chapter 3, I look at one of the primary means of opportunity hoarding, namely, the use of social resources—social, financial, and cultural capital—drawn from family and friends. In this chapter, I provide examples of white job-seekers' extensive use of social resources. The chapter also examines the conditions under which social capital is exchanged among family and friends and the limits of using social capital. Importantly, in this chapter I look at the paradox introduced by the effort required to make use of social capital—namely, that nobody makes it on their own, but nobody makes it without their own effort. I show how effort is then translated cognitively into merit, even though access to social capital is not earned. I also explore in this chapter the inconsistencies in the thinking of interviewees who claim that everyone deserves a chance but who see no relationship between inequality and their own use of social capital and hoarding of opportunities among their family members and friends.

In chapter 4, I examine the legitimating myth of individualism that has so strong a grip on Americans' images of their own lives. I describe the central importance that most Americans place on hard work, effort, motivation, and merit as bases for getting ahead. In this regard, I describe the responses of the interviewees to questions about what most contributed to their life outcomes or to obstacles they may have faced along the way, and I discuss their explanations for inequality, including what makes people rich or poor and what accounts for racial inequality. In this chapter, I also explore the relationship between racial resentment and traditional values, including egalitarianism and individualism. I consider the differences between respondents who use structural explanations for inequality and those who use individualist explanations, and I highlight the importance of personal responsibility in the views held by white Americans with regard to what people must do to make it in the world.

In chapter 5, I turn to the politics of race and to the role of whites in post–civil rights politics. As noted, Myrdal was interested not only in white attitudes toward racial inequality but also in whether whites would respond to the increasing prominence of racial inequality following World War II by actually doing something about it. In this chapter, I discuss the complicated historical context that shaped contemporary racial politics in the post–civil rights period. One of the themes I address in this chapter is the risk that U.S. political parties will lose more white votes than they gain when they compete for the black vote. I examine the role of civil rights in party competition before, during, and after the civil rights movement; the controversy about whether it was racial politics or economics that led to the transformation of the Southern vote; the emergence of religious politics to replace racial politics (and with it the close association that developed between religious conservatives and the Republican Party); the competition for the white working-class vote; the efforts of the Democratic Party to find a third way that would enable them to avoid the costs of their commitment to civil rights; the controversies about the bases of voting behavior; and the competition for various segments of the white vote as it relates to the interviewees in this study.

Beginning with chapter 6, I provide a more in-depth profile of each of the sociopolitical groups among the interviewees and discuss their place within post–civil rights politics. Given that Myrdal assumed that at least some white Americans would be troubled by racial inequality and moved to do something about it, I take a look in this chapter at the interviewees' views about economic inequality and what they think the role of government should be with regard to helping those who have less economically. In my analysis, I argue that concern for obtaining and keeping good jobs drives much of the interviewee outlook about government policy. The interviewees who expressed concern about inequality and who favored government helping the poor were those with liberal politics and those with a favorable outlook in their own economic situation. They also constituted a minority of the sample. In contrast, interviewees who expressed less concern about economic inequality and who were less favorable about government actions to help the poor included both working-class respondents who had themselves been struggling economically and middle-class respondents who were relatively worse off than they might have expected to be given their education. Religiously identified interviewees with conservative politics were also less concerned about inequality and were more equivocal about government's role in helping the poor. The views of these interviewees, however, were less tied to their own economic situation than to an ideology that linked their moral outlook to self-reliance and antigovernment sentiment. Interviewees without firm political views expressed more conservative than moderate or liberal views about inequality and about government help for the poor. I conclude this chapter with a discussion of how these political views are linked to the current competition between the political parties for various segments of the white vote and to the critical concern among whites about maintaining access to good jobs (jobs protected from the market and with wages taken out of competition).

Chapter 7 takes the analysis of interviewee views about inequality and social change a step further by providing information on the interviewee response to questions about taxes and welfare. To get at these issues, I asked the interviewees if they felt that "people like them" got what they deserved from the government and whether they thought they would be "better off" if some people made fewer demands on the government. In analyzing the responses to these questions, I discovered that most interviewees have a very restrictive view of what constitutes the "government," often reducing government to transfer payments like welfare or unemployment benefits. Many interviewees said that they got "nothing" from the government and that they wanted "nothing." Interestingly, the majority of the interviewees claimed that having fewer demands made on the government would not affect them very much. The most conservative groups expressed more concern about demands on the government, while most of the other groups said that it was not a major concern.

Chapter 8 explores the attitudes of the interviewees toward affirmative action, the issue that probably best exemplifies the views about racial inequality. Because those who are opposed to affirmative action policies often claim that it constitutes a form of discrimination against whites, I start the chapter with a summary of interviewee responses to a question about whether they had ever experienced discrimination. I found that the interviewee conceptions of discrimination are very diffuse and are not informed by legal definitions of discrimination. Very few interviewees reported incidents of discrimination that might be covered by the law. To address attitudes about affirmative action, I asked the interviewees about "changes that have occurred in access to education and jobs" for women, African Americans, and immigrants. There were wide variations in the interview responses on this topic, but the general pattern of responses showed more favorable views of changes in access to education and jobs for women, much less favorable views for African Americans, and even less favorable views for immigrants. The responses reported in this chapter show the clearest differences in how the policy views of the interviewees relate to their political identifications.

Chapter 9 revisits the issues that Myrdal raised about why racial inequality would present whites with a moral dilemma that would move them to political action and to support social change. Although I argue that Myrdal was far more prescient in his analysis than some of his critics have acknowledged, I outline in this chapter three major issues that Myrdal could not foresee and that, I argue, have contributed to the American non-dilemma we have observed. Myrdal framed his analysis in terms of the discrimination of whites toward blacks (and other minorities) rather than in terms of the favoritism or advantage that whites provide to each other. Myrdal also had strong faith in the institutional foundations of progressive social change and expected both New Deal politics and unions to have more impact on the transformation of civil rights than has turned out to be the case. And finally, Myrdal underestimated the sustained political influence of the U.S. South in its resistance to civil rights and its ability to continue to shape the political environment of U.S. politics. In my conclusion, I discuss the implications of these issues.

Each section of the book is intended to support the main point, namely, that racial inequality is reproduced in the post–civil rights period, not primarily through racism (of its various types), but rather through the processes by which whites help each other obtain unearned advantages. I further argue that whites' advantage, preference, privilege, or favoritism enables them to support their families and enjoy the kind of life that they think of as reasonable or "fair." Because whites' advantages involve doing good things for other people like themselves and not necessarily (in their consciousness) doing bad things to black people, the whites in this study (and presumably most in the country) do not think of themselves as contributing to adverse outcomes for blacks. They do not perceive any interdependence between their own outcomes and those of blacks, and they do not feel that they have done anything about which they should feel guilty. Thus, when whites in the United States think about the issue of racial inequality, they are puzzled, occasionally concerned, and sometimes angry, but they do not feel the pressures of a moral dilemma that would lead them to support social change. Instead, they feel that, if there is a problem, it is incumbent on blacks to address it themselves, to take responsibility, to work harder, to be persistent, and to have hope. While some may feel that the government should do more, most feel that the government has either done what is necessary or sometimes has done too much.

Given the sense among whites in the United States that racial problems are embedded in the black community and have very little to do with them (that is, with whites), there is a strong consensus among most whites that blacks need to help themselves if they are to achieve the promise of the civil rights movement. When whites think about blacks helping themselves rather than relying on government, however, whites do not have in mind their own use of social and cultural capital that has allowed them to gain advantage and unearned privilege. Instead, they think about a job "market" in which everyone who tries hard enough can participate and in which the "best" person should win out. As will be seen in this book, however, most whites try to find ways to protect themselves from the market, and they try to take their wages out of competition; thus, when they affirm that "equal opportunity" should be extended to blacks and that blacks should be responsible themselves for their own economic outcomes, the meaning and implications of that commitment to the principles of civil rights are not at all clear.

Until the current political context, many had taken for granted that the civil rights legislation already passed, the court cases already won, and the attitudes about civil rights expressed in national surveys by whites were settled issues. In recent years, however, many have been surprised at the fragility of these past successes. The institutional foundations of the civil rights movement have been attacked, resisted, and eroded through a long political struggle that has been orchestrated from above but responded to from below. Competition for segments of the white vote has been a key part of this political struggle. In this book, I try to show why there is no moral dilemma among whites because of racial inequality and therefore how and why whites' political commitments are tenuous and unsettled on the issue of civil rights. To create the kind of moral dilemma that Myrdal anticipated and thus gain the political support of whites for policy as well as principle requires a different understanding of how racial inequality is reproduced. It also requires a resolution of the conflict between labor rights and civil rights, a resolution that will protect both white and nonwhite workers rather than placing both in increasing jeopardy. I hope that this book provides some insight into these important issues.

Chapter 2

Jobs, Opportunities, and Fairness: The Stakes of Equal Opportunity

> If I had worked every day and my job was constant and I didn't . . . I had one steady job, I think my life would be a lot less complicated, and my goals would be pretty much set, because my goal in life is just to live comfortably and take care of my children.
>
> —A union painter from New Jersey (D012 NJ M WC)

> I think the average working guy in the United States should be able to have his own home paid for. He should be able to have some money in the bank when he retires. . . . Now granted, I've told you, I've had a lot of help, but a lot of other people have had help too. . . .
>
> I witnessed a lot of change in my lifetime. . . . When I graduated from high school, there were any number of companies in this area that paid a competitive wage. There aren't now. You know, there's nineteen or twenty people out there would take my job in a heartbeat, because they're working for a company that's even meaner, that's paying them $7 an hour, is less concerned about their health and safety on the job. . . . About the '80s, things got grim around here. Companies folded, moved south. A lot of people were shafted. . . . I'm glad I'm not a kid trying to get started today.
>
> —A factory worker from Ohio (E307 OH M WC)

These working-class men told important stories that revealed a great deal about what is at stake for those who are subjected to the uncertainties of the labor market. Further, the contrast in their life situations highlights both what being protected from market competition means for many white workers and how difficult it is sometimes to hold on to a middle-class lifestyle for workers who cannot find a stable job protected from the market. Both men were union members, but neither of them was in ideal circumstances. The New Jersey man belonged to a union, but he could not get jobs that paid union wages. In contrast, the Ohio man, also a union member, had a steady work history, but faced constant challenges in an aversive work environment and had to deal with the downsides of labor-management relations. In this chapter, I explore what is at stake for workers who are vulnerable to the vagaries of the job market, what workers think of as the appropriate goals for them to pursue, and how opportunity hoarding works as a strategy for obtaining their goals. In the next chapter, I discuss the extensiveness of opportunity hoarding and its limitations.

The work history of the New Jersey man quoted at the beginning of the chapter illustrates how precarious life can be for some workers. Although this interviewee was able to obtain a number of unionized jobs in different firms, he suffered the consequences of companies attempting to undermine or remove themselves from paying union wages and to circumvent safety rules and regulations to save costs. Some of the companies he worked for closed or moved elsewhere (often to the South). Other former employers went out of business after safety violations were found and the government moved in. A number of the jobs that he had held were extremely dangerous, especially in terms of exposure to chemicals, and yet he often dismissed or set aside his concerns about safety because he needed a job that would allow him to support his family.

This New Jersey man started out in a job he obtained with the help of his brother, but that first employer closed because of safety violations. Unfortunately, his initial experience was not unique. Throughout a history of holding low-skilled factory jobs, this interviewee faced losing his job to plant closings, being laid off, and being fired. His best job was as a unionized truck driver, but he lost that job after being caught with drugs. With the help of his brothers and friends, he found a series of new jobs, but again experienced plant closings and other forms of job instability. At the time of the interview, he explained, yet another brother had helped him get into the painters' union (which involved paying a substantial entrance fee and yearly dues), but he and many other painters could not make ends meet while waiting for union jobs because many employers did not want to pay union wages and benefits. Thus, to get by, he and others worked "off the union books" whenever they could and "off the tax books" as much as possible, often adding the pay from their cash jobs to the unemployment insurance payments they collected when the union could not provide enough work. Thus, although his union wages were protected from the market, the protection was meaningful only when he could get union jobs. This interviewee had worked only two months at union jobs during the year he had belonged to the painters' union, so he was worried about what might unfold in his future. Undoubtedly, as he observed himself, his life would have been much less complicated if he had been able to get a job that paid a living wage, provided benefits, and offered him some stability. His inability to work steadily put him and his family at risk. Undoubtedly, he would have been in an even more difficult situation had he not had a number of brothers and friends who could sometimes bend rules to help him get another job when each one ended.

The Ohio man, in contrast, had held a unionized job with one firm for most of his life. He was fortunate in being able to work steadily, receiving medical benefits, accumulating a pension, and enjoying some of the extras in life, like vacations and hobbies. He was painfully aware, however, that if not for the protection that the union contract offered him in this company, there were many other people who would have liked to have his job and would have taken it "in a heartbeat." When he talked about jobs with a "competitive wage," he really meant a living wage, since it is the people making "$7 an hour" whose wages are more subject to competition. As he described it, a worker making $7 an hour (which was substantially above the minimum wage at the time of the interviews) could neither live a comfortable life nor build any economic security for the future. A person in a job at $7 an hour, he said, would have loved to have a job like his, which paid more than twice that amount. Without the protections that the union contract provided him, he said, "there but for the grace of God go I."

The steady job in a large, unionized company placed the Ohio man in a very different financial situation than the man from New Jersey. But the Ohio man did not come by his job easily. After flunking out of college, he was able to obtain his factory job only because during the labor shortage created by the Vietnam War his medical problems (obesity) kept him out of the military. Hence, he was still at home to take advantage of an opportunity for a job to which he otherwise would not have had access. Even so, he received the job offer only after going back to the employment office at the company every week until they finally hired him.[1] Despite having this job, with strikes and layoffs, he and his wife were able to own their own home only after her family first rented and then later transferred ownership of a house to them for the amount of rent they had paid.

Although the Ohio man tried a number of times to finish his college degree, he was not able to complete the degree requirements while working full-time in the factory. The company placed him on swing shifts and was not willing to be flexible so that he could finish getting his degree. At several points along the way, the company made things even more difficult for him. Despite his frustration with company policies—and one incident in which, he said, the authoritarian posture of his boss reduced him to tears—he did not quit the company even when he had other job opportunities because he valued the pension plan, the medical benefits, and the income, which was higher than he could have earned in many starting managerial or teaching jobs. As he (E307 OH M WC) explained when asked about whether he deserved the kind of life he had now:

> I have worked . . . I don't miss [work very much]. I volunteer for the overtime. I know people have worked a lot harder than I have and have a lot less. They didn't work for a Fortune 500 company. . . . So I'm fortunate in a lot of ways. I think my pension is pretty secure . . . supposedly it's completely funded the way it is right now. I'm lucky in that way. I've had relatives that worked at [another company] here in town, and they spent as much time laid off as they did working, which doesn't allow you to accumulate wealth, because everything you get saved up, you eat up when you're laid off. I've only been laid off three times. . . . And I know what a stress it is. Even if you have money in the bank, you're hoarding it. You don't want to spend it, because . . . the uncertainty, you don't know how long you're going to have to rely on it. I told somebody the one time I got called back to work, it's really sad to be so damn glad to get back to a job you hate so much. But that's the way it is.

Steady employment at a job that earned enough money to pay the bills with a little left over and included medical insurance and a pension was the goal of most workers. Meeting this criterion was the dividing line between being middle-class and living in poverty. It was also the issue that most determined my interviewees' political outlooks and the intensity of their views.

What's Fair in Life When You Do What Is Expected?

Neither of these working-class men expressed an interest in being rich, perhaps because they did not believe it to be possible. Like most of the interviewees, they conceived of a comfortable life as being able to pay the bills and have some economic security. Although both of these men were working-class, middle-class interviewees told similar stories, as did women as well as men. For example, a middle-class project engineer from Ohio (B017 OH M MC) said, when asked about what is fair for people to expect out of life "if they do what they are supposed to,"

> You ought to be able to expect that if you're willing to work and put in an honest day's work and start that through school . . . to make an honest wage, one that can sustain you and your family. Beyond that, if you come up with the great American dream or design something and get rich or hit the Lotto even, that's fine. When those opportunities stop or dry up is when I think you can have a big problem. . . . Not everybody expects to get rich. They expect to be able to make a living. . . . But if you deny them those opportunities because you're saying now you're not worth what you used to be worth . . . I think that that aspect of it is not fair. If you make it so that there aren't any of those jobs anymore that you can sustain a low-middle-

> class living, blue-collar lifestyle. . . . You still have to create those opportunities.

When asked further about these views, however, this middle-class man backed off of what seemed to be a concern with the growing economic inequality in the country and said that opportunities do exist for people. He also expressed a concern that trying to do something about improving job prospects for blue-collar workers would lead to "taking rights away from another group of people."

Similarly, a middle-class real estate appraiser from New Jersey (D067 NJ M MC) said: "I think everyone should have a decent house to live in. . . . And enough money to put food on the table, the roof over their heads, some clothes on their back, and are able to enjoy some of the simpler things in life at least." This interviewee also backed off his concern when asked if there were some people who did not have such things. Instead, he began to raise questions about whether such people were trying hard enough, or had no family support, or maybe had opportunities that they "blew" when they had their chance.

Women expressed a similar view of what is fair in life. A very wealthy corporate executive from Tennessee (G521 TN F MC) said: "They should expect being able to do more than just get by. And they should expect, if they are contributing, and by that I mean I don't care what kind of paying job they have, if they are contributing, they should expect respect and people to be fair with them." A working-class homemaker from Ohio (E303 OH F WC) had a similar view of the issue: "I think you should be able to make a decent living, not spoil yourselves, but at least be able to get what you want now and then. And retire and be able to have a decent income when you retire, to live comfortably without having to scrape and scrimp." A working-class Tennessee clerical worker (G504 TN F WC) said it simply: "Just to live comfortably, I mean, not have to live paycheck to paycheck. Be able to have a little money in the bank."

Comments about getting by, living comfortably, and having a little extra were typical when the interviewees were asked about what is fair in life. Over 40 percent of the interviewees gave such responses when asked what is fair for people to expect out of life if they "do what they are supposed to." Another 22 percent of the interviewees (especially political conservatives and the working class) said that what is fair is having an opportunity to work and that "you get out of it what you put in." For example, a working-class woman from Tennessee (G523 TN F WC) who worked as an allied health professional had this to say: "I think you are gonna get out of life what you put into it. You get out what you put into it and what you expect. I am not sure what is fair. I think that question goes along with the popular American attitude of expecting the world to owe you something, and we don't hear that in this house." A politically liberal working-class Ohio woman who worked as an office cleaning person (E301 OH F WC) also made this point: "You get out of life what you put into it. I think it would be fair to assume that if you work hard, you can obtain a home. I think that's fair thinking. I think it's fair to assume that you would be a productive human being. I think that's the most important thing, that you're productive."

Such comments affirm the strong belief—perhaps held especially strongly by whites—that opportunities are available to those who make an effort in life (Kluegel and Smith 1986). Such comments also confirm a fairly strong belief that those who "take advantage of opportunity" should be rewarded for it with a comfortable or decent lifestyle, one that includes a sense of dignity and the ability to meet basic needs. As the middle-class project engineer from Ohio put it, people should be able to earn at least a "low-middle-class living" or be assured a "blue-collar lifestyle"—meaning a reasonable, not extravagant, lifestyle in which they can pay their bills, provide their children with opportunities for growth, and enjoy life to some degree, including a "decent" retirement.

The Route to Being Protected from Market Competition

If a decent or comfortable lifestyle is the goal of those who have "done what they are supposed to," one of the key questions was how the interviewees believed that such a goal is achieved. Based on their life stories, it seems that most interviewees relied on hoarding opportunities by drawing on the social resources available to them—if the opportunities were worth hoarding. Opportunities worth hoarding were those that provided pay or benefits that enabled the kind of lifestyle they envisioned. Indeed, most of the interviewees quoted earlier engaged in opportunity hoarding:

- Despite not having a job until after college graduation because of poor grades, the project engineer from Ohio got his first postcollege job in the company where his father was a supervisor after his father made a phone call to encourage a colleague to interview his son.
- The real estate appraiser from New Jersey got a summer job at a bank during his last year of college after his father talked with a friend. Then, following graduation, this interviewee went into business with his dad. Although he left the business after a decade because he realized that there was no possibility of income growth in the business, he was able to develop skills in this job that later were helpful to him in obtaining a job after completing his MBA.

- The corporate executive from Tennessee inherited money from her family and had the luxury of not having to settle into a career for a number of years. She obtained a master's degree in teaching but decided not to pursue that line of work. Then, after several other jobs, she went back to graduate school with the help of friends who were instrumental in initiating a new program at the university she attended, but she did not finish the doctorate she had planned. Instead, she worked at different jobs, none of which engaged her interest. Finally she landed a job she loved at a large company through networking with people she knew from several avenues.

In contrast to these interviewees who often found jobs with the help of friends and connections, many of the working-class women quoted earlier obtained jobs from newspaper ads, by going door to door, or with the help of employment agencies (including temporary work). Jobs that do not pay a living wage or do not provide benefits seem less likely to be hoarded, but even some of the working-class women interviewees had help along the way:

- The homemaker from Ohio got her first job at a business owned by neighbors, but after that she used an employment agency to get the job she kept until she left the labor force to take care of her son.
- The Tennessee clerical worker obtained most of her jobs from newspaper ads or through employment agencies, but after being fired from a company that was engaging in marginally legal activity, she was afraid she would be blocked from further employment. She was able to find a new job, however, when a friend put in a good word for her in the company where the friend worked.
- Before getting training, the allied health professional from Tennessee found retail or babysitting jobs through ads in the paper or by going door to door. But when she was trying to get established in the field of her training, she had the help of a friend with whom she had gone to school; this friend told her about a position and provided a recommendation that led to her being hired into her current job.
- Despite family support that would have enabled her to go to college, the Ohio woman doing office cleaning did not do well enough in school to take advantage of the family assistance. She obtained several of her early jobs through newspaper ads, but once she had children she needed more flexibility and eventually found a suitable job that she could do out of her home after a friend told her about the work and how to get started. Her efforts to multiply her income by doing double or triple duty with several different companies took a toll on her health, however, at which point a friend (whom she had

directed to a part-time job in the same field) later helped her get her current job.

In a pretty consistent pattern, the interviewees often obtained jobs with higher pay and better benefits with the help of family or friends, but sometimes found jobs that did not pay enough to support a family through more formal means (ads, direct applications, employment agencies). In other words, the jobs most subject to market competition were the ones for which connections did not matter as much; as one male factory worker from Ohio (E304 OH M WC) said in his interview, "One job is as bad as another." For "good" jobs, however, job-seekers endeavored to draw on social resources that would give them an inside edge and help protect them from market competition. In the rest of this chapter, I explore more fully what opportunity hoarding means. In the next chapter, I look at the prevalence of opportunity hoarding and how and when social resources are used by job-seekers.

Opportunity Hoarding and Merit

Unlike the working-class factory worker in Ohio, very few of the interviewees could count on a job in which they could plan to work for thirty-five years, assume a "fully funded" defined-benefit pension, and earn seniority. Furthermore, jobs like his are fast disappearing. Case in point: the company where this interviewee worked announced (presumably after his planned retirement) that it was closing the plant after a century of being the primary employer in the city—one that supported many local charitable organizations that bore its name and promised "lifetime" health and retirement benefits to the employees who stuck it out. Yet companies like this one are now opening plants in lower-wage areas, contracting out for services that used to be provided in-house, and sometimes producing abroad rather than paying the wages that unionized employees have negotiated over the years. Some companies are also trying to renege on their promises of lifetime benefits, and they have been finding support from the courts, which have allowed them to dismantle their existing retirement and health benefit programs (Said 2004). Hence, the protections afforded by unionization, licensing, and tenure are eroding in the current economy, and only a few of the interviewees in this study had jobs with even the eroded version of those kinds of protections.

However, the interviewees were not necessarily subjecting themselves to market competition. Instead, they sought an inside edge, often through the help of their family or friends using whatever influence they might have had to pass along good jobs—that is, jobs as good as they had access to—to people they knew. Charles Tilly (1998) conceptualizes opportunity hoarding as a broad concept that defines any effort by a group of people to reserve a valuable resource for members of their social group. It encompasses in his view everything from professionals fighting to define who can do their type of job to the well-to-do passing along inherited wealth, but the primary example of opportunity hoarding is passing along jobs to people within the same social group or network (Waldinger 1996, 1997). Describing an example of chain migration from a small town in Italy to an area in Westchester, New York, Tilly argues that the Italian immigrants passed along economic opportunities to fellow countrymen (or women), thus creating an economic niche that came to be identified with Italians. He cites this example as a "classic case of opportunity hoarding" (or "categorical inequality") that operated as follows:

> Members of a categorically bounded network retain access to a resource—in this case, a set of employers, clients, and jobs—that is valuable, renewable, subject to monopoly, supportive of network activities, and enhanced by the network's modus operandi. Matching the category Italian-Americans to the business of landscape gardening sequestered opportunities for poor Italian peasants and their descendants, but it also fenced off those opportunities from other people, including the growing number of black residents. . . . It reinforced Italian identity as a basis of everyday social relations. (Tilly 1998, 151–52)

The concept of opportunity hoarding is often used interchangeably with Max Weber's concept of social closure. The emphasis with regard to opportunity hoarding, however, is that of reserving opportunities for members of one's own social group, whereas Weber (1968, 341–42) describes social closure as more a matter of keeping others out:

> One frequent economic determinant is the competition for a livelihood—offices, clients, and other remunerative opportunities. . . . Usually one group of competitors takes some externally identifiable characteristic of another group of (actual or potential) competitors—race, language, religion, local or social origin, descent, residence, etc.—as a pretext for attempting their exclusion.

Although it may seem that these concepts are just different sides of the same coin, there is an important distinction. Exclusion, as in discrimination, is illegal, but inclusion, through opportunity hoarding or favoritism, is not illegal and thus does not carry with it the same legal remedies for those who feel they are adversely affected (McGinley 1997).

The concept of opportunity hoarding has often been associated with ethnic enclaves and niches, but it need not be so specific. It can proceed, as Roger Waldinger (1996, 171) describes it, "through informal ties among established workers and the younger members of their core networks." In the post–civil rights period, core networks are more likely to be residentially based than ethnically based, at least for native-born white workers. People look to those in their families, neighborhoods, or churches, to those with whom they went to school, or to those with whom they have worked in current or past jobs. To the extent that these institutional settings are ethnically based, then people also look to coethnics for information about opportunities. In general, help is given to those who are thought of as "like us."

Within a social capital framework, the boundaries of core networks are defined by those with whom one feels a sense of obligation, identity, and reciprocity. People enjoy the benefits of living within a community, and they draw social resources from community members. They also develop obligations to provide social resources to others in the community. These exchanges may be specific, with two people understanding that help from one will be followed by help from the other. Or the exchanges may be generalized, with the understanding that helping behavior is for the good of the community and as the community is strengthened, one will eventually benefit from the social resources accumulated among family and friends (Putnam 2000).

In the post–civil rights period in the United States, it is the very fuzziness of these boundaries that makes the sense of inclusion more meaningful than exclusion in the everyday cognitive experiences of most whites. But the reality of racial segregation in whites' core networks creates outcomes that do not extend often or far across racial lines. Like most of the people in my study, whites in the United States have very limited contact with African Americans or other nonwhites, so when they think about a job opportunity that someone should know about, they do not often think of African Americans, since there are few in their networks. Thus, what appears to be a totally random outcome of friends helping friends turns out to be a structured outcome with racial content. Tilly (1998, 151) describes how this process is structured: "However much the experience of any particular migrant might seem to depend on chance and individual taste, the experience took shape within stringent limits set by preexisting contacts."

Undoubtedly, African Americans—like all identifiable social groups—help each other too, but there are fewer social resources in their communities and fewer institutional sectors from which they can draw social resources (Parks-Yancy 2010). From the African American point of view, this is because whites have hoarded opportunities for themselves and excluded African Americans from access to those opportunities. Of course, that is the substance of what the civil rights movement was intended to address. African Americans mobilized for "jobs and freedom," meaning that they wanted to have access to the kinds of jobs that whites passed among themselves and they wanted to be protected institutionally in the same way that whites had come to take for granted.

Both the laws and the academic literature frame the complaints of African Americans in terms of their exclusion rather than in terms of white inclusion. That is, they focus on discrimination, by which they mean specific and intentional acts of exclusion of blacks by whites. But exclusion is a consequence of opportunity hoarding. Exclusion is neither opportunity hoarding's main intent nor the primary means by which it operates. Hoarding means gathering to oneself, perhaps with little thought about the negative consequences for others. It is only when others call attention to the negative consequences for them and demand to be let into the process that their concerns become politically relevant. For those who have been engaging in the hoarding, such demands for access cause discomfort and often anger, precisely because the hoarding behavior itself arose in order to preserve resources that are "valuable" to them and to those toward whom they feel a sense of obligation.

Thus, to the extent that civil rights legislation and court rulings interfered with the ability of whites to hoard access to good jobs, whites experienced these changes as a substantial loss to their resource pool and felt themselves to be adversely affected. In that context, this sense of loss caused anger and resistance on the part of whites to civil rights policies. Most whites thought of the civil rights movement only as outlawing discrimination (the active exclusion of blacks), not as outlawing the sort of favoritism that whites showed toward each other (the active inclusion of whites). Given this framing, whites could be both supportive of the civil rights movement and opposed to the government's efforts to impose solutions that would affect the ability of whites to protect their access to jobs and economic resources.

It is in this context that one has to interpret the arguments made frequently by the interviewees in this study that what is fair is for the "best person" to be chosen for a job. In their conception, an employer making a hiring decision is confronted with two potential candidates (perhaps one black and one white), and the employer must choose the best person for the job. This image of decision-making in the job market, of course, is far distant from how decisions are made in this context or otherwise. As Herbert Simon (1947) argued in his classic work, decisions in organizations are not the product of reviewing all relevant information and maximizing or choosing the "best" solution. Instead, according to Simon, most decision-makers "satisfice" by choosing the first, reasonably acceptable solution that they encounter. The same is true in the labor "market," to the extent that it functions at all like a market. Rather than finding the "best person" from an exhaustive search of all potential applicants, employers often attempt to reduce their search costs by hiring the first acceptable candidate who has the necessary qualifications. In this regard, employers are often complicit with employees in hiring friends and neighbors of current workers, because doing so reduces the search costs for the employer and creates a debt on the part of the employee, who may then participate in both socializing and monitoring a new hire whom he or she has recommended.[2]

This image of decision-making in hiring as maximizing or choosing the "best person" for the job is also far distant from the way the interviewees got their own jobs. I heard very few, if any, stories from interviewees about having been the best person for the job that he or she obtained. Instead, they often spoke of having been given a chance to "get in the door" and then learn the job after being hired. In the stories told by the interviewees, opportunity hoarding was evident in all types of organizations and for all types of jobs, but especially for jobs that provided benefits and reasonable pay. These interviews suggest that most jobs are obtained through the help of family and friends, whether the company is a civil service employer, a company that has declared its commitment to being an "equal opportunity employer," or a small family-owned firm. Interviewees told me that one did not get a job in the school system or a city agency without knowing someone. The same was true for jobs in the skilled crafts, especially the construction unions, where interviewees explained the need to know the business agent or the panel of members who screened applicants. Even in hiring situations that involved formal test-taking, interviewees told me, those on the panel or committee would make subjective judgments and give higher scores to friends and relatives. Thus, applicants who ended up with the "highest scores" may have benefited from being given extra credit in the scoring process by those who were looking out for their interests, as several interviewees told me had occurred in their own experience.

Sometimes interviewees got a job through contacts because an employee in a company had "expropriated" the company's jobs for the benefit of his or her family members or friends. For example, an employee would know that someone was leaving the company and would tell a family member to apply for the job before it was otherwise made public. Sometimes that employee would lobby for the friend or relative; in other cases, he or she would simply make a phone call or put in a good word. Some clever employees found ways around nepotism rules, such as asking a friend in the company to hire a relative and then reciprocating the favor. Job applicants also have an inside edge when a family member or friend can tell them what is likely to be on a test, how to do the job, what to look for in the interview process, and, often most importantly, when the hiring is being done. Several employees who got jobs in the U.S. Postal Service had family members who could help them prepare for the required civil service tests, and they could influence the score given on the subjective part of the test.

Interviewees told of the same sort of influence coming into play with promotions. For example, a police officer described his experience when the police chief wanted to promote a favored candidate. Despite the formal requirement that the candidate be interviewed by a panel of senior officers, it was obvious, according to the police officer I interviewed, that the candidate had been given both the questions and answers in advance and was then judged to "merit" a high score. The panel members were told to ask only the questions that the chief had given them, and the candidate was fully prepared with the answers considered appropriate according to the guidelines provided to the panel members.

Although the interviewees often disapproved of these practices, especially when the favored candidate was not someone with whom they identified or felt comfortable, such stories were considered neither exceptional nor especially scandalous. Instead, they described these practices as "the way things are" for those who were "in the know." As Tilly (1998, 151) notes with regard to the disparate fates of those from the same Italian village who ended up in different types of jobs and achieved different levels of success depending on where they immigrated to and the process by which they were incorporated into the community: "Ability, determination, and prior wealth or education certainly seem to have mattered little, while the presence of a relative who could provide aid and information mattered a great deal. That presence, however, was not a lucky coincidence, but the pivot of an extensive migration system."

Not surprisingly, this is not the way the interviewees saw their lives. They did not think of their lives in terms of patterns or networks that linked whites to each other and provided unearned advantages. Indeed, they strongly believed that it was their ability and determination—not their access to unequal opportunity—that had most affected how their lives turned out. For many of the interviewees, civil rights policies had undermined the fairness of the system. Although they thought it was fine to outlaw discrimination (defined as the exclusion of black people), they were opposed to policies that they believed provided advantages for African American or other minorities (defined as the inclusion of them). Such views, of course, ignored the advantages that whites themselves sought and through which most had obtained jobs throughout most of their lives.

Opportunity Hoarding and Politics

Although all of the interviewees described similar processes in getting jobs, their political views varied. Some interviewees were angry about how the civil rights movement had affected people like themselves, although they generally talked about it in more general terms rather than as "civil rights" per se. In contrast, others thought primarily about how the civil rights movement had affected others, most likely because they did not feel that it had affected people like themselves very much.

Although these distinctions are only partially affected by education and income, the most notable differences among my interviewees in points of view regarding civil rights were between the working-class "racists" and the rich white liberals. More than any other group of interviewees, the working-class "racists" were likely to depend on jobs that had been taken out of market competition if they were to enjoy middle-class lifestyles. Like the working-class man from Ohio whose job situation was described in the beginning of this chapter, members of the working class can live the kinds of lives that they envision as fair only if they can get jobs that provide benefits, that ensure reasonably steady employment, and that pay wages above the market rate for people with their level of education. Such jobs for the working class are typically jobs that are unionized or otherwise protected from the market. In other words, like the man from Ohio, the working class need jobs that pay closer to the $16 an hour that he was making and not the $7 an hour that he said would not be enough to support a family.

The importance of being protected from market competition was underlined by another working-class interviewee, a surveyor from Ohio (B008 OH M WC). When asked about economic inequality, he specifically tied jobs with good pay to unionization:

> Well, '70s come along, and the working-class people kept getting the union raises, and believe me, all the raises that America got come directly straight from the unions. They didn't come from anybody that says, "I think Joe over there needs a raise." Well, if Joe wasn't a nephew or a cousin, he was never going to get a raise. So the unions got the economy up to a certain grade . . . they created a real nice pay scale, good working conditions, everybody was working that wanted to work. . . . Well, those people don't like that. So they did something about it.

This interviewee believed that employers purposely slowed down the economy in order to undercut union demands. Thus, it is not just the ability to get a unionized job, which has been critically important for working-class people, but being in a union that can limit the competition from the labor market. As the same working-class man from Ohio (B008 OH M WC) said: "If you have a million jobs and you have 900,000 workers, those 900,000 workers, their pay is going to go straight to the ceiling. But if you have a million jobs, and you have two million workers, they're going to be held down."

For the working class, civil rights represents an expansion of the number of people looking for a limited number of good jobs—that is, jobs that in their view will allow them to live a decent life. Those who find such jobs harder to get risk the kind of vulnerabilities faced by the New Jersey painter mentioned at the outset of this chapter.

In contrast, rich white liberals who all had college degrees (by definition) were often in the kinds of professional or managerial jobs that have fared best since 1973 (that is, in the period after wages for non-college-educated men stagnated, while incomes for professional and managerial employees rose). Even though their jobs were increasingly uncertain with corporate downsizing and business failures, few among the rich white liberals attributed these difficulties to the civil rights movement or to the government policies of the 1960s, perhaps because their jobs were not often subject to competition from blacks; fewer blacks had the same level of education from schools of the same quality as they had, and few blacks had had the types of job experiences that made them as likely to do well in competition for similar jobs. In fact, only a handful of the rich white liberal interviewees described having had difficulty finding a job or keeping a job, and of these, only one—a government employee—mentioned affirmative action (actually diversity) policies as a possible constraint on his career. The others who were either unemployed at the time of the interview or had faced more than temporary unemployment at various points in their careers mentioned a range of factors as causes, including family responsibilities, alcohol addiction, office politics, competition (in jobs in the arts), and, in one case, being a woman. They did not, for the most part, raise concerns about civil rights policies having resulted in people who did not deserve it taking their jobs.

Thus, while both of these groups of interviewees engaged in opportunity hoarding and both groups benefited from job market assistance from family and friends, civil rights policies had the most severe impact on the ability to hoard opportunities for the working-class "racists" and less so for the rich white liberals. To the extent that civil rights policies expanded the competition for good jobs, especially for the working class, those policies opened these jobs up to more market competition—that is, to "equal opportunity." In other words, if the working-class "racists" did not get the kinds of jobs that protected them from the market, they would have had to compete in the job market with low skills and poor educational backgrounds. Although the rich white liberals might have felt some impact of affirmative action or diversity programs in their companies on people like themselves, very few instances of such a situation were reported. Further, when things did go wrong in the job market, most of the rich white liberal interviewees could draw on extensive social capital that made it more likely that they could find new jobs if for some reason they were affected by such policies.[3]

The same distinction operated in reverse, however, for middle-class conservatives and working-class liberals. Despite the fact that the middle-class conservatives should also have had more options available to protect themselves from any outfall from affirmative action or diversity policies, their political views did not lead them to see it that way. Similarly, the working-class liberals should have been just as vulnerable in their job situations as the working-class racists, but their politics also did not lead them to see it that way. Whereas the middle-class conservatives were not sympathetic to blacks or to the poor, the working-class liberals often expressed both tolerance and support for the poor. For example, a Tennessee man who had dropped out of college and worked as a web designer (G513 TN M WC) said, when asked whether those who have less have a right to expect government help: "I think everybody should be equal. If they need help, they should get it." In contrast, a New Jersey insurance adjuster (D040 NJ M MC) who was also a college graduate said, when asked the same question about whether people with less have a right to government help, "No. I personally don't. I am not for politics. I understand people have circumstances, but I think things have moved beyond where everyone needs public assistance in order to benefit themselves." Not surprisingly, both of these groups were small compared to the larger proportion of people in the same job situations in my sample who had more predictable political views. I explore more fully what may set these groups apart in subsequent chapters.

There are also very distinct views with regard to civil rights policies among both the religious conservatives and the religious nonconservatives. The religious conservatives expressed views that were very similar to the working-class "racists" with regard to government policy and civil rights. For example, the manager of an insurance office in Ohio (E311 OH M MC), whom I categorized as a religious conservative, said, when asked whether people who have less should be able to expect help from the government:

> No . . . I think the government has a responsibility to help groups of people to better their lives . . . health, housing, those kinds of things, but I guess I disagree with the federal government setting up programs just for certain groups of people . . . to help them get a leapfrog effect over another group of people. . . . [*What do you have in mind?*] Maybe quotas . . . schools or employment firms having to hire a certain amount or group of people, specific ethnic group of people . . . the best person . . . should get the job.

The religious nonconservatives expressed views that were closer to the views of rich white liberals. For example, a New Jersey management consultant (D044 NJ F MC) said, when asked about whether people who have less should expect the government to help them:

> I think to an extent, yes. . . . If you are a single mother trying to raise children, then you probably deserve some measure of help from the government. If you've . . . become unemployed and need to collect for some pe-

> riod of time, or if you become disabled and need to collect for some period of time. . . . I think there is probably a lot of people that take advantage of those, but . . . I think it's our responsibility as a nation to help the folks that are less fortunate.

The fact that 80 percent of the Protestant evangelicals (including both the religious conservatives and the religious nonconservatives) among my interviewees considered themselves conservative (and were among the most conservative of the interviewees), of course, raises questions about what it is about their religious views that would seem to have such an influence on their political views. Again, the differences between these two groups of coreligionists is explored in subsequent chapters.

The apolitical majority in my sample expressed views that, as expected, were in the middle—between the views of those who were more conservative and those who were more liberal. For example, a male factory worker from Ohio (B011 OH M WC) said, when asked if some people make too many demands on government:

> Oh, yeah. I'd say probably at both ends of the spectrum. . . . I would say business naturally likes to gain all the benefits that they can through naturally buying senators and congressmen. . . . They want to affect policy. And then I'd say probably as we look at welfare, that end of it, I'd say those people . . . naturally they don't have the money, but they have the clout as "Hey, we're a big group, and we need to be taken care of."

As is true in this case, many of those who were categorized as the apolitical majority would often see both sides of the fence, while at other times they either had no opinion at all or disavowed any interest in political issues. For example, a New Jersey crossing guard (C012 NJ F WC) said, when asked about changes that have occurred in education and jobs for African Americans, "I don't have an opinion on that either. . . . I mean, I'm basically not a very opinionated person about many things. . . . Political issues I couldn't care too much about." Although some members of the apolitical majority expressed an interest in politics, their views were usually not consistent and were sometimes on both sides of the same political issue. More often, the apolitical majority members, like the New Jersey crossing guard, were not especially interested in politics and did not give it much thought.

One of the claims that I make in my analysis is that the political views expressed by the interviewees are linked to their views on civil rights. To explore this connection more explicitly, I compared the sociopolitical groups that I defined in this study on a measure of racial resentment that includes four of the six items used by Kinder and Sanders (1996) to measure this concept. As can be seen in figure 2.1, the political views of each

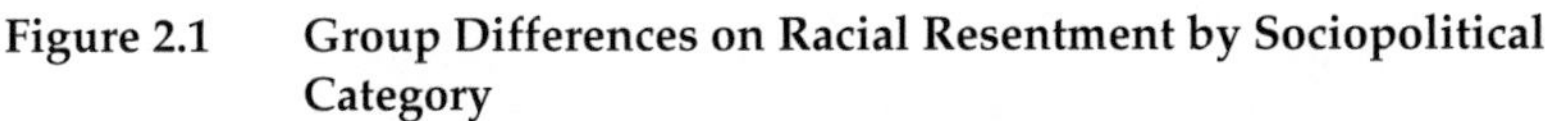

Figure 2.1 Group Differences on Racial Resentment by Sociopolitical Category

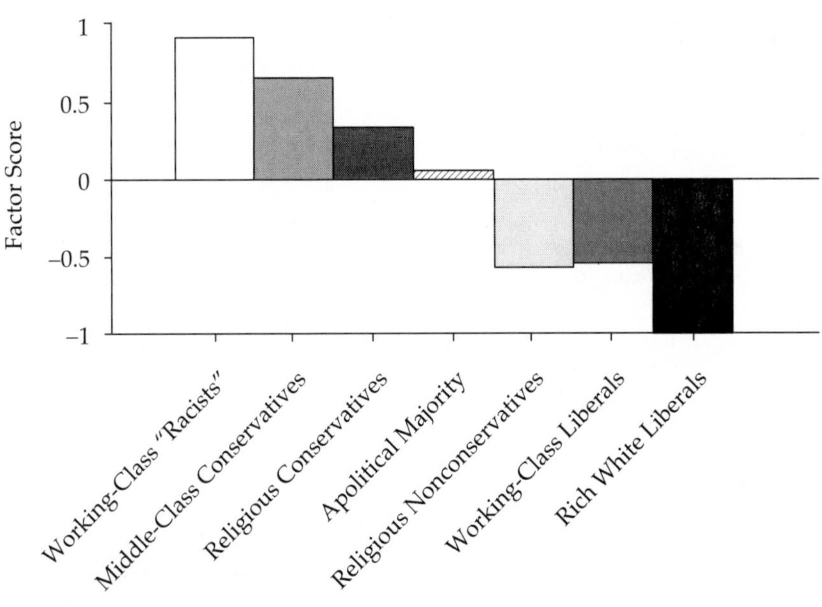

Source: Author's compilation.
Notes: The bars represent the factor score for each group for a measure of racial resentment including the following four items (factor loadings in parentheses). All items range from 1 = "not at all" to 7 = "a lot" and begin with the stem: "To what extent do you believe that . . ."

1. ". . . most people who receive money from welfare programs could get along without it if they tried?" (0.738)
2. ". . . that because the Irish, Italians, Jews, and many other minorities overcame prejudice and worked their way up, blacks should do the same without any special favors?" (0.837)
3. ". . . it is really a matter of some people not trying hard enough and that if blacks would try hard they could be just as well off as whites?" (0.850)
4. ". . . generations of slavery and discrimination have created conditions that make it difficult for blacks to work their way up in life?" (0.629, reverse-coded)

The factor analysis includes only one component with an Eigen value of 2.362 that explains 59 percent of the variance in the items.

sociopolitical group are tied to their racial attitudes and, I would argue as well, to their concerns about how the civil rights movement affected the ability of people like themselves to hoard opportunities that they viewed as valuable resources.[4] Groups with more conservative politics are more racially resentful, while those with more liberal politics are less racially resentful. A pairwise comparison between groups indicates that the apolitical majority is more similar to the conservative groups than to the liberal ones. The bases of these distinctions among groups are explored further in the chapters that look in more detail at the political views of the sociopolitical groups identified in this study.

Conclusions

Most of the interviewees in this study believed that what is fair for people to expect in life if they "do what they are supposed to" is having their basic needs met and being able to live a comfortable and "decent" life. The presumption was that those who do their part, who make an effort, and who stay out of trouble should expect to be treated with respect and that they should enjoy rewards that are commensurate with their contributions in life. Some also felt that there should be assistance from government if misfortune falls, but this is a point on which there was division. A sizable minority of the interviewees said that "life's not fair," that people "should not expect anything," or that each person has to make his or her own luck. Nevertheless, the predominant view was that there should be a fair reward for a fair effort—or as we used to say, "a fair day's wage for a fair day's work."

The views expressed by the interviewees were not especially egalitarian. A number of them indicated that they were not concerned about how rich people might be, but only about how poor they are. The interviewees nevertheless expressed the hope that inequality is not so extreme as to threaten the decency of life for those who try their best. Most of the interviewees clearly believed that they themselves had "done what they were supposed to," and therefore they expected to be able to have a decent life. Because of the uncertainties of life, however, it was also the case that most of the interviewees had endeavored with a great deal of persistence to find opportunities beyond or protected from the market. The interviewees told life stories that suggested that they not only hoarded opportunities but also drew from the opportunities that others hoarded on their behalf.

Although none of the interviewees expressed guilt about the opportunity hoarding in which they had participated, it is interesting that a number of them signaled to me through their body language or tone of voice their recognition that the inside advantage they had received, when it was available to them, was perhaps not quite fair. Most told me about such assistance only when I probed for more information. They did not otherwise offer the information openly, and sometimes after they had recounted an example of inside advantage, they would wink or turn their head or give me a look that implied, "You know how it is." Most often, however, if they heard themselves say something about knowing someone or getting help from someone or getting an extra boost because someone looked out for their interests, they would tend to dismiss or discount or otherwise minimize such advantages. A typical statement was: "That just got me in the door. Then I had to prove myself."

By and large, the interviewees either did not acknowledge or seemed rarely to think about the fact that perhaps there were blacks or other minorities who also might have wanted to get in the door and be able to prove themselves. Instead, most of the interviewees thought of their own experience as the exception, as the occasional and clearly atypical route to a job like theirs; never did I hear expressed an awareness that their getting a job through extra-market social resources was somehow integrally related to a potential black applicant not getting a job for which he or she might have been equally qualified. Instead, if the issue arose, the interviewee was more likely to question the credentials of black applicants and decry the interference of the government in making employers hire unqualified people into jobs that the interviewees clearly implied should rightfully be given to qualified white applicants. Interviewees expressed such views even while declaring that "everyone deserves a chance" and "it is not right to discriminate against anyone."

Thus, as noted, the gap in the views of the interviewees was not so much between a commitment to the principles of civil rights and opposition to civil rights policies—although the interviewees did express exactly these views on many occasions—but more important, between the fact that they lived lives of "unequal opportunity" (opportunity hoarding) even while declaring a commitment to "equal opportunity" as the principle of fairness. In fact, most of the interviewees expressed a great deal of anxiety about the prospect of having to compete equally in the market and being subjected to market competition. Like the working-class man from Ohio whose story opens this chapter, some would say things like, "I'm glad I'm not a kid trying to get started today." Or like the man from New Jersey also described at the beginning of the chapter, some would express dismay that they could not get a "steady job" that would allow them to "work every day." Hence, the interviewees were aware at a visceral level of what was at stake if they were not able to benefit from the opportunities that took them out of market competition and gave them an inside edge. They were not aware at a cognitive level, however—nor perhaps at a political level—of the extent to which the opportunity hoarding in their own lives was neither benign nor a reflection of just the way things are. They did not see how the advantages they enjoyed might constitute disadvantages for those who were not part of the same networks or part of the same communities. To them, getting help from family or friends was the exception, not the rule. The interviewees saw it as a private experience, not a public one. Getting such help was recognized as getting a break thanks to a family member or friend. But there was no sense in which the interviewees saw it as the reproduction of racial inequality—as the reproduction of white privilege.[5]

Before leaving this topic, however, it is important to note that the idea of subjecting more workers to market competition for jobs is not a benign suggestion either. Allowing more people to compete for the same jobs does drive down both wages and working conditions, as noted by the Ohio interviewee who talked about the importance of unions to the economic well-being of working-class people. Institutional protections from market competition are necessary in order for most workers to live a "decent" life.[6] Introducing into the market more workers who are desperate for jobs and willing to work for less has always been a threat to workers who are working at "decent" but not extravagant wages, and finding new and cheaper sources of labor has been a favorite strategy of employers to undermine the effectiveness (the rents) of worker demands.[7] These issues are even more salient today because of the great expansion of international trade and the movement of jobs around the world (Freeman 2007). Thus, we need to remember that there is tension between labor rights broadly defined and civil rights, and virtue is not necessarily associated with one side or the other. This tension can be reconciled only if the institutional protections of labor rights are extended to other people through civil rights, not by using civil rights to undermine labor rights and destroy workers' institutional protections. Unfortunately, a large segment of the white working class has experienced the civil rights movement precisely in this way—as having led to policies that undermine their hold on decent jobs and decent pay, not as having led to the extension of decent jobs and decent pay to other people.

Race relations are complex in the United States in the twenty-first century. To understand how racial inequality is reproduced, we must consider the favoritism or advantage that white workers provide to each other, not just the discrimination or racism toward blacks. Racial inequality is not reproduced primarily through racial attitudes in the post–civil rights period. Importantly, we need to understand how whites share privileges with each other, how they hoard opportunities, and how they draw from and use social capital in order to "get ahead" and gain advantages. In other words, we need to understand both the structure and the social psychology of racial inequality, as well as the fact that accepting the principles of civil rights does not mean supporting civil rights policies. Further, we must look beyond racial attitudes altogether and consider the changing nature of politics in the post–civil rights period—a time when competition for white votes has played a critical role in the competition between the parties. In the next chapter, I examine the prevalence of opportunity hoarding in the exchange of social capital among whites, and I also explore more fully the circumstances under which social capital is used and how it is conceived.

Chapter 3

Community, Networks, and Social Capital

[And how did you get that job?]

I was working at a lumberyard here . . . my friend's father owns it. . . .

I went and got a job at [an industrial firm]. . . . I met a guy down at the shore in a summer house that was a union representative. . . . I was waiting to get into the skilled trades . . . in fact, the supervisor lives [here]. It was just a matter of time, but the plant closed. . . .

I did get three months [at a truck factory] . . . that was from a guy I knew down at the boatyard. . . .

[I did odd jobs with a guy who had worked at the industrial plant]. . . .

A guy from [nearby town] whose father was a [supervisor] at [the industrial company] had his own sons on the job. . . . He said there's a process. You just don't get hired overnight. . . . He must have had a good access because [in this company] you get hired by seniority. . . . So he must have had a little weight for somebody to hire me . . . to be hired first. . . . They ask you for overtime first for the rest of our lives. . . . That's why I was hired a week before everybody. . . . They basically told me to wear like a tennis shirt, looking like you're very athletic, because they know you'll get into the [higher-paying job]. . . . It's a difference of probably at least $30,000 a year. . . . I really don't know how they hired. . . . It seemed like somebody knew somebody, though.

—A disabled industrial worker from New Jersey (D009 NJ M WC)

This blue-collar worker from New Jersey got help throughout his career from people he knew in the neighborhood, on the job, or through leisure activities. His mother had a college degree, and his father had attended some college classes but worked in a blue-collar job. The interviewee was not all that interested in school. By playing a lot of sports, he had been able to generate enough cultural capital to get by in high school, but his lack of conscientiousness in school took its toll subsequently. Although he started at a community college, he flunked out his first semester, and afterward, like his father, he took a blue-collar route.

Despite his blue-collar job, this interviewee had a lot of social capital. He still lived near where he grew up, so he knew many people in the neighborhood and surrounding area. Although he worked in blue-collar jobs, he could draw on both the resources and the knowledge of a middle-class lifestyle from his relatives with college educations and more professional jobs. Further, because his networks extended beyond his family and immediate surroundings, he could extend the range of possible opportunities for himself, which apparently paid off in that he was able to gain access to unionized jobs at relatively high pay for someone with his level of education. He was also able to use his social capital to benefit his children. Despite his own school experiences, he worked at keeping his children focused on schoolwork, insisted that they participate in competitive sports, and provided the resources for them to attend top-ranked colleges (one in the Ivy League). His choices, however, came at a relatively high personal cost. The blue-collar job that depended so much on seniority also required that he work a lot of overtime, often going for days without sleep. He ended up having a very serious accident on the job that ended his ability to work at that company.[1] Although it took several years, he was finally successful in getting a substantial settlement from the company, and he was using the funds from that settlement to pay the college tuition for his kids.

The Use of Social Capital in Finding Jobs

While this interviewee was perhaps especially successful in multiplying his opportunities through social connections, his experiences were not atypical. On the contrary, his experiences were quite common among the interviewees in this study. Most had help of some sort most of the time throughout their careers. As was the case for this New Jersey blue-collar worker, there are various kinds of help on which people can draw. Help may come in the form of information (someone telling you of a job opening that may not be publicly known to others yet, or about how to apply or what to expect in getting a job), influence (someone putting in a good word for you that may sway the decision-makers in your favor), or direct opportunity (knowing the person who makes the hiring decision, who then acts in your favor). In the case of this man, being told about how to dress to signal his ability to handle the higher-paying jobs in the company was an example of getting valuable information. The union representative he met who recommended him for his first industrial job is an example of the use of influence. Having a good word from someone like this who has obvious power in the workplace or who has a respected position can make the difference in whether one gets a job. Getting the edge in seniority at his last job or being hired by his friend's father in his first are examples of direct access to opportunity.

Social capital also entails social solidarity, which is important because it determines who is likely to help whom. Not everyone known to the union representative would be given the same assistance, nor would the father of a friend go out of his way for just anybody to make sure that he was hired first so he would be first in line in seniority. These kinds of favors are made for those with whom one identifies, for those who are considered insiders in one's social networks, and for those who one believes to be trustworthy enough to return the favor to others in the community without violating the group's norms. As is often the case, the ties that lead to meaningful opportunities can be very close ties, such as the friend whose father owned a lumberyard (in this case probably also someone with whom the interviewee played high school sports). At other times, the ties are more distant, but there is enough of a connection in the social interactions that acquaintances are willing to share information about opportunities or to allow an acquaintance to use their name. In many cases, it may be random luck in that the interaction takes place when an opening becomes available and known, so the match is made in the happenstance of interaction.

There are patterns, however, that do not depend on chance or taste, but that take shape, in Charles Tilly's (1998, 151) words, within the "limits set by preexisting contacts." Or, as Pierre Bourdieu (1985, 250) argues, such exchanges of social capital must characterize "recognition of the group membership which it implies." This is especially the case when opportunities are exceptionally valuable and scarce, such as those that were available to the New Jersey blue-collar worker. The jobs he was able to get paid at the top end of the scale for blue-collar jobs and provided substantial health and retirement benefits and skill development. Most importantly, these jobs were protected from the market and, as such, also continually subject to threat from technological change or outsourcing. Indeed, his first industrial job ended when the plant closed, and he left his last job when he got injured. Although his injury resulted from what seemed like an accident, the very structure of the work rules created the conditions that made accidents likely: if he had turned down excessive overtime and gotten enough sleep, he could have been bumped out of his higher-paying job, so he overextended himself for fear that someone else would be able to take his place. In the end, that in fact happened, but not because he lost his position in the seniority line. Instead, he lost his health and well-being. Making some workers undertake a lot of overtime rather than hiring more workers is also part of the pattern of drawing boundaries around who has access to valuable resources within a social group and defending or protecting the boundaries so that the resources stay within the purview of those who are considered group members.

Although the boundaries of access and exclusion are especially evident in unionized environments, the same general principles apply to other work situations as well when the jobs available are valuable. Thus, when it matters, friends and family help each other gain access to opportunities that enable them to live decent lives. You hear that someone is leaving a job, and immediately you think of who among your friends or acquaintances might match that job and want to know about it. You hear that the company is going to expand, and you find out the name of the contact person so you can tell a friend who may want to apply for a newly created job. Because you work in a job at a particular company and have come to understand how the inside rules work, you pass along that information to the son or daughter of a neighbor who is now looking for a job, sometimes at the parents' request. You have a casual conversation at church with a fellow parishioner and find out that he or she is out of a job or about to get laid off, so you share with that person possible pathways and offer your help should it be needed. That is how most people in the United States get jobs, in all kinds of companies, industries, and sectors, whether private or public, small or large, good jobs or lousy ones (Waldinger 1996).

For example, the director of a city government agency in New Jersey (D026 NJ M WC) obtained most of the jobs he had held throughout his career from connections with people he met at school or in service organizations. He described several of these connections in his interview:

> I became an Eagle Scout. . . . They have an Eagle dinner . . . and they found me a [person] who actually knew [about the job field in which I was interested]. . . . And I met him, and I proceeded to work with him on Saturdays and then during the summer for about seven years. . . .
>
> My "in." The in isn't what you know; it's who you know. The in was that I went to school with a woman that worked there. . . . Of course, she gave her boss at the time a good recommendation for me. . . .
>
> I went there for an interview. . . . When I was done with that interview, I went for a tour of the building. Down the end of the hall, I looked and saw somebody that I knew. . . . The woman there I went to school with gave me a good recommendation, and I ended up getting the job. . . .
>
> My job changed. . . . [The same woman whom I knew facilitated my moving into her section]. . . . So I got switched. . . .
>
> [One of the people I worked with] called me up. . . . He says, "I've been here six years. I know you want this job. . . . So I'm letting you know it's going to be open."

As this interviewee indicated, he had an "in" at all of the jobs that he had had since high school. People liked him. They believed in his capabilities, and they were willing to help him when he needed help, based on their sense of connection with him. In two of his jobs, he had had difficulties with political leaders who wanted him to make decisions in their interests, which he was not willing to do. Under these circumstances, when he needed to move to another job, there was someone else within his extended network who provided information, used influence on his behalf, or otherwise provided support.

The same kind of assistance was helpful to a New Jersey woman working as a billing clerk in a medical office (D036 NJ F MC). Through two marriages and several children, she wanted to work at jobs that provided her with flexibility and that she enjoyed. Help from her family and friends provided her with opportunities that she might not otherwise have had. When asked how she had gotten her jobs, her story included the following trajectory, beginning with her first job as a schoolteacher:

> The old stories are true about knowing somebody who is a board member. . . . She knew me from [the town]. . . . She was my Brownie leader. . . . [She contacted] the school and said, "Interview her," and it was sort of done that way. . . .
>
> Someone was starting a sales [company] for homemade [products] . . . and they needed somebody to do the home at night parties. . . . I don't know exactly how I got involved with her, but I did that for quite a while. . . .
>
> And another friend said, "Hey, I have a job in my office, in a doctor's office, would you like to do that part-time?" . . . So I did that part-time, and I really liked it. . . .
>
> So I was like out of work for, I don't know, maybe half a year, three-quarters of a year, and I found a part-time job [at a doctor's office]. . . . I went there as a patient . . . and his wife and I had gotten very friendly . . . and I think I asked for it, you know, asked her if she ever needed help . . . I was there for twelve years. . . .
>
> [I began to teach art classes in my home.] . . . I . . . had no credit of my own, borrowed $3,000 from a friend's credit union and opened up my own [business] in the basement so I could hold my own classes and still be home. . . . [*How did you get customers?*] . . . Oh, word of mouth. It spread like crazy. . . .
>
> In between all that, a friend who . . . a woman who was coming to [my art classes] and knew that I had these part-time hours was quitting a banking job because she was pregnant, and she was looking for someone to watch her son. . . . I started doing child care, so now I had three part-time jobs. . . .
>
> [Then my sister had two babies], then during the daytime I would go to my sister's and give my sister a helping hand . . . we had this little day care center going. . . .
>
> A friend of mine worked at [another doctor's office] right up the street [from where I had worked]. And she knew I needed a job. . . . And she said,

> "It is a terrible place to work and don't hold it against me, but I could use somebody at the front desk." So I went there. . . .
>
> She subsequently left and went to [another doctor's office]. And after she got herself established there, she called me up and said, "Do you want a job here for $2 more an hour?" So I went and worked [there]. . . . She's gotten me two jobs. . . .
>
> It was funny because, while I was [at the previous doctor's office, I] got real tired of commuting very quickly. . . . [I went to an employment agency, and they sent me to a doctor's office where I had interviewed for a job six months before.] . . . Three of the four doctors had already interviewed me and said, yes, we liked her back then, let's take her now. So I got the job [easily].

This interviewee, like the others, found most of her jobs through friends, family, or acquaintances who were willing to help her. Even though she was trained as a teacher, she wanted more flexibility so that she could raise her children, and she was able to accommodate those needs by putting together several part-time jobs while she was still married. Once she divorced, she needed full-time work and again turned to her friends to see if anyone could help her, and they did.

A similar history is evident in the life of a working-class woman from New Jersey who worked as a customer service representative (D025 NJ F WC). She had had only one job throughout her career, and she had gotten the job with the help of her mother:

> I also worked for the same company that my mom did. . . . I'll have twenty years with them. . . . I started in high school on a work program. My mom called one of her friends and said [I] was looking for a job. She's like, "Oh, no problem, send her down." I went down there. I knew the lady since I was like two years old. . . . We have the best union in New Jersey for retail. . . . Right now I'm making almost $14 . . . right below $14 an hour. Excellent benefits, dental, medical, eyeglasses, lawyers. Where am I going to go?

Despite the fact that this woman had no college education, and by her own admission, no other marketable skills, she was able to gain access to a job that paid her a living wage, with full benefits, because of her mother's sponsorship. At the time of the interview, she was also living in a house that her family had owned in the same neighborhood where she grew up. Thus, her living situation had been substantially subsidized, and she was able to get a job where her wages were protected from the market, so even though she had never married and was living alone, she was able to support herself in a safe neighborhood. Unfortunately for her, she had gotten hurt on the job several months before the interview and had not worked since.

An Ohio interviewee who worked as a supervisor in a cleaning business (E315 OH M MC) also described the help he had received throughout his career:

> I don't know if I've taken the path of least resistance when it's come to finding a job, but I've never really been in the job market. And the times that I have been, I wasn't successful in finding a position, and I got frustrated and said, well, let me go talk to this person and see if they know of something that I can do. And it wasn't just networking, but it was to see if I could do something with them, that is, to work with [a friend in a current business], because I know [him]. It wasn't the same as interviewing with IBM or with Xerox or with somebody else. I never had the opportunity to, or never made the opportunity to, have those interviews.

Never having been in the job market, it turns out, is not unusual for many whites in the United States, at least not for a major portion of their lives. Like this upper-middle-class man from Ohio, many whites look for people they know who might be able to help them get a job or a promotion or skills that will improve their job prospects, and contrary to the image and rhetoric about competition in the labor market, they make a concerted effort, to the extent that they can do so, to avoid having to subject themselves to market competition.

The Extent of Social Capital

These interviewees' use of social capital is not substantively different from that of the other interviewees. Figure 3.1 provides information on people who got help (defined here as any combination of information, influence, and opportunity) for each job over their careers. The figure shows the proportion of people who received help in the first job, the second job, and so on, up to the tenth job. Obviously, not all interviewees have had ten jobs, so the number of people for each job differs. About 60 percent of the interviewees across regions got some kind of help getting their first job, and then the proportion rises slightly over the course of their careers, with between 70 and 80 percent of the interviewees across regions getting help in their job searches later in their careers. Although the actual numbers vary, the proportions are still high, showing that the majority received some kind of help most of the time throughout their lives.

Figures 3.2 and 3.3 show the proportion of interviewees receiving help with each job by class and by gender. Surprisingly, there is very little distinction by class: both middle- and working-class interviewees received help about 60 to 65 percent of the time in the early years (that is, with jobs they held while in high school or college) and 70 to 75 percent of the time

Figure 3.1 Proportion of Interviewees Receiving Help Getting a Job (Including Information, Influence, and Opportunity), by Location of Interviews

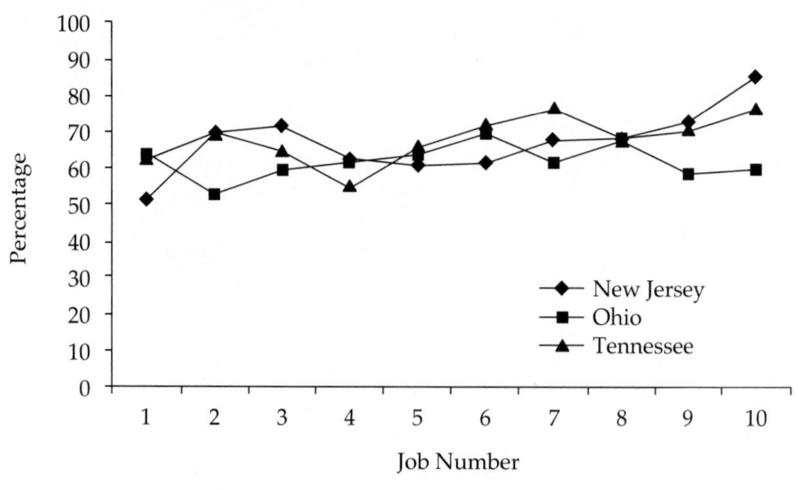

Source: Author's compilation.
Note: The numbers represent each job from the first to the tenth job. Because not all interviewees had ten jobs over their careers, the base number for the percentages varies across the number of jobs.

toward the end of their careers.[2] Although some variation occurs, there is little substantive difference by class. In contrast to the patterns by region and class, there does appear to be a difference in the proportions who received help by gender, with men receiving help somewhat more often than women at most periods of their careers. Only about half of the women reported receiving some help getting a job in the early years, in contrast to about 65 percent of the men. Although the proportions for both genders rise slightly over the course of the career, the gender difference in the availability or use of help in getting a job persists. For those who have had ten or more jobs, both proportions begin to trail off in terms of the amount of help received after about the tenth job, but this could be a reflection of the small number of cases as the number of jobs increases. Based on the information provided by the interviewees, it seems clear that women are less likely to get help with getting a job than are men, because women's jobs are less likely to pay a family wage. In that sense, women are more likely than men to hold jobs that are subject to market competition and therefore pay lower wages. Women's jobs are also less likely to be unionized. Thus, there seems to be less incentive to use up social capital for jobs that are not especially scarce and that are no more difficult to get without help than with it. Even so, women reported

Figure 3.2 Proportion of Interviewees Receiving Help Getting a Job (Including Information, Influence, and Opportunity), by Class

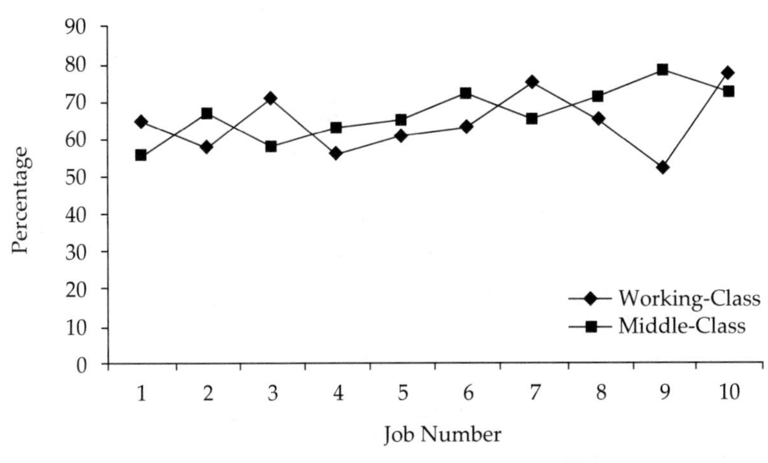

Source: Author's compilation.
Note: The numbers represent each job from the first to the tenth job. Because not all interviewees had ten jobs over their careers, the base number for the percentages varies across the number of jobs.

Figure 3.3 Proportion of Interviewees Receiving Help Getting a Job (Including Information, Influence, and Opportunity), by Gender

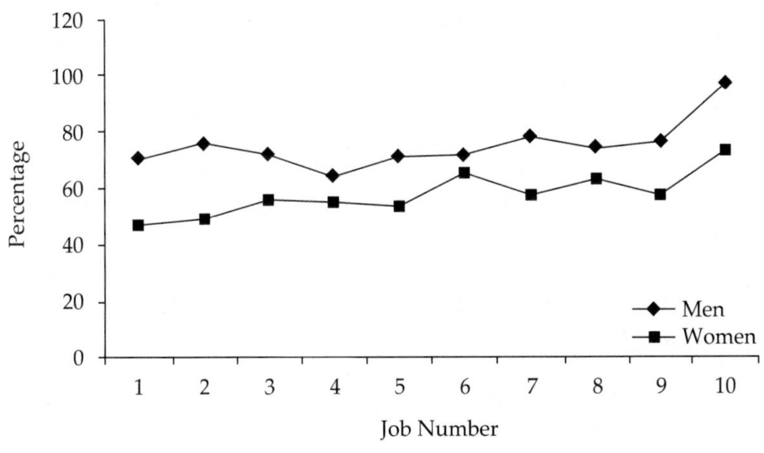

Source: Author's compilation.
Note: The numbers represent each job from the first to the tenth job. Because not all interviewees had ten jobs over their careers, the base number for the percentages varies across the number of jobs.

getting help in finding a job at least half the time in the early years, and then in greater proportions over time.

The average proportion of jobs for which interviewees received help is over 68 percent throughout their careers, with the average for women at about 61 percent and the average for men at almost 75 percent.[3] The average proportion of help for the working-class interviewees is just over 67 percent, and the proportion for middle-class interviewees is almost 70 percent. The overall proportion for the Ohio interviewees is just over 65 percent, for the New Jersey interviewees over 68 percent, and for the Tennessee interviewees almost 72 percent.

These proportions are somewhat higher than those found for professional, technical, and managerial employees in Granovetter's (1995) study: he found that about 48 percent of those under the age of thirty-four in his sample found jobs through "personal contacts," as did 64 percent of those over the age of thirty-four, for an overall average of 56 percent. Data for about one-third of his sample were collected in personal interviews and about two-thirds by use of a survey (for which it would not be possible to follow up with additional questions). Further, his sample was restricted to those who had changed jobs within the five years previous to his data collection.

There are other differences between my study and Granovetter's that may account for the different estimates. First, Granovetter's data were collected in 1969, which was during the tight labor market of the Vietnam War. The use of social capital may have been less necessary to find a job at this time when jobs were plentiful. I asked respondents about all of the jobs they had held over their lives since high school, so my data include periods of both low and high unemployment and both tight and loose labor markets. Second, Granovetter restricted his sample to professional, technical, and managerial employees, whereas my data include those from across the labor force. Professional, technical, and managerial employees are more likely than most other people in the labor force to use school placement services (at least that is apparently true for the few engineers, for example, in my study). Third, Granovetter was interested in the importance of personal contacts compared to more formal procedures for looking for a job, whereas I was interested in the extent to which personal contacts contribute in some way to an inside edge in finding a job. Granovetter's categorization of the use of personal contacts was thus very restrictive, such that he coded a mix of formal and informal means as formal rather than as personal contact. In contrast, I included any mention of assistance from someone in providing information, influence, or opportunity as an indicator of social capital.

Finally, it may be that I probed more explicitly for information about whether the interviewee knew someone on the job, because I often found that those who said that they had gotten a job by "just applying for it" were subsequently able to recall the involvement of a friend or acquaintance whom they had not thought to mention initially. For example, a middle-class high school drama teacher from New Jersey (D039 NJ F MC) described two jobs that she had held. The first one she obtained "through the paper. It indicated summer help." When asked whether she knew anyone at this job site, she replied, "No. Ironically, though, when I went to the interview, her brother had graduated from [the same small school where I went to college]." For the second job she described, she also began by looking in the paper.

> Actually, before I [had that job], I was with a local agent here in Jersey, which was right down the street. Actually, it's still there. . . . Um, I just applied, you know, looked in the paper, sent my résumé. Ironically, again, this man, he was the agent. He owned the shop. His daughter had worked for [the same company] where I was coming from, so there was a lot of names that were familiar to him that were familiar to me, accounts that I had handled that actually were his daughter's when she worked there. So I went there.

Obviously, one cannot know the extent to which these sorts of causal connections might influence the hiring decision, but there is every reason to believe that they can make a difference. In this regard, Granovetter and I both agree that trying to get this kind of information from survey data with fixed responses, especially on the telephone, is likely to substantially underestimate the extent to which networks or connections come into play in finding a job. It is quite likely that surveys about job search strategies greatly underestimate the influence of personal connections in job finding (Granovetter 1995). They also may partly reflect only those instances where the respondent felt that the help was effective in the job search, which undoubtedly would add up to fewer instances than the number of times when the contact made a difference.

When Help Is Not Needed

There appear to be three occasions when help from family or friends in the job search process is not evident. First, as noted, sometimes the jobs are not valuable enough to use up social capital resources to get them. Because their jobs typically pay less, more women interviewees than men talked about just going door to door to find a job or looking in the paper and replying to an ad. Women used such search processes during their high school or college years, when most of their jobs were in retail sales or in restaurants. Second, some interviewees, especially those with college degrees in technical or specialized fields, used school placement services to find their jobs; for these job applicants, friends were not as necessary because the school record provided information on their job capabilities. Even so, recommendations or references were undoubtedly necessary. Moreover, teachers and staff in school placement services often steer applicants to either better jobs or less valuable ones. For example, Deirdre Royster (2003) found that teachers are more likely to help white students from a vocational high school find jobs than they are to help black students. Third, some interviewees told of obtaining jobs during periods of labor shortage (for example, during the Vietnam War), when there were more jobs available than workers. In tight labor markets, connections may not be needed to find a job, although those with good networks might have greater access to the most valuable jobs.

Each of these situations is represented in the interviews for this study. For example, a working-class woman from Tennessee (G531 TN F WC) had a number of jobs as a waitress or bartender (which is higher-paid than a waitress) in her early years. About half of the time, she got a job because someone told her of an opening or put in a good word for her. Many other times connections were not necessary. For example, when asked about how she got a waitress job in her early career, she said: "Just went and probably found it in the paper . . . and went and applied." Similarly, those who graduated from engineering programs or even from high school training in, for example, dental hygienics or auto mechanics were able to get jobs through the placement services at their schools. For example, an Ohio engineer (E306 OH M MC) said, "I was kind of intrigued by the industry they were in, the things they were doing. You know, I attended an on-campus interview, and they invited me to visit the company here." Two male factory workers from Ohio got jobs in companies during the Vietnam War when workers were otherwise scarce. One was the working-class man mentioned at the outset of the last chapter (E307 OH M WC): "I would have never gotten into [the company I did] because of my weight without the Vietnam War. So that was a big factor in my getting hired [there]." For interviewees like these, especially at early stages of their lives, inside information, having someone to put in a good word, or knowing the person doing the hiring was neither necessary nor likely (although most did draw on social capital at other points in their careers). It is useful to note that even in some of these cases the interviewees had social capital available to them, but did not use it, either because they did not need to or because it would not have helped much anyway.

The Competence to Use Social Capital

Some interviewees needed and wanted the use of social capital, but were not themselves able to use it effectively. For example, a New Jersey interviewee (D010 NJ F MC) had high aspirations but an undistinguished college record at an undistinguished local school. Despite having a professional father who evidently tried his best to help her find a good job at one of the major companies where he had contacts, she could never get a job offer from these contacts and finally ended up taking a job in retail sales. When asked about the job search process, she said: "Oh, I must have went on twenty interviews with all these different companies. . . . And a lot of them I got because of the reps that came into my father's office. . . . Both my mother and father would talk to people for me. . . . I got so turned off. I didn't want to be in sales anymore. I came to that realization."

Other interviewees would have had social capital available to them, but their youthful transgressions or their own poor choices had kept them from availing themselves of it. For example, a New Jersey man (D029 NJ M WC) came from a working-class background, but his father had invested in the right stocks and ended up making enough money to pay for the college educations of the interviewee and his siblings. The interviewee, however, got involved with drugs and alcohol in his younger years and ended up not going to college. Now working as a laboratory technician, he described that earlier period:

> I probably could have done a lot more with my time. . . . I think at the end of high school you start with a lot of marijuana, and you know, you start partying, and then that's why I probably never went to college. . . . I was working, making money, having a good time. . . . I did sound for bands . . . that was an exciting time, but I think I probably stagnated my life for five or ten years wasted. Instead of where I probably should have been going to school, instead I was hanging out in bars and getting high.

After spending time in a number of working-class jobs, the interviewee finally went back to college, but did so in "dribs and drabs," as he called it. At the time of the interview, he was still trying to finish his degree.

A working-class woman from New Jersey (D022 NJ F WC) had a similar experience. Her parents would have paid for her to go to college, but she did not have the confidence to act on their offer. Now working as an insurance administrative assistant, she said, when asked about whether she had considered going to college:

> I hadn't really planned on it. I thought about it, and I think in high school I didn't have a very . . . a sense of direction, and I think that if I spoke to my guidance counselor more or if we discussed anything about college, I think that would have helped me. It would have pointed me in the direction of going to college right after high school. . . . I think there was a fear about it, actually about going and not knowing what to expect. My mother and father offered to send me.

Instead of college, this interviewee got married young, had several children, and then ended up divorced and struggling to raise her children on her own.

A few interviewees reported that they would have had the use of social capital, but that it was no longer available to them because someone else had gone to the same sources and then not done a good job or failed to follow through. Consequently, the social capital that would have been theirs was dissipated or withdrawn. For example, an unemployed engineer in New Jersey (D001 NJ M MC) said:

> My uncle was going to mention my name to someone he knew [at a nearby large company] . . . like an old boyhood friend or something like that. But I think it turned out my cousin was also looking for a job. . . . I guess my uncle had also given his son's name in, but at a totally different level. This was just general, you know, ditch-digging type stuff, and he had worked there for a very, very short period of time and just quit afterwards and . . . at that point my uncle was like, "Well, I already used up this thing once. It didn't turn out too well. I don't really think I should pursue this again."

A working-class man from Ohio who worked as a surveyor (B008 OH M WC) told a similar story, though he had searched more broadly for someone who could give him the necessary "in" and thereby circumvented the unwillingness of his father to help him:

> My dad helped my brother-in-law get in there. Well, he helped my . . . brother. He got a job at the [industrial firm] as soon as he turned eighteen. The next brother, he got a job as soon as he got out of high school . . . and they quit. They made a bad [impression]. . . . So here come me, and he decided if I wanted a job, I had to get it on my own.

He did not, however, get it "on his own." Instead, he found a friend who had a relative in a decision-making position in the company, and the friend was willing to put in a good word for him with his relative. After contacting his friend's relative, the Ohio man (B008 OH M WC) said, he went to the company office, "and I told them who told me to come there, and they says, 'Hang on a minute, and we'll just have you go back here and talk to him.' So I went back and talked to him, and he says, 'Well, fill out this application.' He says, 'You'll probably start in a week or two.'" This interviewee thought of himself as having gotten this job on his own because it was his own social contacts who helped him when he needed it. As he said: "I might have actually knowed 25 percent of [the people in the county]. My kids, they tell me that I know everybody. . . . I'm not a person that really cares a lot about education. One of the reasons might be because I know so many people."

All of these interviewees had more social capital (and other social resources) available than they could effectively use. Some did not need it. Some were not themselves competent to use it. Some passed up the opportunity to use it because of various distractions. Therefore, it is even more noteworthy that such a large proportion of those in need of jobs do utilize social capital to give themselves an edge and gain access to jobs that are valuable or hard to get.

Perhaps even more noteworthy is that almost all of the interviewees in this study used social capital to find a job at some point in their lives. In fact, only two interviewees from the 246 (fewer than 1 percent) did not discuss having received any job help during their lives. One of these two was an engineer who had no jobs in high school and then used a college placement service to find her first and only job. The other was also a college graduate and also female. This interviewee had a trust fund that paid for her college expenses, so she did not have to work during high school or college. She quit school after her second year to get married, and then she continued work toward her degree later in life. Although she had had a number of jobs, she claimed to have answered ads for all of them and not to know anyone or to have had help from anyone in obtaining any of the jobs she had held. Obviously, these are the exceptions. The overwhelming majority of the interviewees could draw on social capital to help them find jobs at least once in their lives, and most had help at many points along the way. Hence, even though for any given job the average proportion of interviewees who had extra help in their job search was 68 percent, almost everyone got help from time to time.

Financial and Cultural Capital

Those who exchange social capital also frequently exchange financial resources. The offer of financial capital from one group member to another is for the same purpose as the exchange of social capital, namely, to pass along valuable resources that will improve the social position and well-being of the recipient and strengthen the community. Based on the interviews in this study, I include within financial capital three different types of resources: (1) receiving cash or other goods that have monetary value as gifts or as an inheritance (including being provided with a car, house, or other property); (2) being provided with loans of cash or other resources, sometimes with interest and sometimes without, although almost always below the market rate; and (3) having expenses covered or goods or services provided that save recipients from having to cover the costs themselves (for example, paying for tuition, buying groceries, and providing free babysitting while the recipient works or goes to school). Having access to these kinds of financial resources obviously is likely to improve the economic circumstances of the recipient. That is usually the reason for providing such resources.

For our purposes, what is most important about having access to such financial resources is that the capacity to provide them to family members or friends is often the result of past opportunity hoarding. If your parents were able to obtain jobs that paid a living wage and provided sufficient benefits to allow the accumulation of enough financial resources to share or pass along at death, then you become the beneficiary of their opportunity hoarding. Whites in the United States are substantially more likely than blacks to accumulate wealth, through owning homes and stocks and bonds, accumulating savings, and having pension or insurance benefits.[4] The greater wealth that whites are able to accumulate enables them to assist their children in securing a decent economic future. And they are able to do so because they benefited from opportunity hoarding in the previous generations.

Wealth helps parents provide their children with advantages. It helps parents live in communities that are reasonably secure and offer amenities that improve the lives, skill development, and networks of their children. Of course, children who are able to do well and learn more are better positioned to obtain good jobs or gain entrance to competitive colleges and universities. Those with good jobs are more likely to have children who grow up to have good jobs, and the cycle of inequality therefore continues. Perhaps equally important is that those with financial assets tend to live in communities with a lot of social and cultural capital, so financial resources can be extended and made more valuable because of the connections that they facilitate.

In this study, 91 percent of the interviewees mentioned receiving some form of financial capital from relatives or friends. Of the twenty-four interviewees who claimed not to have received any financial capital during their lifetime, 78 percent were working-class. Of those who did receive some form of financial capital, 58 percent were middle-class and 42 percent were working-class. Hence, unlike with social capital, there is a class difference in access to financial capital. Even so, a high proportion of both the working-class and middle-class interviewees reported having received financial resources in some form from family and friends. In most cases, interviewees received small amounts of money when they ran short, especially in the early years when they were trying to get established. Many were either given a car or given help with buying a car (which is often the means to get to and from a job or school). Many lived at home after finishing school and either paid no rent or paid reduced rent. For those who went to college, parents often contributed to or paid for tuition and living expenses. When the interviewees had children, they often got help with babysitting from relatives, especially in short-term arrangements. And many received some form of inheritance, often at least the family home (or some portion of the assets from its sale) or resources from whatever assets the parents or other relatives had accumulated.

For example, a middle-class teacher from Ohio (B001 OH M MC) inherited money from both his parents and his grandparents. He also got a loan at below-market rates from his parents to buy his first house. Despite limited education, his grandfather had been a middle manager in a major company, so he was able to accumulate financial resources and live a middle-class lifestyle. His father, a blue-collar worker, had been able to raise his child in one of the better school districts in the area because of the financial resources provided by the grandfather. The resources provided by his family enabled the interviewee to work at a middle-income occupation and still bring his children up in one of the best neighborhoods in the city, while his wife stayed out of the paid labor force in order to be available to the children. Along the way, his parents and grandparents provided other financial support—for example, by purchasing a house that they rented to the interviewee at less than market rate. The interviewee and his wife were eventually able to buy a comfortable home in one of the nicest areas of the city, in a good school district, and they were able to raise their children in an upper-middle-class lifestyle on one income, with a trust fund in place to provide for the children's college educations.

Although this Ohio interviewee received substantial financial resources from his family members, the type of help he received was not especially unusual. For example, a Tennessee woman who worked in clerical jobs (G504 TN F WC) grew up in modest circumstances, especially after her parents divorced, but she still received financial help from time to time. Her parents bought her first car and provided some financial help for her to attend a community college. Her husband's parents helped with child care so that she could work and also gave the couple money for a down payment on a house.

Other interviewees received similar resources from their families. In addition to receiving cars, tuition, babysitting services, and occasional loans or gifts, some interviewees lived at home after they graduated from school (high school or college, depending on how much education they received), often without paying rent or while paying substantially reduced rent. When this arrangement was made at the outset of a career, it enabled the interviewee to accumulate resources to get started in life. At other times, the interviewee sought help after an unfortunate life event, like a divorce or a job loss. Some parents saved the rent money their child had been paying and then gave it to him or her as a cash gift when the child was ready to move on with life. Parents or other relatives also subsidized business start-ups. Many interviewees received small gifts of cash or other assistance (as when relatives took over loan payments or bought them groceries and clothing), favorable loans (or loans cosigned by a relative), inheritances (of houses, money, or financial securities), and, for a few fortunate interviewees, trust funds. A few parents or other relatives were able to use their influence to get a better deal for a child making a major purchase (such as a car or an apartment or house). Of course, the parents of a number of the interviewees paid for weddings and other celebrations, saving the interviewee the costs of such events and enabling him or her to receive the gifts and walk away with what would often be a substantial nest egg.

Many interviewees also benefited from the cultural capital that they derived from their families and neighborhoods or from uses of financial and social capital that provided them with valuable experiences. Most interviewees were able to get an education from a decent school system, and of course some were able to attend an excellent school system. The interviewees were able, then, to take their educational credentials to the job market or to offer them when drawing on social capital. As James Coleman (1988) notes perceptively, social capital and other social resources contribute to the development of human capital among people in a community. Many interviewees were able to use the social resources available to them to live in desirable communities and purchase and decorate their houses in a way that communicated that they were decent, upstanding people who contributed to the community (Kefalas 2003). Further, by growing up and then living in communities with available social capital, many interviewees were also able to develop over time a presentation of self that marked them as competent and worthy (Bourdieu 1985; Ridgeway 2001).

In a few cases it was evident that the interviewees received additional opportunities because of how they looked—that is, they literally embodied cultural capital. For example, a middle-class male from Ohio who worked as a lab technician (B004 OH M MC) said of himself:

> Well, yeah, basically luck peppered with being taught good manners and good posture, and not being terribly ugly, being acceptably good-looking. . . . And well, I do comb my hair. . . . Well, from readings I've done and other things I've heard about, I suspect that that is part of it. . . . I'm a white guy. I have what some people would consider a good sense of humor; it can be pretty strange, but I know when to do it right. And like I said, the manners . . . the discipline part really pays off I think. . . . Yeah, they're all contributing factors. . . . Because I would be polite. . . . And I think people have a tendency to cut a little slack for someone like that, you know, a teacher or somebody like that. That's my feeling, and I bet it's probably true.

This interviewee was not being arrogant. He was simply trying to explain what he thought made a difference in some people gaining more advantages in life compared to others. A psychologist from New Jersey (C003 NJ F MC) had some of the same kinds of experiences and self-perception. She said:

> And I was a little bit powerful, because I was sort of popular. . . . I don't know why I was popular. . . . But I realized that how I looked in the outer world . . . I think that I am an attractive person. There's a certain . . . I don't know, charisma . . . I have a certain energy. . . . Yeah. I guess I was cute and . . . I realized when I think about it . . . I was always well liked.

This interviewee was able to use her likability in her career where she gained access to powerful jobs and promotion opportunities that were undoubtedly based on both her accomplishments and the fact that people liked to be around her. So cultural capital is sometimes the result of having access to social and financial capital, and sometimes it is the cause. All around, those who gain access to social resources are likely to have better lives if they are able to use those resources to good effect.

I am not, of course, suggesting that parents should not help their children, and I recognize that there are cultural norms of beauty and desirability that would be hard to counter. Two specific points should be noted, however, about the social resources that are widely transferred within families and across generations and about the ways in which social and cultural resources are shared within groups. First, as noted, parents (or communities) are able to provide such resources because previous generations were often able to obtain jobs protected from market competition. That is, they benefited in the previous generation from hoarding opportunities. Second, although consciousness of the extent of help from families and neighborhoods should be as widespread as the help itself, it is not. Instead, most interviewees described the help they received only when asked specific questions; they otherwise did not offer the information. When asked how they got to where they were in their lives, they did not point to the social, cultural, or financial resources provided to them by others. Instead, they highlighted their own efforts and achievements. As expressed by the Ohio blue-collar worker whose father had refused to help him but who knew one-quarter of the people in the county, they came to believe that they had done it "on their own"—through their own motivation and talents.

Thus, few of the interviewees expressed any awareness of the advantages that inheritances, loans, gifts, or deferred expenses provided to them. Because in most cases the financial capital provided assistance but not a livelihood, the interviewees did not think of themselves in the same way they thought of those who, they said, were "given everything." Instead, they thought of themselves as fortunate, and sometimes they expressed gratitude, but hardly any of them acknowledged the importance of the resources available to them—whether social, financial, or cultural—as the factors that made the most difference in what happened in their lives.

Gender Issues

Although the impact of gender roles was evident in the life histories of the interviewees, they did not seem to have much effect on the key issues that are of concern in this study. Both men and women tended to think that any remaining problem with racial inequality stemmed from the residual prejudice of "those racists." Both men and women claimed to believe strongly in equal opportunity, even though most had availed themselves of unearned advantage in their own lives and, like most others, they primarily sought ways to get ahead or to get advantages in their own lives and those of their children or family members. Both men and women were also likely to express strong individualist values. They believed that they themselves got to where they were in their lives because of their hard work, talent, and persistence, even though they tended to seek out and use social resources from their families and neighborhoods when they could or when it mattered.

Some differences in the views expressed by men and women are evident, and there are therefore gender differences in the composition of the various sociopolitical groups that emerged from the interviews. In general, men were more likely to show up in the working-class "racist" and religious conservative categories, while women were more likely to show up in the working-class liberal and religious nonconservative categories. Further, when analyzed in regression analyses, men were likely to express more racially resentful views than were the women interviewees. Most importantly, however, men were more likely than women to report that they had had help at some point along the way in getting a job (the average for men was about 75 percent of the time and for women about 60 percent), although both received help with getting jobs the majority of the time over their lifetimes.

The main distinction between the life histories of the men and women interviewees had to do with how gender had shaped women's life chances compared to men's. Women's jobs were less likely to pay a family wage, and hence it did not seem to matter as much for women to try to get an inside edge in the jobs that they obtained. Although most interviewees sought advantage most of the time, sometimes the job did not really warrant it, because one job was just as bad as another. In these circumstances, the women interviewees talked about just going from door to door until they found a job, usually working in retail sales or as a waitress. Professional women and women whose jobs provided benefits and decent salaries, however, were just as likely to gain access to such jobs through the use of social resources as were men. In other words, these women, like men, were helped along by having social connections to people in their families, among their friends, in their neighborhoods, and through membership in civic or religious organizations to find jobs, but when any job would do, women would sometimes go looking for a job without availing themselves of such help. Perhaps they did not want to use up their chips, so to speak, when the job did not pay much, or perhaps they were more interested in jobs that were convenient in terms of location and hours and so went looking for the job instead of for the social tie. Further, for those looking for jobs in retail or in restaurants (that is, jobs providing low pay and requiring low skill), there may sometimes have been more jobs available than people who wanted them; it would not have been necessary at those times to draw on social networks in order to find a job that would fit their needs. And it may have been that such jobs were easier for them to find because they were white.

Men rarely settled for these kinds of jobs if they had any other options. Men apparently considered access to a good job, with benefits and decent wages, as more important than it was for women, and more so than women, they used the help of their family and friends, both early in their careers and even more later on. It also may be the case that the kinds of jobs that men wanted were more likely to be hoarded than the kinds of jobs that women wanted, and so access to such jobs, which were usually not readily available to just anyone who happened to apply, had to come through some form of social connection. That is, they were protected from or kept out of the market. This was generally the case unless there was a labor shortage and jobs were plentiful. When jobs were plentiful, not every job could be filled by friends and acquaintances, so some people were able to get jobs to which they otherwise might not have had access. For example, several of the men in the study who were able to obtain unionized factory jobs that paid relatively high wages and offered good benefits for men without college degrees were hired during the Vietnam War, when companies were not able to be choosy about whom they hired. Several of the interviewees who benefited from these circumstances were aware that their timing was right, and they commented that they might not have gotten the same kind of job if the labor supply had not been so tight.

Gender came into play in another fundamental way in the life histories of these interviewees, but it did not have much to do directly with their views on racial inequality. More than was the case for men, the life circumstances of women were affected by who they were able to marry—

positively when their husbands made relatively good money, and negatively when their husbands were not able to secure stable and well-paid jobs or when their marriages fell apart. Especially for those women who were not married when responsible for young children, gender was the most important factor in defining what happened in their lives. Most such women were often dependent on the resources available from their families, and in general most were able to move on to an acceptable life situation only if they could find another husband to provide for themselves and their children. There were a number of women interviewees who started but did not finish college—and so might, on their own, be considered working-class—but because they married a man in either a professional or managerial job, they were able to live a middle-class lifestyle.

For many (perhaps most) of the women interviewees, marriage was the gateway to a middle-class (or upper-middle-class) lifestyle. As long as they were able to stay in the marriage, their life circumstances depended on their marriage partner, not on what they themselves brought to the labor market, nor on the social resources that they could draw on directly to get themselves into good jobs. A dramatic example was evident in the life of one female interviewee who described herself as a "trophy wife" (E353 OH F MC). In recounting her job history, she described doing both her own job as a secretary and her boss's job. When her boss left, she wanted to be officially promoted into his job, or at least be paid what he was being paid, but the company was not willing to acknowledge her work. She described it this way:

> I'll never forget this. . . . [I asked] why don't they pay me for the work I'm doing, because I'm doing his job. He's no longer even there. I've got my job and his job, and I [said], "Just pay me what you were paying him. Don't pay me for two jobs, just what you were paying him. Why won't you do it?" And his answer was, because we don't have to. Because we don't have to.

Later this woman ended up marrying a top executive in the same company and ultimately inherited his fortune, which established her in a very affluent lifestyle. When asked whether she deserved the kind of life she had now, she said that she did, because, as she explained,

> I gave up a tremendous amount . . . a lot of my youth. . . . I didn't realize what I was doing at the time, but I did because once . . . even before we were married, I was moving in a world with older people. Now there were advantages. I traveled a lot with him and that kind of thing, but there's a chunk of time gone out of my youth. And the fact that I didn't have kids. . . . I probably would have, had I married anybody else.

This interviewee said that it had taken her a long time to accept and understand her situation, but she clearly believed that there was no other way for her to have the lifestyle she wanted except through marriage because her employer would not pay her for the work she was doing.

For many of the women interviewees, if their marriage to a man with a good income ended, they were in a much more vulnerable situation, and the situation did not change for some of them unless they found another spouse. For most, children complicated their labor force experiences and their life situations as well. Although, of course, most had welcomed their children, children also presented a financial burden for the woman who found herself alone because her marriage fell apart or ended. Thus, for most of the women in this study, despite the many changes in recent decades in women's paid labor force participation and the increasing salaries of white women compared to men, a relationship with a man made the difference in their ability to live a decent lifestyle and to maintain it, especially if they had children and especially if the man with whom they had a relationship had a job that was protected from the market. Women in the paid labor force also had a better chance at a decent life if they were able to find jobs that were protected from the market and therefore had benefits, more job stability, and better pay. All workers are vulnerable to employers' efforts to undermine the security that workers have tried to foster and to economic changes that further undermine access to good jobs. Women as well as men in the study, therefore, endeavored to protect themselves as much as possible from market exigencies.

The labor market experiences of women in the sample may have had some influence on their attitudes toward race and economic inequality in that they were less racially resentful and more egalitarian than were men in the sample. Perhaps their greater vulnerability in the labor market, on average, made them somewhat more open than men to the occasional need for government assistance and for a social safety net. Men, however, seemed to have more to lose if their efforts to hoard opportunities were adversely affected by the civil rights movement, since their jobs often paid more and had better benefits. That might help explain why men's attitudes were more tinged with racial resentment and conservative politics than seemed to be the case for women. Even so, sometimes women interviewees, recognizing their vulnerability when they perceived that their husbands' jobs were affected by government civil rights policies, expressed conservative, anti-welfare, and anti-government views as well. For example, an Ohio homemaker (B021 OH F MC) who was classified in the middle-class conservative group made this comment:

> I think the white male is the biggest minority anymore. I honestly believe that. Because if you're female, you have a shoo-in, just because you're fe-

> male. And if you're female and you're black, you've really got it. You know, if you're male and you're black or Hispanic or whatever. And I feel sorry for the lowly white male out there anymore. I really think they're the ones that are the minority.

Thus, although gender was not a major factor in differentiating the interviewees with regard to their views of inequality and fairness, it did sometimes come into play because of the social relationships between men and women and the extent to which some women depended as much as men on jobs that were protected from the market and that paid a family wage.

Nobody Makes It on Their Own, but Nobody Makes It Without Their Own Effort

Social capital only exists in the relationships among people. The exchange of social capital creates social obligations on the part of community members to help each other. Although such obligations can be powerful in their effect, they are not necessarily consciously considered, nor are they always visible to those on the receiving end of obligations. When the interviewees recounted their life histories, it was only after follow-up probes (being questioned, for example, about who they knew or who might have helped them) that information on their access to and use of social capital and other social resources came out. Their social capital was otherwise rarely mentioned when they were asked for their life stories. Even when they talked explicitly about help they might have received, they often dismissed or discounted its role in their lives and emphasized instead their own individual contributions to their success—hard work, motivation, adaptability or persistence—and sometimes their blessings.

The disabled industrial worker mentioned at the beginning of this chapter (D009 NJ M WC) who had had help from many sources in getting jobs throughout his life said, when asked whether he had earned his current place in life, "Oh, I worked seven days a week all of my life. Yeah, I've earned everything I've got. . . . I've been a go-getter all of my life. So, yeah, I have no regrets at all." Further, when he was asked what had most contributed to his having the kind of life that he had now, he said, "A lot of energy." Similarly, the city agency head (D026 NJ M MC) who also had received a great deal of help from friends along the way said, when asked whether he deserved his current place in life, "I've put in a lot of time. I've worked since I was sixteen. I do a lot of things I don't get paid for. Yeah, I've gone through school. I've got the degrees. I've taken the tests. I put in the time. Yeah."

The same attitude was expressed by most of the interviewees. For example, a construction manager from Tennessee (G518 TN M MC) got a number of jobs after friends or family members put in a good word for him or through connections with friends and acquaintances. When he was asked whether he earned or deserved his place in life, he said, "Yes, because all that I have is that which is accrued as a result of the work that I have done." And a self-employed truck driver from Ohio (E339 OH M WC), who had gotten at least three jobs where friends or family members worked, said: "I've earned everything I have. . . . I've worked for everything I've got."

Those who did acknowledge some help did not give it much weight in how they conceived of their life outcomes. For example, the project engineer from Ohio (B017 OH M MC) who got a job where his father worked (after his father made a phone call on his behalf) said of his situation: "I spent a lot of extra hours in there. . . . I earned my keep and more. . . . I think the first thing is probably the initial good work ethic. Hard work pays off and so forth. It might not get you the job, but you will be able to keep it. That's one of those things that helps you make your other opportunities." Although he alluded to the help he had received from relatives, like others who acknowledged any such help, he focused on his own work ethic, his hard work, and his ability to "keep" the job rather than on how he got the job. Similarly, an Ohio teacher (E316 OH F MC) emphasized her ability to prove herself rather than the help she got to get in the door. When asked whether she had earned her current place in life, she said:

> I think so . . . because I had to work to get myself through the high school I wanted to go to. I had to work to get myself through college. It was my grades and everything that got me the scholarships and that to get where I was. . . . I may have had some help getting my first job, but I think that I proved myself in that first job enough to get me my second job, which is where I'm really happy. So, yeah, I think I got here on my own accord.

Across most of the interviewees there was a strong sense that all outcomes in their lives had been the result of their own efforts or were justifiable because of the choices with which they had been faced. And indeed, in most cases that was certainly true. But what most of the interviewees did not see or acknowledge was that it had been possible for them to make their efforts in the first place only because family or friends provided them with help that gave them an extra edge or advantage that moved them to the head of the line when hiring was done. Even those who acknowledged that they might have received some help to "get in the door" stressed that they had proved themselves or worked hard to earn their place. And most did not mention or seemingly did not recall the help they had received when asked how they ended up in the life situations they had achieved. Instead, what was salient to them was the effort they themselves had expended, the hard work they had undertaken, and the uncertainty that had faced them at various times in their careers. The efforts undertaken on their behalf by family, friends, and acquaintances were not especially salient to them and, in most cases, were not mentioned unless I specifically asked about them.

For example, a well-to-do dentist from Ohio (E357 OH M MC) earned money to help pay for school through jobs he obtained from family and friends. Despite initially low grades as an undergraduate, his persistence paid off, so that he was able to get admitted to professional school, albeit at the last minute and off the waiting list. In addition to helping him get jobs, his family helped pay for his schooling, and then his networking efforts led to his getting started in his own practice after he obtained his degree. When asked whether he had earned his current place in life or deserved the kind of life he now had, he said: "I would say that I worked very hard to be where I'm at. I've worked hard to get to my level of income. But a lot of it has been due to a lot of smart decision-making, doing things that I felt from a financial standpoint were real prudent. . . . I would say, yeah, I deserve it because I've put a lot of time and effort into it, but at the same time it's not what drives me."

Like most of the interviewees, especially those who had done well in their lives, this interviewee emphasized his continual efforts, his self-motivation, and his ability to manage money and invest wisely. Getting help from family and friends is so taken for granted, so much a part of the way people get jobs, and so much in the background of consciousness that hardly anyone thinks to mention it when asked about their lives. Instead, they highlight the things they did in response to this help, not the help itself.

Even those whose every job was the result of inside information, a good word, or a friend who had a job to give them thought of themselves as having done it on their own. If they did not go to college but ended up in a unionized blue-collar job with benefits, they pointed to their skills and their work ethic, not to the brothers or fathers or uncles who helped them get in the door. If they were able to attend college, they mentioned the hard work they did to get through, not the tuition that their parents paid or that they could pay themselves because of the jobs they got through neighbors or relatives. In subsequent jobs, when networking and professional connections may have mattered more, the interviewees highlighted the skills they had developed and the reputations they had earned, not the people who may have provided them with an initial break or step up. Because they thought of such assistance as "just getting in the door," their own efforts, motivation, and persistence seemed to be far more important in their thinking about their life outcomes than the efforts made on their behalf or their access to valuable social resources. Hence, most of the interviewees believed that "nobody makes it without their own effort," but they gave little attention to the fact that "nobody makes it on their own."

The Social Psychology of Social Capital Exchange

Attributing success to our own efforts is consistent with our well-documented psychological tendency to attribute causes to what are called dispositional factors (that is, personality, character, or other such "internal" causes) rather than to situational factors (the circumstances under which the actions might have taken place). We also tend to take credit for our successes but to deny responsibility for our failures, as well as to overemphasize our own contributions to whatever positive outcomes occur.[5] In other words, there is both a self-centered bias (taking more than our share of credit for jointly produced outcomes) and a self-serving bias (taking more credit for our successes than for our failures) (Fiske and Taylor 1991). Even for those who receive a great deal of help throughout their lives, their own efforts are more salient than help that they might have received. Given these tendencies, even taking the initiative to look for someone to help, showing up when opportunities are given, or following through when an offer is extended are interpreted as acts of laudatory personal effort and motivation. The circumstances that made such acts possible are often not consciously considered. Instead, the respondents' own efforts are salient, especially if there were challenges, uncertainties, or obstacles to obtaining and using the opportunities available.

Having to put forth the effort led the interviewees to believe that they did it on their own. In contrast, there was much less memory of or importance attached to a friend talking to the boss on their behalf, or a neighbor hiring them for an initial job. As a case in point, the working-class surveyor from Ohio (B008 OH M WC), who knew 25 percent of the county and who used his connections throughout his life to get a series of jobs, still believed that he was "on his own": "You mostly help yourself. . . . If you don't do it on your own, you're not going to get it done." It is apparent in these interviews that social psychological processes translate the use of social capital (and other social resources) into advantages that are then interpreted as being the result of hard work, talent, effort, motivation, and persistence.

Although the interviewees were conscious of the efforts that they themselves had made and were much less conscious of help they had been given along the way, a number were nevertheless quite conscious of assistance given to blacks. For example, a New Jersey administrative assistant (D022 NJ F WC) who had gotten jobs with the help of her cousin, her neighbor, and a friend believed that she was denied help that was available to blacks: "I think that they need to even it out a little bit. I think that even though . . . somehow I feel that there's more opportunity for African Americans than there is, say, for me." Similarly, a heavy equipment operator from Ohio (B022 OH M WC), who got his own job at a company where a friend of his wife's was doing the hiring and who had previously held jobs where family members or friends worked, said:

> Now they have an apprenticeship program that, say, an average white man can't get into that apprenticeship, because they have to take so many women, so many blacks, so many Spanish. I mean, that's not right. . . . Because I've known quite a few people that . . . they try to get their young kids in there for the four-year apprenticeship, and a lot of the young men couldn't get in to get it. But they would give it to the women and the blacks, and how is that fair?

As suggested by this interviewee, the extra help they may have received when looking for a job or trying to help their own relatives get jobs was considered appropriate and expected, but when nonwhites or women were given access to jobs from which they had previously been excluded, that was considered unfair or unbalanced.

Thus, the self-serving and self-centered biases that characterized the interviewees' views of their own life histories often contributed to their supporting the principle of civil rights but opposing the policies that might bring it about. When many of the interviewees therefore declared that "everyone deserves a chance," they often meant by that something different when thinking of their own lives than when describing what they thought public policy should address. As the Ohio heavy equipment operator (B022 OH M WC) said: "Okay, it should be an opportunity for anybody. Not just because they're a black or a woman or whatever. If that person is qualified . . . they should have to take a test, put it that way." As far as I could tell from his own life history, this interviewee did not himself take tests before getting the jobs he held. Instead, he looked for family and friends to get him in the door or to put in a good word for him.

The same disconnect between how the interviewees viewed their own lives and how they described what rules or procedures should be applied to others was evident in the story of the Ohio interviewee (E315 OH M MC) who had complained that he had never been in the job market because he had gotten most of his jobs through the help of friends. At the time of the interview, he was working as the manager of a cleaning business owned by his friend. He said of test-taking: "I don't think that if I've got a better score, and I use 'I' in the general sense . . . if someone has a better score than an Afro-American, and the Afro-American gets in as opposed to the white person that has the better score. That's not fair. And vice versa." When explaining his own situation, however, he felt comfortable explaining: "I'm not the greatest student in the world, but I happen to think I'm a pretty good person. If you just looked at my grades, no, I'm not equal to a lot of people. But if you look at the things that I've done in my career and the things that I've done in my community, I've done some things. It's more than just my grades, my scores." He also mentioned that his daughter got into law school despite having test scores on the "lower end of the distribution," and yet he felt that what was fair was that people get what they deserve. Thus, it is clear from this example that our psychological tendencies to attribute outcomes to dispositional factors, to inflate the contributions that we make to various outcomes, and to take credit for successes instead of failures all shape our view of what is deserved.

As is evident from these several examples, the interviewees also reflected another psychological tendency, namely, to be more concerned with potential loss than with likely gains (Kahneman and Tversky 1979). Perhaps especially because the additional help or inside edge that the interviewees received throughout their lives was not visible or salient to them, the prospect of losing out on an opportunity seemed to hold a heightened salience for them, because they assumed that opportunities offered to blacks or women were at the expense of whites and men. Thus, despite these white interviewees' access to extensive social resources, they expressed displeasure that opportunities were being offered to blacks and women, but they took for granted the opportunities offered to themselves.

Social Capital: Merit or Advantage?

Because there is neither a systematic way in which help is given nor a clear path to follow, the interviewees, like most people in this country, had been "on their own" when it came to finding the opportunities that might give them a step up or a way forward. Yet the help they might have sought was patterned in that the people with whom they came into contact were likely to be people like themselves in important ways (Bourdieu 1985). In the stories told by the interviewees, it was clear that there had been multiple pathways through which they might have found help and no certainty about which pathway might lead to the most positive outcomes. Many, perhaps most, interviewees had found extra help from family members: fathers and mothers, brothers and sisters, aunts and uncles, and others more distant. Many relied on the goodwill of neighbors or friends. Social ties developed in school, at church, or in neighborhood organizations that provided a rich source of information and influence and often direct opportunity. It was usually these sorts of ties, closer to home, that the interviewees had available to them at the outset. As they "got in the door" and then took advantage of the opportunities that were offered, they then used the ties that they developed on the job, in their professions, or otherwise through more distant ties. This is not to say that family, friends, and neighbors became less useful, but rather that networks were extended and broadened over time. In other words, over their careers people found opportunities from multiple sources and often from unexpected ones. They used these advantages as they accumulated to help their children get ahead as well.

Although it is easy to see that the interviewees had people to help them when they needed to earn some money or when they wanted to get started in a career, it may not be evident why we should think of this as advantage rather than as merit. After all, as many of them said, once given a chance, in their judgment, they used it well. But the existence of help and the use of help do not differentiate those who sought help and those who did not. Some actively looked for someone to help them, often knowing that there might be fruitful outcomes to seeking it out. Others received help even without asking, because someone who had assistance to give thought of them.[6] The outcomes were no better for those who sought help and received it than for those who received help without seeking it. Further, a number of interviewees received help even though they apparently made bad choices or took a wrong turn. In fact, it was precisely because these interviewees had taken a wrong path that the help was offered to them, often by family members who felt they needed to change their direction in life.

For example, a New Jersey man (D024 NJ M WC) had flunked out of college, worked off and on for a number of years, got in trouble with the law, and moved out of state because he lost his driver's license in New Jersey. After he got married and had a child, however, his uncle told him that if he returned to New Jersey, he would get him a job. Now an assistant stockbroker, he said of his experiences before his uncle made the offer for him to return home: "I did a lot of things. . . . I bounced around. . . . I worked with . . . my friend . . . and [did] whatever I could get. I wasn't really into anything really, you know, big time. . . . I was hanging around with people that weren't very good to be hanging around with . . . so I got in a lot of trouble. . . . We were going nowhere." Despite this uneven start and his poor choices, this interviewee was able to get a job that paid reasonably well, provided benefits, including a retirement plan, and allowed him to support his wife and children and move into a new house in the neighborhood where he grew up. He was cognizant of the need for opportunity, but he also believed that it was his ability to prove himself that made the difference:

> Well, you have to get the opportunity. They have to feel that you can do it, and then you have to get the opportunity to do it, and then once you get the opportunity, you have to do the job. . . . Oh yeah, it's a good job. It's, with everything, profit-sharing, the pay, there's not too many jobs that you're going to find and you're going to make that kind of money, you know. Especially with no education.

This is just one of a number of examples of interviewees who started out with misdirection, poor performance, or blocked mobility and then found a way, with the help of family and friends, to get into a reasonably secure job with pay and benefits that fit their needs. Another example is an Ohio interviewee (E326 OH M WC) who was discouraged from going to college by his high school counselor because of poor grades and low test scores; he decided to give it a try anyway, only to drop out when he had difficulty completing the language requirement. He then got a series of jobs with the help of his father and friends, but he found the work hard and the hours unacceptable: "I was just kind of drifting. I didn't have any goals. I didn't know what I wanted to do at the time. I didn't know what direction I was going. So I just kind of just made my money, spent my money. I saved a lot, but I still spent it and just enjoyed life." However, his wife and her whole family, including her father and brothers, worked for a government agency, and he began to think of this as a favorable alternative. Despite not previously doing well in school, he did very well on the civil service test. It is likely that his wife and family members gave him tips on what to expect on the test. After some period of waiting, he was able to get a job at a government agency and support his family. As he said: "It was just something—it was a good job. . . . I had a family, and it was a stable job. I went for it."

There is no way to tell how these interviewees compared to others who might have wanted the jobs that they were able to get, but it is undoubtedly the case that other applicants might have been able to do well on the tests they took with a bit of coaching, to learn the job with enough support and patience, and to have the motivation and commitment to turn their lives around if offered a way out of dead-end jobs or poor life choices. Although the interviewees in this study were the ones who "got in the door" and were given a chance to "prove themselves," others might have done so as well if given the chance. Thus, help was made available and often led to substantial improvements in the life situations of interviewees who did not themselves seek out the help. As already noted, help was sometimes offered to those who were not competent to use it or who screwed up after it was offered. Hence, getting help was not determined by who merited it, but by who had access to help at the right time in their life.

An added dimension to the advantages of getting in the door and having the chance to prove oneself is that many jobs are stepping-stones to other jobs and many provide skill development and experiences upon which one can build. In other words, getting help from family and friends often provides cumulative advantages that position one for additional benefits over time. Those who get in the door can develop skills and credentials that enable them to get the next job and the one after that, and as their skills develop they have a better chance to be the "best person" at successive periods of their career. Although there are a surprising number of people for whom there is no clear career path, even these people gain advantages from getting in the door, because they are able in the process to develop a work history. The skills learned in early jobs often lead to subsequent jobs in similar or related fields.

For example, a Tennessee man (G505 TN M MC) worked at various jobs while in high school, all of which were at companies where either friends or relatives worked. Then, during college, he was able to get a summer job with a major company where a neighbor was a sales representative. Following college, he was offered a full-time job by the same company. He worked at that job for a number of years until the company reduced its workforce, and then he was able to get a similar job at a different company through connections with one of his customers. Such stories were typical in the lives of the interviewees.

In each step of the career path, getting the job required that the interviewee show some effort ("nobody does it without their own effort"), but in the vast majority of cases it also involved an inside edge or the added benefit of getting information, influence, or opportunities from someone else ("nobody does it on their own"). Although sometimes the extra help was not used because one job was as bad as another or because jobs were plentiful and extra help was not needed, most of the time finding someone to help was the pathway taken by interviewees into the labor market and the means by which they moved from position to position. Although not everyone did well or moved up, the availability of social resources helped protect them from the vicissitudes of the labor market. Indeed, the purpose of seeking the help of family and friends was to avoid the consequences of market competition, since most would have preferred not to face "equal opportunity" but rather to know that they could "get in the door."

Doesn't Everybody Do It?

The extensiveness of the help provided to the interviewees in this study and the prevalence with which it was offered raises an important question, namely, doesn't everyone help their own family and friends? Furthermore, perhaps we should both expect and applaud such assistance, since it shows a sense of responsibility and self-sufficiency. There is a great deal of evidence that, in fact, everyone does help their own when they can and to the extent that they can, but that is the rub. If some groups have been able to hoard opportunities for the benefit only of people like themselves and if the opportunities they have hoarded are not theirs to claim, then there may be a public interest in addressing such behavior. Indeed, this is the essential aim of the civil rights movement: to gain access to "jobs and freedom" that had previously been reserved only for whites.[7] Civil rights policies and programs are, in effect, a means to provide social resources to those who do not otherwise have them in their families or communities. For blacks and for others, civil rights programs make up for the lack of social resources that others gain from the legacies of past opportunity hoarding (Parks-Yancy 2010).

Framing the civil rights movement and subsequent legislation only in terms of making it illegal to keep blacks out therefore ignores the primary process by which racial inequality is reproduced, namely, through the help and assistance that whites give to other whites. Civil rights programs and policies, in a very real sense, interfered with the ability of whites to hoard opportunities for themselves, their children, their family members, and their neighbors. Because civil rights programs attempted to spread the access to good jobs and other such opportunities to more people, it increased the competition that whites had to face in order to obtain good jobs. In other words, by trying to create "equal opportunity" for access to jobs, the civil rights movement undermined the "unequal opportunity" that some whites had previously enjoyed and that many needed to access a middle-class lifestyle. It is presumably for this reason that so many whites have resisted the implementation of government programs that are intended to provide access to good jobs, to preparation for jobs, or to neighborhoods where such resources would be available to blacks and other minorities as well as to whites.

Although everyone might make an effort to help their own to the extent that they can, not every group is equally positioned to provide such help, and not every member of a group is equally effective at following through on good intentions. A study by Katherine Newman (1999) found that nonwhite workers in a fast-food restaurant were reluctant to recommend their friends for jobs because they were afraid that their own job might be jeopardized if the friend did not do good work (see also Smith 2007). To provide the kind of help that makes a difference, one must have some security on the job and sufficient access to social capital so that if something goes awry, other prospects are likely. Whites have broad-based social capital that cuts across a range of industries, occupations, and geographical areas. In most sectors in the United States, they are dominant in the sense that they control most of the positions of authority and have substantially greater access to resources. Those who "get in the door" therefore have a strong incentive to believe, and to project the belief to others, that their selection was based on merit, not on favoritism. To the extent that these levels of achievement represent the hoarded opportunities of the past, it is reasonable to expect that public policies might constrain how access is given and to whom.

Among the interviewees, there was little consciousness of the role played by access to social capital, despite the widespread access to and use of social capital to improve job prospects and to provide steppingstones to better opportunities. Each individual treated his or her own experience as the exception rather than the rule. Each used certain language about the help they had received from family or friends—that it "just" got them in the door, for instance—and emphasized having "proved" themselves after the fact. Even academics tend to promulgate a certain image with their use of language: for instance, the image that people find jobs in a competitive and free "market." The use of such language suggests that labor market outcomes are similar to winning a contest in a fair and open competition. While some attention has in fact been paid to the informal means by which some people get jobs, the research findings seem to underplay how often and how widespread the use of such means is.[8] Certainly, most interviewees did not give these processes much explicit attention. They not only did not highlight the fact that they had gotten jobs with the help of family and friends most of the time throughout most of their career, but often actively dismissed or minimized such help. Instead, they talked about individual achievement, individual merit, and individual effort and motivation. The focus on the individual instead of the group and the personalization of outcomes that are embedded in collective relationships represent another aspect of the reproduction of racial inequality without the need for racism. That is the issue to which I next turn.

Chapter 4

The American Dream: Individualism and Inequality

[Do you think that if people try hard enough they can make it in the world?]

Heavy-industry vice president from New Jersey (D013 NJ M MC): "Yeah . . . I think you have to keep searching. . . . There is a biblical relation, you know, right? Ask and you shall receive. . . . It's all biblical."

Self-employed truck driver from Ohio (E339 OH M WC): "Yeah, if you want something, you gotta work for it . . . no matter what."

Drywall deliverer from Ohio (B006 OH M WC): "Oh yeah. You can do anything you want. . . . You've just got to keep going at it."

Chef from Tennessee (G515 TN M WC): "It's kind of a racist remark, but I think that they can if they really wanted to. I think some people try not to make it. They feel better being unhappy."

Attorney from New Jersey (D062 NJ M MC): "Absolutely, because making it in the world means achieving the things that are important to you. . . . I think everyone can achieve that if you work hard enough."

Retiree from Tennessee (F020 TN F WC): "I don't think there is anything you can't do. Only we've had a lot of good examples in people that never even finished high school, like Sam Walton, who has wanted something and has made something of himself. So I think you can."

According to two-thirds of the interviewees in this study, everybody can make it, no matter what, because this is America, because everyone has the same opportunity, because there is something for everyone, because only those who give up fail, because they have heard stories that prove the point, because they have experienced it in their own lives, and because even if you have to pay the price, sacrifice, or face obstacles, succeeding is really a matter of wanting it enough. Further, they said, there are government programs to help those who need a boost, education is available to those who put forth the effort, and there is always an opportunity to change directions if you are on the wrong path. While some questioned what it means to "make it" and others acknowledged that for some it was harder than for others, the overwhelming majority of the interviewees espoused a firm belief in the ability to achieve the American dream with enough hard work, persistence, and determination. They said that you might not end up wealthy, but you can have a satisfactory life, put food on the table, and support yourself and your family.

The interviewees held views consistent with those of the majority in the country. According to James Kluegel and Elliot Smith (1986, 100–101), most Americans believe that "opportunity for economic advancement is widely available, that economic outcomes are determined by individual efforts and talents (or their lack), and that in general economic inequality is fair." Kluegel and Smith label this set of beliefs the "dominant ideology," the belief that making it in America results from individual factors, especially hard work, motivation, and effort. In this chapter, I examine the interviewees' explanations for how people "make it," and I also explore how political and racial attitudes frame beliefs in the American dream. Political attitudes clearly differentiate the interviewees. Those with more conservative political views were those most insistent that anyone can make it, any time, with enough hard work and effort. Those with more liberal political views expressed concern as well about the hardships that some people face and the obstacles that might interfere with their access to opportunity. But even the liberal respondents attributed success to hard work, and many expressed the view that others can use such strategies for getting ahead. Perhaps most noteworthy in these responses is that the principles cited by the interviewees as the way to get ahead differed significantly from the stories they told about their own lives.

In addition to the belief in the efficacy of hard work and motivation, the interviewees argued that it is never too late to start and that tomorrow is always another day—that is, no matter what the circumstances you have to face, you can pick yourself up and change things. These beliefs are consistent with the four tenets of the American dream as spelled out by Jennifer Hochschild (1995, 18): (1) regardless of background or potential obstacles, anyone can pursue their dreams anytime; (2) making a sufficient effort leads to a reasonable chance of a successful outcome; (3) what determines success is what is under one's own control, that is, effort and motivation; and (4) achieving success reflects positively on one's character.

Within this complex of beliefs is both an appeal to the self ("do not give up," "you can do it") and a challenge ("opportunities exist," "how things turn out is in your hands"). This sort of optimism and belief in the unlimited possibilities of willpower seem to have a mobilizing effect for many Americans, and they also create social pressure in many communities for people to find a way forward despite what might otherwise be thought of as poor options (Benabou and Tirole 2002; Louria 2005). For example, a lawn and garden equipment salesman from Ohio (E313 OH M WC) said, when asked whether one can make it through hard work: "Yeah. Because I think there's a lot of opportunities out there, and all you've got to do is put your mind to doing something. I'm not saying that everybody has to go to a secure college or anything like that, but there's just a lot of opportunities out there if you want to go get them." This interviewee's grandparents were both schoolteachers, and his father was a supervisor in the factory of a large company. The interviewee originally planned to go into a professional field, but his grades and test scores were not encouraging. Instead, following high school, he worked at a gas station owned by a friend, worked at an orchard owned by neighbors, and then took a job at a body shop to which a friend had referred him. After his father talked with the owner of a repair shop, he got a job there and worked at it for several years, before finally starting his own shop with the financial help of his parents. He also went to school for an associate's degree (that he was never able to finish) with tuition support from his grandparents. There is presumably a big gap between "putting your mind to it"—his characterization of the abundant opportunities available to those who want them—and having access to abundant social resources such as he experienced.

A young musician (G517 TN M MC) who went to Nashville to try to make it in the music business said, when asked about whether one could make it with hard work, "Absolutely. Because I think will and work ethic and persistence severely outweigh talent and knowledge and education." In high school, this interviewee got a number of jobs in restaurants where friends worked. In college he was able to get a part-time job at the large company where his father worked that helped him pay his way through school. After college, he got a job through a friend to do sales in a music store, while playing on the side. He had since learned that in the music business it is all about networks and friendships, so he got most of his jobs in music after meeting people who could hire him or put in a good word for him. For example, he got one of his first regular gigs after one of the patrons in the bar where he was working mentioned his name. He felt that this gig provided him with a lot of experience, but it kept him out of town and away from the kind of unannounced opportunities that are so important in the music industry. Hence, he quit this job and went back to his previous job, until he was hired away by a former coworker. The new restaurant where he worked was closer to Music Row, had a clientele that included more musicians, and was run by managers with whom he was able to work out a flexible schedule so he would have a lot of days free to play and build his music career. As his networks developed he was able to get more jobs through word of mouth, and as his experience developed his name was more likely to be mentioned to those who needed someone to play. When asked whether he had "earned" his current place in life, this young musician said, "I worked very, very hard to get where I am. Yeah."

In both of these cases, the interviewees drew on the social resources of family and friends, and although both presumably did their part when the opportunities were made available, they did not "make it" just by hard work. As they themselves described it, their hard work was combined with the opportunity to develop their skills, gain experience, and meet people who could offer jobs on which to build their careers. These two cases are similar to many others in this study. Although 68 percent of the time the interviewees obtained jobs with some kind of help from extra-market social resources (75 percent of the time overall for men and 61 percent for women), most did not mention this kind of help when they thought about whether people can make it by trying hard. Instead, they called attention to motivation (Tennessee manager [F005 TN M MC]: "It's a matter of want to"), persistence (Tennessee electronics technician [F015 TN M WC]: "You only fail if you give up"), determination (New Jersey party sales manager [D063 NJ F WC]: "Determination and focus can create anything"), and the abundance of opportunities (Tennessee homemaker [G537 TN F WC]: "There is something for everyone"; Ohio heavy equipment operator [B022 OH M WC]: "Everybody's got the same opportunity"). Although some pointed to obstacles or to hardships, most did not view these as an excuse not to make it: (Ohio door-to-door advertising salesperson [E302 OH F WC]: "You need to always look on the good part"; Ohio order entry clerk [E352 OH M WC]: "No matter what the situation, you can make it out"; Ohio unemployed interviewee [E362 OH F MC]: "Most can overcome a lot"; and Tennessee travel agent [F022 TN F WC]: "Everybody has obstacles—you need to trust in the Lord and help yourself").

Not only did the interviewees attribute life outcomes to individual effort, but most specifically rejected explanations that attributed such outcomes to structural factors, such as poor schooling, low wages, or exploitation by employers. For example, a male schoolteacher from Ohio (B016 OH M MC) had this to say about people being poor: "You know, what can you say? I have been a low-wage person. If you do a good job and you work hard, you won't be a low-wage person all of your life. Every place has to have low wages for somebody, because they do less important work. . . . Private industry is only going to provide jobs that they think they can use to make money. . . . If they provide jobs that they don't need, they'll go broke." Similarly, the CEO of a small business in Ohio

(B010 OH M WC) said: "If you're working somewhere that you don't like, then you should change. . . . Here at this company, we have a hundred people. I can't say, oh, just because I want to do my part, I'm going to increase that to two hundred people . . . and then go bankrupt in a year. . . . It doesn't necessarily work that way."

Other interviewees said that if low-wage workers did not like their jobs, they should just go elsewhere. For example, a Tennessee graphic designer (G520 TN M WC) said, with reference to people who are poor, "They're not trying to pull themselves from where they're at. . . . If you don't like the projects, leave. You see. It is not like you are surrounded by a barbed-wire fence. You have to go out and make it happen." Like these interviewees, most Americans believe that individuals are the masters of their fate, with outcomes dependent on how much they try, how much they want it, and how persistent they are. Most do not think about these issues with regard to who helped them and how they might have gotten an inside edge or an unfair advantage compared to those without the necessary connections or social environment.

Getting Ahead: How One Earns a Place in Life

To provide more clarity about the interviewees' conceptions about making it or getting ahead, I compared the responses of the sociopolitical groups that emerged in the interview process on three questions about their life situations: (1) whether they had earned or deserved their current place in life, (2) what most contributed to the life that they had now, and (3) whether any obstacles had prevented them from achieving everything that they had hoped. The questions were open-ended. I read through the responses to identify the most frequent explanations, and then I coded the responses into these categories. Most interviewees gave a single explanation, although about one-third gave more than one. Tables 4.1 to 4.3 include those responses that were given by more than 5 percent of the interviewees. Overwhelmingly, "hard work" was the most prevalent answer to why interviewees believed they had "earned" their current place in life. Although there are some variations across the sociopolitical groups, there are fewer differences than similarities in the responses to this question. More than 80 percent of the middle-class conservatives and the religious nonconservatives, more than 60 percent of the religious conservatives, working-class "racists," working-class liberals, and rich white liberals, and more than half of the apolitical majority said that they had earned their current place in life because of their hard work. For example, a retired attorney from Ohio (E308 OH M MC; whom I categorized as a rich white liberal) said, when asked if he had earned

Table 4.1 Responses to the Question "Why Is That?" When Asked, "Do You Think That You Have Earned Your Current Place in Life?," by Socio-economic Category

Type of Response	Religious Conservatives N = 46	Working-Class Racists N = 30	Middle-Class Conservatives N = 11	Apolitical Majority N = 92	Religious Nonconservatives N = 11	Working-Class Liberals N = 14	Rich White Liberals N = 42	Total N = 246
Percentage of sample	12%	4.5%	19%	37%	4.5%	6%	17%	100%
Hard work	61	63	82	54	82	64	69	64
Got some help	11	0	27	12	9	7	12	14
Blessings	15	3	9	9	27	7	7	10
I deserve better	9	27	27	10	0	7	2	10
No one deserves	9	20	27	9	0	7	5	10
Not given anything	9	20	27	9	0	7	5	10
Luck	4	0	0	9	0	0	12	8
Made bad Choices	4	13	9	5	9	0	0	5

Source: Author's compilation.
Note: Responses do not add up to 100 because miscellaneous responses are not included, and each respondent may have given more than one response.

Table 4.2 Responses to the Question "What Has Most Contributed to the Kind of Life You Have Now?," by Sociopolitical Category

Type of Response	Religious Conservatives N = 46	Working-Class Racists N = 30	Middle-Class Conservatives N = 11	Apolitical Majority N = 92	Religious Nonconservatives N = 11	Working-Class Liberals N = 14	Rich White Liberals N = 42	Total N = 246
Percentage of sample	12%	4.5%	19%	37%	4.5%	6%	17%	100%
Hard work	13	27	18	25	9	29	50	27
Family values	20	20	18	23	27	29	12	21
Motivation	20	20	45	16	9	7	19	19
Husband/spouse	13	17	18	11	18	7	12	13
Education, intelligence	11	3	9	8	0	0	26	10
Persistence	2	0	9	11	18	29	12	10
Managed money well	13	7	18	4	9	21	7	9
Help, inheritance	4	3	0	2	0	14	19	8
Blessings	22	3	0	2	18	0	2	7

Source: Author's compilation.
Note: Responses do not add up to 100 because miscellaneous responses are not included, and each respondent may have given more than one response.

Table 4.3 Responses to the Question "Have There Been Any Obstacles in Your Life That Have Prevented You from Achieving Everything You Had Wanted?," by Sociopolitical Category

Type of Response	Religious Conservatives N = 46	Working-Class Racists N = 30	Middle-Class Conservatives N = 11	Apolitical Majority N = 92	Religious Nonconservatives N = 11	Working-Class Liberals N = 14	Rich White Liberals N = 42	Total N = 246
Percentage of sample	12%	4.5%	19%	37%	4.5%	6%	17%	100%
No obstacles	24	10	36	20	27	29	29	23
Lack of education	13	20	0	17	18	50	10	17
Self-imposed obstacles	13	23	27	9	9	21	19	15
Lack of help, goals	11	3	0	15	9	7	12	11
Divorce, early pregnancy	13	17	0	10	18	14	7	11
Family problems	11	10	18	15	9	0	5	11
Health problems	9	23	0	12	0	7	7	11
Poverty, unemployment	7	17	18	11	9	0	2	9
Lack of social skills	7	0	27	7	0	7	12	8

Source: Author's compilation.
Note: Responses do not add up to 100 because miscellaneous responses are not included, and each respondent may have given more than one response.

his place in life, "Absolutely . . . I've worked hard in school. . . . I worked and saved my money to be in this position. . . . It takes a lot of time and dedication. . . . There's been a lot of sweat that's gone into it." Similarly, an Ohio owner of a small trucking firm (E321 OH M WC; whom I categorized as a working-class "racist") said, when asked the same question, "Definitely . . . because I've worked since I've been eight, nine, ten years old. I've given up a lot of stuff that other kids have had. . . . I worked for everything I've got."

Aside from "hard work," the groups differed in the answers they gave for why they had earned their current place in life, underscoring the different social positions of the groups and the differences in their life experiences. Although "hard work" was by far the most prevalent response, both the religious conservatives and the religious nonconservatives pointed as well to their blessings. For example, an Ohio electrical engineer (B003 OH F MC; whom I categorized as a religious conservative) said: "I believe that everything I have is just God's mercy in my life. It's like a cloud of favor." A preschool supervisor from Ohio (E330 OH F MC; whom I categorized as a religious nonconservative) said: "I think I've been blessed with this kind of life. . . . I think I'm privileged, and I think I'm lucky to be here."

A different pattern is evident for the two nonreligious conservative groups, the working-class "racists" and the middle-class conservatives. "Hard work" was for both the most prominent response, but they were also likely to say that they deserved much better outcomes than they had obtained, that no one deserves anything in life, and that no one had given them much in the way of help. For example, the working-class housepainter from New Jersey (D012 NJ M WC) mentioned in chapter 2 who had hoped for more steady work said: "I think I deserve a little better. . . . I went through that . . . with the drugs. . . . It set me back. . . . I've been very patient, but I'm still waiting for the better break." In general, the job and financial circumstances for these two groups were less favorable than for others in their same class position, namely, the working-class liberals and the rich white liberals.

When asked about whether they had earned their place in life, a small proportion of the interviewees acknowledged that they had received help. A perhaps unusual example is from an Ohio woman who described herself as a "trophy wife" (E353 OH F MC; whom I classified as a rich white liberal). She mentioned the inheritance she received from her deceased husband as the key factor in enabling her to live an affluent life, but she also said that she had earned her current place in life because she "gave up a tremendous amount." The Ohio factory worker (E307 OH M WC) mentioned in chapter 2 who had the steady, unionized job also acknowledged the help he had received: "Boy, we've had help. . . . My mother- and father-in-law helped us. My parents helped us. . . . We wouldn't be where we're at now if it wasn't for that." Those who acknowledged that they had had help made reference primarily to money they had received from their families and not so much to the connections that might have helped them get jobs.

A somewhat different pattern emerges when the respondents were asked what "most contributed" to their current life situation (table 4.2). The respondents gave less prominence to hard work, although it was still the first or second most prevalent response for rich white liberals, working-class "racists," the apolitical majority, and working-class liberals (tied with family values and persistence for the last group). A Tennessee musician (G517 TN M MC) combined the two concepts when he explained what contributed most to his life outcomes: "Probably the infusion of a good work ethic by my parents. I think that counts for just about more than anything as far as developing general character." The three most conservative groups (religious conservatives, working-class "racists," and middle-class conservatives) also frequently mentioned family values or their own motivation. For example, an insurance adjuster (D040 NJ M MC; whom I categorized as a middle-class conservative) said: "I think probably my commitment. . . . I've always . . . given 110 percent. . . . And I take a lot of pride in what I do." Rich white liberals mentioned motivation as well as their education and intelligence. Family values were mentioned also by the apolitical majority and religious non-conservatives. Working-class liberals said family values, persistence, and good money management contributed to their current life situations.

Overall, the interviewees primarily pointed to hard work when asked about whether they had "earned" their current place in life, but when asked to think more specifically about what had led to them having the life they had now, they added to hard work the importance of family values, motivation, and, for some, education, persistence, or money management skills. It was mostly the two most liberal groups, rich white liberals and working-class liberals, who indicated that the help they received or resources they inherited had been a central factor in their current life situation. Even among these groups, however, only a small proportion gave this response. Thus, despite the fact that the overwhelming majority of the respondents had had significant help in their lives in obtaining jobs, paying their bills, and getting through challenges or hard times, they attributed their life outcomes to their own character more than to their access to social resources. Conspicuously absent from the explanations given by most interviewees was the value of social capital for finding jobs, although a few mentioned financial help from their families. Hence, when they thought about whether others could make it, they also pointed to issues of character: wanting it, being motivated, being persistent, and expending effort.

These views were also evident when the respondents were asked about potential obstacles in their lives. The most prevalent response to this question was that there were no obstacles. Twenty percent of the apolitical majority, one-quarter of the religious conservatives and religious nonconservatives, and about one-third of the working-class liberals, rich white liberals, and middle-class conservatives said that they had not really faced obstacles. For example, a carpenter from Tennessee (G529 TN M WC; whom I categorized as a religious conservative) said with regard to whether he had faced obstacles: "No. I achieved everything I wanted out of life. . . . I've exceeded [my goals]." Another sizable proportion of the interviewees said that any obstacles they might have faced were of their own making. This was true of the working-class "racists," the middle-class conservatives, and both the working-class liberals and rich white liberals. For example, an Ohio interviewee who was self-employed in the landscaping business (E354 OH M WC; whom I categorized as a working-class "racist") said about obstacles in his life: "Some self-inflicted . . . not going and getting the degree . . . not taking the use of the GI bill and getting that degree." These responses suggest strongly the perception that life outcomes are the result of individual circumstances, sometimes defined by choices made or efforts expended, occasionally defined by luck. The working-class "racists" among the seven sociopolitical groups were the least likely to say that they had faced no obstacles.

Working-class liberals were the most likely to say that their lack of education had been a significant obstacle for them. Middle-class conservatives pointed to their lack of social skills as an obstacle that had kept them from achieving their life goals (and indeed, a number of these respondents did seem to be socially awkward). Other obstacles said to have caused difficulty for some of the interviewees included divorce or early pregnancy, family problems, or health problems (including getting hurt on the job). Most of the interviewees discussed such issues as if they were the result of bad luck or perhaps bad choices that they had made. It is interesting that lack of help or lack of social resources, though mentioned by some, was not an especially salient reason given in the interviewees' explanations for their life outcomes.

The American Dream: Individualism, Egalitarianism, and Racial Resentment

The sentiments expressed by the interviewees reflect an individualist framing of life issues. Their responses were personal in tone and outlook, and they mentioned their own efforts, motivation, and persistence but included institutional or collective factors only with regard to education and family issues. Few mentioned class, race, or gender when discussing the factors that had contributed to their life outcomes. Their responses did not consider the structural factors that may impinge on the lives of people who are trying to make it, nor did they consider the social relationships among groups that may make getting ahead easier for some than for others. When thinking about their lives, most did not mention help they had received from family and friends, nor did they mention their efforts to seek such help when they needed an edge in finding a job.

Some may argue that the wording of these questions invoked individualist responses. It is possible, for example, that words such as "earned" or "deserve" call forth a response about the importance of "hard work," but that is not necessarily the case with the question about "what most contributed to your having the life outcomes that you did." Further, given the life stories that the interviewees had just recounted, one would expect them to mention in their responses that they had a lot of help from family and friends. Although some respondents talked about the role of their families, they mentioned having learned family values more than having received family assistance. Especially given the extent to which social connections seemed to be consequential when the respondents were looking for jobs, it seems significant that only one in seven interviewees thought about either help or inheritances from which they had benefited. These responses reflect the framing that the respondents used to interpret their lives. Despite patterns that might exist at the aggregate level, life outcomes for any given person are not guaranteed and, indeed, depend on hard work, motivation, and persistence. Life outcomes also depend, however, on help from family and friends, but this part of the story largely dropped out when the respondents thought about their lives.

Racial Resentment and Traditional Values

The interviewees' faith in hard work as the means to having a good life was evident when they talked about others as well, not just when they talked about themselves. Specifically, an individualist perspective framed their political views about what the government should or should not do for those who are poor or disadvantaged, and even more so with regard to government policy on racial issues. In this chapter, I want to revisit and expand the analysis of racial resentment that I mentioned in chapter 2 so that we can better understand how racial politics and traditional values come together for the sociopolitical groups in this study. Interviewees with liberal views constituted a minority of the sample. They were also the only interviewees who discussed structural rather than personal issues in talking about their political views. For example, an upper-middle-class writer from New Jersey (C006 NJ M MC; a rich white liberal) said, when asked if people can make it through hard work:

> I think some people can, but not all people. . . . There's definitely an edge for people who come from certain kinds of economic and ethnic and racial backgrounds. . . . If your background is wealthy and you're white and your education is good, you're in much better shape than somebody who's not. And I think that's built into the society very, very rigidly.

This interviewee pointed to the advantages that made it easier for him than for others: "I never really had a problem finding a job, finding something to do . . . but I had . . . I came from a family where people were educated. I went through a good school system. I went through good colleges. And so I think I had an advantage."

Most of the interviewees did not share his views when they talked about the relationship of hard work to life outcomes. Instead, most interviewees insisted that making it depends on individual effort: how much people try, how much they want to succeed, and whether they persist in their efforts. Most did not talk about advantages and disadvantages when thinking about this question, especially not with regard to themselves.

In previous discussions of the policy views of whites, there has been controversy about whether the primary determinants of support or opposition to civil rights policies reflect racial attitudes (especially racism) or instead reflect traditional American values. In these analyses, measures of several key concepts, including racial resentment (as a measure of a type of racism), egalitarianism, and individualism, have been compared as explanations for white policy views. To explore these issues in this sample, I used items from the American National Election Studies (ANES) to construct measures of these concepts (by combining the individual items into scales). The items are listed in the appendix to this chapter. As we saw in chapter 2, the sociopolitical groups in this study vary in terms of their racial resentment, although as a group, the respondents were less racially resentful than a national sample from the ANES. Levels of racial resentment among the respondents in this study do vary, however, in line with their political views, with more conservative respondents showing greater racial resentment than those with more liberal political views. For the measure of egalitarianism, I followed the lead of David Sears, P. J. Henry, and Rick Kosterman (2000) in dividing the measures into two components, which they call "more equal" and "gone too far." "More equal" is a measure that indeed taps egalitarian values, while "gone too far" is a measure of inegalitarian values with regard to civil rights policy. In the analyses here, I used these value measures as dependent variables in regression analyses that included gender, education, and income as control variables and the sociopolitical groups as dummy variables. I used the rich white liberal group as the reference

Table 4.4 Regression of Attitudes Toward Inequality, on Demographic Factors and Sociopolitical Group

Independent Variables	Racial Resentment	More Equal	Gone Too Far	Individualism	Racial Resentment
Constant	–0.068	1.318	–0.317	–0.207	0.117
Education	–0.165***	–0.055	–0.080	–0.108+	–0.109**
Income	–0.031	–0.136**	–0.002	0.063	–0.070
Gender (male)	0.259*	0.000	0.021	0.182	0.186*
Working-class racists	1.341***	–1.074***	0.926***	0.429	1.013***
Middle-class conservatives	1.571***	–0.835*	1.383***	0.381	1.204***
Religious conservatives	1.117***	–0.804***	0.986***	0.595**	0.718***
Apolitical majority	0.758***	–0.727***	0.725***	0.443**	0.476**
Religious nonconservatives	0.332	0.239	–0.217	–0.354	0.109
Working-class liberals	0.067	–0.294	0.017	0.012	0.052
More equal	—	—	—	—	–0.087+
Gone too far	—	—	—	—	0.108*
Individualism	—	—	—	—	0.385***
R-squared	0.373	0.073	0.153	0.046	0.546

Source: Author's compilation.
$^{+}p < 0.10$; $^{*}p < 0.05$; $^{**}p < 0.01$; $^{***}p < 0.001$

category because they tended to be the most distinctive group with regard to their politics. The regression analyses are shown in table 4.4.

Of particular note in this analysis is the fact that the apolitical majority cluster with the more conservative groups. Working-class "racists," middle-class conservatives, religious conservatives, and the apolitical majority were all significantly more racially resentful than rich white liberals, while religious nonconservatives and working-class liberals were not different from rich white liberals.[1] The apolitical majority tended to be traditional and family-oriented, and generally they were not especially interested in social and political events outside their neighborhoods. When asked about political issues, they were likely to align themselves with those of a more traditional and conservative outlook and not with the more liberal respondents. Illustrating this point is the ambivalence of a middle-class male purchasing agent from New Jersey (D018 NJ M MC; included in the apolitical majority) when asked whether government should help those who have less economically:

> That's one of the tougher social questions of our ages. From my early left-wing leanings . . . I fully believe the government should help all its people. . . . And then I got right-wing, and now I'm for . . . I don't know what . . . I believe the government's for the good of the people, and I think they should help those less able. But I'm not so sure at what extent. . . . I'm a

believer in self . . . you've got a . . . responsibility. Only you have the ability to change things.

In addition to racial resentment, the short survey I gave to the interviewees also included questions that have been frequently used to measure egalitarianism and individualism (see, for example, Sears, Sidanius, and Bobo 2000; see the appendix to this chapter for a list of items used in these scales), including Sears, Henry, and Kosterman's (2000) measure of egalitarianism ("more equal") and their measure of inegalitarianism ("gone too far"). I reproduced these measures in my analyses and also created a measure of individualism (see also Kinder and Sanders 1996).

Table 4.4 also shows the regression of "more equal," "gone too far," and individualism on the sociopolitical groups and the control variables. As can be seen from the middle columns, the results of the analyses of "more equal" and "gone too far" are mirror images of each other. Net of the demographic characteristics of the groups, working-class "racists," middle-class conservatives, religious conservatives, and the apolitical majority were less likely to be egalitarian ("more equal") than were rich white liberals, and they were more likely than rich white liberals to believe that we have "gone too far" in trying to create equality within the country. Not surprisingly, religious nonconservatives and working-class liberals do not differ from rich white liberals in their views about egalitarianism on either measure. Note, however, that the results for individualism are quite different. Religious conservatives and the apolitical majority appear to be more individualist in their responses than rich white liberals. The other groups do not differ statistically on the measure of individualism, and this analysis explains very little variance in the individualism scale. I take these results to mean that individualism prevails so extensively in this country that there is little differentiation, at least among whites, on these values, as evidenced as well by the fact that there were hardly any groups who were less individualist than rich white liberals.

I also regressed the measure for racial resentment on the other value scales, and surprisingly, I found that individualism is the value with the strongest effect on racial resentment, net of egalitarian values. Adding these values as predictors, however, does not change the significant differences between the groups, nor the effects of the other demographic characteristics. It is perhaps noteworthy that this last equation explains more than half of the variance in the racial resentment measure. Working-class "racists," middle-class conservatives, religious conservatives, and the apolitical majority were all more racially resentful than were rich white liberals, even controlling for other political attitudes. Males were also more racially resentful than females, and those with less education were more racially resentful than those with more education. Beyond the group and demographic effects, those who were more individualist were more racially resentful, as were those who believed that we have "gone too far" in our efforts to bring about racial equality.

Across these analyses, the predictions of racial resentment explain more variance than those that predict egalitarianism or inegalitarianism and far more than the prediction of individualism, suggesting that racial resentment is what differentiates these groups the most. Thus, it appears from these analyses that the strong individualist framing of the interviewees in this study reflects adherence to traditional values, but these values seem to be strongly related to racial attitudes. As suggested by Sears, Henry, and Kosterman (2000), these attitudes are highly interrelated rather than alternatives to each other. As seen in this analysis and in others throughout the book, the results for this sample are consistent with the analyses by Michael Alvarez and John Brehm (2002, 116), who argue that in reference to a wide range of policy issues, "white Americans' responses are driven primarily by two core principles, modern racism and egalitarianism." The implications of the variations on racial resentment and egalitarian values can be seen in later chapters when I discuss the interviewees' views of public policy issues.

These attitudes can be seen in the responses of a working-class interviewee from Ohio (E342 OH M WC; included in the apolitical majority category) who was enrolled at the time of the interview in a semiprofessional program. He felt that it was not fair for people who are economically less well off to expect the government to help them, in part because he felt that such people take for granted the help that they receive and do not do their part in working for what they get. He said:

> There's a low-income housing project. . . . It's an all-black residency place. . . . [Every year the housing authority has to replace hundreds of thousands of dollars of plumbing fixtures] because all they do is just bust it up with sledgehammers and bust out windows. . . . They know that it's going to be provided for them, so they don't have to respect it. . . . Now, there's other people out there, such as your welfare people that don't want to work or want to stay in bed all day long, and all they have to do is go downtown and fill out an application and that's about the end of story. It's as easy as one, two, three, you know. And people that do work, they're helping to support them, and I don't feel that it's right. . . . There are too many blacks that take advantage of it. . . . If they want to be equal, let them do their equal share of work. I think they use it to an advantage.

Even if not representative of the country as a whole, and although the sample includes only U.S.-born whites, it is striking how politically conservative the interviewees in this study are, as reflected in their responses to questions about inequality; it is all the more striking given that my sample had a larger proportion of college-educated respondents than would be true of a nationally representative sample and given that the respondents were less racially resentful on the survey measures than is evident in national samples. Further, despite significant political events over the last few years, it is striking as well that the ideological views of the population have remained relatively stable. The 2009 Pew report (Kohut 2009, 15) on trends in political values and attitudes notes, for example, that there is a "fundamental stability in overall political and social values."

Should Government See to It That Blacks Get Fair Treatment?

To further examine the attitudes toward inequality in my sample of U.S.-born white adults, I include another set of analyses. I used as a dependent variable an item commonly used to predict policy attitudes in the American National Election Studies, namely, whether "the government in Washington should see to it that blacks get fair treatment in jobs" (see table 4.5). A positive score on this scale means that it is not the government's business to ensure fair treatment in jobs for blacks; a negative score means that the government should see to it that blacks are fairly treated. Compared to rich white liberals, both religious conservatives and working-class "racists" were more likely to think that it is not the government's business to ensure fair treatment in jobs for blacks. The other groups did not differ from rich white liberals on this scale. Interestingly, middle-class conservatives did not cluster with religious conservatives and working-class "racists" in this analysis. I further added racial resentment, "more equal," "gone too far," and individualism to the equation one at a time and then all together. Racial resentment almost fully mediates the effects of religious conservatives and working-class "racists" on the views of government responsibility toward blacks, as does "gone too far." "More equal" partially mediates these effects, but religious conservatives still stand out in believing that it is not the government's business to ensure fair treatment for blacks. Individualism, however, does not work well in mediating these effects, and individualism itself is only marginally significant as a predictor of the views on government responsibility toward blacks. Surprisingly, the effects for middle-class conservatives become substantially negative (that is, supportive of government effort) when controlling for all of these political values together. Also of interest is that gender has no effect on these views, and that these political attitudes do not mediate the effects of education or income.

When all of these values are included in the equation at the same time (last column of table 4.5), it turns out that the feeling that we have gone

Table 4.5 Regression of Attitudes Regarding Whether the Government in Washington Should Ensure Fair Treatment for Blacks, on Demographic Factors and Sociopolitical Group

	Should Government Help Blacks?					
Independent Variables	(1) Basic Model	(2) Basic Model Plus Racial Resentment	(3) Basic Model Plus More Equal	(4) Basic Model Plus Gone Too Far	(5) Basic Model Plus Individualism	(6) Full Model
Constant	3.507***	3.513***	3.902***	3.646***	3.555***	3.864***
Education	–0.314**	–0.232*	–0.330***	–0.274**	–0.299**	–0.224*
Income	0.188*	0.202*	0.149+	0.196*	0.184*	0.168+
Gender (male)	0.023	–0.092	0.011	0.004	–0.029	–0.050
Working-class racists	1.109*	0.536	0.810	0.682	0.997+	0.072
Middle-class conservatives	0.138	–0.601	–0.128	–0.563	0.059	–1.115+
Religious conservatives	1.215**	0.691+	0.963*	0.719+	1.091**	0.280
Apolitical majority	0.410	0.027	0.099	–0.043	0.247	–0.278
Religious nonconservatives	–0.397	–0.550	–0.573	–0.781	–0.442	–0.945
Working-class liberals	–0.520	–0.543	–0.573	–0.502	–0.533	–0.547
Racial resentment	—	0.472**	—	—	—	0.299+
More equal	—	—	–0.324**	—	—	–0.207+
Gone too far	—	—	—	0.510***	—	0.442***
Individualism	—	—	—	—	0.213+	0.019
R-squared	0.112	0.149	0.138	0.173	0.124	0.191

Source: Author's compilation.
Note: Higher scores mean that the respondent believed that it is not the government's business to ensure fair treatment for blacks in obtaining jobs; lower scores mean that the respondent believed that the government should ensure such fair treatment.
$^{+}p < 0.10$; $^{*}p < 0.05$; $^{**}p < 0.01$; $^{***}p < 0.001$

too far in promoting equality has the most significant effect on the views of government responsibility toward blacks. Racial resentment and "more equal" have marginally significant effects net of the effects of "gone too far," but individualism has no explanatory effect in these analyses. Of course, it is not surprising that those who feel that the government has already gone too far in promoting equality would also feel that it is not the government's business to ensure fair treatment in jobs for blacks, especially net of their feelings of racial resentment and their (in)egalitarianism. Individualism plays almost no role in these analyses. Instead, fundamental views about racial politics appear to drive the view of the government's responsibility toward blacks. Although only the two most conservative groups believed that the government should stay out of the issue of trying to ensure fair treatment, there was also not much sentiment in the direction of the government seeing to it that blacks are fairly treated.

A 2007 report from the Pew Research Center for the People and the Press found that, despite the fact that 70 percent of Americans said that they supported affirmative action, 45 percent felt that we had "gone too far in pushing equal rights," while 62 percent opposed the use of racial preferences to improve the position of blacks (Kohut 2007, 39–40).A working-class respondent from New Jersey (D024 NJ M MC) who worked as an assistant stock broker and who otherwise said that he believed that the government should help people who need it and that everyone should have a home and food to eat, nevertheless also said, when asked about changes that have occurred for African Americans over the last several years: "I think there's reverse discrimination that goes on. . . . Well, if you're a black female, you're going to get into a college before my son's going to get into a college. . . . I'd say it's a typical situation."

Structural Versus Individual Explanations for Inequality

Finally, I examine the differences among these groups and the interrelationship between racial, political, and traditional values in several other ways. Given the very strong individualist frame by which the respondents qualitatively discussed their views of inequality, I examined who among them was more likely to explain inequality in structuralist terms (for example, in terms of exploitation, poverty, poor schools, and so on). For this analysis, all of the respondents were asked to choose answers about why people are rich, why people are poor, and why there is racial inequality, using the category choices provided in Kluegel and Smith (1986). Each interviewee was to choose only the two explanations that were most persuasive to him or her. I created a variable based on the items that Kluegel and Smith defined as structuralist (as opposed to in-

Table 4.6 Regression of Structuralist and Individualist Explanations for Inequality, on Demographic Factors and Sociopolitical Group

	Structuralist Reasons		Individualist Reasons	
Independent Variables	(1) Basic Model	(2) Basic Model Plus Political Attitudes	(1) Basic Model	(2) Basic Model Plus Political Attitudes
Constant	2.399***	2.033***	3.634***	4.010***
Education	–0.052	–0.108	–0.042	0.149
Income	0.032	0.062	0.001	–0.040
Gender (male)	–0.086	–0.007	–0.053	–0.128
Working-class racists	–1.049**	–0.393	0.411	–0.180
Middle-class conservatives	–1.041*	–0.395	0.780+	0.220
Religious conservatives	–1.009***	–0.615+	0.454	–0.073
Apolitical majority	–0.725**	–0.263	0.508+	0.121
Religious nonconservatives	–0.223	0.097	–0.055	–0.315
Working-class liberals	–0.272	–0.205	–0.186	–0.280
Racial resentment		–0.271*		0.149
More equal		0.269**		–0.167+
Gone too far		–0.060		0.059
Individualism		–0.148		0.241*
R-squared	0.049	0.158	0.006	0.077

Source: Author's compilation.
+$p < 0.10$; *$p < 0.05$; **$p < 0.01$; ***$p < 0.001$

dividualist) explanations for wealth or poverty and those that are characteristic of discrimination (as opposed to motivational) explanations for racial inequality. The items are listed in the appendix to this chapter. As can be seen in table 4.6, working-class "racists," middle-class conservatives, religious conservatives, and the apolitical majority were far less likely than rich white liberals to offer structuralist explanations for inequality. Further, when we add the measures of political and racial values, we find that the differences in the use of structural explanations among the groups are almost fully mediated by racial resentment and by "more equal" (with religious conservatives still less likely than other groups to use structuralist explanations, even after controlling for their political values). As Kluegel and Smith found as well, structuralist explanations for wealth, poverty, and racial inequality are not prevalent in Americans' views.

I also constructed a measure for individualist explanations for inequality (for example, lack of motivation, lack of effort) using the same procedure (items are listed in the appendix). The regression for individualist explanations for inequality, however, is not the mirror image of that for structuralist explanations. Instead, we find very little differentiation among the groups with regard to individualist explanations for why people are rich or poor or why there is racial inequality. Hardly any variance in the individualist responses is explained, and the groups did not differ much in their use of individualist explanations (with middle-class conservatives and the apolitical majority being marginally more likely to use individualist explanations than rich white liberals). Not surprisingly, when we add the measures of political attitudes, we find that those who were more individualist in their values were also more likely to give individualist explanations for inequality.[2] These results suggest that individualism is more of a universal component of U.S. culture. As Kluegel and Smith (1986) argue, it is the "dominant ideology." In contrast to the individualism that forms the dominant ideology in beliefs about stratification and racial inequality, structural explanations are salient only for a small minority of the sample—those with more liberal politics. In other words, respondents with liberal values, like those with moderate and conservative values, are similarly influenced by individualism in their views of inequality, but only those with liberal views also think in terms of structuralist explanations for inequality. The sample in this analysis includes only whites, but Kluegel and Smith found that, although there are variations, especially on explanations for racial inequality, these patterns are evident among nonwhites as well.

Religious conservatives and working-class "racists" stood out in terms of their conservative views about both policy and race relations, but middle-class conservatives and the apolitical majority frequently expressed similar views. These views are readily found in the open-ended responses to the interview questions, as well as in the survey responses to the questions from the American National Election Studies. The interplay of these values can perhaps best be seen in the detail of the explanations given for why people are rich, why they are poor, and why there is racial inequality in the country (Kluegel and Smith 1986).

Why Are People Rich or Poor and Why Is There Racial Inequality?

Using the choices the respondents selected from the Kluegel and Smith (1986) lists, I compiled a count of the explanations that respondents found most compelling for why people are rich, why they are poor, and why there is racial inequality. Across the sample, the views about why people are rich did not differ much across the groups. As can be seen in table 4.7, most respondents said that people are rich because of their personal qualities: personal drive and risk-taking and initiative. While a fairly large proportion across all of the groups also said that people are rich because of inheritance, many who gave this response minimized its

Table 4.7 **Responses to the Question "What Are the Reasons That You Would Say Are Most Likely to Explain Why People Are Rich?," by Sociopolitical Category**

Reasons for Being Rich	Religious Conservatives N = 46	Working-Class Racists N = 30	Middle-Class Conservatives N = 11	Apolitical Majority N = 92	Religious Nonconservatives N = 11	Working-Class Liberals N = 14	Rich White Liberals N = 42	Total N = 246
Percentage of sample	12%	4.5%	19%	37%	4.5%	6%	17%	100%
Personal drive, risk-taking	70	63	91	67	46	79	83	71
Inheritance	46	60	46	67	46	57	67	52
Initiative	50	43	36	50	46	21	31	44
Talent	15	13	18	29	27	21	19	22
Good luck	20	10	36	16	9	7	19	17
Political pull	7	10	0	9	27	7	10	9
Take advantage of poor	4	3	0	3	0	7	7	4
Dishonest	9	23	9	7	0	0	0	7

Source: Author's compilation.
Note: Responses do not add up to 100 because miscellaneous responses are not included, and each respondent may have given more than one response.

importance by saying that people who are not talented will usually lose the money that they inherit. Thus, the respondents said that if people remain rich, then they are also talented, even if they started out with inherited money. As a female electrical engineer from Ohio (B003 OH F MC; a religious conservative) said: "Money inherited from families might make you rich, but if you're not wise, you're going to lose that money." Inheriting money, although a structuralist explanation, did not elicit much negative sentiment from the interviewees, because they believed that continuing to be rich also relies on initiative, effort, and talent.

Further, there is a kind of romanticism about the rich that was expressed by a number of the interviewees. Some of the comments, for example, created biographies of the rich that are not consistent with the historical record. A male quality control manager from Ohio (B002 OH M MC; also a religious conservative) said, when asked about why people are rich:

> Look at the guy that owns Microsoft. That guy started off with nothing. Now the government wants to take everything away from him because he got too successful. . . . I think if you have great ability or talent, nothing will stop you. I don't think the American economic system takes advantage of the poor. I think it takes advantage of the rich, personally.

The founder of Microsoft, Bill Gates, was, of course, the child of a prominent attorney in Seattle, attended Harvard, but left to start his company. Interviewees with more politically liberal views said similar things about the rich. For example, a computer consultant in New Jersey (D058 NJ F MC; categorized as a rich white liberal) said: "I think that if you really, really work hard and you think of something that nobody thought of and you are willing to bet on yourself in some way, I think that it happens. I think that it happens every single day. . . . I don't believe in bad luck." Thus, the overwhelming majority of the interviewees, both conservative and liberal, said that the primary reason that people are rich is because of personal drive and willingness to take risks. Strikingly absent from the understanding of why people are rich was a more critical view. Hardly any of the respondents said that people are rich because of political pull (the highest proportion was 27 percent of the religious nonconservatives), very few said that being rich is the result of taking advantage of the poor, and very few said that people are rich because they are dishonest. (The working-class "racists" mentioned dishonesty, but hardly anyone else did.) All in all, these interviewees had very favorable views of the rich.

Correspondingly, the interviewees had very unfavorable views of the poor (as evidenced by some of the quotations at the beginning of this chapter). Table 4.8 provides a summary of the interviewee responses

Table 4.8 **Responses to the Question "What Are the Reasons That You Would Say Are Most Likely to Explain Why People Are Poor?," by Sociopolitical Category**

Reasons for Being Poor	Religious Conservatives N = 46	Working-Class Racists N = 30	Middle-Class Conservatives N = 11	Apolitical Majority N = 92	Religious Nonconservatives N = 11	Working-Class Liberals N = 14	Rich White Liberals N = 42	Total N = 246
Percentage of sample	12%	4.5%	19%	37%	4.5%	6%	17%	100%
Poor attitude	63	53	82	58	73	53	62	59
Lack of thrift	41	33	9	28	36	21	14	28
Lack of effort	33	30	46	30	18	21	12	27
Low wages	17	23	27	29	18	36	12	23
Drugs, alcohol	22	7	0	21	9	7	7	15
Lack of ability	9	13	9	16	0	7	14	13
Prejudice	4	3	9	13	9	14	33	13
Poor schools	9	7	9	4	18	21	29	11
Poor health	9	3	0	7	9	0	12	7
Bad luck	0	7	0	7	9	0	10	5
No jobs	7	7	9	0	0	0	2	3
Exploitation	2	7	0	2	9	0	5	3

Source: Author's compilation.
Note: Responses do not add up to 100 because miscellaneous responses are not included, and each respondent may have given more than one response.

about why people are poor. The most prevalent response from both conservatives and liberals was that the poor have attitudes that keep them from getting ahead in life. For example, a New Jersey real estate owner (D056 NJ F WC; whom I categorized as a working-class "racist") said: "That goes back to the welfare problem where generations are on welfare. They don't know anything else. Their fathers did it before them, so that is basically, that is their attitude: they don't have to work." Her comments, however, are not so different from those of a female Ohio high school drama teacher (B023 OH F MC; whom I categorized as a rich white liberal), who said: "You only know what you know. And if you come from a background where you're poor and everything is centered on that and your attitude is, 'We're going to just live off the [government].'... And the government gives her more for each baby she's had.... They're going to go on welfare just like [their parents]."

Liberal interviewees were somewhat more likely to talk about poor schools and prejudice with regard to why people are poor, but there was a fair amount of overlap with conservatives in the way liberals framed their explanations for poverty. Similarly, the more conservative interviewees were somewhat more likely to say that lack of thrift and lack of effort were reasons why people are poor, but the differences between conservatives and liberals on explanations for poverty were not substantial. Both conservative and liberal interviewees said that low wages contribute to poverty, but some also said that if people do not like their jobs, they should simply leave and find another one. Hardly any of the interviewees attributed poverty to exploitation by rich people or to the unavailability of jobs. Thus, there was almost no difference among the interviewees in this study in the reasons they gave for why people are rich, and there were only marginal differences in the reasons they gave for why people are poor.

There was more variation in the responses across the groups with regard to reasons for racial inequality than there was in their responses regarding why people are rich or poor. These results are reported in table 4.9. Both conservatives and liberals said that blacks lack the skills and abilities to compete successfully with whites. Religious conservatives also said that blacks have not prepared themselves enough, but surprisingly, so did the apolitical majority and rich white liberals. Otherwise, the responses regarding racial inequality diverged by political group. The more conservative groups were far more likely to deny that racial inequality exists and to claim that blacks no longer face unfair conditions. Conservative groups were also more likely than the liberal groups to say that blacks need to "act like other Americans" (a phrase taken from the Kluegel and Smith [1986] study), whereas the liberal groups never gave this response. In contrast, the liberal groups were more likely to say that racial inequality exists because of the "same old discrimina-

Table 4.9 Responses to the Question "What Are the Reasons for Racial Inequality?," by Sociopolitical Category

Reasons for Racial Inequality	Religious Conservatives N = 46	Working-Class Racists N = 30	Middle-Class Conservatives N = 11	Apolitical Majority N = 92	Religious Nonconservatives N = 11	Working-Class Liberals N = 14	Rich White Liberals N = 42	Total N = 246
Percentage of sample	12%	4.5%	19%	37%	4.5%	6%	17%	100%
Lack of skills and abilities	26	30	64	39	27	43	38	36
Same old discrimination	20	7	18	34	55	50	43	31
Blacks are not acceptable to whites	9	13	18	21	27	43	38	22
Blacks haven't prepared	28	17	18	21	18	14	21	21
Blacks no longer face unfair conditions	24	33	27	16	9	0	5	17
Blacks need to act like other Americans	26	27	27	13	0	0	0	14
Whites get opportunities	13	3	0	10	18	7	19	11

Source: Author's compilation.
Note: Responses do not add up to 100 because miscellaneous responses are not included, and each respondent may have given more than one response.

tion," and the intensity of this perception among liberal groups made it the most prevalent response for those with liberal views. The liberal groups were also more likely than the conservative ones to say that racial inequality exists because blacks are not acceptable to most whites (which they claimed about other whites, not themselves). Thus, there seemed to be far greater distinction between the responses of conservative and liberal interviewees with regard to racial inequality than there was with regard to the rich or the poor—further strengthening the suggestion that these political differences overlay differences in racial attitudes.

The responses to these questions about inequality, as is true in the life stories of the respondents in general, suggest that the respondents as a whole did not find much of a problem with advantage. They generally believed that advantage is earned, and if not, that it will be short-lived. Their views of the poor were somewhat more divergent: rich white liberals were more likely to believe that low wages and prejudice contribute to making people poor, while conservative groups gave more credence to blaming the poor themselves for lack of effort, lack of thrift, and the use of drugs or alcohol. Most respondents, across groups, cited inappropriate attitudes on the part of the poor as a reason for their poverty.

There was more divergence in the explanations for racial inequality. The conservative groups denied that racial inequality still exists, or they pointed to the failings of blacks themselves and argued that blacks should act like other Americans. In contrast, the liberal groups were more likely to argue that discrimination is a major factor and to say that blacks are simply not accepted by most whites. Both liberals and conservatives were about equally likely to say that blacks lack the skills necessary to compete equally with whites. Overall, many of the white respondents in this study did not consider inequality to be a problem at all, and if they did, they framed it in terms of disadvantage (sometimes self-imposed). In general, the respondents did not think about inequality in terms of advantage, but rather celebrated the rich and defended their rewards because of their purported drive, risk-taking, initiative, hard work, and great ability.

Conclusions

The strong beliefs of most of the interviewees in this study that anyone can get ahead, that people get what they deserve, and that no matter what the obstacles, anyone can always improve his or her own life, are supported by a pervasive belief in individualism (that people who work hard are those who get ahead and that those who do not make it have only themselves to blame) combined with a predominant inegalitarianism in political attitudes. These sentiments are quite consistent with what Kluegel and Smith (1986) and Hochschild (1981) found several decades ago. These researchers noted the strong adherence in the United States to what Kluegel and Smith called the "dominant ideology" and what Hochschild called the "American dream." The interviewees in this study seemed uniformly to hold to these beliefs. Such views seem to be reinforced by interviewees' reactions to the civil rights movement, as reflected, for instance, in the view expressed at the beginning of this chapter by one interviewee that there are some who "try not to make it" (as well as the interviewee's comment that this was probably a "racist" remark). As Teixeira and Rogers (2000) document, the 1960s led to a dramatic decline in confidence in government. Although the political attitudes on a range of issues in the country may be trending toward more liberal views (Greenberg 2004), these do not offset the decline in support for government action and the suspiciousness of many white Americans toward anyone concerned with issues of equality and "fairness" (Greenberg 2008).

One might wonder how the pervasive individualism and inegalitarian views of whites relate to the egalitarianism associated with American culture and the American dream. Hochschild (1981) provides one explanation, namely, that Americans believe in equality before the law, but not in equality within the family or in the economy. Even if this is true, there are still points in U.S. history when egalitarian social movements on behalf of the poor or the disenfranchised have gained wide support (Piven 1977). The 1960s was one such period. Based on the responses of the interviewees in this study, however, it seems that, following the 1960s, a reaction set in that changed the nature of any such commitments to the poor or disadvantaged. There is a political story here that will be addressed in more detail in the next chapter. Suffice it to say that an active political countermovement arose to reframe the politics of the 1960s and endeavored to turn the country back from liberalism. I argue that it is precisely because liberal views seemed to be so widely and positively received as the 1960s moved forward that a countermovement was initiated (Massey 2005; Mendelberg 2001).

Personal Responsibility and Racial Inequality

There are other themes running through the American dream that have as much to do with white views of inequality as they do with white views of blacks or of civil rights: the themes of personal responsibility and the need to persist against adversity. A substantial body of research suggests that parents, spouses, and others play a role in shaping the motivation of loved ones to learn or persist at difficult tasks, trading off encouragement with threats depending on the circumstances. The targets of such efforts themselves engage in self-motivation strategies to manage their own sense of self (Benabou and Tirole 2002). In this regard, it seems that the freedom and openness of American society make it necessary to keep the pressure on, so that those who face less favorable circumstances are not tempted to forgo their responsibilities and take what might look like an easier road—for example, toward crime, substance abuse, or welfare (Benabou and Tirole 2002, 2006). While the American dream expresses the promise of rewards for those who make the effort, themes of personal responsibility and the need for persistence despite adversity seem to be closely aligned in the minds of many Americans.

In the post–civil rights period, the theme of personal responsibility was used politically to reframe an understanding of the government's role in addressing inequality. As a consequence, confidence in government declined sharply (Teixeira and Rogers 2000). The responses of the white adults in this study seem to reflect these political sentiments: they not only were rather negative about the government's role in addressing inequality but also strongly emphasized personal responsibility and effort, even against obstacles. Successful political messages to respondents like these undoubtedly must address the concerns they seem to raise about the need for personal responsibility, persistence, and effort, while also making a case for the role of the government. In addition, attention must be given to issues of advantage as well as issues of disadvantage if these efforts are to have any substantive effect.

Presenting a special challenge for progressive politics is the fact that so many white Americans (and possibly Americans in general) have given so little attention to structural issues regarding inequality—and indeed, structural explanations have little salience even in understanding their own lives. The strong belief that life outcomes are about values and motivation and personal character, divorced from social relationships, the distribution of resources, and the workings of social institutions, is hard to counter given the pervasiveness in American culture and psychology of the belief that people are the masters of their fate and can change history by strongly asserting their will. Kluegel and Smith (1986, 201) expressed the problem well in their analysis of views on stratification:

> Consistent with the prevalent and stable tendencies of white Americans to deny structural causes and to attribute poverty to individual failings, it seems quite clear that most whites do not see black poverty as an important part of the "race problem." To most white Americans the fact that blacks make up a disproportionate share of the poor because of past race discrimination (if this fact is recognized at all) does not constitute a problem in need of a solution, because most white Americans do not believe that poverty itself presents any structural limits to opportunity.

Although racial attitudes clearly underlie current political views on issues like inequality, there is more to understanding the absence of structural explanations for inequality in American culture. Americans apply individualist explanations to their own lives. They fail to see or acknowledge the structural resources that they themselves draw on in their own efforts to "get ahead" or to "make it" in the world. And they find structural explanations for the life situations of others neither compelling nor credible compared to the explanations that make sense to them, namely, that life outcomes are the result of hard work, effort, persistence, and motivation. These issues need to be addressed by those who care about issues of inequality.

Addressing racial inequality in an American context is a complicated endeavor because it involves politics, sociology, and psychology, all intertwined. There is a strong self-serving bias in the views that white Americans (indeed, all Americans) have of themselves when they claim that it was their talent, hard work, and persistence that provided them with favorable life outcomes. At the same time, there are surprisingly few in this study among those with less favorable life outcomes who blame the system or the ill will of others for their circumstances. Instead, they attribute their difficulties to poor luck, poor health, poor choices, and sometimes to poor timing (for example, being young and foolish). Thus, white Americans construct a story of their lives in which they have been the masters of their fate, even though they drew on substantial social resources from family and friends at many points along the way. By highlighting their individual accomplishments and minimizing or forgetting the social dimensions of their good fortune, most white Americans hide from themselves the extent to which their embeddedness in social institutions that favor whites contributes substantially to their ability to strive for and achieve their dreams. Even those who have some understanding of their good fortune tend to attribute their life outcomes to good luck and good upbringing more than to inheritance, social capital, or getting an inside edge from those who provided information, influence, or material support along the way.

The Dominant Ideology and a Counter-Ideology

I argue that it is the very hiddenness of the social resources available to white Americans that allows them to gain confidence, social status, and motivation to keep at it, but there is a paradox in this situation as well. Not only did the interviewees in this study not think much about the social networks that had assisted them throughout their lives, but when confronted with such notions, they also denied explicitly that networks or connections or social resources had had much effect in their lives. Yet, in order to draw on and use social resources, one must be skilled in developing them, identifying them, and knowing how to use them. Hence, these interviewees, like others I am sure, both knew and did not know how their lives were embedded in social networks. It was not part of the story they told about their lives, yet they practiced their skills in developing social ties, taught these skills to their children, and were careful to guard these prerogatives if they ever felt that they were being challenged or threatened. Thus, these interviewees were embedded in social relationships. They invested in extending and fostering these relationships within their communities and in their careers. They drew on these affiliations when they were in need of an inside edge for getting a job or improving their opportunities, and they hoarded opportunities for those who were within their own social networks and for whom they felt some sense of obligation. Indeed, social networking and building social capital are topics now taught in a number of business schools and through professional training, and of course, new technologies are making the building of networks both more explicit and more extensive.[3]

When the interviewees in this study told their life stories, however, these social relationships faded into the background and did not come to mind when they thought about the factors that contributed to their life outcomes; these relationships were not a salient part of the stories they had to tell when they talked about jobs or skills. To see the world otherwise would have taken both effort and experiences that would have called into question the dominant ideology. Interviewees who constructed stories that incorporated access to social resources into the story line had to develop a political framework through which to see the functioning of the social relationships in their lives and among the groups of which they were a part. Kluegel and Smith (1986) made the same point: in order to see the effects of social relationships on life outcomes, they argued, one must develop a "counter-ideology" in which group relationships are linked to the distribution of resources and to the institutions that maintain the advantages of some groups over others. Many of the interviewees in this study who recognized the effects of social structure on inequality had experiences in their lives in which they were able to get out of their own social environment and see across social boundaries.

For example, a young Ohio woman who worked as a supervisor in a predominantly black day care center (E330 OH F MC) talked about how her politics began to change as she encountered different ideas and different people through college and then in the labor force:

> My college education ... actually they pulled me from conservative to moderate ... I was thinking in terms of ... like that's the last time I probably gave serious thoughts to why I believe what I believe. ... My politics are becoming, evolving as a result of my experiences in the inner city. ...

> My mom . . . was a civil rights activist. . . . I have been very strongly influenced by her. . . . My dad was always on the other side saying you can say all those things, but if you ever had to work with, and he'd say black people, well, then you might have a different view. My only objection was well, you're right, that may be true. But I can't tell you yet. Well, now I feel like an adult, and I can say, no, it's not true. I do work with them, so hah!

Based on what we can see from the interviews in this study, however, even this counter-ideology has a twist. Even those interviewees who understood the importance of resource distribution to maintaining and reproducing the social relationships among groups nevertheless sought to remove themselves from the story. They attributed the problems that might exist among groups to the ill will or political sins of other groups, but not to themselves. They attributed the problems of racial inequality to, for example, "those racists," by which they meant the other groups, but rarely did they include themselves in the story line about how racial inequality is reproduced and how whites obtain and maintain advantages that enable them to "get ahead"—that is, into more favorable circumstances than most others with whom they are likely to compete.

In this regard, the rich white liberals, who in general espoused the most liberal politics and who were more likely to use structural explanations for inequality than most of the other interviewees, nevertheless did not differ much from the other interviewees in terms of their own use of social resources, their perception that they got ahead through their own efforts, intelligence, and motivation, and their commitment to the view that hard work is the primary route to life success. Thus, when they talked about problems in society such as the plight of the poor or their concerns about racial inequality, they tended to frame the source of the problem as prejudice or racism. They did not generally see their own advantages as having contributed to the disadvantages of the poor or racial minorities. That is, they recognized their own good fortune (and generally attributed it to their hard work and commitment to making good use of the opportunities with which they were provided). They expressed a concern about those who are less fortunate. They also talked about what government ought to do and what "those racists" need to do, but their analyses were not turned toward themselves or toward those in their neighborhoods. Their concerns, instead, were turned outward, toward working-class whites (for example, toward the types of people I identify here as working-class "racists"), toward older generations of whites who, in their view, have not yet accepted the principles of the civil rights movement, or toward misdirected and ill-informed others whom they perceived as standing in the way of a just society. It should be noted, of course, that the working-class "racists," in turn, perceived people like the rich white liberals as contributing to the country being on the wrong track.

To understand the political dynamics that make it possible for white Americans to both know and not know how advantage works, we need to consider how the ideas expressed by the interviewees in this study fitted into and shaped the politics of civil rights, both leading up to and then subsequent to the civil rights movement. Even that small proportion of the interviewees who developed structural explanations for inequality had an implicit political analysis that framed the problems of inequality in terms of the prejudice and ill will of others rather than in terms of the structural relationships among groups in society and with regard to how these structural relationships affect their access to social, financial, and political resources. In the next chapter, I explicitly discuss the role of race in U.S. politics as a framework for examining the role of each group of interviewees in post–civil rights politics. Given Myrdal's (1944) presumption that the American dilemma would lead white Americans, especially in the North, to support political change, my story about the American non-dilemma would not be complete without examining the role of groups like those among my interviewees in the political dynamics of post–civil rights politics and their views of public policies that affect racial politics. Partisanship, voting patterns, and some political attitudes have all been reconfigured in the post–civil rights United States. I argue in this book that such political changes are the result of the relationships among groups in society and of their perceptions of the effect of the civil rights movement on people like themselves. I endeavor to make that case in the next part of this book.

Appendix

Racial Resentment (factor scores of the following items from Kinder and Sanders 1996)

> Most people who receive money from welfare programs could get along without it if they tried. (0.738)
>
> Because the Irish, Italians, Jews, and many other minorities overcame prejudice and worked their way up, blacks should do the same without any special favors. (0.837)
>
> It is really a matter of some people not trying hard enough, and if blacks would try hard they could be just as well off as whites. (0.850)
>
> Generations of slavery and discrimination have created conditions that make it difficult for blacks to work their way up in life. (0.629, reverse-coded)

More Equal (factor scores of the following items from Sears, Henry, and Kosterman 2000)

Our society should do whatever is necessary to make sure that everyone has an equal opportunity to succeed. (0.700)

One of the big problems in this country is that we don't give everyone an equal chance. (0.812)

If people were treated more equally in this country, we would have many fewer problems. (0.786)

Gone Too Far (factor scores of the following items from Sears, Henry, and Kosterman 2000)

We have gone too far in pushing equal rights in this country. (0.667)

This country would be better off if we worried less about how equal people are. (0.783)

It is not really that big of a problem if some people have more of a chance in life than others. (0.732)

Individualism (factor scores of the following items from Kinder and Sanders 1996)

Most people who do not get ahead have only themselves to blame. (0.656)

If people work hard, they almost always get what they want. (0.851)

Hard work offers little guarantee of success. (reverse-scored) (0.680)

Most people who do not get ahead in life probably work as hard as people who do. (reverse-scored) (0.495)

Any person who is willing to work hard has a good chance of succeeding. (0.775)

Even if people try hard, they often cannot reach their goals. (reverse-scored) (0.565)

Government Help for Blacks (Response to the following item, scored 1 to 7, from American National Election Studies database (available at http://www.electionstudies.org/)

Should the government in Washington see to it that blacks get fair treatment in jobs, or is this not the government's business?

Structuralist Reasons for Inequality (count of structuralist explanations included among the top two reasons given for questions about the reasons for people being rich, for people being poor, or for racial inequality, based on Kluegel and Smith 1986)

Structuralist reasons why people are rich:

- Money inherited from families
- Political influence or "pull"
- The American economic system allows them to take unfair advantage of the poor
- Dishonesty and willingness to take what they can get

Structuralist reasons why people are poor:

- Failure of society to provide good schools for many Americans
- Low wages in some businesses and industries
- Failure of private industry to provide enough jobs
- Being taken advantage of by rich people

Structuralist reasons (discrimination) for racial inequality:

- Job opportunities just go to whites
- Same old discrimination
- Blacks really aren't acceptable to most whites

Individualist Reasons for Inequality (count of individualist explanations included among the top two reasons given for questions about the reasons for people being rich, for people being poor, or for racial inequality, based on Kluegel and Smith 1986)

Individualist reasons why people are rich:

- Personal drive and willingness to take risks
- Hard work and initiative
- Great ability or talent

Individualist reasons why people are poor:

- Lack of thrift and poor money management skills
- Lack of effort by the poor themselves
- Lack of ability or talent
- Their background gives them attitudes that keep them from improving their condition
- Loose morals and drunkenness or drug addiction

Individualist reasons (motivation) for racial inequality:

- Blacks haven't prepared themselves enough
- Lack of skill and abilities

- Blacks no longer face unfair employment conditions; in fact, they are favored
- Black people push too hard for civil rights
- Blacks need to act like other Americans

Chapter 5

The Transformation of Post–Civil Rights Politics: Race, Religion, Class, and Culture

> [My father got transferred to New Orleans when I was in middle school.] I went to public school. The school I was in was racially mixed, and I had some very wonderful black friends. I'll never forget being yanked out of school one day. They came and pulled us out of school. [*Who's "they"?*] Administrators. And they said we had to go to another school because of this policy, and I had to be bused, like twenty-five miles to school. . . . I had to catch a bus at six in the morning and didn't get home until after dark. So that was the first government thing that affected my life. I was a fifth-grader. It was pretty horrible. [*How did your parents respond to that?*] They didn't understand why. . . . I think they realized at once that we were exhausted, we couldn't do our work well. My dad left that job. We didn't make our year down there. . . . We moved back to New Jersey.
>
> —A homemaker from New Jersey (C002 NJ F MC)

THE civil rights movement disrupted the institutional patterns by which whites lived their lives. Although busing induced perhaps more resistance than other civil rights policies, any policies that affected white lives were resisted, and not only by those directly affected. Despite the general acceptance of the principles of civil rights that eventually emerged in the country, the efforts of the federal government to implement programs and policies to support both the legislation and the growing court enforcement of civil rights led to the mobilization of political opposition that affected the political commitment, loyalty, identity, and behavior of various segments of the white population.

In this chapter, I try to sort out the arguments set forth, both historically and for the present, to explain the transformation of party politics that resulted from the civil rights movement. I try to provide a context to understand the party competition for various groups of white voters, especially the white working class, evangelical Christians, professionals, and independents. These groups are all represented by the sociopolitical groups in this study. In subsequent chapters, I discuss the views of the interviewee groups with regard to various policy issues. Seeing these responses within the larger context of political change in the country, I believe, makes it easier to address Myrdal's (1944) expectation that whites would undertake political change to eliminate racial inequality because of the moral dilemma they would face.

In this chapter, I examine the role of race in the creation of party coalitions, both before and after the civil rights movement, that led to the current parity between the two major parties nationally.[1] The parties' competition for the white vote has been the center of their efforts to re-create a winning and, they hope, majority coalition. Controversies over the interpretation of these changes have been both animated and challenging. As both Democrats and Republicans have faced difficulties in holding together a winning coalition of voters, they have also faced internal competition between party activists and moderates—in the Republican Party between conservative activists and moderates and in the Democratic Party between liberal activists and moderates. Providing an analysis of the larger political context should help make the content of the interviews more understandable and help explain specifically how the structural circumstances of different groups of interviewees led to their political attitudes and behavior with regard to inequality.

The Racial Underpinnings of Contemporary Politics

Black Voting Rights and Party Realignment

In the competition between political parties, race has not always been the central concern, but it has always been a defining issue in terms of how the parties organize winning coalitions at various levels of government (Frymer 1999). It has long been a strategy in U.S. politics to hide or suppress issues related to race in order to maintain a coalition around economic or social issues. For example, in the early part of the nineteenth century Martin Van Buren succeeded in building a national Democratic Party that could address critical economic issues by avoiding the differences between the North and the South over the issue of slavery. In doing so, Van Buren was instrumental in creating rules for adopting the party's platform that required support from both the North and the South. The Republican Party, in contrast, was organized in 1854 on the issues of "free soil, free labor, free men," but by bringing slavery to the fore, the Republicans initiated what Van Buren and others had feared—namely, the threat that the country would break apart, as it nearly did during the Civil War. As the "Party of Lincoln and Grant," the Republican Party was identified as the party that supported black interests and also as the party of the Civil War and Reconstruction. Paul Frymer (1999, 8) argues that Republicans found themselves with a precarious hold on electoral victory until they cut a deal that ended Reconstruction and effectively abandoned the South—and black interests—to the Democratic Party.

According to Frymer, with Southern blacks moving to participate politically following the Civil War, the Republican Party had to confront the same issue that the Democrats had faced before the war—the threat to their viability posed by their attention to black interests. Through Reconstruction, the Republican Party experienced the possibility of losing more white votes than it gained from blacks whenever it openly formed coalitions with or supported black political interests. Consequently, the Republican Party collaborated with Democrats to end Reconstruction and to look the other way as the Democratic Party in the South instituted Jim Crow laws that ended the ability of blacks to vote. In doing so, the Republican Party was able to win all but four presidential elections from the end of Reconstruction until Franklin D. Roosevelt's election in 1932. Van Buren's solution to "sectional differences" (in other words, the slavery issue) was to create a national Democratic Party that forged collaboration between Democrats in the North and the South. Roosevelt's success with the New Deal and the continued success of the Democratic Party after the 1930s depended on this coalition.

During the period when blacks were disenfranchised and concentrated in the South, neither party needed to attend much to their interests, but the parties could not ignore the effects of blacks in the political process, first because of slavery and subsequently because of Reconstruction, Jim Crow, and the civil rights movement. Although blacks moved into the Democratic Party in the New Deal realignment, Democrats were able to maintain an electoral majority only by focusing on class issues rather than on race. Of course, many blacks could not vote during this period, at least not in the South. The support of Southern Democrats often required excluding blacks, for example, from New Deal programs and keeping racial issues off the political agenda (Katznelson 2005; Quadagno 1994). Thus, through the long period of Democratic electoral dominance in the twentieth century, Democrats too ignored the interests of blacks. Frymer (1999, 44) argues that blacks became "captive" in the Democratic Party, just as they had previously been captive within the Republican Party: "'Electoral capture' refers to any politically relevant group that votes overwhelmingly for one of the major political parties and subsequently finds the primary opposition party making little or no effort to appeal to its interests or attract its votes." Frymer argues, in other words, that for either party, being associated too closely with black issues brings up the prospect of losing more white votes than it can gain in black votes; consequently, each party has a strong incentive to minimize its association with black interests in order to maintain a coalition that represents the "white median voter."

Frymer further argues that blacks are unique in the way that they are captured in the electoral process. It is worth quoting his argument at some length because it provides a backdrop to my discussion of race and politics remaining intertwined in the post–civil rights period:

> I argue that the primary reason for African Americans' electoral capture is the worry of national party leaders that public appeals to black voters will produce national electoral defeats. The perception among party leaders that important blocs of white voters oppose the political goals of African Americans influences party leaders in ways simply not comparable to the perceptions about other potentially captured groups. Disagreements over race do more than limit the ability of white and black Americans—who might otherwise have similar economic or social interests—to join in a coalition. Precisely because racism is so divisive and repelling, African Americans are in the unique position of not being able to join in the give-and-take of normal coalition politics. Party leaders recognize this divisive quality and are reluctant to reach out to black voters, since doing so often results in a larger loss of white voters from their existing electoral coalition. They fear making appeals to black voters, because they fear that the salience of blacks will overwhelm an electoral coalition of white voters united by largely economic concerns. Thus, party leaders have incentives to ignore black voters, and as such are willing to lose the black vote. Given this situation, black leaders cannot represent their voters as a "swing vote," even in close national elections and even if their numbers can influence state or local elections. Party leaders not only believe that appealing to black votes may actually decrease the party's total vote, but that it also will alter entirely the makeup of both parties' coalitions. (Frymer 1999, 10)

There are several points in this argument that need to be highlighted: that the experience of African Americans is unique in U.S. history in their effect on party politics; that party leaders are willing to lose the black vote because they fear that reaching out to blacks will undermine their coalition and lose them more white votes than they would otherwise gain from blacks; and that there is no easy coalition between the interests of the white working class and blacks because of their common economic interests. Specifically, the Democratic Party can support class-based policies like job creation, wage growth, health insurance, and protectionism, but it cannot also support policies that address the access of blacks to jobs, education, housing, and social welfare without invoking a reaction from white voters and a potential loss of white votes. At the same time, external circumstances have contributed to a situation where the Democratic Party cannot avoid addressing exactly the kinds of civil rights policies that have created these tensions, and Democratic Party activists have aggressively pursued an explicit civil rights agenda.

Thus, this political dilemma has been especially problematic for the Democratic Party in the post–civil rights period. Until the civil rights movement, the Democratic Party was able to form a winning coalition by combining Northern and Southern Democrats and focusing more on class than racial issues to avoid the trade-off between white and black votes. These challenges have since worked to the advantage of the Republican Party, which has been able to appeal almost exclusively to white voters.[2] As long as whites constitute such a large percentage of the electorate, and especially with the demographic concentration of white and black voters in different locations, Republicans can win national elections with a strategy that appeals primarily to whites. In contrast, the Democratic Party has to form a biracial coalition to win elections, and this has been difficult. The challenge has been compounded because redistricting has created majority-minority districts in which black representatives have had an incentive to move to the left, complicating the ability of Democrats to attract white votes in such districts. Further, because population movement and economic activity have increased in the South, the region's influence on national politics has strengthened rather than dissipated over the post–civil rights period.

According to Earle Black and Merle Black (2002), the Democratic Party needs about 40 percent of the white vote, combined with about 90 percent of the black vote and 60 percent of the Latino and other nonwhite vote, to win elections, but the more the party appeals to nonwhites, the less likely it is to gain the necessary white votes. Especially in the South, the Democratic Party has failed to gain the necessary level of white votes in most elections since 1964.[3] For most of the post–civil rights period, the Republican Party has appealed to white voters through coded racial messages to win national elections. This strategy has enabled Republicans in most post–civil rights elections to hold the "solid South" (that is, the white South), while gaining enough white support in the Midwest and the Mountain West to win the electoral college vote. Thus, because of the significance of the South in size and politics, Republicans have been able to win national elections, and they have done so by playing up racial divisions, albeit in coded and implicit forms (Mendelberg 2001).

Race and Politics Since World War II

The United States has never been free of racial politics, but some periods have been more consequential than others for bringing racial issues into the political foreground. In the post–World War II period, most scholars begin with the civil rights movement of the late 1950s, but racial politics was gaining in importance even earlier. (Of course, as Edward Carmines and James Stimson [1989] argue, one could trace the argument back to the origins of slavery). For our purposes, the relevant events begin with the global political dynamics brought about by World War II. Myrdal (1944, 1020) pointed to the restructuring of the American economy toward globalization, the influence of anticolonial movements around the world, and the Communist Party's influence in racial politics during the Depression as factors that would push whites in the United States to address racial inequality because, he said, "lynchings and race riots are headlines in Bombay [and Oslo]."

The political mobilization of blacks during World War II (most notably A. Philip Randolph's threatened March on Washington in 1941) and after the war (for example, the militancy of black soldiers returning home), as well as the emerging Cold War in which it was believed that the state of U.S. race relations increased world support for Russia, all contributed to President Harry Truman's decision to support a civil rights package in the Democratic Party platform of 1948 and subsequently to desegregate the military. Truman's support for civil rights, however, led Strom Thurmond, then the governor of South Carolina, to walk out of the Democratic National Convention; subsequently, he formed the States' Rights Party (later known as the "Dixiecrats") and challenged Truman in the presidential election, with the intent of undermining Truman's election bid and throwing the election into the House of Representatives.[4] Although not successful at that juncture, Thurmond's actions would be consequential later on.

Thurmond returned to the Democratic Party in the 1950s, but he made race the hallmark of his early political career. Among other things, he orchestrated the writing of the "Southern Manifesto" following the 1954 *Brown v. Board of Education* decision. Under the guise of protecting states' rights, nineteen Southern senators and seventy-seven Southern congressmen signed the "Manifesto" (with the obvious allusion to communism) to urge resistance to the implementation of the Court decision. These actions were so thoroughly imbued with racial politics that few would doubt the relevance of civil rights as the driving factor. Yet Thurmond's actions during this period were part of a chain of events that continued to reshape U.S. politics and that had a racial subtheme (Edsall and Edsall 1992). Thurmond and a fellow Southern senator, Jesse Helms from North Carolina, would later be active in the efforts to resist and perhaps turn back the civil rights movement, which they would do in part by helping to mobilize the "Religious Right" and turn racial politics into religious politics. They were both instrumental in linking different parts of the conservative movement and forging greater coherence in the efforts of various groups to revive a new conservative politics in the wake of the liberal movements of the 1950s and 1960s.

According to Carmines and Stimson (1989), a building block of this political transformation was the Senate election of 1958, which occurred in the midst of the emerging civil rights movement but before the passage of the 1964 Civil Rights Act. As they document, until this period, it was the Republican Party that was most associated in the minds of the public with liberal positions on race, and the voting records of congressional members support this view. The 1958 Senate election, although not specifically about racial issues, led to victory for a substantial number of liberal Democrats who replaced liberal Republicans, especially in border states. Until the 1958 election, the Democratic Party had a balance between Northern and Southern Democrats, which made it impossible for the party to summon either the will or the capacity to support more liberal civil rights policies. After this period, and especially by the time of the Democratic landslide of 1964, Democrats who voted liberal on civil rights held a substantial majority in the Democratic Party (68 percent by 1965 to 1966, up from 44 percent in 1957 to 1958), while the proportion of civil rights liberals among Republicans declined substantially (31 percent by 1965 to 1966, down from 91 percent in 1957 to 1958) (Carmines and Stimson 1989). The same pattern was evident in House elections, albeit slightly later. As Carmines and Stimson (1989, 69, 72) conclude regarding racial politics: "Republicans were always more liberal than Democrats before the mid-1960s, always more conservative after."

The 1958 election cannot be divorced from the contextual events at the time. President Dwight Eisenhower was apparently reluctant to take an active stand on civil rights, but he too was forced into action by the 1954 Supreme Court decision *Brown v. Board of Education* and the Southern resistance to its implementation. When, in 1957, Orval Faubus, the governor of Arkansas, ordered the Arkansas National Guard to block black students from entering Central High School in Little Rock—an event among many that was witnessed on television by millions of Americans and around the world—Eisenhower had to federalize the Arkansas National Guard and call in members of the 101st Airborne Division of the Army to implement the Supreme Court order to desegregate the schools. Eisenhower also introduced a civil rights act in 1957, but its provisions were gutted by the Southern chairmen of congressional committees. Thurmond filibustered the bill for twenty-four hours and eighteen minutes, which stands as the longest filibuster in Senate history.

President John F. Kennedy also trod lightly on racial issues, after a close election in which he won by little more than 100,000 votes and received less than a majority of the popular vote.[5] But despite Kennedy's hope to avoid a confrontation on race, the strategy of civil rights activists was to create a national crisis that would necessitate action on the part of the federal government (Morris 1993; Payne 1995). Kennedy endeavored, to no avail, to get the Southern governors putting up the most resistance to protect the Freedom Riders who were engaged with civil rights activists in the South. Kennedy, like Eisenhower, also had to call out the National Guard—in his case, in Alabama, to implement the order to desegregate the University of Alabama.

The televised speech that Kennedy gave in June 1963 to explain his decision may have convinced Southern Democrats that the federal government was unavoidably resolved to desegregate Southern schools. In echoes of Myrdal (1944), Kennedy referred to the incompatibility of sending soldiers to West Berlin and Vietnam without regard to race and then denying citizenship rights to blacks in the United States. Kennedy associated the issue of civil rights with morality and even alluded to "the Golden Rule" as a justification for his actions. Both Southerners and Northerners alike would have recognized the scriptural reference:

> The heart of the question is whether all Americans are to be afforded equal rights and equal opportunities, whether we are going to treat our fellow Americans as we want to be treated . . . if, in short, he cannot enjoy the full and free life which all of us want, then who among us would be content to have the color of his skin changed and stand in his place? Who among us would be content with the counsels of patience and delay?[6]

Kennedy alluded to the rights to public services and accommodations, to education, jobs, and housing, and to the right to vote. As Myrdal had done, Kennedy said that the credibility of the United States in world politics would be jeopardized if "we preach freedom around the world . . . [and] that this is a land of the free except for the Negroes." Kennedy's speech was made only a month after Alabama governor George Wallace's "Stand in the Schoolhouse Door" to prevent the integration of the University of Alabama, and just two months before the famous 1963 March on Washington. Kennedy was assassinated only a few months later, but these events set the stage for the critical 1964 election and for Johnson's subsequent legislation on civil rights and voting.

The Johnson-Goldwater election of 1964 was clearly a watershed in the crystallization of the Democratic Party's role on civil rights, but equally important, the election also represented for the Republican Party a significant step away from being the party of civil rights. This was especially true in the South. President Lyndon Johnson was famously reported to have remarked when he signed the Civil Rights Act of 1964 that the Democratic Party would lose the political support of the South for a generation. Indeed, it seems that he was being far too optimistic: the shift in Southern politics has lasted far longer than a generation and has had profound implications for U.S. politics. Given the increasing—and unavoidable—commitment of the Democratic Party to civil rights, Southern whites began to search for a means to maintain their political control. Johnson won the largest popular vote total ever, causing the Republicans to fear that the Democrats could become an electoral majority without needing the support of the South. As Carmines and Stimson (1989, 76) argue, "The 1964 elections began the process, now nearly completed, of purging Lincolnism from the GOP."

Johnson's opponent in the 1964 election, Sen. Barry Goldwater of Arizona, came from the conservative wing of the Republican Party, which had until that point been subordinate to moderates within the party.[7] The increasingly visible Democratic support for civil rights provided the issue on which Goldwater thought it was possible to split the Democratic Party and prevent the long-term domination of Democrats in national politics. Strom Thurmond was one of the first Southern Democrats to move to the Republican Party. As such, he advised Goldwater on the campaign and helped develop what came to be known as the "Southern strategy," which was intended to capture conservative white Southerners for the Republican Party on the issue of race.[8] Goldwater voted against the Civil Rights Act of 1964, although before he ran for president he had voted for the Civil Rights Acts of 1957 and 1960. Ryan Sager (2006, 44) attributes his change of heart to political calculation of where he was most likely to garner votes: "In 1962 he'd famously said that the GOP should 'go hunting where the ducks are'—as in pandering to white, southern, racist voters." Indeed, Sager credits Goldwater's vote against civil rights as the reason he carried the five states of the Deep South that had previously voted for Strom Thurmond in his 1948 Dixiecrat run for president.

Goldwater was resoundingly defeated in the 1964 election, both by more moderate and liberal Republicans, who either sat out the election or voted for Johnson, and of course by Democrats. Although the results were disastrous for Goldwater and for the Republican Party in 1964, his strategy broke "the tie of southern whites to the Democratic Party," which, as Carmines and Stimson (1989, 188) argue, "would later be helpful to Richard Nixon in 1968 and 1972 and decisive for Ronald Reagan in the 1980s." Political developments following Johnson's 1964 win were also instrumental in putting into play the dynamics that would eventually lead to a renewed effort and coordination among conservatives to turn the country back from liberalism. None of this was inevitable, but the efforts of people both in the South and elsewhere to create institutions, a social movement, and political resources to change the politics of the country were mobilized by the end of the 1960s. The three streams of the conservative movement—anticommunism, libertarianism, and anti–civil rights—began to work together in various contexts to create a new conservative movement and, ultimately, to take over the Republican Party.

The White Working Class Versus Civil Rights in the Democratic Party

The 1964 Democratic convention highlighted the conflict over civil rights, especially in the South, when delegates from the Mississippi Freedom Democratic Party challenged the legitimacy of the regular Democratic delegation from Mississippi on the basis that blacks had not had the right to vote and therefore the regular party delegation was illegitimate. The compromise that President Johnson and Vice President Hubert Humphrey proposed as a resolution failed and led to most of the regular Mississippi Democratic delegates leaving the convention and throwing their support behind Barry Goldwater. These events, however, led to new party rules against discrimination by future delegations, which then affected the representation at the 1968 convention in Chicago.

The year leading up to the 1968 convention was volatile. There were race riots across the country that began right after the passage of the Civil Rights Act; opposition to the Vietnam War intensified (leading Johnson to withdraw from the election in March 1968); and both Martin Luther King Jr. and Sen. Robert Kennedy were assassinated in the months prior to the convention. The prospect for violence at the convention was so great that the Democratic Party tried to make arrangements to move the convention out of Chicago to Miami, but Mayor Richard Daley threatened to withdraw his support for Humphrey if the convention was moved.

The convention pitted Mayor Daley's conservative urban political machine (representing white, working-class ethnics) against an array of left-wing political groups demonstrating against the war and in support of a liberal agenda on civil rights. Even though Hubert Humphrey was a strong supporter of civil rights in the party, his support of Johnson's war policies and his willingness to support the Democratic Party regulars in 1968 placed him on the opposite side of the party activists who were pro–civil rights, antiwar, and liberal or left in their policies. The experience of pitting party regulars against party activists encapsulates the challenges within the Democratic Party (and increasingly today within the Republican Party as well). The party regulars, grounded in the white working class and urban political machines, were perceived, with good reason, to support the Vietnam War (and the defense-industry spending and jobs associated with it), and they were perceived by the activists as obstacles to the full implementation of a civil rights agenda.

The conflict was evident in the confrontation between antiwar student protesters, hippies, and countercultural liberal activists and people like George Meany (the former head of the carpenters' union and then president of the AFL-CIO, who actively supported the Vietnam War) and hard-hat construction workers. Especially after the violent suppression of protests by the Chicago police under Richard Daley at the 1968 Democratic convention, the activists within the party portrayed the party regulars as the primary "enemy."[9] Tensions also developed between local political leaders and civil rights activists when the Economic Opportunity Act of 1964 called for "maximum feasible participation" of community members in Johnson's War on Poverty. When local administrations seemed to subvert the intent of the law, funds were administered through the community action agencies, bypassing the control of local—and often Democratic—politicians. The local politicians were inevitably white, while the community activists were often minority, or at least primarily supporting minority interests.

Anger over the success of Humphrey's nomination in 1968 led to a motion to create a Commission on Party Structure and Delegate Selection, which Sen. George McGovern of South Dakota headed (as part of a compromise to appease the antiwar factions). By the time of the 1972 convention, the shift was under way for the party activists to control the nomination process and the representation at the convention by putting more emphasis on primaries and caucuses rather than deals by party regulars. The social movements of the period, through successive rule changes, were able to wrest party control from the party regulars, undermining the influence of unions, urban machines, and the white working class within the party. As a result, party activists who opposed the war and pushed for the implementation of civil rights and greater representation of minorities, women, and other "interest groups" were able to gain significantly more influence in the party. The success of Democratic Party activists created a great deal of concern among party leaders, especially after George McGovern won the nomination in 1972 and then went on to lose by one of the widest margins in history to Richard Nixon. From 1968 until 2008, only Jimmy Carter and Bill Clinton, both Southern governors, were able to overcome these challenges and win the presidency. In both cases, they did so by running against the "old" Democratic Party (grounded in urban machines and the white working class) and presenting themselves as the new generation of Democrats (especially after the Reagan presidency and the completion of the transformation from the Democratic to the Republican South).

The Wallace Campaigns and the Emergence of the New Right

The electoral success of Alabama governor George Wallace in the presidential races of both 1968 and 1972 took many people by surprise and, again, encapsulated the contrast between the liberal and leftist activists in the Democratic Party and the backlash among white conservatives, union members, and leaders of big-city Democratic administrations. Wallace gained a substantial number of votes across the country, but he was not able to win the nomination or the election, nor was he able to capture enough votes to throw the election into the House of Representatives. Thus, although the Wallace campaigns showed the potential for mobilizing the white working class on the basis of racist appeals, his campaigns also showed the limits of racist organizing in the aftermath of the civil rights movement. Nevertheless, by showing that the political landscape of the United States could be changed, the Wallace campaigns were highly significant in the post–civil rights period (Carter 1996). As a consequence, a small group of wealthy conservatives funded an effort that they built from the Wallace campaigns to change the direction of the country.[10]

Richard Viguerie is one of the key figures of what was called the New Right. Viguerie started his career working for Billy James Hargis, a far-right televangelist, staunch anticommunist, and one of the first among fundamentalist ministers to urge political action through his radio and TV ministries.[11] Hargis was a member of the John Birch Society, a prosegregationist, and one of the first televangelists to be denied tax exemption because of the political activity he urged on his listeners.[12] Subsequently, Viguerie worked with Wallace on direct mail and polling, and it was from the base of his massive mailing list that the New Right endeavored to build its movement.

Wallace ran as a Democrat in 1964 when he won 11 percent of the primary vote nationally (with Johnson receiving only 18 percent, as most of the delegates were unpledged before the convention). Significantly, in 1964 Wallace received 30 percent of the Democratic primary vote in Indiana, 42 percent in Maryland, 34 percent in Wisconsin, and even 8 percent in New Jersey. Hence, his appeal was not only in the South. In 1968, when he ran on the American Independent Party ticket, he again received 11 percent of the national vote. Richard Nixon apparently believed that Wallace's campaign would take more votes from Republicans than Democrats, so he reportedly cut a deal with Wallace before the 1972 election in which Wallace agreed not to run again as a third-party candidate. Instead, in 1972 and 1976, Wallace ran again for president in the Democratic primary, with surprising success (Sager 2006, 50).[13] In the 1972 election, even with the assassination attempt in May of that year that paralyzed him, Wallace garnered 24 percent of the vote in the Democratic primary, compared to 26 percent for Humphrey and 25 percent for McGovern. In 1972 Wallace won the primaries in Florida (with 42 percent of the vote and winning every county), Maryland (39 percent), Michigan (51 percent), North Carolina (50 percent), and Tennessee (68 percent). He also gained significant support in states he did not win, including Indiana (41 percent of the vote), West Virginia (33 percent), New Mexico (29 percent), Wisconsin (22 percent), Pennsylvania (21 percent),

Oregon (20 percent), Rhode Island (15 percent), Nebraska (12 percent), and even California (7.5 percent).

In 1976, with Wallace running in the Democratic primary, Viguerie and Howard Phillips, another key member of the New Right, tried to take over the American Independent Party to use it as a base to build the new conservative party they had as a goal. They abandoned the effort to create a third party, however, when Ronald Reagan rejected the idea of running as a third-party candidate (Phillips 1969). The New Right therefore renewed its efforts to take over the Republican Party.[14] In doing so, they organized their campaigns around the Southern strategy followed earlier by Goldwater and Nixon, which used coded racial language and implicit appeals to white voters in the South. Thus, the same struggle was under way in the Republican Party as in the Democratic Party, although among Republicans the conservatives were pushing aside the moderates, whereas in the Democratic Party the liberals were pushing aside the moderates. Party activists from the social movements of the 1960s (both those who created the movements and those who reacted against them) wrested control in both parties from party regulars. The activists won in both parties, with right-wing activists driving out moderates within the Republican Party and left-wing activists gaining control over moderates in the Democratic Party.

The White Working Class in Kansas and Elsewhere

The Republican Party's success in 1968, after what appeared to be a significant Democratic hold on the electorate in 1964, occurred in the context of the Wallace campaigns. The Wallace vote came disproportionately from young, blue-collar, and lower-income white men, including union members. This is why the New Right leaders believed it might be possible to create a new party of conservatives and why they were anxious to take over the American Independent Party in 1976 as a vehicle for doing so, but they soon turned their attention instead to taking over and transforming the Republican Party.

A great deal of attention has since been given to white working-class voters in the discussions of the transformation of post–civil rights politics. The Edsalls' (1992) book is the most explicit in making the argument that race has been at the center of the realignment between the Democratic and Republican Parties. According to their analyses, race pervades all of the policy issues of most concern to the majority of voters in the aftermath of the civil rights movement, especially after taxes became more prominently of concern following the oil crisis and subsequent inflation in the 1970s. The Edsalls note:

> Republican victories have . . . relied on reducing or eliminating Democratic margins among white voters to the degree necessary to convert what was a minority Republican coalition into an election-day majority. . . . The target voter is the white, working and lower-middle-class northern or southern populist, and the fundamental strategy is to break him or her loose from traditional Democratic moorings. (Edsall and Edsall 1992, 22)

The appeal to populism among Republicans is evident in Reagan's folksy style, in the "aw shucks" presentation of self of George W. Bush, and in the rise of political figures like Sarah Palin and the Tea Party movement in the post-2008 period. Specifically, Republicans have endeavored, using common folks rhetoric, to attract blue-collar, white, working-class voters from the Democratic Party by appealing to their anti-elitism and anti-intellectualism, even while the Republican Party has primarily supported the interests of business and the very wealthy. In this context, the Democratic Party has lost support among white working-class voters, and some, like the Edsalls, believe that it has lost this support because of the attention it has given to minority—specifically black—interests. These commentators do not argue that the Democratic Party should not have supported civil rights, but they claim that the party went too far in supporting "interest groups" with a liberal agenda of rights. Some have also expressed dismay that the Democratic Party has not addressed the increasing deterioration of life in the inner city and the presumed dysfunctional behavior of many inner-city residents, but at the same time has ignored the economic and class interests of the white working class.[15] Teixeira and Rogers (2000, 32) further argue that the white working class is "America's forgotten majority" and that no party can win elections without the support of the white working class.

Perhaps the most noted argument along these lines, however, is Thomas Frank's book *What's the Matter with Kansas?* (2004). Frank argues that the white working class in Kansas has been successfully mobilized on the basis of social and cultural issues by conservative Republicans to vote against their own economic interests, because the Democratic Party has adopted a more centrist and probusiness posture that is perceived as elitist and offends white working-class voters. Frank says that racism on the part of the white working class is not the source of their dissatisfaction with the Democratic Party, but rather that the Democratic Party has become too liberal on social issues while not representing the economic interests of the working class.[16] Frank's argument, in this regard, is consistent with that of Green (2000) and others that white evangelical Protestants abandoned the Democratic Party because of cultural and social issues rather than because of race.

Larry Bartels (2006) challenges Frank's claim about the politics of the white working class. Contrary to the claims of Frank and others, Bartels finds that the decline in Democratic support among the white working class has been minimal outside the South. In showing that it is primarily the white working class in the South that left the Democratic Party, Bartels also provides evidence that this political transformation is undoubtedly related to the changes in racial dynamics in the South in the post–civil rights period. The end of Jim Crow, the expanded right to vote for blacks, and the inability of Southern whites to stop enforcement of desegregation in public facilities all contributed to the movement of Southern whites into the Republican Party. In his analyses, Bartels finds that it is moderate- to high-income members of the white working class who have been more likely to abandon the Democrats both in and out of the South, but most of the change has been Southern white Democrats becoming Southern white Republicans. Bartels's claim also challenges Teixeira and Rogers (2000), who argue that these changes are not limited to the South.[17]

The movement of Southern whites into the Republican Party occurred only after the prior generation of Democratic politicians in the South was replaced by a new generation that had to form a biracial coalition to win and only after the New Right took control of the Republican Party away from Northern moderates during the Reagan administrations. As Bartels (2006, 224) concludes:

> While it is true that white voters without college degrees have become more Republican in their presidential voting behavior over the past half-century, that trend is almost entirely confined to the South, where the historical commitment of the Democratic Party to civil rights in the early 1960s precipitated the end of the long, unnatural Democratic monopoly of the Jim Crow era. Not much mystery there.

Bartels argues that there is now more differentiation within the working class by income level (higher-income members of the white working class being less likely to vote Democratic), but more convergence among whites by education level (those with college degrees being more likely to vote Democratic and becoming more like the white working class in their affiliation). According to Bartels, although there has been a somewhat greater influence of social and cultural issues on voting, these changes have affected those with college degrees more than working-class voters. He further finds that economic issues have been more salient influences on the vote choices of working-class whites. Bartels also finds that the images of the parties held by the white working class are not consistent with Frank's claims that the Democratic Party abandoned the interests of the white working class. As Bartels (2006, 212, italics in original) summarizes:

> I found that less affluent voters attached much *less* weight to social issues than to economic issues, that they attached much *less* weight to social issues than more affluent voters did, that the apparent weight of social issues increased substantially over the past 20 years among more affluent voters, but *not* among those in the bottom third of the income distribution, and that the apparent weight of economic issues among less affluent voters *increased* rather than decreasing as Frank's account would suggest.

In further analyses, Bartels (2006, 222) finds that white voters describe their economic views as being closer to the Republican Party (that is, as more conservative than the position taken by the Democratic Party) and their social views as being closer to the Democratic Party (as more liberal than Republicans and, on some issues, even more liberal than the Democratic Party). This pattern is the opposite of what Frank claimed.

The political allegiance of the white working class has been of special importance in the competition for an electoral majority. States with large numbers of white working-class voters therefore have been hotly contested in presidential elections, and this has made most of the Midwest a battleground for electoral politics, especially because other areas of the country have more consistently leaned toward one party or the other. These affiliations have been changing in recent years with population growth in different areas of the country, but the Midwest is still critically important for the Democratic Party to win at the national level.

From Racial to Religious Politics: White Evangelicals and the Republican Party

Among those white Southerners who moved from the Democratic to the Republican Party in the post–civil rights period were white fundamentalist or evangelical Christians, a key target of the New Right organizing efforts.[18] These groups of religious conservatives had not been actively engaged in politics prior to this period, so their political alignment with the Republican Party is part of a much larger political story. Specifically, the New Right targeted white religious conservatives as part of its effort to capture the Republican Party and challenge the emerging liberalism in the country (Jorstad 1981; Lienesch 1982; Weyrich 2003). The New Right was successful in doing so: white Protestant evangelicals are now the core of the Republican Party (Green 2000).

Following Watergate, the Democrats won the White House again in 1976 with the election of Jimmy Carter, who ran as a "new Southern governor" and who was supported by religious conservatives and rural voters. Carter's ability to gain votes in the South contributed some urgency to the New Right's goal of building a new conservative movement. One of the precipitating events that facilitated the efforts of the New Right was the Carter administration's decision to deny tax-exempt status to the "Christian academies" that had arisen in the South to resist school desegregation and to the Christian broadcasting companies that had become increasingly more political in their messages (Jorstad 1971, 1981). Sager (2006, 49) argues that this one event carried "more weight than one might think" and notes that "the incident spurred the Reverend Jerry Falwell and social-conservative political strategist Paul Weyrich to form the Moral Majority in 1979."

When Ronald Reagan was elected in 1980, he appointed William Bradford Reynolds, who helped in Reagan's election as governor of California, as assistant attorney general for civil rights. Reynolds was hostile to civil rights leaders and laws, and he endeavored to reverse the Carter ruling by supporting tax exemption for Southern Christian schools.[19] The Supreme Court ruled against such exemptions, but the efforts of Reynolds and others in the Reagan administration contributed to the alignment of the Religious Right with the Republican Party. As Carter (1996, 57) explains: "Conservative white evangelicals had begun their exodus to the Republican Party in the 1960s and 1970s, but the threat to their tax-exempt status did much to motivate the religious right, and Reagan's support for their cause increased their tilt toward Republican conservatism in the years that followed." This realignment was not an easy process, but it was ultimately a successful one:

> It was only through painstaking organizational efforts and large commitments of financial resources that the Christian Right was able to attract a large number of conservative Protestants into Republican party politics. . . . Conservative religious leaders such as Jerry Falwell, Pat Robertson, and Ed McAteer were strongly encouraged and actively assisted in the formation of evangelical political groups by the leaders and operatives of the highly conservative secular political movement known as the New Right. (Layman 2001, 44)

The New Right received substantial monetary support from conservatives like Joseph Coors, Nelson Bunker Hunt, and Richard Mellon Scaife, among others (Jorstad 1981; Massey 2005). Their explicit agenda has been to turn the tide back from liberalism and energize a new conservative movement. The alliance with prominent conservative ministers was a calculated and strategic move on their part to further their antiliberal agenda and to build the base of the Republican Party. As Michael Lienesch (1982, 409) explains:

> Far from a "grass-roots" uprising, the religious right was organized from the top down. At the apex stood the New Right strategists who set much of the original agenda for their less sophisticated Christian recruits. . . . The

> New Christian Right is far from the model of the irrational mass movement. Despite frequent flurries of public protest, most of the movement's efforts have been private and intensely pragmatic. The Christian conservative lobbyists were originally concerned with protecting the Christian schools from Internal Revenue Service investigations over the issue of racial imbalance. The television evangelists were frightened by persistent rumors concerning government regulation of the Christian broadcasting industry. Many ministers, Falwell among them, were worried about tax regulations involving church properties.

New Right leaders such as Richard Viguerie and Paul Weyrich worked with people like Jerry Falwell to set up the Moral Majority and later the Christian Coalition. The first director of the Moral Majority was Bob Billings, who had organized the National Christian Action Council to oppose the IRS ruling that "Christian schools" could not claim tax exemption as long as they failed to desegregate. Viguerie (1979, 14) explained the appeal in the New Right publication *Conservative Digest:* "[The IRS] wants to tax Christian schools that won't set racial quotas for their student bodies." The link between civil rights and the rise of the Religious Right seems fairly clear in this statement. The New Right, in support of the Christian Right, also endeavored to create an array of other organizations that fostered conservative policies regarding the family, abortion, women's rights, and prayer in schools, all of which have contributed to the success of the Religious Right and heightened its influence on Republican politics (Guth et al. 1996). The primary goal was to create a conservative movement; the vehicle for doing so was to mobilize white religious conservatives and to work through their influence with their congregations.

The creation of the Religious Right by the New Right was also directly tied to the conservatives' goal of taking over the Republican Party. After an initial meeting between Jesse Helms, Jerry Falwell, and others, Edward McAteer, the founder of the Religious Roundtable, organized something called the National Affairs Briefing, which met before the 1980 Republican convention in Dallas, where Ronald Reagan was nominated. The meeting brought together most of the key figures among white conservative Protestants, many of whom went on to work more actively to build the Religious Right movement. Ronald Reagan spoke at the meeting, using a line that mobilized support for him among fundamentalists and evangelicals, "I know you can't endorse me. But . . . I want you to know that I endorse you" (Martin 1996, 216).

For a long time the political dynamics that contributed significantly to the transformation of post–civil rights politics were largely hidden, but as the effects of these dynamics became more evident, and especially when the right held power across branches of government, more attention was given to both the players and the strategies that enabled them to become a significant political influence. There are now a number of political organizations whose goals are to ferret out the people, organizations, political strategies, modes of influence, and connections of the right-wing movement in the United States. Thus, we know more about how these social movements emerged than we did previously. Groups such as People for the American Way, TheocracyWatch.org, and Religious Right Watch post information on their Internet sites about the right-wing people, organizations, sources of funding, and political strategies, perhaps especially those identified with the Religious Right.

The research of groups like these has confirmed that a small group of wealthy individuals and the foundations and advisory groups they control have provided the resources to fund the "culture war" that has persuaded conservative religious leaders to encourage conservative political views and participation on the part of their congregations and listening audiences. Essential to the mobilization of the Religious Right, however, were the efforts of Southern whites to defend the creation of "Christian academies" against the "immorality" supposedly evident in public schools and their efforts to keep government from interfering with religious freedom and decisions about children and families (that is, to keep the government from desegregating their schools). Thus, the railing against contemporary culture and the government's presumed role in encouraging or permitting immorality can be translated as opposition to the federal government trying to enforce desegregation, especially in public schools. Defense of the family and traditional roles for women is always tied, of course, to conservative movements, but in the South such concerns are also linked to the attacks on public schools and, by association, the attacks on desegregation.

Given the role of televangelism and megachurches in the South and the ideology of states' rights in the opposition to any federal enforcement of civil rights legislation, it is not surprising that the Religious Right emerged at least initially as a Southern movement. Through the array of right-wing organizations promoting the culture war, however, the politicization of conservative Christians and their realignment with the Republican Party spread beyond the South. Even so, the South is still the heart of this transformation, as is evident in current patterns of party affiliation and voting.

Race or Economics As the Driver of Change in the South

Carmines and Stimson (1989) provide evidence of the major role played by race during this period in the realignment of the Democratic and Republican Parties through a gradual process of what they call "issue evolution." They argue that the South was transformed because of an evolutionary process based on racial politics rather than as the result of the kind of "critical elections" with which some political scientists have concerned themselves in their definition of political realignment. In contrast to Carmines and Stimson, Alan Abramowitz (1994, 1995; Abramowitz and Saunders 1998) argues that racial attitudes were not good predictors of party identification; instead, concerns about the welfare state and national security had more impact in the transformation of the South. I argue that the role of race in the mobilization of the new Republican Party is undeniable.

Not only were the campaigns of Goldwater and Nixon both shaped by their efforts to gain white votes in the South on the basis of anti–civil rights positions in the guise of states' rights, but the efforts of the Republican Party to follow on the coattails of George Wallace to capture disaffected working-class whites also had racial content, even if coded or masked. The shift of Southern Democrats into the Republican Party began when the Democratic Party took a more active role in support of civil rights. The shift began gradually (it "evolved"), but it accelerated after Reagan's election. It is useful to remember that Ronald Reagan's national debut occurred in the speech he made on behalf of Goldwater in the 1964 campaign. Then, after undertaking many anti–civil rights efforts when he served as governor of California, Reagan subsequently launched his 1980 presidential campaign with a speech near Philadelphia, Mississippi, the site where three civil rights workers were murdered in 1964.[20] Carter (1996, 55–56) describes Reagan's record on racial issues as "abysmal" and adds that Reagan "never met a civil rights bill he liked."

Resistance to school desegregation, opposition to civil rights legislation, and localization of the realignment from the Democratic Party to the Republican Party in the South surely suggest that the main political changes following the civil rights movement had a great deal to do with race. Yet several factors have contributed to the claims that racial politics are not at the heart of the political realignment since the post–civil rights period: the party realignment occurred gradually, rather than precipitously in response to the 1964 election; the movement of Southern Democrats into the Republican Party did not become widespread until after Reagan's elections; and there is ambiguity in the link between racial attitudes and party identification, voting behavior, and other policy preferences. Further, the greater attention given in later years to cultural and moral issues, combined with antigovernment rhetoric, has further complicated our understanding of the role played by race in these political changes. Each of these issues, however, has been addressed in research on the role of race in the political realignment from the Democratic to the Republican Party in the South.

David Lublin (2004, 214), for example, argues that economics played a larger role than racial attitudes in the movement of Southern white Democrats into the Republican Party, because Southern whites did not differ much in their racial attitudes. Thus, despite strong opposition to the implementation of civil rights legislation among most Southern whites, there was only gradual movement of whites into the Republican Party and party identification had an ambiguous relationship to racial politics. Prying Southern Democrats away from the Democratic Party was not an easy task, because membership in the Democratic Party was not just a reflection of popular sentiment but, importantly, was embedded in local and state political institutions that controlled political resources and maintained what was effectively one-party rule in the South. Lublin makes several arguments about how the process unfolded. First, he argues that the Democratic Party's support for civil rights at the national level led Southern blacks to move into the Democratic Party, but initially did not cause Southern whites to leave because, on issues of race, the Democratic politicians in the South in office at the time of the civil rights movement did not differ significantly from Republican politicians at the time.

Second, Lublin argues that even with the passage of the Voting Rights Act, which enfranchised blacks in the South, it was not until the older generation of Democratic politicians began to be replaced by a younger and more racially liberal generation that Southern whites felt the need to change parties. Specifically, Lublin argues that as the Democratic Party increasingly faced the need to form biracial coalitions in order to win in the South, whites fled to the Republican Party. Third, he argues that because of the similarity in the racial views of white Southerners across parties, differences between the parties on economic issues (and to a lesser extent on cultural or social issues) became more salient in the post–civil rights period, leading to more consistency between policies and party identification at this time. In summary, Lublin claims,

> When candidates from the two major parties do not disagree about an issue, their positions cannot spur partisan change. . . . The rise of race as a national question destroyed the old southern political system, but it did not assure that racial issues would assume center stage in the new one. . . . Affluent southerners and believers in economic conservatism were the first to rally to the Republicans as a result. Economic issues promoted most Republican growth in the wake of the Civil Rights Movement. (Lublin 2004, 214)

Even so, the role of racial attitudes in the movement of Southern whites from the Democratic to the Republican Party is complicated. Lublin (2004) uses patterns of party identification and voting by district as well as data from the American National Election Studies to compare policy views of Southern Democrats and Southern Republicans in order to make the case that economic issues were more important than racial ones in the emergence of the Republican South. Nicholas Valentino and David Sears (2005) also use ANES data, but they compare Southern whites with non-Southern whites on the relationships of symbolic racism, ideological conservatism, and various policy preferences over time to party identification and voting. In contrast to Lublin, they argue that Southern whites are stronger adherents of symbolic racism than whites in the rest of the country; that the racial views of Southern whites became more closely linked to party identification over time, whereas this did not happen outside the South; and that symbolic racism is a better explanation for the changes in party identification and voting among Southern whites than cultural or social explanations and a better explanation than general conservatism (Valentino and Sears 2005).

The issue regarding the realignment of the parties is tied up with the argument within the research literature about whether the opposition to welfare state policies—and, specifically, opposition to policies that benefit blacks—is defined by race or by traditional values. It is also an element of the controversy regarding the principle-policy gap (Sears, Sidanius, and Bobo 2000; Sniderman and Carmines 1996, 1997). Showing that Southern whites exhibit more symbolic racism than whites elsewhere in the country, however, may not settle the issue about the relative role of race compared to "culture" or economic views in the political realignment of the post–civil rights period because measures of symbolic racism have sometimes been confounded with policy views.[21] It is clear that the loyalty of Southern whites to the Democratic Party was premised on the assumption that the Democratic Party would need the cooperation of the South to support its policy agenda and that in exchange the Democratic Party would not interfere with the "Southern way of life" (that is, the racial stratification of the South). As the Democratic Party of necessity became more explicitly supportive of the civil rights movement, including support for the desegregation of schools and public accommodations, white Southerners began to abandon the Democratic Party, albeit gradually and in the guise of moral issues.

The Role of the South in the Republican Realignment

An understanding of political change in the South leads to understanding of political change in the rest of the country. The South is the largest region of the country, making up 30 percent of the population and 56 percent of the electoral votes needed to win the presidency. Further, in the post–civil rights period, the South has continued to have disproportionate influence on national politics, just as it had disproportionate influence before the civil rights movement. If Republicans are able to maintain their dominance in the South, they need only 31 percent of the electoral votes outside the South to win the presidency (Black and Black 2007). Further, the Southern advantage has been growing with population movement away from the former Rust Belt and the North to sunnier areas of the country. Successive reapportionment, directed by Republican-controlled statehouses, has also favored Republican candidates, extending their representation in the House beyond what it otherwise would be.

As long as white Southerners aligned themselves with the Democratic Party, the Democrats represented a substantial majority of likely voters, while the Republicans were a minority party that could win in the post-Depression era only under unusual circumstances, such as when they nominated a former war hero and political moderate, Dwight Eisenhower (Black and Black 2002, 382). But once white Southerners abandoned the Democrats and moved into the Republican Party, relative parity was created between the two parties, giving Republicans an opportunity to be competitive in national as well as state and local elections. Outside the South, the changes in party identification have been relatively minor. Bartels (2008a) found that among whites with college degrees, the presidential vote for Democrats has actually increased overall, while among whites without college degrees the Democratic vote has decreased by 6 percent—almost all of the decrease being in the South.

Black and Black (2002, 4) argue that the party realignment reflects racial politics. As they say, "The central political cleavage, as ancient as the South itself, involves race." They further conclude: "Any realistic understanding of southern campaigning must address its racial structure. Although explicit racial appeals have diminished, race profoundly shapes the ways in which politicians assemble winning coalitions" (382). In fact, Black and Black are quite explicit about this point: "Race clearly trumped economic class in separating core Republicans from core Democrats. At the grassroots, religious right whites anchored the Republican party, just as black southerners did the Democratic party" (373). This conclusion is reinforced by the analyses of Valentino and Sears (2005), who also find that attitudes of symbolic racism are associated with a change in both party identification and voting over time for Southern whites, but not for whites elsewhere in the country.

It is important to understand in this analysis, however, that the claim that race has been the primary driver of the political realignment in which white Southerners have played a major role does not mean that explicitly racial attitudes or explicitly racist campaigns have been evident in Southern politics. The post–civil rights political campaigns have all used coded language to avoid explicitly talking about race (Gilens

1995; Mendelberg 2001). Even the Wallace campaigns were framed in terms of states' rights, as was Reagan's Philadelphia, Mississippi, campaign speech.

Thus, in this sense, Lublin (2004) is correct. After the initial vociferous and violent resistance to the civil rights movement failed both to stop the growing public sentiment in favor of civil rights—even in the South—and to stop the persistent efforts by the federal government and the courts to enforce desegregation in the South, political resistance took alternative forms. Most important in this regard was the withdrawal of many Southern whites from the public school system and the creation of the private system of "Christian academies" across the South that grew in size, importance, and competition with the remaining public schools. Those who mobilized around this issue defended it on the basis of freedom of religion and freedom from government interference in religion, but the issue was clearly desegregation. Such schools were created as a means to oppose the desegregation intended by the movement for black civil rights.

Although a great deal has been written about the religious motivations of the New Right (and some of these activists later claimed to have been converted to evangelical Christianity), the New Right leaders who encouraged and trained the Religious Right to get involved in politics were closely associated with well-known right-wing politicians such as Strom Thurmond, Jesse Helms, and Ronald Reagan, and their initial actions toward remaking the political landscape were about creating a conservative movement, not about supporting religious goals as such. Racial politics in the guise of religious politics was a vehicle as much as a motivator of the new conservative movement, but racial politics could be a vehicle for this movement because of the response of Southern whites to the efforts to implement civil rights policies.

Further, the political goals of the New Right were not, of course, limited to the South. Starting there was simply an expedient way to mobilize an already disgruntled constituency and a means to gain access to the political and organizational resources available through Christian broadcasting and fundamentalist and evangelical churches. In other words, racial issues put the parties in play, but the motivations for the New Right's attempt to capture the Republican Party were political more than racial. They were trying to counter the success of the liberal Democrats and moderate Republicans in controlling the White House, but they did so through a Southern strategy that was possible because of the resistance to the civil rights movement. These efforts were helped along by the group of supporters around Ronald Reagan, which included, among others, Joseph Coors, who was a member of Reagan's "kitchen cabinet" and among the first to provide financial support for the organizations developed by the New Right, the Religious Right, and the newly emergent conservative movement overall (Jorstad 1981; Massey 2005; Weyrich 2003).

The Democratic Leadership Council Versus the "Democratic Wing of the Democratic Party": The New Class Versus the Working Class

As the realignment of the South from the Democratic to the Republican Party became more complete, Democratic "regulars" who had lost influence in the Democratic Party, especially those from the South, began to push back on some of the Democratic Party reforms from 1972 that they felt had made it more difficult for Democrats to win the presidency in a general election. These efforts came to fruition in 1985 with the creation of the Democratic Leadership Council (DLC). The DLC was concerned that, with the new Republican South, elections at the presidential level and increasingly across the South would be highly competitive, perhaps even leading to a "permanent" Republican majority. DLC members attempted to outmaneuver the party members who kept nominating liberals in the primaries (George McGovern, Michael Dukakis, and, more recently, John Kerry, although he was himself a member of the DLC) and then losing definitively in the general election. The DLC endeavored to transcend the distinctions between the old party regulars and the party activists of the 1960s by creating a "third way."

The DLC was organized by two staff members of Rep. Gillis Long from Louisiana. The organization included elected officials in the House and the Senate, governors, staff members from various political offices, and other prominent politicians.[22] According to the "New Democrat Credo," the goals of the organization were as follows:

> In keeping with our party's grand tradition, we reaffirm Jefferson's belief in individual liberty and capacity for self-government. We endorse Jackson's credo of equal opportunity for all, special privileges to none. We embrace Roosevelt's thirst for innovation and Kennedy's summons to civic duty. And we intend to carry on Clinton's insistence upon new means to achieve progressive ideals. . . . We believe that economic growth generated in the private sector is the prerequisite for opportunity, and that government's role is to promote growth and to equip Americans with the tools they need to prosper in the New Economy. (Democratic Leadership Council 2001)

Especially in an information age and with the advent of globalization, the DLC felt that the success of the Democratic Party required a transformation in politics, especially with the parity between the parties created by the movement of white Southern Democrats into the Republican Party.[23]

The leadership of the DLC also helped created the Progressive Policy Institute (PPI) in 1989 as an educational and research organization to help create a policy agenda to counter the work of right-wing organizations such as the American Enterprise Institute (AEI) and the Heritage Foundation, which had created the "Mandate for Leadership" that served as a road map for Ronald Reagan's first term.[24] The Progressive Policy Institute helped articulate the goal of creating a new type of politics in terms of a "third way" that stepped away from the left-right distinction, especially with regard to the role of government in the economy.

The "third way" was an effort by the "New Democrats" to bridge the race-versus-class divide that had separated party regulars from party activists. Among other things, the third way—fostered by the policy positions of the DLC—rejected the automatic alliance between organized labor and the Democratic Party, as well as the automatic defense of social welfare policies that were associated with the legacy of the 1960s. Further, in support of globalization and twenty-first-century economic expansion, the "New Democrats" sought and accepted support from large corporations, especially those in the new economy, including support from the investors and inventors associated with such enterprises. Hence, the two most controversial policies supported by the Clinton administration were the North American Free Trade Agreement (NAFTA) of 1994 and welfare reform, enacted in 1996. Organized labor opposed NAFTA and the social service industry opposed welfare reform, but President Clinton supported—indeed, fought for—both of these policies, even though the policies were expected to have adverse effects on blue-collar workers, on the one hand, and on the other, minorities and the poor, both key parts of the Democratic coalition. It is in this regard that the Clinton administration was seen as centrist or as moving to the right and thus raising the skepticism of party activists on the left toward the DLC approach to politics.[25]

The fact that Bill Clinton was elected president twice was not necessarily seen by party activists as a confirmation of the DLC approach; critics from the left argued that although Clinton won the presidency, he did so with Ross Perot running on a third-party ticket, and even so, under his administration, Democrats lost the Congress.[26] Further, because Al Gore was also closely associated with the DLC (he was Southern, moderate, and oriented toward technology and the new economy as well as the environment), his ultimate loss of the election in 2000 led to the renewed debate during the 2004 election about whether Democrats should "move to the center" in an attempt to appeal to independents and moderate Republicans or whether they should recapture the New Deal coalition by speaking from the "Democratic wing of the Democratic Party"—that is, renewing their historical emphasis on class, blue-collar workers, organized labor, and social welfare policies.[27]

The controversies within the Democratic Party, especially evident in the 2004 election, highlighted the difficulties that the party has had holding together a coalition that includes minorities (and especially blacks), the white working class, and an increasing number of professionals. As the Republican Party has moved right, professionals—or "New Class" members—have turned to the Democratic Party. The third way proposed by the DLC was intended as a way to avoid a direct confrontation between the interests of blacks and other minorities and the white working class, but in transcending the "left-right debate," this strategy also ran the risk of losing both constituencies, rather than just one of them. Hence, members of the DLC endeavored to hold together the Democratic coalition, not so much by re-creating the New Deal coalition, but by bringing together a set of constituencies that would change the nature of the debate rather than fight the battles of the 1960s. The difficulty with this strategy, of course, was that the party activists who gained control from the party regulars during the controversies of the 1960s and through the 1972 reforms did not buy into the efforts of the DLC to return more influence to party leaders in the nomination process, nor did they accept efforts to reduce the control of party activists, especially on the left. The struggle during the 2008 election over the role of the "super-delegates" in the nomination process was about these issues.[28]

To some extent, the DLC strategy has been to put the issue of class-versus-race back in the shadows, hidden away from view, while using the language of the third way, the bridge to the twenty-first century, and the emphasis on rights with responsibilities. Despite the criticisms of this approach by party activists, Bartels's (2008a) analysis of the political attitudes of white working-class voters and their images of the two parties seems to show that the DLC's message comes closer to the values expressed by the white working class—namely, more centrist on economic issues and more liberal on social issues—than to those of party activists. While Bartels found a decline in support for Democrats among higher-income members of the white working class in the South, others have found both a decline of support and a lack of consistency in support for the Democratic Party among members of the white working class overall (Greenberg 2004). This does not mean that the white working class necessarily votes Republican, but instead, it may mean that they do not vote at all, which could still undermine the chances of Democrats to win elections. The DLC therefore has endeavored to reframe the image of the Democratic Party by bringing it closer to the more conservative economic views of the population and closer to the more liberal views of social and cultural issues that the population appears to hold. In this regard, the DLC perspective has come closer to the views of whites in the general population. Yet, subsequent elections have shown the riskiness of this strategy in that efforts to align what otherwise are incompatible interests also have made the Democratic Party vulnerable to the culture war mounted by the Republicans, as well as to the disgruntlement of components of the Democratic coalition, who can choose to vote Republican, to vote for a third party, or not to vote at all. Indeed, the DLC itself has suffered from these tensions. Even original founding members have distanced themselves from the DLC, which no longer plays the central role in the efforts to moderate the influences within the Democratic Party that it did originally.[29] Specifically, the tensions between race and class—between civil rights and labor rights—continue to create major issues for the Democratic Party.

Political Attitudes Versus Political Behavior

Understanding the political views of the American public, however, has not been easy, despite the constant polling and availability of twenty-four-hour news media focused on electoral politics. The long-standing controversy among political scientists about whether the political views of the population determine their voting behavior—and indeed, whether the population has consistent political views in any form—continues to cause confusion among political commentators. Philip Converse (1964) long ago argued that American voters are not very well informed about either candidates or policies, but instead tend to vote based on the influences of family and friends and by party identification. More recently, John Zaller (1992) has updated Converse's notions about the average voter. He finds that there is wide variation in the policy knowledge held by voters, that only those who are more knowledgeable use political information to evaluate policies, that most people construct their political views when the issues are raised, and that those who construct policy preferences use recent and readily available information in the process. Michael Alvarez and John Brehm (2002) argue further that voters' political preferences depend on the interaction between their knowledgeability and their values: (1) for some kinds of issues, such as abortion, voters are highly ambivalent, because they are not able to reconcile the discrepancies between the policies and their values; (2) for other policies, such as those dealing with race, voters are highly uncertain, often not being sure what they believe or how their values should be applied in specific situations; and (3) on issues such as views of government, voters are more likely to have equivocal views in which they both support and oppose different aspects of policies, again, depending on their level of knowledgeability. It seems clear that many political analysts, especially in the popular media, have a very simplistic view of what voters know and pay attention to, as well as the extent to which they hold consistent values that translate explicitly into political support for a given party or candidate. Even in these sophisticated analyses, the measure of voter knowledge is quite limited (with two or three answers to questions such as the number of Supreme Court justices constituting the measure of political knowledge).

It appears instead that very few people pay much attention to politics, that most people know little about the candidates, and that even fewer know any details about specific policy positions (to which candidates contribute by always giving ambiguous and carefully worded responses so that it is difficult for listeners to determine exactly where they stand on controversial issues). Fewer people still have clear and consistent views that translate easily into support for candidates who presumably hold similar views. Further, research by Christopher Achen and Larry Bartels (2004) finds that voters also do not reliably vote retrospectively, meaning that they do not base their votes on the outcomes provided by a given administration. Instead, voters rely on recent experience, making it possible for administrations to pander to voters near election time but to otherwise escape accountability for their actions while in office. Neither political party is especially responsive to voter preferences at any rate, so closer attention to the political positions of party candidates may not translate into enacted policy once elected (Bartels 2008a).

The recent confusion about the polarization of the electorate and the supposedly unprecedented levels of controversy within the Congress seems to stem from a misunderstanding both of the meaning of political values and of how those values do or do not translate into political behavior. Although the trends in political attitudes have been toward more liberal views on most policy issues, this does not mean that support for Democratic candidates is guaranteed or automatic. The views of most voters are not necessarily clear or consistent, and importantly, they are not easily translated into associations with specific candidates or a party identification. Further, given the inattention of most voters to the specifics of elections and candidate positions, their votes are also likely to be heavily influenced by the framing provided to them in the media (including recent efforts to influence political outcomes through the use of the Internet; Gilens 1999; Kinder and Sanders 1996; Mendelberg 2001) and by contemporary events that invoke the salience of some values and preferences more than others (for example, war, terrorism, changes in the economy, or environmental threats).

The impact of voter preferences and values also depends on where voters are located, because the structure of the electoral college makes the popular vote less important than the vote within each state. Since support for one party over the other is so lopsided in most states at this point, overall voter preferences, especially when only weakly tied to political behavior at the voting booth, do not provide any guarantees about the outcome of elections. Of course, these issues are also superseded by the concerns about who gets to vote, who counts the votes, and whether voter access and vote counting are somehow compromised. Efforts by Republican governors in a number of key states to make it harder for those parts of the population who are likely to vote Democratic to register and then vote are just the latest steps to try to manipulate the vote to make it more difficult for an electoral majority to emerge.[30] The bottom line is that liberal-trending political values do not mean that voters will support Democrats. There are many connections between political values and political behavior that are unpredictable and easily influenced by media and events, and these connections have an impact only in the context of specific political structures. Finally, the connection between political values and political behavior is fragile, ambiguous, and often inconsistent in any case.

The "50/50 State"

One of the reasons that the controversy between regulars and activists within the Democratic Party has remained so heated is because after the transformation of the Democratic to the Republican South, both party identification and voting patterns have shown a close division between the two parties in electoral votes in presidential elections. One of the most detailed and careful analyses of these patterns is Black and Black's *Divided America: The Ferocious Power Struggle in American Politics* (2007). Black and Black argue that after the white South moved into the Republican Party, presidential elections became highly competitive across the country. Although each party has a geographical stronghold, the electoral votes each party is likely to win are closely divided. They find that the Republican Party has had a substantial advantage in the South and in the Mountain and Plains States, while the Democratic Party has substantial advantage in the Northeast and the Pacific Coast States. Only in the Midwest do they find evidence of likely party competition: states in this region having been nearly at parity in terms of support for the two parties. Black and Black further argue that such a division between the parties has never happened previously in U.S. history.

Until the 2008 election, it was the Democrats in the post–Civil Rights period who were at a slight electoral college disadvantage, but soon after the 2008 election, some argued that it was the Republican Party that now faced this challenge. Democrats have had to gain the support of a more disparate set of groups by race-ethnicity and class in order to win elections than the Republican Party, which has become more ideologically consistent and white following the take-over that drove most moderate Republicans out of the party. Critics have recently cited the Republican Party's lack of diversity—including some of its own members who now believe that the "whites-only" strategy may no longer work. Some also argued that demographic changes over the last several decades now favor the Democrats, both because of the faster growth of population groups that identify with the Democratic Party and because of the concentration of these groups in states with larger electoral votes (Judis and Teixeira 2002; Judis 2008; Teixeira 2010). The Democratic Party cannot, however, take for granted that it has now pulled together a "permanent" electoral majority, and predictions that it has seem premature.

Although the Democrats won in 2008 with the candidacy of Barack Obama, they did so in the context of the Bush administration's failures: the worst economic crisis since the Great Depression, two wars going badly, and domestic policy failures of the Bush administration such as the problematic response to Hurricane Katrina. Even in this context, Obama won only 43 percent of the white vote and overall only 53 percent of the popular vote. Yet in 2010—the very next election after 2008—the momentum shifted back to the Republicans (as had occurred as well after the Democratic landslide in 1964). Obama was able to win the 2012 election in the context of continued economic difficulties, but only after a very hard-fought campaign. While in 2012 Obama won all but two of the states he had won in 2008, he also gained a smaller proportion of the popular vote and a smaller proportion overall of the white vote than he had received in 2008. Obama won most of the Midwestern states—which the Democrats had lost en masse in 2010—again in 2012. Winning the Midwestern states in 2012 was presumably in reaction to the efforts of Republican governors in several of these states to undermine collective bargaining rights and because of the social movements that were mobilized as a result. In these events, class issues became more significant than racial divisions. Further, the support of the Obama administration for the auto bailout that saved the American auto industry and even higher turnout and support from nonwhite voters delivered the Midwest and the election to Obama in 2012. The fierce competition between parties and a divided electoral vote noted by Black and Black (2007) continues, however. Further, efforts to change the rules for eligibility to register and vote and even for the implementation of the vote, such as cutting early voting days or having a limited number of voting machines available in heavily Democratic districts (which may have backfired for the Republican Party in 2012), constitute a battleground for election outcomes, even where Democrats might expect to have majority support in the population.[31]

Going forward, both parties have to be concerned about whether their attention to the interests of any given subgroup in their coalition might turn off voters who would otherwise have supported them. For the Democratic Party, attention to black interests has always been problematic, but efforts to suppress the support for civil rights are no longer feasible, especially given the notable importance of the Latino vote as well as that of African Americans in 2012. The Democratic Party has to somehow bridge the gap in the interests between race and ethnic minorities and the white working class in future elections where the economic circumstances may vary, while retaining the support of upper-middle-class professionals. Doing so by shifting the frame to New Class issues risks losing support from both minorities and the white working class, but leaning toward one or the other of these constituencies has its own risks for the Democratic Party. The Republican Party faces similar issues with white evangelical Protestants and the Tea Party movement, since support from other voters appears to erode when they give too much attention to the policy preferences of these groups.

Both parties have to be concerned with not only the possibility that some of their constituents will support the other party but also the risk that voters who should be counted for one party or the other will stay home. The outcome of both the 2010 and 2012 elections, for example, seemed to be determined primarily by which constituencies were mobilized. There is also the potential threat of third-party candidates who can influence the outcome of elections. None of these challenges, however, begin to address the honesty of the election process, who controls the election machinery (both symbolically and actually) in critical areas of the country, and, importantly, who is allowed to vote and who counts the votes. In that regard, the elections of governors--whose administrations count the votes—across the states is a critical part of the outcome of presidential elections. An additional threat on the horizon, especially for the Democratic Party, is the recent push to change the rules and split the electoral votes proportionally in those states like California where Democrats otherwise appear to have a secure majority. Going forward, there will be continued competition between Democrats and Republicans for various segments of the white vote--notably, the white working class, professionals, and religious conservatives--but success in attracting white voters will have to be weighed against the likely support from minority voters from various groups and in various locations.

Both parties are insecure in their ability to capture a majority of voters and maintain their electoral coalitions, and both face internal opposition about the best strategies for accomplishing their goals. The Republican Party has to assess the viability of its continued whites-only strategy, which relies on the concentration of support in the South, in rural areas, and in sparsely populated states. If the Republican Party can hold on to and count on the support of the "solid South" (which seems problematic after the elections of 2008 and 2012), it needs less than one-third of the electoral votes outside the South to win the presidency (Black and Black 2007). Although it now appears that Democrats can concentrate on winning presidential elections without the South (Schaller 2006), the Democratic Party cannot win without the Midwest, the support of which has shifted back and forth since the 2008 election. Many independents left the Republican Party and voted for Obama in 2008, but they swung back to the Republicans in 2010. In 2012 Obama received fewer votes from independent voters, but he still won Midwestern states with the support of working class voters. To win going forward, the Republicans need the support of the independents and moderates who were pushed out of leadership in the party, but holding on to support from moderates works against the party's efforts to hold its base of religious conservatives and the new anti-intellectual, working-class populist movement that has been fostered to oppose the Obama administration. Thus, the electorate continues to be divided and seemingly up for grabs depending on the economic conditions in the country at the time of a given election and each party's ability to mobilize political support around issues as they emerge close to an election.

Although the Democratic Party supposedly benefits from current population trends, one challenge to holding the coalition of likely Democratic supporters together is the need to address seemingly incompatible interests, especially between race and ethnic minority voters versus the white working class, and both in the context of the growing importance of upper-middle-class professionals to the Democratic Party coalition. To the extent that the Democratic Party visibly supports policies and programs that are favored by and benefit racial and ethnic minority voters (for example, opening access to jobs, education, and housing where blacks have been excluded or expanding the social safety net), it risks losing the support of white voters, especially the white working class, but to the extent that the party focuses on traditional class issues that are of concern to the white working class (especially policies that protect the job rights of white workers at the expense of minorities), it risks losing (or demobilizing) both the party activists who have promoted civil rights policies and the minority vote. Despite the focus on class issues in the 2012 election, however, the minority vote intensified rather than withdrew. The party's efforts to transcend this dilemma by focusing on New Class issues that might appeal to upper-middle-class professionals has been especially challenging during times of economic crises. The way forward is certainly not clear, and the competition within both parties to frame the debate has been muddled at best.

The Democratic Party cannot win the presidency without the support of working-class whites in large Midwestern states, nor can it win without doing well in states with large Latino populations. Further, it must mobilize strong voter turnout and support from African Americans in large urban areas. The party must meet these goals, however, without losing the support of upper-middle-class professionals and without undermining the support of independents (many of whom are the moderates who were driven out of the Republican Party). Although a declining proportion of the population, whites are still a majority, and the elasticity of whiteness makes predictions about future demographic alignments uncertain. For example, the vast majority of Latinos define themselves as white, so their political affiliations may be less certain as native-born Latinos rise in proportion to immigrants within the Latino population. The political affiliations of Asians are similarly uncertain: on the basis of class, they are more similar to whites than to other minority groups, but their political sentiments have so far aligned more with minority voters.

The Democratic Party must bridge race-ethnicity and class in order to hold together its coalition, and despite the growing diversity of the population, it must compete successfully for enough white votes to win elections both locally and nationally. The Democratic Party has failed to meet that standard many times in the last several decades. Understanding the political attitudes of various segments of the white population, especially with regard to inequality and civil rights, is an essential part of resolving the contradictions and dilemmas for the Democratic Party. Of course, understanding political attitudes in and of themselves is not sufficient for understanding and predicting political behavior, but it is a necessary step for understanding the political landscape in the post–civil rights period. The interviewees in this study were asked about their views of a wide range of political issues, but particularly about inequality and fairness. The distinctive—and contradictory—views expressed by the various sociopolitical groups that emerged from the interviews in this study map to the different political groups among whites that are especially of concern in the commentary about the politics of the future. Equally important, understanding how each of these groups fits into post–civil rights politics is essential to understanding their views of public policy and their views about inequality, especially racial inequality. The political views expressed by the interviewees within this study are shaped by their relationships within a structure of inequality and by how their life circumstances had been affected by the policies offered by each political party. Most important in this regard was the ability of the various groups of interviewees to gain access to jobs whose wages were taken out of competition and which could be protected from the market. I turn to these issues in the next three chapters as I describe in more detail the views of each of the key sociopolitical groups and provide an overview of their views of inequality and fairness, especially with regard to civil rights.

Whites in Post–Civil Rights Politics

In this chapter, I have examined some of the historical influences on the interplay of race and politics that has characterized the ongoing controversies in the post–civil rights period. The current strong support of black voters for the Democratic Party has kept alive some of the same issues that party politics, according to Frymer (1999), had to confront in the nineteenth century, namely, how to attend to the interests of blacks and other minority voters without losing more white votes than are gained from minority voters. While the Democratic Party struggles to bridge the conflicts between race and class, the Republican Party has been able to use racial subtexts to mobilize white voters who had previously identified with the Democratic Party, but the racial nature of support for the Republican Party has been masked, in part, by a shift in the framing of politics from race to religion. In this transformation, however, the Republican Party created its own dilemma by risking the support of key parts of its coalition when the party became too identified with the policy preferences of the Religious Right or the anti-intellectual and populist Tea Party movement.

I have also highlighted the importance of the South to contemporary politics. As the largest region of the country and the heart of the Republican Party in its political identification, the South continues to have substantial influence in national politics. Even though in the 2008 election support for Republicans eroded somewhat in the South and the Mountain West and Democrats captured most of the Midwest, in the 2010 election the Democrats lost in the areas of the South where they had previously gained strength and also lost almost all of the Midwest. In 2012, the Democratic Party again won most of the Midwest. The subsequent ferocity of efforts to undermine the Democratic coalition by finding new ways to recruit the white working class is a reflection of these dynamics. Both the New Right and the Religious Right are products of Southern influences and politicians, although their funding comes from wealthy individuals across the country. The financial support for groups like the Tea Party movement comes from the same wealthy individuals who previously fostered the growth of the Religious Right, but as in that effort, controlling the outcomes of these mobilization efforts is not always straightforward. Even the Democratic Leadership Council—which endeavored to push back some of the electoral reforms within the Democratic Party that had given more influence to party activists so that party leaders could regain influence in the nomination process—emerged out of a concern by Southern politicians that, with the loss of the white Democratic South to the Republican Party, Republicans would become a permanent majority party.

Indeed, the Republican ascendancy in the South has led to a highly competitive political environment in which the two parties are fighting a "ferocious struggle" to gain a "permanent" majority (Black and Black 2007). This situation has contributed in the last few years to an image within the country, and especially within the media, of the population as polarized and to the idea that there is a culture war that defines opposing sides in policy preferences across the country, although the supposed content of the cultural divide has been shifting back and forth from "guns, gays, and God" to deficits and taxes, the size of government, and immigrants, especially in the efforts to attract the white working-class vote outside the South. The ferocious struggle has developed, however, even though political opinion in the country has not been polarized but instead has trended toward more liberal views, especially on social and cultural issues, and even though the population's economic preferences have changed little, despite the major changes that have occurred in the country and the world (Kohut 2009). The downturn in the economy in late 2008 and the constant crises that subsequently derailed hopes for a quick recovery added to the competitiveness between the parties, and as the close competition between the two major parties has continued unabated, the stakes of each election have remained high.

The illusion of a polarized population does not match the underlying reality of political attitudes, but neither does the commentary following the 2008 and 2012 elections that suggested that the country would soon be unified in support of the Democratic Party. The two political parties are still highly competitive in national elections and largely dependent on how national and international events—especially the world economy—affect political support in the Midwest and Southwest. How the parties fare in future elections may also depend on whether the Democratic Party can bridge its ongoing internal conflicts regarding race and class—or whether it can shift attention to the New Class. On this, the future is yet to be written. Although a declining proportion of the projected future population, neither party can win without substantial support from white voters, and the competition for various segments of the white vote affects the lives of the entire population. Further, the trade-offs that each party faces in gaining the support of one group potentially at the expense of another have to be carefully weighed in all political contests. Both building a winning coalition and holding it together when it counts are challenges that continue for both parties.

The traditional assumptions about how class position affects political identification and behavior have become more ambiguous, especially within the white population. The Republican Party has made significant inroads with the white working class, which has historically been affiliated with the Democratic Party, at the same time that the Democratic Party has gained significant support from upper-middle-class professionals, who previously were core constituents of the Republican Party. Even white religious conservatives present something of a puzzle since most were Democrats before they moved so quickly to the Republican Party. The political support of each of these groups depends, in part, on how each party addresses the interests and concerns of racial and ethnic minorities, how visible and forthright that support is, and whether political support translates into public policies that affect the ability of various groups to protect themselves from competition within the labor market so they can provide a "decent" lifestyle for themselves and their family and friends in these uncertain times. In the next several chapters, I discuss the views expressed by the interviewees in this study on economic inequality, the role of government in general, and specific public policies such as taxes, welfare, affirmative action, and immigration. In my analysis, I show specifically how racial attitudes interface with politics and how both are shaped by the efforts to obtain good jobs that are protected from market competition.

Chapter 6

The White Electorate: The White Working Class, Religious Conservatives, Professionals, and the Disengaged

[If a group of people have less economically than others, is it fair for them to expect the government to help them?]

Graphic designer from Tennessee (G520 TN M WC): "No, it is not the government's job. The government is not there to be our babysitters. The government is there to run the infrastructure of the country and that is it. . . . They end up looking at the government as kind of like the omnipotent parent. . . . It costs all the rest of us money, and it breeds weak people. . . . All it does is encourage them to keep doing it, and they're completely nonproductive members of society."

Health care executive from Tennessee (G521 TN F MC): "As a community . . . we have a right to expect that people should not have to go without food, clothing, and housing, and some level of health care. . . . I don't know that it should be to the government as much as I think, I do believe to some extent I am my brother's keeper. So to that extent I think the government has a responsibility."

THE contrasting political views of these two Tennessee interviewees set the boundaries for the political differences among the interviewees in this study. The graphic designer felt that the government providing help for the poor just makes them weak and encourages irresponsibility, while the health care executive thought of the poor as members of the community with whom those who have the means to do so should share their resources. The economic circumstances of these two people were very different, and that seemed to have affected their political views. One might think that the health care executive who had more income and resources would not want the government to address inequality, perhaps for fear that government policies would undermine her favorable situation. Further, one might think that the graphic designer who was more vulnerable economically would welcome government attention to issues of inequality, with the expectation that he might need such help someday. In this study—and consistent with current political trends—we find just the opposite. I categorized the graphic designer as a working-class "racist," while the health care executive is one of the rich white liberals. Those with marketable skills and access to extensive social networks seem to adopt more liberal politics. Those who have to compete for jobs with less education or skills, and probably with social networks that are less dense or valuable, are more cautious about politics and especially want to hold the line against the government getting involved in decisions about whom employers can hire or reward. I interpret the views expressed by liberals like the health care executive as reflecting the hope that things will be right in the world, albeit often outside the confines of their own neighborhoods. I interpret the attitude of working-class conservatives like the graphic designer as not wanting anything to interfere with their ability to get help from their friends and family members when it comes to getting a job.[1]

Jobs were a constant theme in the political views expressed by the respondents. Jobs are key to the kind of life one is able to live. The interviewees espoused the value of hard work, believed that they themselves had attained their life goals because of their own hard work, and formed judgments about others on the basis of their perception of how hard they worked. Having a job is imperative for a good life, according to the interviewees, and having a good job—defined as one offering benefits (medical insurance, a pension, and other aspects of a safety net) and paying a salary that allows one to live comfortably and have a little extra after the bills are paid—made the difference in the kind of life that they could hope for and in what they could offer to their children and family members. Some of the respondents were concerned about public policy and paid attention to the news media and to what was going on among politicians, while others focused on their own lives and left the powers-that-be alone to do whatever they would. When asked to comment on broad policy areas and to reflect on their preferences and their interpretations of political events, the respondents' comments reaffirmed their belief in the dominant ideology—as defined by Kluegel and Smith (1986)—and their suspicion of anyone who suggested alternative ways of thinking. As discussed in chapter 4, the dominant ideology includes beliefs that "opportunity for economic advancement is widely available, that economic outcomes are determined by individual efforts and talents (or their lack), and that in general economic inequality is fair" (Kluegel and Smith 1986, 100–101).

Importantly, in speaking of economic opportunity and individual effort, these interviewees were referring to whether people are working in paid employment. Thus, preparing for a job, gaining access to a job, and keeping a job were central concerns of the respondents in this study and, indeed, of most Americans. As shown earlier in this book, however, this ideology creates the story line for whites in the United States (and for most Americans) that individual hard work is what makes the difference in whether people get good jobs and have decent lives. The actual experience of their lives, however, is determined by their embeddedness in group-based social networks that provide an inside edge in obtaining jobs that are protected from the market and whose wages are taken out of competition, to the extent that obtaining such a job is possible for anyone in recent decades. Because of the ever-present competition between employers and workers over the structure and compensation afforded by such jobs, almost everyone in this country has come to experience a constant uncertainty about their ability to continue in jobs that allow them to live a decent (or even affluent) lifestyle, and thus most Americans have become perennially vigilant regarding any threats that might undermine their access to jobs that provide these kinds of rewards.

Segments of the White Electorate

In this chapter, I outline the interviewees' views on inequality and the role of government in helping those who have less economically. I also link their political views to their concerns about maintaining access to good jobs. In the subsequent two chapters, I discuss the interviewees' views on various public policy issues, such as taxes, welfare, affirmative action, and immigration. Through these chapters, I hope to provide a profile of white Americans that will help us understand not only the nature of the life situations they face, but also the relative structural position of each sociopolitical group and how structure and culture have come together to shape post–civil rights politics. Because the groups that I identify in this study are consistent with the major groups of whites targeted by the two major political parties, understanding their views of inequality and what constitutes fairness should be of interest. I argue, for example, that in order to understand why some whites feel an obligation to support the agenda for civil rights while others stay disengaged or actively oppose civil rights policies, we need to understand how civil rights policies have affected their access to good jobs and their ability to protect themselves from market competition, both directly and indirectly. This chapter begins to provide that explanation.

Myrdal expected that at least some whites in the North would be so conflicted by the growing acknowledgment of racial inequality that they would become part of the movement for social change. Although some whites did join the civil rights movement, I explain through these chapters and the conclusion why support for civil rights has more often been for principles than for policies that make a difference. In the analysis, I hope to show why most whites are not moved to political action because of a moral dilemma regarding racial inequality. It is important to note, however, that the larger context played a significant role in determining the economic conditions for various groups of whites and therefore perhaps also their political responses. The effects of civil rights policies and the growth of a neoliberal political agenda that adversely affected working-class jobs were not simultaneous. Civil rights policies had their greatest effect on black job prospects from 1964 to 1980, while neoliberalism and the growth of globalization began to affect working-class jobs especially after 1980. There is a link between these two developments, however, as I have argued throughout the book. Implicit racial messages were used to mobilize a new conservative movement, so racial politics played a key role in the development and support of neoliberal policies that have threatened the ability of white workers—especially the working-class "racists"—to gain or hold on to jobs protected from market competition.

In this chapter, I discuss the groups of white voters who have been most targeted by the two political parties—the white working class, religious conservatives, professionals, and independents or the disengaged—but I do so within the categories that emerged in the interviews. As noted in chapter 1, the way I have constructed these groups reflects the intersectionality that their lives represent in terms of class, social position, and ideology. Although I did not create these groups theoretically but rather defined them in terms of what stood out in the interviews as reflecting distinctive views, they turned out to be politically meaningful groups. As can be seen in table 6.1, these groups differ in important ways. Both working-class "racists" and religious conservatives are disproportionately male, while the religious nonconservatives are much more likely to be female. Both middle-class conservatives and working-class liberals are somewhat more likely to be female, while both the apolitical majority and the rich white liberals are evenly divided by gender.

There are also regional differences among the groups, and the respondents' political attitudes reflect, in part, the culture and demographics of the geographical areas where the interviews were done. I conducted only about two-thirds as many interviews in Tennessee as in Ohio and New Jersey because of the limited amount of time I could spend in Tennessee. Most of the rich white liberals were from New Jersey, whereas the largest proportion of both the religious conservatives and the religious nonconservatives were from Tennessee. The Tennessee sample also had fewer working-class interviewees because the area where I conducted the interviews has a concentration of government offices and colleges and universities. Most of the working-class "racists," the middle-class conserva-

Table 6.1 Demographic Characteristics of Socioeconomic Groups Among the Interviewees

Dimension	Working-Class Racists	Middle-Class Conservatives	Religious Conservatives	Apolitical Majority	Religious Nonconservatives	Working-Class Liberals	Rich White Liberals	Total
Percentage of sample	12%	4.5%	19%	37%	4.5%	6%	17%	100%
Gender								
Male	65	46	59	50	27	43	52	52
Region								
New Jersey	36	36	15	46	9	14	62	38
Ohio	48	55	39	37	18	43	24	37
Tennessee	16	9	46	17	73	43	14	25
Income								
Less than $30,000	19	0	7	15	9	7	2	11
$30,001 to $50,000	32	9	15	23	36	36	5	20
$50,001 to $75,000	29	27	28	33	18	43	21	29
$75,001 to $100,000	10	27	15	11	18	7	17	13
$100,001 to $200,000	10	36	26	11	9	7	17	15
More than $200,000	0	0	9	7	9	0	38	11
Politics[a]								
Liberal	19	0	0	18	9	64	60	23
Moderate	36	46	0	60	91	29	36	41
Conservative	45	55	100	22	0	7	5	36
Economic situation[b]								
Bad	57	30	26	20	9	21	2	23
Okay	20	60	22	42	36	36	10	30
Good	23	10	52	38	55	43	88	47

Source: Author's compilation.
Notes: Responses may not add up to 100 because of rounding error.
[a]Self-defined.
[b]Coded responses to question: "How are groups like yours faring in the United States these days?"

tives, and the apolitical majority were from New Jersey or Ohio. The area where I conducted interviews in Ohio is primarily industrial (albeit with many of those jobs disappearing), so a larger proportion of the working-class groups were from Ohio.

There were differences among the groups of interviewees, of course, in both occupation and family income, because I defined the groups, in part, by education and class. There is variability, even so, within the groups. Income varied by geographical region as well, so the income differences should be interpreted within that context. The respondents' self-perceptions of their economic condition were more skewed than the actual income differences. By far, the rich white liberals were the most affluent among the interviewees, while the middle-class conservatives were somewhat less affluent than the rich white liberals. The rich white liberals included doctors, lawyers, business owners, executives in major corporations, government workers, and some with more modest jobs who had either inherited money or married well. Although also college-educated, the middle-class conservatives, on average, were not as well off, and they were employed in a range of occupations, including two managers in major companies, a small-business owner, and a salesman, as well as a nurse, a homemaker, several interviewees working part-time, and one who was unemployed. Although almost all of the rich white liberals thought of their economic situation as good, most of the middle-class conservatives thought that their situation was only okay, or even bad.

Both working-class groups had more modest incomes, but this was especially true for the working-class "racists," who were the least well off financially among the interviewees. For example, the working-class "racists" reported the lowest incomes in general, and even though I conducted the interviews before the major downturn in the economy in 2008, they were already overwhelmingly more likely to describe their economic condition in very negative terms. By their self-reports, the working-class "racists" were in much less favorable economic circumstances than the working-class liberals. The working-class "racists" included people in such jobs as carpenter, police officer, gas station owner, maintenance worker, welder, waitress, truck driver, and salesman, plus a few people who were retired or unemployed. In contrast, the working-class liberals included such jobs as building contractor, self-employed construction worker, clerical worker, small-business owner, web designer, and computer technician.

Both the religious conservatives and the religious nonconservatives had incomes that spanned the distribution, but both were concentrated in the middle, with the religious conservatives slightly more affluent than the religious nonconservatives. For both groups, a slight majority indicated that their economic situation was good, but at least one-quarter of the religious conservatives indicated that their economic situation was unfavorable. The religious conservatives included teachers, engineers, nurses, some managers, and a few executives, but also factory workers, salesmen, a carpenter, clerical workers, and a few homemakers. The religious nonconservatives included such occupations as teacher, technician, management consultant, minister, government worker, and deputy sheriff.

The apolitical majority had incomes that ranged over the distribution, but they were weighted more toward the modest end. Their perception of their economic situation was also varied, with about two-fifths indicating that their situation was good, while one-fifth indicated that it was bad. The apolitical majority included such occupations as teacher, clerical worker, chef, purchasing agent, nurse, customer service worker, factory worker, bookkeeper, programmer, office manager, hairstylist, librarian, and actress; this group also included some who were unemployed, but also an accountant, two attorneys, a dentist, and an actuary.

I defined the groups more by the content of their interview responses than specifically by their income, and thus it is expected that the self-description of their politics would be consistent with these distinctions. There are some discrepancies in these numbers, however, in part because not all of the respondents understood the meaning of the terms "liberal," "moderate," and "conservative," but also because sometimes respondents described themselves in particular ways but their interview responses suggested political views inconsistent with that self-definition. The majority of the rich white liberals and working-class liberals reported their politics as liberal. By definition, all of the religious conservatives defined their politics as conservative, while most of the religious nonconservatives defined their politics as moderate. The majority of middle-class conservatives defined their politics as conservative. The working-class "racists" leaned toward conservative politics, although more than half defined themselves as either moderate or liberal. The apolitical majority were primarily self-defined as moderate, although their views spanned the political spectrum.

In table 6.2, I provide a summary of the interviewees' responses to questions that revealed their views about inequality and the role of government. I discuss these in more detail in the profiles of each group, but here we can compare the groups in terms of how they thought about these two critical issues. As can be seen in the table, rich white liberals and working-class liberals stood apart in their expressed concern about economic inequality, while a majority of working-class "racists" and middle-class conservatives indicated that they had no concerns about inequality. Interestingly, a majority of the apolitical majority disavowed concern about economic inequality as well, and nearly half of the religious conservatives said that they were unconcerned about inequality.

Table 6.2 Coded Responses of the Socioeconomic Groups to Questions Regarding Inequality and Government Help

Dimension	Working-Class Racists	Middle-Class Conservatives	Religious Conservatives	Apolitical Majority	Religious Nonconservatives	Working-Class Liberals	Rich White Liberals	Total
Percentage of sample	12%	4.5%	19%	37%	4.5%	6%	17%	100%
								Average
Inequality[a]								
No	55	70	46	54	36	21	10	43
Maybe	7	10	22	9	18	0	8	11
Yes	38	20	33	37	45	79	83	46
Total								100
Government help[b]								
No	71	64	38	38	27	14	12	37
Maybe	29	36	51	40	36	29	24	37
Yes	0	0	11	22	36	57	64	26
Total								100

Source: Author's compilation.

Notes: Responses may not add up to 100 because of rounding error.

[a]Coded responses to question: "To what extent are you concerned about the existence of economic inequality?" with follow-up, "And why would you say that is the case?"

[b]Coded responses to question: "If a group of people have less economically than others, is it fair for them to expect the government to help them?" with follow-up, "And why would you say that is the case?"

The religious nonconservatives tended toward a liberal view on concerns about inequality, but their views were more moderate than those of the two liberal groups.

The same general pattern characterizes the views expressed about the role of government in helping the poor. A majority of both rich white liberals and working-class liberals felt that it is fair for those with less economically to expect government help, whereas a substantial majority of the working-class "racists" and the middle-class conservatives argued that government help is not warranted, even though both of these groups found their own economic situations challenging. The other three groups were in between with regard to this question: the modal response of the religious conservatives and the apolitical majority was that government help is not warranted except in restrictive circumstances (and in general, they leaned more toward the conservative end of the distribution), while the religious nonconservatives were somewhat more likely to endorse a role for government in helping the poor.

The interviewee comments that I include here are illustrative of the general content of the interviews for each group. In my discussion, I endeavor to show how the political attitudes of the interviewees were affected by their life situations and specifically how their racial attitudes seemed to be affected by their access to (and perhaps their ability to hoard) jobs that were protected from the market. I end with a discussion of the impact of the political attitudes of these groups on the competition for white votes —specifically, the votes of the white working class, religious conservatives, professionals, and independents—in the post–civil rights period. I present the groups from those least concerned about inequality to those most concerned about this issue. Thus, I start with the working-class "racists" and end with the rich white liberals. For each group, I provide examples of their responses to questions about whether they are concerned about economic inequality and whether they think it is fair for those who have less economically to expect government help.

Working-Class "Racists"

The interviewees in the working-class "racist" category seemed to be especially vulnerable to the changing economy, and they were openly and intensely resentful toward blacks for taking what they defined as "their jobs." I did not place all the members of the working class I interviewed in the category of working-class "racists," but rather reserved this category for those who were especially outspoken and animated about their views of blacks and the inner-city poor. These interviewees were often explicitly racist in their language. As previously discussed, they showed up as very racially resentful compared to other groups on the questions from the American National Election Studies (see table 4.4). Although civil rights policies were a target of their anger, they were surprisingly silent about issues like globalization and the politics of neoliberalism. In fact, many had bought into the antigovernment rhetoric that pervades the neoliberal agenda.

These members of the working class felt especially aggrieved by the civil rights movement, although they, like everyone else, argued that they supported the principles of civil rights (and "equal opportunity"). For example, a retired factory worker from Ohio (E304 OH M WC) said, when asked about changes for women and minorities: "They have a lot more opportunities today. . . . I think that's great. They should have. . . . I don't think anybody should be discriminated against. . . . If a job comes up, the best man gets it, no matter what color he is, or man or woman." When asked, however, whether a black person could ever be the "best man," the interviewee said, "In my mind, it would probably be very seldom." Thus, although the interviewees strongly expressed the principle that jobs should go to the "best person" or to the "most qualified," they felt that blacks often get jobs that they do not deserve, and they felt that these jobs "belonged" to them, their kids, or their friends and neighbors. The same retired factory worker, for example, told stories about his company having hired blacks who then would not do the work and who eventually walked away from the jobs because of the adverse working conditions. As he said, "The blacks come in and they just . . . they didn't want to work. They didn't want to work there, didn't like the kind of work, and they hired them all the time."

These working-class interviewees were explicitly antiblack (unlike the religious conservatives, who used coded language and talked in terms of morality and faith instead of in terms of race). Many working-class "racists" had stories to tell about conflict with blacks, such as having been beaten up by blacks at some point growing up, or having personally observed blacks getting jobs that they did not deserve or not doing the job because they "don't want to work," or knowing employers who were afraid to fire blacks because of the "NAACP," even though blacks, they said, are slackers and are incompetent. For example, an Ohio welder (B018 OH M WC) told the stories of his experiences with blacks that had contributed to his very negative feelings toward them:

> They called me a honky. I says, "Fuck you, nigger." I'm not one to sit and cower from blacks, I'm not afraid of them. I went to school with them. They proceeded to come over. They beat me up pretty good. . . . I really got no use for the race, I really don't. I didn't have a prejudice bone in my body until I went to high school. Once I got in there, they'd cut into the lunch line. "Get out the way, honky." There'd be fighting, pushing. They cause their own problems, 90 percent of them. . . . I'm sorry, but as far as I'm concerned, that is a trash race. You can say I'm prejudiced. I am. . . . I

> learned it from being with them, from being around them. . . . A lot of them work at [the same company as me] because they got the NAACP. They can't do anything to them. They run . . . discrimination, discrimination. . . . So the company says, "Push the white guys. Let the blacks alone."

Interviewees like this fellow were especially angry that, in their view, blacks slack off with an attitude, which makes them even angrier when they think about it. A working-class woman who worked as a custodian and was also from Ohio (E312 OH F WC) made the following comment when asked whether those with fewer economic resources should expect government help:

> No. I don't like that at all . . . to just sit back and say. "Give me, give me, give me because I'm poor." . . . I have a real hard problem with black people for the fact that they have this black college, and black this, and black that, black soul train, black this . . . you don't see things that are just white. . . . And they are always like, "Well, you know, you made slaves of our family," and blah, blah, blah. I don't like to even hear it. I mean, it just sickens me to even hear it.

In response to the same question, a carpenter in New Jersey (D003 NJ M WC) responded similarly:

> I'm thinking about the downgrading of the exams for . . . the lowering of the standards for the exams for civil service to the black people. . . . I don't think that's right. If they're stupid, they're stupid. Let them get stupid jobs. . . . I don't think they should help at all.

His comments were not isolated. The question had been about poor people, not specifically about blacks, but it triggered in these respondents their resentments about government support that they felt goes undeservedly to blacks. Many other interviewees whom I classified as working-class "racists" responded with a similar tone.

As discussed in earlier chapters, many of the working-class "racists" told stories about attempts to get a job or to help someone else get a job (often a family member) that involved cronyism, favoritism, or nepotism. Sometimes the interviewees talked about how unfair it was for blacks to get jobs because the government mandates "quotas," even though they themselves, their children, or other family members got jobs through various kinds of personal connections. These respondents were often able to get into jobs that paid a living wage, many with good benefits and some level of job security, because of network ties to friends and family who could put in a good word for them at the companies where they worked and sometimes could help them circumvent the screening process (for instance, by giving them copies of the test, providing test answers, bending the rules, or otherwise giving them an extra hand). Such inside advantage was provided to several interviewees even though they either could not read or had poor reading skills; in addition, a number who obtained jobs this way described themselves as not having done well in school. Confident in their ability to do a good job and committed to the value of hard work, they all felt that they deserved these jobs that were supposed to go to the "best person," and they did not see their use of inside advantage as contradicting their view that the best people should get jobs. Further, because using social capital on behalf of family members and friends is such an important part of the white working class's ability to maintain a decent lifestyle, especially with such jobs disappearing around them, these respondents were angry not only when they felt that they had been excluded from a job to which they felt entitled but also when they felt that they could not help their children or other family members gain access to desired jobs. They maintained this anger even when many of these jobs proved to be insecure. Most of the interviewees who had experienced plant closings, layoffs, or company bankruptcies did not attribute these problems to globalization, capitalist greed, or mismanagement; instead, they were angry that blacks were taking jobs that they did not deserve—that is, blacks were taking "their" jobs.

These working-class interviewees believed that the government coddles blacks, allows them to be lazy, and provides more help than they deserve. Perhaps that is one reason why two-thirds of these interviewees said no when asked whether it is fair for those who have less economically to expect government help, and many said that a work requirement should be attached to any form of aid. For example, a woman from Ohio (E318 OH F WC) who was not employed at the time of the interview said:

> If they sit around and wait for that check to come, no. . . . I used to be on food stamps, and that depended on my husband's income, but these people nowadays that just sit around because they are going to get welfare checks or food stamps that's going to come to that door, rather than them going out that door. . . . That makes me mad. . . . If people are just sitting around the house and keep having babies to get that money, no.

A New Jersey woman (D056 NJ F WC), a real estate owner, provided a rationale for these views: "I don't think that everyone should be on the same level. I think that people who work hard deserve to have a little more. . . . I resent people who take advantage of . . . help."

Given the economic vulnerability of the working-class "racists," one might think that they would be more supportive of having a social safety net available for people who get into economic difficulty, but apparently these interviewees made these comments with an image of the black poor in mind, rather than their own economic situation. Further, they were clearly thinking of welfare rather than unemployment insurance or the kind of temporary help that some of them had sought and felt was warranted (for example, food stamps or funds from the Women, Infants, and Children [WIC] program). In their presentation of self, they all indicated that their own need for help had been temporary and that their situation was distinct from that of the people who "just sit back and wait for a check." They further underlined their views by indicating that they did not necessarily believe in equality and that there was no reason to worry about inequality because there will always be rich and poor.

The working-class "racists" were especially proud of being good workers, but they expressed anger at the fragility of their hold on a middle-class lifestyle and their vulnerability because of poor health, industrial accidents, swing shifts, and dangerous work. A number of the interviewees experienced these circumstances in their own life histories. Yet many felt that anyone who wants to can always get a job and that obstacles do not matter. They believed that life outcomes are a matter of persistence and hard work. Several interviewees said that although the jobs available might not be good jobs or jobs they would want, any job would provide a place to start and then lead to better jobs. This view of jobs, they felt, was not one shared by poor blacks, whom they believed would rather live off of the government by staying on welfare. In spite of such sentiments, a few interviewees told me about jobs that they themselves would not take and about the times when it had not been worth it to them to take a job that either was dangerous or paid too little. For example, an Ohio waitress (E317 OH F WC) had been on welfare for five years while her son was small after a troubled relationship had led to a divorce. She only got off welfare when she remarried. When asked whether people with less economically should expect government help, she said: "No. They should get what they work for. . . . I believe if you have to be on welfare, they should make you work." Even so, recounting her own experience, she did not take a job while on welfare. As she said:

> I was just trying to raise my son. I did try to get jobs, but what I would have gotten paid. . . . I had to have car insurance. My mom got me a car for $150, but I still had to have car insurance, pay a babysitter, be able to pay my water, sewer, gas, electric, rent, all that. I would have been in the hole, and I would have gradually drowned, because I couldn't have kept my head above water. There would have been no way. I didn't want on assistance, but there was a trap. There was like no way out.

Thus, as is evident in a number of the interviews, this respondent applied rules or principles to others that she did not apply to herself and that she did not follow in her own life.

The views expressed by the interviewees about the rich, in contrast, were quite generous. The rich, they said, deserved everything they earned because they were "so smart." For example, a Tennessee woman who worked as a route salesman (F026 TN F WC) said: "The rich got rich because they either did things smarter or worked hard, and it wasn't necessarily handed to them." This view was expressed as well by the owner of a small industrial equipment company in Ohio (E350 OH M WC): "Anybody that achieves that status, that's what they've worked for. If they've got an idea in the back of their head that makes them rich, and nobody else followed through with it, then they should be rewarded for it." A truck driver in New Jersey (D052) reinforced this view: when asked if he was concerned about economic inequality, he said: "I don't believe in equality in anything. . . . [It] doesn't bother me in the least."

The working-class "racists" portrayed government leaders as not looking out for their interests. These interviewees were also very resentful of black leaders who call attention to racial issues and who seek government benefits for black people—at the expense, they felt, of whites. They hated Al Sharpton, were not very favorable toward Jesse Jackson, and in general thought that the country should stop talking about race, should not give it much attention, and should punish those who try to call attention to it. They did not think that poor blacks deserve anything from the government because they fundamentally believed that poor blacks are lazy, have not tried hard enough to succeed, waste the opportunities they have been given, are not responsible parents, have no work ethic, and are ungrateful for the help they have been given.

Even so, while many of these interviewees identified themselves as conservative in their politics, a number described themselves as liberal, because of their class identification and involvement in their unions. Hence, this group was somewhat internally split. Its members tended to be conservative, but when mobilized on class issues, their views were more consistent with those of liberals. In general, however, to the extent that race was salient when they talked about government, they drew more on their conservative side and either did not vote at all or voted Republican. Most of the antagonism expressed by working-class "racists" was directed toward the government and toward blacks. Although there was some hint in their views of dissatisfaction with liberals and snooty people, generally the working-class "racists" celebrated the rich and thought the rich get what they deserve.

Middle-Class Conservatives

The responses of the middle-class conservatives (all of whom had college degrees), like those of the working-class "racists," often had a racial subtext, although their comments were not quite as explicit as those of the working-class "racists." For example, in response to the question about whether it is fair for those with less economically to expect government help, a female school system development officer from Ohio (B013 OH F MC) said: "The whole issue of welfare and all of that, I have a problem with. . . . I don't want to label it as a black community kind of thing, but I think some of the leadership in the black community isn't doing them any justice at all either. I think . . . the people that are speaking for them, sometimes are just way off base." Race also was incorporated into the response of an Ohio nurse (E336 OH F MC) to the same question. She said:

> I don't want to get ethnic about it, but I think mainly the black people, and a lot of poor whites, but I can gear it more toward blacks. I'm real tired of hearing about how they were slaves. . . . They weren't slaves. Their mothers weren't slaves. Their great-great-grandfather was a slave, and I didn't have a damn thing to do with it, and neither did you. . . . I even hear it where I work. . . . Basically, we don't have a lot of blacks working in our operating room, but there are some. And I do not feel they are discriminated against at all. . . . The average white male is almost more discriminated against than the black people, because they gotta have numbers and they gotta have so many blacks. And it doesn't matter if you have a better education. . . . I don't find that fair.

The general tenor of the middle-class conservatives' remarks is exemplified in a comment made by an Ohio business executive (E338 OH M MC): "I don't think anybody should expect anybody to help you. . . . The government has set up a system that has set up expectations. . . . Life is not fair. . . . I think that everybody can help themselves, and people who are healthy and can get out and work, but want subsidies, I don't think they deserve it." There clearly seemed to be a racial component to his comments about who would want subsidies.

Middle-class conservatives argued that economic inequality was not a concern of theirs, that there will always be economic inequality at any rate, that they did not begrudge the rich or necessarily want what they have, and that ultimately people should help themselves. For example, the Ohio nurse (E336 OH F MC) said about economic inequality: "I'm not worried about it. . . . I look a little more up to the person who worked hard for his money, rather than the person who was handed it. . . . It's not your fault that John D. Rockefeller was your father. No, I don't have a problem with that." The middle-class conservatives, like the working-class "racists," also were generous in their assessment of the rich. For example, a Tennessee salesman (G505 TN M MC) said:

> There's always been rich people . . . and usually, in most cases, the rich people have really worked for what they have. . . . Bill Gates . . . that's where creativity and ingenuity and being able to step out and try something that nobody's trying or nobody's doing. . . . If it wasn't for Bill Gates doing what he's done and making computers accessible, I probably wouldn't have one. Does he deserve to be one of the richest men in the world for it? Yeah . . . he has that right.

This view was summed up by a male small-business owner in New Jersey (D030 NJ M MC): "I am not concerned that we are not all equal. I think if you work hard and you did your stuff, took a chance, and did all of your stuff, I don't begrudge anyone to make a dime."

Despite having college degrees and middle-class lifestyles, only a few of these interviewees were in highly prestigious jobs. A number were working part-time or were out of the labor force, and some were in jobs that did not match their initial aspirations. Despite their own apparent feelings of vulnerability, they were opposed to the government providing help to those with fewer financial resources, and they disavowed a concern about economic inequality. Several of the middle-class conservatives' comments raised issues of race, even when the question did not specifically ask about it, thus suggesting that when the middle-class conservatives thought about the economically disadvantaged, they had racial minorities in mind.

Middle-class conservatives had adopted a politics of conservatism that presumably offered them some psychological assurance that their efforts would be rewarded if they persisted and that they belonged in the middle class. In other words, although the structural circumstances of their lives and their "objective" economic circumstances might not have determined their politics, strictly speaking, their perceptions of their economic situation seemed to have influenced how they thought about issues of inequality and fairness.

Religious Conservatives

Even though most Christians, like most people in general, are not especially political, do not know much about political issues, and may not belong to and perhaps have never heard of some of the organizations that were created in the emergence of the New Right, they nevertheless have been affected by the new politicization of conservative Christians. White evangelical and fundamentalist Protestant Christians (the religious conservatives in my study), in general, have become identified with the Republican Party, have mobilized their members to vote Republican, have been elected to school boards and state political organizations, and now constitute the Republican base, even though organizations like the Moral Majority and the Christian Coalition have long since disbanded (in part because of the strong reactions within the electorate against their influence in the political arena).

Religious conservatives are among the most politically conservative groups in my study. Further, the Protestant respondents who espoused conservative religious beliefs tended to have similar political views in all three regions where I did interviews. Thus, although the movement began in the South, it has now spread beyond that region to the rest of the country. Their politics is characterized by strong anti-government, anti-tax, and anti-welfare rhetoric. Like most of the other respondents, religious conservatives profess a belief in civil rights and express generally positive attitudes toward the changes brought about by the civil rights movement. Yet, as shown in table 4.4, where I examined the position of the various sociopolitical groups using questions from the American National Election Studies and measures drawn from Sears, Henry, and Kosterman (2000), religious conservatives are also significantly more likely than rich white liberals to hold racially resentful views and to believe that government has gone too far in support of civil rights.

Despite the subtext on race in their political views, the comments of religious conservatives focused primarily on their self-identity as Christians and were usually framed in moral terms. In that sense, these views reflect the shift from racial to religious politics that occurred with the emergence of the New Right and the Religious Right. For example, while many of the other interviewees had difficulty understanding the question when I asked which groups or categories they would place themselves in, most of the religious conservatives readily called attention to being Christian and being closely involved in their church. This response suggests that most thought of themselves as a group (unlike many of the other respondents). Some were clearly aware of the political dimension of being a conservative Christian, and they claimed that, as a group, they were embattled or even persecuted. For example, a middle-class manager from Tennessee (F005) said about his identity as a Christian:

> Economically, I suppose we're faring as well or better as most everybody. . . . From a religious standpoint, we're probably not faring as well, because we're viewed more negatively today. . . . Christians are . . . becoming a minority . . . maybe not physically persecuted, but certainly verbally and every other way. And put down upon and misrepresented and so forth. . . . It's not fashionable to have a relationship with God or to speak of God, certainly not in public, anymore.

Similarly, an unemployed teacher in Ohio (B007 OH F MC) said: "Christians are being told they don't have a right to the same freedom of speech as the rest of the people, because they don't like what they're saying. That's wrong. It's the pendulum swinging too far the other way." These and other religious conservatives often justified their political views by claiming that their views were grounded in what the Bible says or what God intended.

When asked whether it is fair for those who have less economically to expect the government to help them, religious conservatives were likely to say that people should help themselves, that others should not have to pay for their mistakes, and that too much is expected of government. For example, a retired schoolteacher (B016 OH M MC) said: "I think the government shouldn't be in the employment business; it should be in the governing business." Similarly, a manager from Tennessee (F005 TN M MC) said:

> I personally don't believe that's the role of government to redistribute wealth. . . . National security, very limited government, in my opinion, is the role of national government. . . . The great social programs, in my opinion, have been a disaster. They have not been successful at all. All they've done is create more people dependent upon the government.

A number of the religious conservatives thought that people should take care of themselves, that opportunities are available for those who are willing to work, and that it is not "healthy" for government to provide help, because we "should look to ourselves," in the words of a Tennessee construction manager (G518 TN M MC). One religious conservative interviewee (D013 NJ M MC) insisted that this view is biblical. He said, when asked whether the government should provide help to those who have less economically: "No . . . it depends if they want to become somebody . . . you're really debilitating people. . . . Instead of giving them fish, teach them how to fish. . . . That's where you're giving them a greater value. . . . It's in the Old Testament. . . . Christ . . . envisioned people being the charitable causes, not the government." Of course, the Bible does not include this aphorism, but the respondent was convinced that his views are supported by the Bible. Another interviewee, a Tennessee materials specialist (G527 TN F MC), also was convinced that the Bible provides the justification for her views: "I go to church. I read my Bible, and I study, and you know, the Bible says that you work, not just men, but the woman in Proverbs who worked and sold her fields. . . . And that is what God expects all of us to do. And to expect the government to give you something for which you haven't worked is ridiculous." The views of religious conservatives about government help can be summarized in the comments of a pharmaceutical sales manager from Ohio (E314 OH M MC): "I think there are too many people who . . . expect the government to do too many things for them, as if the government is their lifesaving vehicle. The government doesn't owe anybody anything."

These sentiments carried over, of course, when the religious conservatives were asked about whether they were concerned about economic inequality. A number of the religious conservatives noted that the Bible says that there will always be poor people, and thus they felt that there was not much that could be done about the situation. For example, a middle-class quality control manager from Ohio (B002 OH M MC) said: "You're always going to have it though . . . even the Bible says that. You'll always have that. And it's just the nature of capitalism. You're always going to have people who make poor choices." Another manager in Tennessee, who worked for an industrial firm (G525 TN M MC), also viewed inequality as a matter of choices: "I think in any society, you will have those who are the movers and shakers, and [it does] not matter what restraint you put on, they are going to be successful. And there's others that don't select to make those choices to be that motivated."

Other religious conservative interviewees thought that inequality is the result of motivation, effort, and experience. A New Jersey homemaker (C002 NJ F MC), who had been trained in a professional field but was not in the labor force at the time of the interview, put the issue in context:

> Inequality implies that everybody should be the same, and I believe in capitalism. I believe in being rewarded for what you're willing to work for. . . . I'm deeply concerned about the poverty . . . the drugs . . . that whole underworld. . . . I really believe there's nothing the government can do to stop that. . . . It's got to come from one-on-one relationships with kids. . . . Honestly, the adults need the training more than the kids.

A Tennessee administrator (G503 TN M MC) personalized the issue: "No, I guess I don't get too hung up on it, looking at what somebody else has or doesn't have, because I think a lot of what you have is what you make of it."

A number of the religious conservatives also noted that rich people deserve what they have and that it is not appropriate to try to take it from them. For example, a working-class Tennessee man who worked in his wife's family business (G529 TN M WC) said: "I don't think that everybody owes a poor person anything. I don't think that somebody rich has something that is mine. . . . It would be different if it was communism or something . . . however, that isn't the way our society is." Another middle-class man from Tennessee (G534 TN M MC), a salesman, was more explicit about the notion of the rich having earned what they have: "The Bill Gates and the Steve Jobs of the world and all those people who just absolutely work their fannies off and are just brilliant people. . . .

But it's not been at the expense of others that I know of . . . of people in the lower economic [level]. . . . I think those people who have made their money in most cases have made their money honestly." Thus, while some of the religious conservative respondents said that they were concerned about economic inequality, most did not think that it was the government's responsibility to do anything about it because inequality, in their view, is the result of poor choices or lack of motivation on the part of the poor and also the result of the hard work and innovativeness of the rich.

In summary, religious conservatives expressed a preference for private services over public ones, including private schools, and charity instead of welfare, consistent with their strong antigovernment rhetoric. The religious conservatives argued that the federal government should have the very limited role of providing national defense and not much else. In this regard, various religious conservative interviewees indicated that the government should not be involved in providing employment and social services or in shaping the economy because they believed in capitalism, not socialism or communism. Further, the religious conservatives said that both jobs and opportunities were available (at the time of the interviews) and that if people had pride in themselves they would do what was necessary to support themselves without government aid. Instead of accepting government help, the religious conservatives argued that people should have to live with the consequences of their mistakes and should have to dig deeper within themselves if they run into trouble because of poor decisions. Although a few acknowledged that sometimes help may be needed, they clearly indicated that it should be limited, temporary, and delivered in the form of services (such as education) rather than money, and that it should depend on a willingness to work.

Thus, although in their comments the religious conservatives, more than the other interviewees, talked in terms of social and cultural issues, their comments were often framed in terms of antigovernment or anti–welfare state policies, with a subtext about race. They did not talk about segregation and the "Southern way of life," but rather called attention to the way the government (meaning specifically the federal government) encourages dependency and irresponsibility, through the expansion of the welfare system, as they affirmed their own support for the value of freedom, capitalism, and the need for self-reliance.

The views of the religious conservatives clearly fit the ideological underpinnings of the New Right and the Religious Right. In fact, it was quite striking that the religious conservatives used such similar language and arguments in each of the three regions where the interviews were conducted—for example, they all spoke about welfare creating dependency and undermining incentives, and all of them mentioned their support for capitalism, defended the rich, and asserted that the only way to have self-respect is to be self-reliant. The similarity in responses across the regions among the religious conservatives (even though there were only a small number of religious conservative interviewees in New Jersey) strongly suggested that these interviewees were hearing these kinds of arguments in their churches, perhaps through the Christian media, and most likely among their friends and family members who were similarly involved in their churches. A number of the religious conservatives, in fact, talked about their embeddedness in Christian communities, about the fact that their friendships were primarily among church members, and about the importance of their religious beliefs to their self-identities.

What is striking about the commonalities in the responses of these interviewees is the political underpinning of their responses. Evangelical and fundamentalist religious groups have in the past been nonpolitical, but the ascendant Religious Right, with the explicit assistance of the New Right, created an interpretation of the faith that became infused with politics in the guise of morality. Thus, even though perhaps only a small proportion of evangelical or fundamentalist Christians are actively involved in the political organizations created by the New Right and the new Religious Right, many such Christians are nevertheless influenced by the ideas of the conservative movement through Christian broadcasting and media and other conservative media, through the influence of the growing number of megachurches, and through the active and intentional efforts of the New Right to organize the new conservative movement through religious organizations. Also important to consider in this regard is that the racial dimension of these politics in the post–civil rights period was expressed by these interviewees in terms of moral arguments about what God intended. In other words, racial politics has become religious politics.

The Apolitical Majority

The group that I am calling the apolitical majority comprises people with a range of political views about issues of race and inequality, but most defined themselves as politically moderate, with a slight tilt toward conservatism. As the label implies, most were not very interested in politics and had not thought much about and did not know much about policy issues, but when asked to formulate an opinion, their views seemed to be more like those of the conservative groups than the liberal ones (as evidenced as well by the regression analyses reported in table 4.4). Of course, the apolitical majority is composed of both working-class and middle-class respondents.

Like most of the other interviewees, many of the apolitical majority interviewees indicated that they supported the civil rights movement and believed that equal opportunity should be available to everyone. Some of the apolitical majority interviewees had rather liberal views about the role of government, and some had quite conservative views, but these interviewees stood out primarily because of their general disinterest in politics and their lack of engagement with most of the political issues that are of concern in this analysis. The primary attitude of the apolitical majority was a "live and let live" perspective. Many among the apolitical majority claimed that they were not very knowledgeable about or interested in politics, while others did not say much about it one way or the other. Even so, in contrast to the rich white liberals, who seemed to care a great deal about politics, and in contrast to the working-class "racists" and the religious conservatives, who were very animated about their antigovernment perspectives, the apolitical majority did not express very strong opinions about political issues. For example, a New Jersey senior trade analyst (D031 NJ F WC) said, when asked if she voted:

> See, I have not. I did vote previously, but I have not voted recently because I figure I haven't followed anything and I'm just gonna vote Republican. I think [my husband is a] Democrat. I don't even know. I don't even care. But eventually I would like to actually see people who are running [for office] and read up on them and to myself form my own opinion and not do it based on what someone else is telling me.

These interviewees, like the majority of Americans, tended to go about their lives, taking care of their families, going to their jobs, and mostly dealing with whatever came their way. They did not tend to stand out as either leaders or followers. They had opinions, but they were likely to preface their comments with phrases such as "I guess," "I don't know," or "Maybe yes, maybe no." This sort of tentative expression of their opinions can be contrasted with the responses of religious conservatives, who readily answered most political questions, claimed certainty in their answers, and expressed a strong belief that their way of seeing the world was in conformity with the way God intended things. The tentativeness of the apolitical majority can also be contrasted with the tone taken by the working-class "racists," who were equally certain of their views and rarely hesitated to provide a response. Similarly, the tentative views of the apolitical majority can be contrasted with the views of rich white liberals, who seemed to have given a great deal of thought to the issues about which they were asked, had reasons to support their opinions, and offered some factual basis for the claims they made. In contrast, the responses of the apolitical majority interviewees were shorter, less expressive, and often inconsistent.

When asked whether those with fewer economic resources should expect help from the government, the apolitical majority interviewees predictably equivocated. These interviewees were not as liberal as the liberal groups, nor as conservative as the conservative groups. About two-fifths said that government help is not warranted because people should help themselves. For example, a small-business loan officer in Ohio (E349 OH M MC) said: "When the welfare system started, theoretically it's a great idea. The problem is . . . when the government gives you something, they take away your incentive to get it yourself. And unless you're just a really motivated self-starter, a lot of people would just sit back and take the handout." Similarly, a musician from Tennessee (G517 TN M MC) said, when asked whether expecting government help is fair for those who have less economically:

> No, I don't believe so. . . . There seems to be . . . in the latter part of the twentieth century, with the New Deal and everything, I think there seems to be less of an emphasis on rugged individualism and the whole "come hell or high water" approach to success, as opposed to "what can be done for me." . . . I feel a little uncomfortable about making a speculation about what that might be like, not having any experience to [draw on].

The rest of the apolitical majority respondents, however, said that the appropriateness of government help depends on the reason. Many said that help should be given to those who are disabled (physically or mentally) or elderly, unable to work and take care of themselves, or facing natural disasters. But the apolitical majority interviewees also said that, if help is given, it should be temporary, limited, and primarily intended to develop skills or provide education and training to help people help themselves. For example, a working-class man from Ohio who worked in order entry for a large company (E352 OH M WC) said, when asked if poor people should expect help from the government:

> I guess it depends on the situation that put the people in that separate group. . . . I mean, if it's because . . . somebody got hurt, and they, let's say, where they were working, they didn't have any kind of disability or anything like that, I'd say yes, the government should probably help them. But for the average person that . . . is able to work and just doesn't want to work, no. I don't think they should help them.

A number of these interviewees commented favorably on welfare reform and said that whatever help is given should have a time limit. Further, most of the apolitical majority interviewees defined the criteria for those receiving government help as trying hard, helping themselves, taking initiative, and trying to get "on their feet." For example, a disabled industrial arts teacher from Ohio (E344 OH M MC) said: "If they are sincerely trying, doing the best they can with their intelligence . . . [and]

need the help, great, no problem. . . . There's got to be a point where these people have to show that they're sincerely making an effort." The apolitical majority interviewees said, however, that those who just sit around, who expect a handout, who do not want to work, and who will not help themselves should not get help. For example, a supervisor at a small company in Ohio (B014 OH M WC) said: "I think that they should expect it, but I think they should have to earn what they expect too. . . . Why can't you bring me a bag of trash, and then I'll give you so much of a welfare check that day. . . . I think the government should help people, but then in turn, it shouldn't be a handout."

Although only a few of the apolitical majority interviewees specifically mentioned African Americans or minority groups, these interviewees alluded to people on welfare in a number of other ways (for example, "people in Newark" or "those in ghettos") that clearly implied that the interviewees primarily had African Americans in mind. For example, a factory worker from Ohio (E307 OH M WC) said with regard to whether it is fair to expect government help:

> I've been discriminated against. Made me madder than hell, so it's out there and it does exist. But somewhere you have to quit blaming the past and take responsibility for your actions too. . . . There are still people with a chip on their shoulder—"we were slaves" and whatnot. Somewhere you have to start taking responsibility for your own destiny.

In addition, many of the apolitical majority interviewees pointed to corruption and said that welfare creates dependency. For example, a Tennessee hairstylist (F004 TN F WC) responded to the question about government help this way: "Why should they expect to have preferential treatment or get our money?. . . They should have to work hard like everybody else. Why get a handout from the government and depend on all of our tax dollars?" Thus, while the apolitical majority interviewees were more likely than the more conservative groups to indicate that government help is sometimes warranted, they expressed concern about the motivation and effort of potential recipients, and they believed that any help should be limited to skill development and also should be temporary.

When asked whether they were concerned about economic inequality, the apolitical majority interviewees were more similar to the working-class "racists" than to the other groups in their responses, but the reasons differed. Whereas both the working-class "racists" and the middle-class conservatives said that the rich deserve what they get because they earned it, argued that life is not fair, and said that there is not much that one can do about inequality, the apolitical majority interviewees said that they were not concerned about economic inequality because they were only concerned about themselves or because they were middle-class and therefore inequality did not affect them. A number of the apolitical majority interviewees said that because there have always been both rich and poor, there is nothing to do about it. But some also said that rich people earned it, that entrepreneurs should be rewarded, and that one should not begrudge or envy the rich. For example, a New Jersey woman (D031 NJ F WC), who worked as a senior trade analyst at a large company, said: "I can't say it necessarily concerns me. . . . You're kind of limited to getting ahead in your own life with your own family that these issues don't necessarily become your own." Another New Jersey woman (D043 NJ F MC), a special education teacher, however, said that she was not concerned about economic inequality because people basically get what they deserve:

> No, not really. I mean, people are rich because they worked hard or they got parents with money or whatever, and that's their right, you know. I think I am where I am because of what I have done. I don't think that I feel jealous or animosity against rich people at all. I think you get what you get, and that's it.

Although the apolitical majority interviewees said that they felt sorry for the poor, they also said that poor people generally are not very motivated or capable, and therefore, if they were given more economic resources, they would not be able to manage them. For example, a self-employed Tennessee woman (G510 TN F MC) said: "In history there's always been rich and poor. . . . People make of themselves what they will. . . . People don't probably change classes very much, and I don't know if that has to do with ambition. . . . [Some] people are leaders, and they will be the ones who succeed."

Even though the apolitical majority interviewees said that they did not want to see people starving or homeless, they also did not think that the government should necessarily redistribute wealth. For example, a New Jersey football coach (D060 NJ M MC) said: "I think that it always is going to exist. . . . I don't think the goal should be to eliminate that gap. . . . I don't think that the government role should be to make sure that everybody has the same pie. . . . Quite honestly, some people can't be responsible. Some people are not cut out to have a bigger piece of pie." Like the football coach, some of the apolitical majority interviewees said that people are not equal and that not everyone should have the same things. That is, they said that they believed in capitalism. Instead of government help or redistribution, the interviewees said that help should come from charity that helps people improve their skills so that they can be independent and self-sustaining.

Only a few of the apolitical majority interviewees suggested that inequality is a concern that requires that something be done, and a few were concerned with the long-term implications. For example, an unemployed cost accountant from Ohio (E358 OH M WC) said, when asked if he was concerned with economic inequality:

> I think there's going to be a rich class, and there's going to be a poor class. I don't think there's going to be anything in between. . . . A lot of us that are stuck in between, the middle class, are going to fall into that poor class, because we're not going to be able to afford, because the rich are just going to outprice everything.

A New Jersey purchasing agent (D018 NJ M MC) thought that the long-term consequences were of concern. He said: "I'm concerned that it can be swayed . . . that it's something that demagoguery will allow us to take advantage of, and I don't think there's anything you can do about it." A similar point was made by another New Jersey man, a real estate appraiser (D067 NJ M MC): "We seem to be losing our middle class. . . . But you need that middle class. It gives you your values, your work ethic, your basic conscience of your nation. At the other ends, it just seems to be extremes."

As the largest of the sociopolitical groups in my study (about one-third of the total respondents), the apolitical majority tended to reflect the average views of whites in the United States. They tended to feel that the civil rights movement was a good thing, but that sometimes the government does too much or does things in the wrong way. They said that they believed that some groups of people may ask for too much or may need to be pushed a bit more, but that they were sympathetic to those who may need help to get back on their feet. In general, they tried to weigh both the pros and cons of most political issues when asked, but they were not very certain about their preferences. Most were confident that they themselves had done their best with their own circumstances. Those from the middle class among the apolitical majority tended to be somewhat more conservative in their views than the rich white liberals who shared their class positions, and those from the working class among the apolitical majority tended to be somewhat more liberal in their views than the working-class "racists" who shared their class. In general, however, the apolitical majority were uncertain in their views, had not given much thought to political issues, and did not seem to read much about political issues or follow the news. For the most part, they were happy to let others in their lives attend to such things.

The apolitical majority rarely thought about racial issues, and they were not very conscious of any particular impact that the implementation of the Civil Rights Acts had had or was likely to have on them. They generally thought that whatever will happen will happen and that there is not much that one can do about it. They wanted things in their lives to be harmonious, for people to be happy, for their family members to be settled in life, and for the world to go about its business. Although some of these interviewees may have voted as part of their civic duty, some indicated that they did not necessarily vote and that they did not care that much about what happens in the political sphere. They thought that politicians will do whatever they are going to do, that some people probably involve themselves too much with such things, and that what is most important is what happens in their own neighborhoods and families. While the apolitical majority sometimes expressed an opinion if asked survey questions about public policy issues, they were just as likely to change their views if they were given more information, and sometimes they backed away from their opinions if they were challenged. In other words, they really did not care that much about politics. They had other things to worry about in their lives.

Religious Nonconservatives

The religious nonconservatives raised some of the same issues as the religious conservatives about the poor always being with us and their uncertainty about whether providing money alone would help, but the religious nonconservatives also were more likely to say that the rich and perhaps the government should help in some way and that that would be a positive thing for the country as a whole. The number of interviewees categorized as religious nonconservatives is much smaller than the number of those categorized as religious conservatives, and it is also important to note that the vast majority of the religious nonconservatives described their politics as moderate. Only one identified as liberal.

Thus, the religious nonconservatives actually made statements similar to those made by the religious conservatives with regard to whether those with less economically should expect government help. Some said that people should work for what they get, that help from the government should be limited to education, that government programs do not work very well, and that money, in and of itself, does not help very much. A Tennessee man who worked as an electronic publishing coordinator (G507 TN M WC) felt that some government help is warranted, but felt that there should be limits on it: "If there are degrees of help . . . then my answer would be yes . . . but I like the idea of welfare being time limited. . . . Part of the welfare system today is the situations engendered by people that just won't change. . . . It's not that they can't change."

A few of the religious nonconservative interviewees expressed somewhat more liberal views about the role of government. For example, a young woman from Ohio who worked as a part-time preschool supervisor (E330 OH F MC) said:

> I work in a low-income area. Nearly everyone I work with is on government assistance. . . . I don't know if they have a right to it, but I'm sure glad the government gives it to them, because I see the good in things. I see people really working hard to turn their lives around or to work toward financial independence, and without government assistance, they couldn't get a start.

A similar sentiment was expressed by a female minister from Tennessee (F012 TN F MC): "I think the government should help. . . . I've just seen people who really did have the need. The government helped them for a while. They got . . . everything straight, and then they took off on their own and did it. They just needed that little bit of help."

The religious nonconservatives had somewhat ambivalent views on economic inequality, but unlike the religious conservatives, none of them said that it was not an issue of concern to them. In general, though they often expressed a view that people should help themselves, they nevertheless also acknowledged that sometimes that is not enough and that there are circumstances that may require a public response. For example, a radiology technician from Ohio (E329 OH F WC) said: "Nobody ever said that life was going to be fair, but as fair as we can make it would be a lot better than what it is." A Tennessee teacher (F007 TN F MC) expressed concern about the existence of inequality, but said that there is really nothing that can be done about it. She said: "You're only on this earth one time, and there are people who get to do whatever they want, and there are people who struggle every moment they're here, but that's kind of the way life is."

There were other religious nonconservatives, however, whose views were supportive of more public action. For example, a middle-class woman from Tennessee who worked in government service (F013 TN F MC) said: "If we don't share our opportunities and our education with people that haven't had those opportunities, then the whole country will not do as well." The Tennessee minister (F012 TN F MC) thought that it was not God's plan to always have poor people. In this regard, her comments are contrary to those of many other religiously identified people in the study:

> I believe that God created us. . . . His plan was for us to have what we needed and that's it. For everyone to have equality, male, female, and in the future of course, different colors, different backgrounds. I think we are supposed to all have equal, so if there's that big gap between rich and poor, then obviously, we're not following God's plan.

Not all of the religious nonconservatives, however, not even those from Tennessee, were quite this concerned with inequality. The Tennessee deputy sheriff (G501 TN M MC) claimed that if money were redistributed, "in ten years it would be back the way it is right now."

The religious nonconservatives were open to possible government help, although they thought it should be temporary. The religious nonconservatives also expressed somewhat more concern about economic inequality. There was no obvious reason why some of the religiously identified people had been less influenced by the social movement dynamics of the Religious Right, nor why they had come to see the world through a more moderate political lens than their conservative counterparts. There may have been some differences in denomination, but I did not specifically ask that question of the interviewees. A few religious nonconservative interviewees described experiences they had had in college that enabled them to work or interact with poor people, and those experiences had changed their view of the world. As discussed by Kluegel and Smith (1986), developing a "counter-ideology" in which one comes to question the existing stratification order seems to be a pathway to more moderate or liberal politics, and this was evidently the case for some of the interviewees in this study. Those who mentioned life experiences that had enabled them to work with or closely observe people whose lives were different from their own, often by going away to college or otherwise moving away from the environment where they had grown up, indicated that these experiences had caused them to ask questions about what they had taken for granted and, in some cases, to come to see the world differently. Such experiences do not conform to the naive version of the "contact hypothesis," namely, that just getting to know people will lead to friendships. Instead, the interviewees who discussed these kinds of experiences often had had an opportunity to see people who were less fortunate than themselves and rather than responding to them with disdain, they instead had thought about their own good fortune and about ways in which good fortune might be shared with others (Brewer and Miller 1984; Fiske, Xu, and Cuddy 1999).

Working-Class Liberals

The views of the working-class liberals and the working-class "racists" with regard to government's role in addressing issues of inequality were almost mirror images of each other. The working-class "racists" were emphatic that it is not the government's role to help people just because they are poor, while the working-class liberals felt that this is precisely what government should do and how government resources should be used. Whereas two-thirds of the working-class "racists" said that the government should not help those who have less economically, more than two-thirds of the working-class liberals said that the government should provide help. The differences in these views seem especially ironic since it was the working-class "racists" as a group who expressed more concern about their own economic circumstances than did the working-class liberals.

For example, an electronics engineer from Tennessee (G533 TN M WC) favored a role for government: "I would like to take part in a government that is there to help people out when they need it. . . . If you play by the rules of our society, if you pay your taxes and are socially responsible, then I think that you can expect some help when you need it." A similar sentiment was expressed by a small-business owner in Tennessee (G512 TN M WC): "I think every person now and then needs a hand. . . . If you help somebody get back on their feet, it's well worth it." A moral dimension to these views was added by a building contractor from Ohio (E368 OH M WC), who said:

> I consider myself a very conservative person. I think we have an absolute obligation to help as many people as we can to have as good a life and to fulfill their potential as much as possible. And that's probably the best thing government can do. But entitlement, no. I think they need to help people fulfill their potential. . . . If there's been inequality, some way to level the playing field.

Working-class liberals said that inequality did concern them, especially with the growing gap between rich and poor. For example, a front-desk clerk at a medical center in Ohio (E359 OH F WC) said the following when asked if she was concerned about economic inequality:

> Oh, yeah, very much. [I am concerned about] the discrimination against the poor people. . . . I just think it's so difficult for them. . . . Why can't we all have the same options? I understand that maybe you were born to a wealthier family than maybe I was, but . . . we can all reach that same goal, but I just think, why is it so difficult for so many to do that.

Another female interviewee, a self-employed construction worker from Ohio (E366), said that she was concerned that the rich have ways to reduce their taxes or to hide their money, which she felt has consequences for others: "Those taxes [could] help out that poor person in the long run somewhere along the line. . . . Our government should be able to help out. When somebody wants to make theirselves better, the government should help." Thus, the working-class liberal interviewees felt compassion for those in difficult circumstances and felt further that it is a main role of government to make sure that everyone has a chance.

Overall, there is a clear difference in the tone of the comments and the views expressed by the working-class "racists" and the working-class liberals. It is not clear, however, what it is that causes these groups to diverge so much in their opinions about government and inequality. The differences between the two groups seem to have more to do with their feelings of vulnerability and how that translates into their political views. Race seems to play a special role in this regard, since many of the working-class "racists" were quite open about their negative attitudes toward blacks, whereas these types of views were not very prevalent among the comments of the working-class liberals, who in fact seemed to have sympathy for and be open to poor people, including blacks and other minorities.

There is another aspect to these views, however, that may also play a role in the seeming incongruity between the economic situation of the working-class "racists" and their denigration of poor people, on the one hand, and celebration of the rich, on the other. The very vulnerability of the working class creates a dilemma for white working-class families that may be distinct from the issues faced by more middle-class families and those with more skills to bring to the labor market: that precarious hold on a decent lifestyle may tempt those who face unpleasant jobs, adverse working conditions, and humiliating challenges to finding and keeping jobs that pay a living wage to give up or to lose themselves in self-medication through alcohol or drugs, irresponsible sexual behavior, or domestic violence. For example, country-and-western songs associated with the poor and working class have some very familiar themes about cheating, drinking, rambling, and restlessness, among working-class men in particular. As Benabou and Tirole (2003) have argued, one of the tasks of parents is to instill confidence in their children while at the same time motivating them to do their duty and take on responsibility. The same may be true in general within families and communities. Ensuring that male members in working-class families accept the role of primary breadwinner may require a delicate balance of nudging and incentives to encourage their effort and persistence and to forestall or head off their giving up or acting out. It may be precisely because the lives of working-class "racists" are so vulnerable that they have to work extra hard to create the belief that effort will be rewarded and persistence will ultimately win out. Further, the white working class's uncertain hold on a middle-class lifestyle may also induce some of them, consciously or otherwise, to draw a firm line between themselves and those they categorize or define as lazy and unworthy. Thus, the strong insistence that those who try will be rewarded and that government help is neither needed nor wanted may reflect the psychological needs of this group of interviewees more than their structural circumstances. In a sense, it may be that psychology trumps structure (in the sense that the psychological need to encourage persistence shapes political views more than the objective class circumstances that might otherwise lead to more support for a government-provided social safety net) when there are strong temptations to give up or walk out. In this regard, the working-class "racists" made a point about their wish to help their children or family members get good jobs, whereas the working-class liberals were more concerned about their children getting a good education and middle-class jobs unlike their own.

Rich, White Liberals

Unlike most of the other groups of interviewees, both the rich white liberals and the working-class liberals expressed concern about the role of poverty and unemployment in the problems of the inner-city poor. They were generally supportive of government efforts to assist the poor and to alleviate the problems of racism. Many attributed the continued problems with race to the legacy of racial discrimination and prejudice on the part of ignorant and selfish people. Sometimes they had in mind the white working class, sometimes the older generation, but in general they assumed it was other people and not they themselves who still held negative views toward blacks. These interviewees were generally more politically informed about issues than were other interviewees. They were more likely to know something about and generally were supportive of affirmative action, welfare state policies, the use of tax money to help the poor and minorities, and the public policies that provide a social safety net.

When asked whether those who have less economically should be able to expect government help, about half of the rich white liberals said that poor people should expect government help, and several said that it was a moral obligation of society. For example, a physician from New Jersey (C005 NJ F MC) said: "You know, I think a lot of us have done okay because our families have helped us, but there are a lot of people whose families can't help them, or haven't been able to, or just are not there." Similarly, a senior brand manager from New Jersey (D064 NJ F MC) said, when asked whether it is fair to expect government help: "I think that it is a helping like teaching a man to fish. . . . It is helping them to have the tools and the support. . . . Yeah, I believe in helping others. Look at . . . how we live. I don't begrudge paying taxes. . . . I think that we are lucky if you look at our country. We pay less taxes than most people are."

The rich white liberals among the interviewees did not seem to blame blacks for their condition, but instead, they felt that there is a lot of wasted talent among blacks because of their being denied opportunity and because they have not been given the quality of education that is necessary for them to obtain good jobs. The rich white liberal interviewees also talked about the contributions that blacks could make to society, and they generally talked about how much better off everyone would be if the government did more to help the poor. For example, a New Jersey builder (C009 NJ M MC) said: "I would like to see the truly underprivileged . . . the truly lower classes of the country, given a chance and at the same time utilized. They're an asset that we don't use. There's a tremendous amount of brain power . . . that just is left alone." This fellow, however, like other rich white liberal interviewees, indicated that there are no simple solutions and that just giving money is not enough. Rich white liberals did not necessarily attribute the problems of poor people to their character, however, but rather cited the larger structural conditions that they face. For example, a New Jersey government worker (D045 NJ M MC) said:

> I have a tremendous amount of difficulty with this. . . . I was ultra-liberal and have been getting more and more conservative on social issues. . . . Part of that is watching the place where I live be destroyed brick by brick. . . . Intellectually I realize that those poor buggers were the victims of economic forces that were far huger than they were. Newark didn't fall apart simply because they were poor and they moved in. Newark fell apart because of what was going on industrially in this country and things that were happening in the South and things that were happening up here with our manufacturing base. . . . I think the only answer to those problems is when we are all eventually beige. . . . In this country we really should be able to provide health care and decent housing for everyone, but I think that has to come with some personal responsibility.

Similarly, other rich white liberals felt that government help is warranted, but that the recipients have a responsibility to help themselves as well. Unlike the working-class "racists" and some of the other groups who made a similar point, however, the rich white liberals acknowledged that government help should be available during rough economic times for those who are struggling, and they defined the circumstances for which help might be needed much more broadly than did the more conservative respondents. For example, a New Jersey social worker (D042 NJ F MC) explained it this way: "It depends on the situation. . . . I see people that are on welfare and, you know, just got into a bad situation . . . maybe a boyfriend or girlfriend that threw them out on the streets, but have been working . . . people that work from paycheck to paycheck, or either lost their job or lost their housing." These types of circumstances did not draw much sympathy from the working-class "racists" or the religious conservatives.

Like the working-class liberals and unlike the working-class "racists," the majority of the rich white liberal interviewees said that they were concerned about inequality, especially because they thought that the gap is getting wider, and because they felt that there are institutional or structural factors that are maintaining or expanding inequality. For example, a Tennessee government worker (F009 TN M MC) said: "Well, the economic inequality is usually perpetuated. . . . The existing statutes . . . basically give each subsequent generation of the wealthy a far better chance to succeed. . . . I don't really see that big of an improvement in the plight of blacks. . . . There's marginal gains by some, but it's getting worse. It's not getting better." Others pointed to structural conditions that should make inequality a concern. As the New Jersey senior brand manager (D064 NJ F MC) said: "I am just concerned that here we are at this incredible stage in our country where there is just so much opportunity, and there is still the same inequality. If you can't help people now, when are you ever going to be able to help them?. . . The poverty line is how much I spend in two months."

Some of the rich white liberals expressed even graver concerns, because they felt that the current state of inequality could lead to threats to social stability. For example, a research technician in Ohio (B004 OH M MC) said, when asked if he was concerned about inequality: "Yeah . . . that there will be a revolution if it is not taken care of. . . . There's a lot of guns floating around out there. How much can you keep someone under your thumb?" Other interviewees thought that inequality would lead to equally dire consequences. For example, a record producer in Tennessee (G516 TN M MC) said: "The more inequality financially, the more crime you're going to have, the more desperation. I see that as a real threat." An unemployed salesman from New Jersey (D038 NJ M MC) made a similar point: "The wider the difference between the rich and the poor, the more unstable the society gets." It is perhaps noteworthy that these comments were made before the economy took a turn for the worse.

Only a small number of interviewees among the rich white liberals said that they were not concerned about inequality. A New Jersey law firm administrator (C004 NJ M MC) said he was unconcerned because he had traveled to other countries where the extremes of rich and poor were much more pronounced than in the United States. As he said, "At least in America the masses are the middle class." A handful of rich white liberal respondents said that they were not especially concerned about inequality because things have always been this way. For example, a manager of a music store in New Jersey (D006 NJ M MC) said: "There's always going to be the haves and the have-nots, and part of that is also some people are industrious and some people are not. Some people are driven, and some people are not."

The rich white liberals were concerned about people learning to get along with each other, and they wanted their children to live in a world with more harmony. They expressed concern about the role of the United States in the world and to some extent saw problems with racial inequality in the same framework they used for problems in the Third

World and poor countries. These interviewees, however, seemed to be particularly concerned about racial inequality and about the disadvantages suffered by blacks in the United States. Rich white liberals talked about the responsibility of government to provide blacks with a better education, with access to good jobs (through programs like affirmative action), with social support for neighborhoods that may need more resources to provide services to the population, and they expressed their willingness to pay taxes to provide such services to blacks and to the poor. None of the rich white liberal interviewees, however, seemed to recognize that perhaps their own special advantages in life had had some effect on the opportunities available to blacks and to the poor. In other words, there was little if any acknowledgment of the interdependence between their life situations and those of blacks and the poor. (This failure to acknowledge that interdependence is consistent with the views expressed by other interviewees as well, although the other interviewees, unlike the rich white liberals, did not express much sympathy or support for government efforts to help the poor.) Concern for the poor and for racial inequality was evident among rich white liberals despite the fact that they were likely to live in the most segregated communities among the places where my interviewees lived, to work in the most segregated workplaces, and to send their children to the most segregated schools. Some (although not all) of the rich white liberals sent their children to private schools, which were even more exclusive in their composition than the neighborhood schools in the areas where these interviewees lived.

All of the rich white liberals had graduated from college (by definition), and for some, their college experience had been an important step in their coming to see the world from the perspective of a counter-ideology. In addition to their experiences in college, some also had worked in civil rights organizations, had grown up in the 1960s, or had worked in volunteer capacities, such as in soup kitchens, church inner-city programs, and other programs intended to help the poor. A few had grown up in families with left-leaning politics. Only a few of the rich white liberals indicated that their religious views had shaped their political views (unlike the religious conservatives). In general, there was no consistent factor that contributed to the more liberal politics of these interviewees. Even so, both the working-class liberals and the rich white liberals, as well as some of the religious nonconservatives, mentioned the importance in shaping their political views of life experiences that had taken them out of their own neighborhoods and allowed them to see how other people live and to meet them face to face.

Perhaps the most important characteristic of the life histories and current circumstances of the rich white liberal interviewees was that, except for their politics, their own lives had not been very much affected by the civil rights movement, and the exercise or enforcement by the government of civil rights policies had not affected their lives very much one way or the other either. Although most expressed a concern about the need for a better society in which there would be less fear and fewer bad things going on, the lives of most of these interviewees would not be affected if blacks were given more or better opportunities. These interviewees already had educational credentials, and their children (if they had them) were all in (or had graduated from) good primary and secondary schools and would go on to college (or had already completed college). Blacks would not have been in competition with most of them for the jobs they had, and there was not much chance that a lot of blacks would be able to afford to move into their neighborhoods. Although a number of the rich white liberals talked about how much better it would be if we lived and worked in a more diverse environment, there was not much likelihood that their own lives would change in this direction with the enforcement or implementation of government civil rights policies. At least one of the rich white liberal interviewees, however, who was among the most affluent in this group, did send his children to an inner-city high school (and paid to do so) as a personal commitment to diversity and inclusion. His actions were clearly the exception.

Although no one is really in a secure job these days, among the interviewees, the rich white liberals were the ones with the most to offer to the job market, with the most stable work histories, with the least to fear from changes in the economy, and with the most available resources to get themselves through a transition if it arose. Indeed, most of these interviewees had extensive social networks that they could draw upon if they found themselves without a job or needing to change jobs or careers. In many cases, there were two incomes in the household, and there was evidence of extensive involvement in the community and in neighborhood or professional organizations where social capital could be developed and used if necessary. In other words, if the government did more in the area of civil rights and helping the poor, the primary effect on rich white liberals would perhaps be that they would have to pay a higher rate of taxes, but most of these interviewees felt that they could do so without much impact on their current lifestyles. In general, few of these interviewees expressed a concern about the level of taxes that they paid or expressed concern about their ability to meet their financial obligations. Their political attitudes were decidedly liberal, with explicit concern for the poor and for racial minorities.

Thus, on the face of it, the rich white liberal interviewees held political views that contradicted their class interests, but as was perhaps the case with the working-class "racists," psychological factors may have interacted with social structure for them. The political attitudes of the rich white liberals seemed to reflect their wish to view themselves more as positive and helpful people than as a privileged class. As was the case with the other interviewees, there is no evidence to suggest that the opinions they expressed were not genuinely held and a core dimension of their view of themselves. As noted, more so than the other interviewees, the rich white liberals were in favorable economic circumstances, had marketable credentials that provided them with some protection from the vagaries of the market economy, and seemed to be aware of and grateful for their privileges (which they perceived as a combination of blessings, luck, and hard work, as noted in chapter 4). Further, these interviewees expressed views that were consistently liberal. Among the interviewees in this study, there were very few who were as well off as the rich white liberals but did not hold liberal political views.

David Wellman (1993, 224) frames the type of responses expressed here by the rich white liberals as a specific type of "white racism," thus putting the analysis into the negative frame (racism and discrimination) that has been prevalent in much of the research on racial inequality. In his analysis, he argues that middle-class respondents draw boundaries that reinforce their privilege without reference to racial stratification so that they can avoid "thinking of themselves as sons of bitches." The rich white liberal interviewees in this study, however, seemed to embrace the ideas of diversity and multiculturalism, and they expressed a wish for a just and harmonious society. It may very well be that the rich white liberal interviewees, at a psychological level, did not want to be thought of as racists, although their motivations may not have been either conscious or intentional. Their liberal views on racial inequality, however, also seemed consistent with the experimental results of Itesh Sachdev and Richard Bourhis (1991). In their analysis of power and status differences among minority and majority group members of small experimental groups, these authors found that the "dominant high status *majority* group members" (emphasis in the original) engaged in discrimination in the allocation of points in their experimental task, but that they also expressed parity (awarding equal points) toward out-group members (meaning that although they maintained their own advantage, they also provided benefits to those in less advantageous positions). Sachdev and Bourhis (1991, 20) interpret this result as follows: "With the security of strength in numbers within a stable intergroup structure, it seems that dominant high status majorities could afford some 'noblesse oblige' toward subordinated low status minority group members." In the context of this study, this combination of discrimination and parity—in a context of advantage—might reflect gaining an inside edge through opportunity hoarding and the use of social capital while at the same time advocating for equal opportunity and support for civil rights policies.

In this regard, the rich white liberal interviewees expressed dismay at the racism of other people ("those racists") and clearly expressed views that were politically liberal and in support of civil rights legislation and policy, but they did so, it seems, from a position in which, more so than other interviewees, they could "afford to be generous." Wellman (1993, 51–52) makes a similar point in his analysis: "Tolerance is not simply an attribute middle-class people learn; it is also a luxury they can afford. . . . The people scoring highest on scales purporting to measure 'prointegration' sentiments are economically the most secure; they are the people least affected by policies directed at minimizing racial inequality." Although I did not in my interviews find that the rich white liberals defended or provided a rationale for the status quo, nevertheless, their comments often implied that the change that was needed had to begin with others (for example, "those racists," often meaning the white working class). The rich white liberals did not, for the most part, suggest the need for changes in their own approach to "getting ahead" or "gaining advantage."

The rich white liberals were more affluent and had a more positive view of their economic circumstances than was true of most of the other interviewees. The rich white liberals also had the highest level of education, often professional degrees, and brought the most skills to the labor market when they needed to find new jobs. Most expressed a belief in both personal and government responsibility for providing a social safety net, and they felt that their tax dollars and government policies should address the needs of the less fortunate. They did not, however, make a direct link between their good fortune and the less favorable circumstances of the poor, nor did they take note of how their own use of social capital and their opportunity hoarding may have affected the lives of others.

In a sense, the rich white liberals were "generous" in their views of the poor and racial minorities and the wish they expressed that there would be less inequality and less exclusion. Further, they wished that "those racists" would cause less conflict and be more welcoming to racial and ethnic minorities. To some extent the political views of the rich white liberals contradicted their class position, in that they held liberal views that often supported redistribution, presumably from the rich to the poor. Their views, however, were consistent with the national trend of more professionals moving from Republican to Democratic affiliations, often because of displeasure with the increasingly right-wing politics fostered by the Republican Party as it has been captured by the right and become less welcoming to moderates (Brooks and Manza 1997). In summary, rich white liberals adopted a politics of liberalism that presumably made them feel like they were part of the solution to the problems of racial inequality, but in a context in which they were probably more removed than most others from any substantive effects of potential enforcement of civil rights policies.

Conclusions

In this chapter, I have tried to provide a profile of each of the sociopolitical groups in the study and to outline how their politics were influenced by their structural position with regard to the labor market and by the impact of the civil rights movement (or more specifically, government policies that support civil rights) on their ability to gain access to good jobs that pay a living wage and provide benefits. For many of these interviewees, the changes in the global economy and the neoliberal policies that undermine institutional protections from the vagaries of the market have had a dramatic effect on their job prospects. It is important to keep in mind, however, that the influences on the politics of these various groups are not only structural. Although structural position affects each group's access to resources, social capital, and institutional privileges, psychological and cultural influences play a role as well. Thus, there are variations in the politics of the groups in this study and in the country at large that seem incompatible with class position more narrowly defined. For example, many people tend to expect that the working class will support the Democratic Party and hold liberal political views because of their economic position, but as is evident in the remarks of the interviewees in this study, that assumption may not always be correct. Right-wing populism is just as likely a result of the political activism of the white working class as left-wing populism, and that seems to have been especially the case since the Wallace campaigns, which appealed to the white working class on the basis of race (although sometimes in the guise of states' rights or morality) (Levison 2012; Teixeira and Halpin 2011). The Republican Party has been relatively successful in gaining support from the white working class when it has been able to introduce racial politics, albeit implicitly, into political campaigns. There are also psychological and cultural dimensions that may influence these responses. To the extent that the white working class needs to encourage its members to stick with unpleasant, dangerous, and low-wage jobs, rather than escape into drugs, alcohol, profligacy, or vagrancy, working-class culture has featured a strong theme of the need for individual responsibility, hard work, and persistence.

The movement of professionals and more highly educated workers into the Democratic Party also seems to contradict the expected influence of class. Although there is still a positive correlation between both education and income and voting for the Republican Party, this association has been modified to some extent with the growing identification of professionals with the Democratic Party. That seeming contradiction is evident in the views expressed by the interviewees in this study as well. Liberals were a minority in the sample of interviewees (as they are in the white electorate in general), and those whose views were most liberal among the interviewees were those who were doing better economically than their counterparts, among both college- and non-college-educated respondents. Those whose own social position is more secure may have a strong psychological incentive to affirm egalitarian principles that seem to support social justice. As Sachdev and Bourhis (1991) found in their experimental studies, the dominant, majority, and high-status group may be in a position to be generous—and may have a psychological motivation for being so—with regard to those in less favorable circumstances.

Party Competition for the White Vote

In the context of post–civil rights politics, various segments of white voters have been targeted by the two major political parties, including the white working class, professionals, white Protestant fundamentalists (or evangelicals), and "independents." Gaining an understanding of how the politics of white Americans is influenced by their views of racial inequality speaks to the expectations that Myrdal (1944) outlined when he suggested that at least some whites would be moved by the growing attention to the incompatibility of racial inequality with the American creed and thus would be moved to support social movements for political change. Although some did so, whites as a group have been more conservative in their political views, and only occasionally and only for some groups (seemingly those who are most secure in their economic and social positions) have they actively supported the movements for social change and racial justice. Understanding the contest for the support of various groups of white voters by the two major political parties helps explain why civil rights have been more about principles than policies and why some whites have been much less willing to support racial equality than Myrdal would have expected.

The White Working Class The white working class shows up in several of the groups that we have identified on the basis of their politics. The working-class "racists" were among the most politically aware and the most animated of the various groups (and thus, were also among those likely to be more politically active), and on issues of public policy intended to bring about greater equality, they were among the most conservative. Although the comments of the working-class "racists" suggested that they would be easily mobilized on the basis of class issues that supported their right to good working-class jobs protected from the market, they were extremely antagonistic about issues of race. They also seemed to be angry with the Democratic Party for its support of civil rights, which they seemed to feel was directed at them and came at their expense. For working-class "racists," there seemed to be a direct trade-off between civil rights and labor rights. They felt that the attention to civil rights undermined their claim to labor rights. Unless the Democratic Party is able to bridge the race-versus-class tensions that have so animated this group, it is unlikely that Democrats will gain the support of the working-class "racists" in future elections. The recent efforts of the Republican Party to directly undermine union rights and protections, however, might shift this group back into the Democratic coalition. Although some members of this segment of the white working class had voted Republican in the post–civil rights period, others may not have voted at all because of their sense of betrayal by both parties.

About one-third of the interviewees from the religious conservative group were members of the working class, and of course, they were also among the most conservative politically on a range of issues dealing with inequality. Almost all of the interviewees in this category were from either Tennessee (about half) or Ohio (almost half), with just a small number from New Jersey. Given that these interviewees strongly identified with their churches and with the interpretations of the Bible that have tied conservative politics to fundamentalist or evangelical religion, it is unlikely that the Democratic Party is going to have much influence with these working-class voters unless something dramatic changes in the political landscape. The other large segment of the white working class in this study is found in the apolitical majority group, which is about half working-class. The main characteristic of this group is that they were not very involved politically and did not care much about politics, but when they were asked to express their views and they took time to think about it, they tended to give conservative rather than moderate or liberal responses. Although the Democratic Party might be able to mobilize this group, to engage them would require overcoming what seemed to be a natural inclination toward more conservative views. Either party would also have to capture their attention—most working-class members of the apolitical majority either were not especially interested in politics or did not have clear policy preferences. It is likely that members of this group would become more interested in political issues in the midst of a national crisis, but of course, the conservative tendencies of the group might also be heightened under those circumstances.

The religious nonconservatives and the working-class liberals were small groups within the study. About one-third of the religious nonconservatives were working-class, many were from Tennessee, and most defined their politics as moderate. Although they expressed somewhat more liberal views on some of the issues that we have discussed in this book, their views on affirmative action–type policies were more like those of the conservatives than the liberals, especially with regard to the changes in access to education and jobs for African Americans and immigrants. The working-class liberal interviewees expressed consistently liberal views on policy issues, including on affirmative action policies (although not with regard to immigrants), but this group was also only a small proportion of the working class (only about 6 percent in this study). They may have been reliable members of the Democratic coalition, but they seemed to function more as individuals than as engaged members of unions or working-class organizations. The interviewees in this study who fell into this category were self-employed, service workers, or semi-professionals. None were factory workers, and few were likely to be union members.

To the extent that the interviewees in this study represented the range of potential voters within the white working class, the Democratic Party is clearly at a disadvantage. Unless the Democrats can bridge the race-versus-class issues and perhaps the religious and secular orientations that are salient to these members of the white working class, these potential voters are likely to remain unreliable members of the Democratic coalition, as they have been since the Democratic Party embraced the civil rights movement.

White Religious Conservatives Another group that has been important in post–civil rights politics is conservative Christians. White Protestant traditionalists have become the core of the Republican Party since the mobilization of the Christian Right by the New Right (Green 2000). Those influences are reflected in the comments of interviewees in this study: 80 percent of those with a strong religious identity expressed conservative politics that included strong antigovernment rhetoric. (I did not include Catholics or Jews in the religious conservative group because the Religious Right has been politically significant among Protestants. Further, very few Catholic or Jewish interviewees talked about their self-identities in ways that highlighted their religious convictions.) As noted, most of the religiously identified interviewees in this study were from the South (Tennessee) or the Midwest (Ohio), but even the few religious conservatives in this study from New Jersey talked the same way about both religion and politics as those from Tennessee and Ohio. The fact that the social and political views expressed by the religious conservative interviewees were so distinctive suggests that their churches have been incorporated into the political movement fostered by the Religious Right, either formally or informally. For example, the view expressed by some of the interviewees that God is against welfare dependency, or that the Bible says that we should teach poor people to fish rather than provide them with fish, seemed to have been shaped by the existing political movement from the right. Such views do not reflect traditional Protestant theology with regard to the poor. The religious nonconservatives constituted only about 20 percent of the religiously identified interviewees in this study, and their politics were moderate rather than liberal.

Their views on affirmative action policies, however, were more consistent with the views of the more conservative groups than the more liberal ones. Thus, to the extent that the religious conservative interviewees reflected the types of views of the conservative religious movement, they are not likely prospects for the Democratic Party in the near future. The religious nonconservatives were less predictable with regard to party politics, but it seems from the views expressed here that their political affiliations depend on the issues that are salient at the time of a given election.

Professionals and the Democratic Party Consistent with recent research on trends in political attitudes, I also found that the most consistently liberal interviewees in my study were the rich white liberals. The members of this group were college-educated, many with advanced degrees. This group was more affluent than the others, as might be expected given their occupational roles, and most of them lived in upscale suburbs with good school systems, public services, and community amenities. Before the civil rights movement, many of these types of interviewees would have been Republican by class position, but in the post–civil rights period, they have been moving increasingly into the Democratic Party. Some evidence suggests that the change in party identification among professionals is partly a reaction to the growing influence within the Republican Party of religious conservatives (Bolce and De Maio 1999a, b). Across a range of issues, the politics of the rich white liberals were liberal, their views were tolerant, and their explanations were more structuralist than those of the other interviewees (in common with the working-class liberals on most issues). This group of voters has become an essential part of the new Democratic coalition, but they seem to be concerned more with social issues (especially civil rights) than with economic ones. Because their class interests and their political interests do not seem to coalesce, the Democratic Party could lose them to third-party appeals if the political compromises made to put together a political majority undermine the sense that the Democratic Party is remaining true to their political interests.

The middle-class conservatives also had college degrees (by definition), but in this sample, they were less economically affluent than the rich white liberals. They were mostly in lower-level white-collar jobs, and some were unemployed or out of the labor force. Their views on political issues were consistently conservative, and they seemed to be especially antagonistic toward nonwhites and toward changes to traditional hierarchies. Based on the views that they expressed, it is highly unlikely that they would join the rich white liberals and support the Democratic Party. Two-thirds of the religious conservatives were also college-educated, but as noted, their politics were firmly conservative and shaped by a political movement that had contributed to conservative interpretations of their religious views. Similarly, about two-thirds of the religious nonconservatives were college-educated, and they defined their politics as moderate. However, they were a much smaller group among the religiously identified in this study.

Independents and the Disengaged The other college-educated interviewees in this study included slightly less than half of the apolitical majority interviewees. The main characteristic of this group was a lack of interest in politics, but when asked for their opinions and given time to think about them, they tended more toward conservative than toward liberal views. It is among the apolitical majority that "independents" are likely to be found. These were the interviewees (and possibly potential voters) who did not have firm views about public policy issues, who did not spend a lot of time thinking about politics, and who did not think politics were very important to their everyday lives. It may be that they could be mobilized by the Democratic Party if the issues could be framed in ways that seem especially to affect family and community life; however, these interviewees seemed to reflect center-right more than center-left politics. Indeed, more former Republicans are numbered among independents in the United States today than former Democrats, and they tend to lean more Republican than Democratic in their political views (Kohut 2009). In this regard, the apolitical majority interviewees in this study were consistent with the profile of independents among the white population based on recent analyses.

The White Vote in Party Politics The rather pessimistic outlook suggested by this analysis for the possibility of the Democratic Party gaining white votes should not, of course, be surprising given that the Democratic Party has not gained a majority of the white vote since 1964. Before that, Democrats had last won a majority of the white vote in 1948. They also received a majority of the male vote in the post–World War II period only in 1948, 1960, 1964, and 1976. Thus, for the Democratic Party to win presidential elections, it must obtain enough of the white vote that when combined with the minority vote (and enough of the male vote so that when combined with the female vote), it can gain a majority. The analysis in this chapter underlines the Democratic Party's dilemma: it can only win when it is able to form a biracial coalition, and it is likely to be successful in doing so only if it can bridge the race-versus-class tensions that have existed in American politics since the beginning. If the Democratic Party attends too openly to black interests, it may lose more white votes than it gains from blacks, but if it gives insufficient attention to black interests, it may fail to get the strong turnout among nonwhite voters that is required for a winning coalition. The Republican Party, equally aware of these challenges, has fostered policies to undermine the political strength of groups that have tended to vote Democratic or to make it more difficult for them to vote.

These tensions have also affected the internal dynamics of the Democratic Party, making it hard to hold together a coalition of groups that perceive their interests and values to be at odds. As discussed in chapter 5, since the advent of the civil rights movement the Democratic Party has been divided between those who want to highlight the commitment to civil rights and those who want to reinforce the commitment to New Deal principles, which address primarily class interests. This division has been evident even within the white electorate and appears to be manifest in the attitudes expressed by the interviewees in this study as well. The rich white liberals believed that racism is perpetuated by groups like the working-class "racists" and the religious conservatives, while the working-class "racists" felt that groups like the rich white liberals have supported policies that undermine their interests. The religious conservatives, to the extent that they had been influenced by the politics of civil rights in the transformation of the South, saw rich white liberals, especially those from the coasts, as threatening their control of the levers of power and privilege within their communities. In the vernacular, they were concerned with maintaining the "Southern way of life."

The Democratic Party has tried at various times in the post–civil rights period to solve this inherent conflict between labor rights (based on class politics, whether in the form of New Deal politics or New Class politics) and civil rights (based on racial politics), but has failed to do so. This has made it difficult for the party to form the biracial coalition that is necessary for it to win elections, especially at the presidential level. In order to win, the Democratic Party must bridge the conflicting interests based on race (civil rights) and those based on class (labor rights). This tension remains within the Democratic Party and was evident in the hostile relations between the campaigns of Hillary Clinton—who represented the New Class or "third way" focus, mixed with an appeal to New Deal politics—and of Barack Obama, who represented the civil rights and social agenda of the party. The fact that Barack Obama has been criticized as a centrist since his election is partly a reflection of this same tension. He has tended to practice the New Class or third way type of politics rather than a politics based on a firm commitment to civil rights and social issues, as hoped for by the left wing of the Democratic coalition.

Although the majority of whites claim to support the civil rights movement and equal opportunity as a solution to discrimination, the uncertainties of the labor market and the constant competitive pressures to lower wages and erode job security have contributed to strategies of seeking unequal opportunity through opportunity hoarding and helping protect friends and family members from the market by giving them an inside edge to secure good jobs.[2] In the post–civil rights period, whites have helped each other, and that is how racial inequality is reproduced, despite the supposed legal protections that have been put in place to end discrimination. Whites do not have to actively discriminate against blacks or other nonwhites. They just have to actively provide information, influence, and job opportunities to other whites. In doing so, they can believe that they are against discrimination and supportive of civil rights. By acting positively toward other whites rather than negatively toward blacks (or other nonwhites), they avoid the moral dilemma that Myrdal thought would motivate changes in American politics. There have clearly been changes in the post–civil rights period, and yet racial inequality is still reproduced. In the current political landscape, racial inequality is reproduced even without the efforts of any (or hardly any) racists.

In the next chapters, I look more specifically at the interviewees' views on a number of key policy issues: taxes, welfare, affirmative action, and immigration. Again, the interviewees were divided in their views on these policy issues, and to some extent there were regional differences between them. Surprisingly, interviewees' opinions about taxes were less predictable than might be expected given the rhetoric that often emerges in contemporary politics, while their views on welfare depended on the political views of each group. Both the more conservative groups and the apolitical ones were fairly uniform in their opposition to affirmative action policies (although they often could not even name the policy, let alone explain its components). Across the sociopolitical groups, most were ambivalent at best and often antagonistic toward the issue of immigration. The liberals and conservatives among the interviewees had predictable views, but importantly, the moderates were more likely than not to side with the conservatives when they were asked to express an opinion. To understand the policy views and political implications of various segments of the white electorate, it is necessary to disentangle the complexities that underlie the thinking of white voters like the ones in this study. That is the topic of the next two chapters.

Chapter 7

Government, Taxes, and Welfare

[Do you think that people like you get what you deserve from the government?]

> Homemaker from New Jersey (D075 NJ F MC): "Why should I be getting anything? Well, we have roads, and we have health services, and Social Security, and education, all the pollution stuff. What else does the federal government do? Oh, the Army. We sort of pushed the Army down the drain. The Army, the Navy, and Air Force, that is very important, and I think there should be more emphasis on that. . . . but I think there is a lot of unnecessary spending."

> Commercial artist from Tennessee (G519 TN M WC): "I pay taxes. There's roads. I'm safe from foreign threats. There's agencies that make sure that there is quality in the food that I eat and the drugs that I take, that the airplanes are operating safely. I have a real problem with people who complain about taxes, because it is as if they think they are getting nothing for their money. . . . So I don't have a lot of sympathy for people who complain that their money is being spent or wasted. It is not being wasted. . . . Overall, you get what you pay for."

These interviewees were almost unique in recognizing that government provides a wide range of services, although the New Jersey homemaker's acknowledgment of this fact was something of an afterthought. The Tennessee commercial artist was especially cognizant of the services that government provides because he had moved from a Northern state to the South and was surprised at how much poorer the service levels were in the Southern state, where he paid lower taxes. In contrast to these two interviewees, many others claimed that they received "nothing" from government. The prevalent antigovernment sentiments expressed by most interviewees represent the one major exception to political attitudes that otherwise have not changed much in the last half-century (DiMaggio 2003; DiMaggio, Evans, and Bryson 1996; Fiorina, Abrams, and Pope 2006; Kohut 2010). Americans have dramatically changed their views about government (Kohut 2010; Teixeira and Rogers 2000).

Figure 7.1 Changes in Public Trust in Government, 1958 to 2010

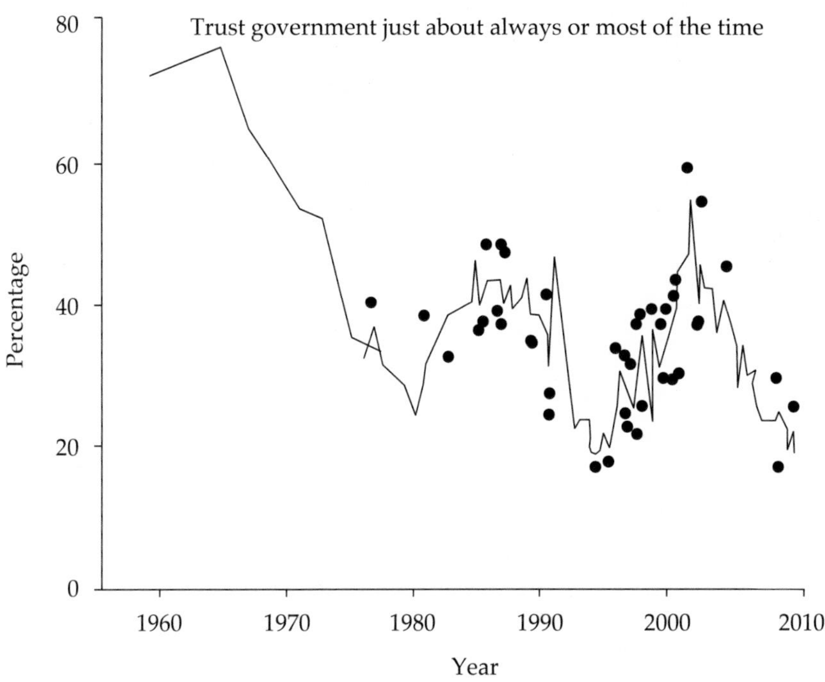

Source: "Distrust, Discontent, Anger, and Partisan Rancor: The People and Their Government," The Pew Research Center for The People & The Press, April 18, 2010, p. 5.
Trend sources: Pew Research Center, National Election Studies, Gallup, ABC/*Washington Post*, CBS/*New York Times*, and CNN Polls.
Note: From 1976 to 2010, the trend line represents a three-survey moving average, with individual data points shown.

Based on national data, the proportion of Americans who said that they trusted the government most of the time dropped from 70 percent in 1958 to only about 20 percent by 2010 (Pew Research Center 2010; see figure 7.1 for a graphic representation of this change). As with all political attitudes, however, the views of government of the interviewees in this study were neither straightforward nor easy to interpret. In this chapter, I provide an overview of interviewee views about government, taxes, and welfare (in each case, getting at these issues somewhat indirectly). In the next chapter, I discuss their views of affirmative action and immigration.

The views expressed by the interviewees in this study followed a predictable pattern. The working-class "racists" and the religious conservatives were critical of government policies in general, expressed more displeasure with the taxes that they paid, and were anti-welfare. On the other end of the spectrum, rich white liberals and working-class liberals were more favorable about government, less concerned about taxes, and more supportive of welfare policies. The religious nonconservatives were generally mixed in their views, leaning either toward a more conservative or more liberal view depending on the issue. Importantly, the middle-class conservatives and the apolitical majority frequently expressed views similar to those of working-class "racists" and religious conservatives, in substance if not in tone. The interviewees as a whole tended toward the conservative side of the political ledger, while the interviewees expressing liberal views were in the minority.

Despite these predictable political differences, the situation is not quite as simple as it may seem. The hold of the dominant ideology on all of the interviewees was so strong that their political views have to be framed within this context (Kluegel and Smith 1986). That is, the beliefs that economic opportunity is available for all, that success depends on individual effort and hard work, and that inequality is an acceptable outcome of a capitalist system overlay the interviewees' views about specific policies. Further, the ambiguities and complexities in how the interviewees expressed their understanding of political issues make interpreting whether they supported or opposed a given policy not quite straightforward.

Even responses to a simple question about whether the interviewees had gotten what they deserved from "government" were not straightforward. The interviewees tended to have a very restrictive view of the meaning of "government," often reducing "government" to transfer payments and more specifically to welfare or other kinds of income subsidies. Thus, if the respondent was not currently receiving welfare or perhaps unemployment insurance, he or she might claim to be receiving "nothing" from government. Although a majority of interviewees indicated that they did get what they deserved from government, many interviewees said that they did not receive anything, did not want anything, did not need anything, and did not expect anything from government. They further said that they would like for government to leave them alone or to get out of their lives. Some also said that they thought others should not get anything from government either. The contradiction between the notion that government provides "nothing" and the expectation as well as the reality that all interviewees received substantial government services is consistent with the view expressed by a participant at a recent political rally who reportedly said to his congressman, "Keep your government hands off of my Medicare" (Krugman 2009). The respondents in this study did not think of the many public services that were necessary in their lives as "government." Services provided by the federal government were certainly invisible to many, but so were the services provided by states and sometimes by local communities as well. Thus, to understand how the interviewees thought about inequality and fairness, especially with regard to racial inequality, we must first understand their very restrictive views of government.

Although the Republican Party has made the mandate of lower taxes and smaller government a constant theme in its political rhetoric over the last several decades, there was limited understanding among most interviewees of how taxes work and the purposes for which they are used. Not only are the services provided by government often invisible, but the interviewees also seemed to be unaware of the relationship between the taxes they paid and the services they received. For example, many interviewees expressed the view that their taxes were too high or that they paid more than their fair share of taxes, and yet they also suggested that the government (unspecified by level) should provide more money for schools, medical care, or local services, or more money to offset local taxes, and that government should have been available to help them when they had needs or were struggling at various times in their lives. Thus, while many interviewees said that their taxes were too high, at the same time they did not want any of their services reduced, and often they wanted services extended or expanded. A number of respondents explained away this seeming inconsistency by claiming that there is so much "waste" in government and expressing their confidence that if government would just allocate their funds better and cut unnecessary spending, there would be sufficient funds to cover the needs they deemed of personal importance.

Despite these views, the interviewees did not necessarily suggest that taxes were a major concern for them. For example, when asked if they would be better off if poor people did not make so many demands on the government, the majority of the interviewees said that it would not affect them much one way or the other. So, despite the often animated attention in the news media to the issue of taxes, the interviewees in this study—even while expressing a wish to pay lower taxes—did not suggest much concern about the need for their taxes to be cut or for government priorities to be reorganized.

Interviewees' views about government and taxes depended, however, on whom they thought of as the recipients of government programs or resources. In general, race was a subtext in many of their views (Gilens 1999; Mendelberg 2001). To get more directly at this issue, I also report in this chapter on the interviewee explanations for the problems in the inner city. As expected, this question invoked more explicitly racial comments, which can be contrasted with the interviewees' more general comments when asked questions about government and taxes that had no specific racial content. The responses revealed that more conservative interviewees opposed any programs that they believed were for the benefit of blacks or other racial minorities. In contrast, the more liberal interviewees were more likely to indicate that such programs are needed, and they were generally more supportive of government efforts to provide a social safety net, including, or perhaps especially, a safety net for race and ethnic minorities.

The interviewee responses on government, taxes, and welfare suggest several things. First, for most of the interviewees, government-provided services were invisible and rarely came to mind when they thought about what they got for their taxes. Further, many interviewees said that their taxes were too high and that they did not get much in return. Yet there was a surprising nonchalance among many interviewees about whether they would be better off if poor people made fewer demands on the government. This juxtaposition suggests that the interviewees' views of government were framed by the ideology of contemporary politics and not necessarily rooted in facts or specific knowledge. Second, the strongest negative sentiments regarding government and taxes seemed to be attached to policies thought to target or primarily benefit racial and ethnic minorities. Thus, this chapter provides evidence that post–civil rights politics is shaped largely by race relations, and as I argue elsewhere in the book, this is because of the effects of civil rights policies on the ever-present competition for jobs. Those whose access to jobs protected from the market is most threatened by the enforcement of civil rights policies are the most antagonistic toward government, especially when those policies are thought to provide greater access and benefits to racial minorities. Those who are least likely to be affected in their own job opportunities by the implementation of civil rights policies are more likely to support liberal social policies on race and, in some cases, to become strong advocates for civil rights.

Do You Get What You Deserve from the Government?

Overall, the interviewees expressed generally negative views of government. In their comments, a number of the interviewees seemed to portray government almost as an enemy, or at best a necessary evil. In the context of the heightened patriotism, often ethnocentrism, expressed by many of the interviewees, this very negative view of government is especially unexpected. Few of the interviewees saw government as a representative of the people acting on their collective behalf and providing a foundation for civil life. Instead, government was seen as an entity that takes their hard-earned money away from them, wastes it on often frivolous and unnecessary extravagances, and gives them little of value in return. Therefore, many of the interviewees expressed the wish for government to be kept at bay, to be limited in scope, and to be cut down in size. With many of the interviewees thinking of government only with regard to transfer payments or direct subsidies rather than in terms of the array of services provided at different levels, it perhaps is no wonder that so many of them thought of government as a net-drain on their resources rather than as a net-positive. The important question, of course, is why and how such an image of government became prevalent in the minds of so many American citizens. I believe that it happened because of the efforts to enforce civil rights policies.

In general, the more conservative respondents were critical of government, more concerned about their taxes, and seemingly disgruntled about what they perceived to be waste and misdirection on the part of government. In general, the more liberal respondents (a minority of the total) recognized the services they received from the government and were more favorable, although a few would have preferred that government reorder its priorities, and others felt that government was not a major factor in their lives. The interviewees, across the political spectrum, had a limited view of what government is and what it should do. Table 7.1 provides a summary of the responses to questions about getting what is deserved from government and about whether the respondents felt they would be better off if poor people made fewer demands on government. I order the responses from the most conservative to the most liberal groups.

Working-Class "Racists"

Given the adverse economic circumstances that many of the working-class "racists" perceived in their lives, it is not surprising that over two-thirds of them said that they did not get what they deserved from the government. Some interviewees had very little to say about this issue, but most of the working-class "racist" interviewees were animated about it. For example, a New Jersey policeman (C010 NJ M WC) said: "I think the government gives too many things. People shouldn't be looking for these things from the government. . . . I think that when assistance became an entitlement, that that's where we started to have problems. . . . We've lost a perspective in America on what poverty is." Similarly, an Ohio salesman (E310 OH M WC) said: "I think we're getting quite a few things we don't want, and most importantly, we're getting too big a bill for it." A Tennessee graphic designer (G530 TN M WC) expressed this view more emphatically:

> What I think we deserve from the government is not much. I don't need the government to help me. Just let me make my own way. The biggest thing I want the government to do is stay out of my life. Keep our military up in case of war. Make sure there are some roads built, and that is pretty much their job. I don't like them coming in taking away rights. . . . Stay out

Table 7.1 Coded Responses of Socioeconomic Groups to Questions Regarding Public Policy Issues

Dimension	Working-Class Racists	Middle-Class Conservatives	Religious Conservatives	Apolitical Majority	Religious Nonconservatives	Working-Class Liberals	Rich White Liberals	Total
Percentage of sample	12%	4.5%	19%	37%	4.5%	6%	17%	100%
								Average
Get what is deserved from government[a]								
No	69	78	38	39	27	21	25	42
Maybe	0	0	9	9	9	21	19	10
Yes	31	22	53	52	64	57	56	48
Total								100
Better off[b]								
No	41	67	31	54	64	70	70	57
Maybe	26	11	28	22	9	10	8	16
Yes	33	22	41	24	27	20	22	27
Total								100

Source: Author's compilation.
Notes: Responses may not add up to 100 because of rounding error.
[a]Coded responses to question: "Do you think that people like you get what you deserve from the government?" with follow-up, "And why would you say that is the case?"
[b]Coded responses to question: "Do you think that people like you would be better off if some groups did not make so many demands on the government?" with follow-up, "And why would you say that is the case?"

> of the normal person's life. . . . I just see a slow trend toward, really socialism. . . . They are basically telling us you are not smart enough to handle your own money or to get your own job or to do anything on your own.

A New Jersey woman who earned a living as a real estate owner (D056 NJ F WC) summarized what many working-class "racists" expressed: "We don't ask anything from the government, and we never have gotten anything from the government."

Despite the generally unfavorable views of government expressed by the working-class "racists," a number mentioned services that they would have liked for the government to provide, even though they said that their taxes were too high and that they thought they should pay less. Some called attention specifically to their local school system, for which they felt that the government should provide more support. Surprisingly, the area that seemed to receive the most attention and support was government-provided or -supported health care. But the interviewees who mentioned it assumed that the taxes they were already paying should be sufficient to cover health care services. An Ohio welder (B018 OH M WC), for example, said: "I think people like us deserve national hospitalization and get taken care of just as good as some politician that drops over and gets taken to the hospital, and they spend millions of dollars to keep the guy going." Another Ohio interviewee, a self-employed truck driver (E339 OH M WC), claimed: "I think the government should do away with the medical monopoly. . . . I think that the U.S. should go to a socialist type . . . where the day you're born, you have insurance. . . . Nobody would ever have to go without medical attention." Another Ohio interviewee (E354 OH M WC), who was self-employed in a landscape business, thought that health care should be made available: "I'm not saying that the government should be providing it. I think that the government should have some type of program set up through these insurance companies, that the insurance company can classify us as a group and give us a group discount." Similarly, a New Jersey waitress (D028 NJ F WC) expressed concern about the issue:

> You know, my main importance is health care. I really don't have anything. . . . I really think we have to have a universal health care system. And somebody better decide to sit down and figure this the hell out. They figured out how to do everything else out there. . . . Why can't they figure this health care problem out is beyond me.

Thus, like a number of the other respondents, many of the working-class "racists" expressed negative views of government and claimed that they got "nothing" from government. These interviewees rarely thought about the services that they undoubtedly received in their neighborhoods or as part of society (such as police and fire protection, education, transportation, parks and recreation, and emergency services). They felt that their taxes were too high and that they should be able to pay less, but they also felt that there should be more government funding available—for example, for schools and especially for medical care. And to the extent that they gave consideration to how to pay for it, they assumed that their current taxes should be able to cover it.

Middle-Class Conservatives

Most of the middle-class conservatives said that they did not get what they deserved from the government. Like some of the other interviewees, many said that they got nothing from the government and that they did not want anything. They claimed that their taxes were too high and that there was too much waste. For example, an Ohio interviewee (E327 OH F MC), a part-time college instructor, said: "I don't know that I deserve anything from the government. . . . We feel that you should work for what you get, and so we've never asked for anything. . . . I'd rather get the government out of my life." A New Jersey small-business owner (D030 NJ M MC) concurred: "No way. I get nothing from the government. I just pay taxes. . . . I couldn't even get a scholarship or anything or financial aid, because, you know, my parents made too much money." The invisibility of government services was pervasive among many of the interviewees: A New Jersey marketing manager (D073 NJ M MC) said: "What do I get from the government? Taxes? You know what, that's a great question. I don't know what I get from the government. I really don't."

Religious Conservatives

Surprisingly, the religious conservative interviewees were not as exercised about the issue of government as the middle-class conservatives or the working-class "racists." The majority of the religious conservatives said that they did get what they deserved from government, albeit often because they said that they did not want anything. Most said that government should be limited in scope and involvement in the lives of the citizenry. For example, an Ohio graphic designer (E361 OH M WC) said succinctly: "I expect nothing. I get nothing." A Tennessee woman (G527 TN F MC), employed as an essential materials specialist, ultimately said that she got what she deserved from government, but she was not especially pleased with the situation:

> I don't expect much crap from the government anymore. . . . I guess we all have a right to expect military protection, roads, schools, whatever. . . . The

> quality of the things that we get from the government is such that we can't expect much of anything, those of us who work for what we have. If you don't work for anything, then you know, then you would get everything from the government.

An Ohio interviewee (B009 OH F WC), a practical nurse, made a similar comment: "I don't know that [the working class is] getting anything from the government as far as that goes. . . . It's the people that don't do anything that get too much from the government that I see."

An Ohio quality control manager (B002 OH M MC) indicated that he was happy when Congress was less able to act because of divided government: "I believe in less government is better government. . . . I guess I don't really see the government playing a big role in my life." A Tennessee manager (F065 TN M MC) claimed that the Constitution should define what government does: "I'm not sure what I deserve from the government other than a few basic things that the Constitution grants me. . . . I'm certainly not getting my bang for the buck in terms of what I'm giving them." An Ohio letter carrier (E326 OH M WC) was similarly concerned about government overreaching: "I think it's too much control. Too many laws. Too much litigation. . . . Government's only supposed to be there [for] national security. . . . Sometimes I think it's becoming almost like big brother. . . . We don't need all this excessive stuff. . . . Half the time, they don't even know what's going on." A New Jersey primary school music teacher (D046 NJ F MC) may have best expressed the overall perspective of the religious conservatives about the issue of government: "I think most Christians don't expect from the government, 'cause that is what the Bible teaches us . . . to rely on God and also do it yourself. He gives you the talent to do so. Render unto Caesar what are Caesar's."

Apolitical Majority

About half of the apolitical majority interviewees felt that services are available, they were doing okay, and they did not want much from government at any rate. In contrast, some felt that they were not getting much of anything, that there is too much waste, that taxes are too high, and that people need to take care of themselves rather than depend on the government. Even those who responded positively to the question put limits on how they thought about government. For example, a Tennessee librarian (G506 TN F MC) said: "Yeah, I have the right to vote. I have the right to protest. . . . Most of the men that are in there have an agenda. What we have to do is watch them. . . . But I think we're still free." A Tennessee man (G517 TN M MC), a musician, raised the issue of political voice: "Yeah. I pay my fair share, and I don't ask for anything in return. . . . I would like . . . a little bit more of a voice than one vote. I think if I could impose the will of not wanting the government to waste my valuable tax dollars." An Ohio billing clerk (D036 NJ F MC) thought that rights were all that she was getting from the government: "Yes. I am getting the rights America is granted. I'm not getting anything more than that, 'cause I haven't been on unemployment for a couple of years."

A number of the interviewees disavowed any interest in handouts, and many claimed that they did not get anything from government and did not want anything, even when they indicated that they got what they deserved. For example, an Ohio insurance office manager (E335 OH F WC) said: "Yes, because I don't want the government to take care of everybody. I think everybody should take care of themselves, and we would be fine." Another Ohio interviewee (E357 OH M MC), a dentist, made a similar point: "I'm getting nothing from the government, but I don't expect anything from the government." Thus, even among the apolitical majority interviewees who said that they did get what they deserved from the government, they often said this because they also said they did not want anything. The few who recognized that they enjoyed the benefits of some government services still had a fairly limited view of what those services were and what it took to provide them.

Those interviewees among the apolitical majority who said that they did not get what they deserved from the government rarely acknowledged the services that government provides and often claimed that their tax dollars were wasted or spent on the wrong priorities. For example, a part-time postal worker from Ohio (B015 OH F WC) said: "I think the government takes a lot and wastes it. . . . I think they could do a lot better if they tried." Several of the interviewees said that they did not get much of anything from the government, but at the same time they identified areas where they thought the government should provide benefits for them. An Ohio door-to-door advertising manager (E302 OH F WC) mentioned the need for government help with schools: "Oh, I don't know if I'm getting anything in particular from the government. I keep giving them my money, and I don't know what I'm getting back for it. . . . I think the government needs to come in and help out with [schools]. The schools are in terrible shape." Another interviewee, an Ohio auto mechanic (E343 OH M WC), raised the issue of Social Security: "Not sure that we're getting a lot from government. As far as, let's take Social Security for instance. I strongly believe that it's not going to be there for me. It's up to me to take care of me." And another interviewee, an Ohio factory worker (E307 OH M WC), mentioned health care: "I don't want too much from the government. Yeah, I'm okay. . . . The big threat ahead of all of us is the cost of health care. That's a real problem." A New Jersey assistant stock trader (D024 NJ M WC) made a comment that seemed to summarize what many of the apolitical majority interviewees believed: "The government doesn't do anything for me. . . ."

They take my money, that's all. . . . As far as I'm concerned, the government just takes money from me."

Apolitical majority interviewees expressed the wish that government would provide health care, Social Security, or money for their local schools. At the same time, many argued that their taxes were too high and they should not have to pay as much as they did. Thus, as was true across the interviewee groups, the apolitical majority interviewees did not seem to make a link between taxes and the services that they received or wanted. Further, many who were not receiving any direct payments from the government claimed not to be getting anything. Yet they certainly did not indicate that they would find it acceptable to cut the services that they already received, and many had a wish list of what they hoped government would do or support, either for them personally or for their communities.

Religious Nonconservatives

A majority of the religious nonconservative interviewees said that they got what they deserved from the government, in part because they did not want government services. For example, a Tennessee electronic publishing coordinator (G507 TN M WC) said:

> The older I get, the more ridiculous I think the amount of income tax is. . . . I don't even want [things from the government]. I don't want to have to pay for it. I don't need it. I don't think others should have it. . . . People like me are getting what they deserve from the government. . . . We don't have polluted streams. . . . I don't think people should expect as much from the government as a lot of them seem to.

Another Tennessee interviewee, an electronics technician (F015 TN M WC), said: "I don't know like I feel like I deserve something from the government other than freedom. But with the amount of money that I give them, I cannot say that I get a return on that. . . . They have taken [Social Security] into bankruptcy. . . . They can't balance a checkbook." An Ohio part-time school supervisor (E330 OH F MC) made the following comment: "For the most part, yes. . . . I'm thinking about when my dad was laid off. . . . He still gets government unemployment. . . . He's getting enough." Only one of these interviewees made a clearly positive statement about what she received from the government, and she was a government employee (F013 TN F MC): "Yes, because I have a better home than I've ever had in my life. I don't have a lot of debt. Our jobs are secure. I have a good education for my child. The infrastructure, like the roads, electrical, all of that is good. I don't really have any complaints."

Thus, although most of the religious nonconservatives said that they got what they deserved from the government, in some cases it was because they did not feel that they had asked for anything or because they did not want anything, and in other cases it was because someone in their family had received direct subsidies (like unemployment or Social Security). Others were more distrustful of government decision-making and skeptical about their prospects for receiving benefits from government actions in the future. Most of these interviewees defined their politics as moderate rather than liberal. As a group, therefore, although the religious nonconservatives were somewhat more open-minded with regard to helping people than some of the more conservative groups, on the issue of government they were not especially favorable in their responses.

Working-Class Liberals

In contrast to many of the other groups, the working-class liberals talked about doing what they needed to, helping where they could, and, in some cases, about just getting by. For example, a New Jersey computer technician (D008 NJ M WC) said:

> I don't think I ask for anything. I'm not getting my homestead rebate. . . . I think it should go to somebody who needs it more than I. . . . Everybody deserves what they get from the government, and nobody should get more and nobody should get less. . . . Thank God I'm fairly young and healthy, and I think I can . . . take care of myself. . . . I don't need the extras from the government or anybody else.

A Tennessee small-business owner (G512 TN M WC) distanced himself from the question: "I really don't think much about the government. I kind of do my own thing. . . . I stay current as much as I can, but I don't get involved in anything." Some self-employed interviewees called attention to the need for health care coverage, whether provided by the government or facilitated by the government. For example, an Ohio construction worker (E366 OH F WC) said: "I really like the fact that Canada doesn't have to pay for any of their medical, that it's free. . . . I don't think it's fair how much we have to pay for our insurance, and I think the government should have more control of it." Most of the interviewees did not see the connection between taxes and services, and many thought of government only in terms of direct subsidies—or in the case of one interviewee, the return she got back from the taxes that she paid (as if a tax return were some kind of subsidy, as opposed to being related to deductions and withholding preferences). Thus, the view of government among the working-class liberals was generally positive, but they still expressed concerns about taxes, a lack of needed services such as medical care, and, for most, uncertainty about how taxes are related to outcomes for people and places.

Rich White Liberals

The majority of rich white liberals felt that they got what they deserved from the government. They mentioned services such as roads, schools, and safety, and some indicated that those people who make more should pay more. Some were concerned about wanting more of a voice in government priority-setting, better-quality leadership from government officials, and honesty from government. A few were concerned about the level of taxes that they paid and expressed concern that they were being punished for their success, while others indicated that they did not want much from government or that they had not thought much about it. A representative comment came from a New Jersey music manager (D006 NJ M MC): "As I wrote my check to the IRS this year, I don't like it, but it is what it is. You make more, you pay more. . . . I wish my taxes were lower . . . but this is America, and I've got a lot of great things to show for it." Another New Jersey man, an attorney (D048 NJ M), said: "I don't have any complaints myself. I think there are people who tend to complain no matter what they have. . . . I don't have a lot of problems with paying taxes. . . . The things we have here as Americans are expensive . . . so I'm paying my taxes without complaining."

A few other interviewees raised questions about the trade-offs. An Ohio woman, who described herself as a trophy wife (E353 OH F MC), said with regard to whether she got what she deserved from government: "Everybody in this country probably is getting shorted a little bit because of the waste in government. . . . The truth of it is, we've all elected the people that are there . . . and we continue to be passive. . . . I guess we do get what we deserve." At the same time, a New Jersey executive (D064 NJ F MC) raised the following concerns:

> I would say that leadership is lacking a little bit. . . . When I think of the government, I don't think of money back from the government. I think more, do I think that they are making the right decisions. . . . I get worried about safety net issues, about pulling back, about the whole welfare thing. . . . What is going to happen when unemployment goes back to 12 percent, which it will someday. . . . I worry about our educational system. . . . I think taking money out of the school systems is not the answer. . . . I worry more about the things that they are doing, the broad things that they are doing.

Another New Jersey woman, a vice president for human resources (D053 NJ F MC), raised questions about what she got from government: "I don't really see the government as giving me anything. The government is just this structure that kind of allows us to be in the United States. . . . But I just want my Social Security. . . . That's what the government owes me." Thus, in general, the rich white liberals were not especially concerned about taxes, recognized the services that they received, were concerned about how wisely the government spends money, and sometimes acknowledged their own privileges and responsibilities as people with higher incomes and more economic opportunities. But even these interviewees were not entirely clear about how their taxes translated into services, nor, in general, were they sure about what government does with the money that it collects.

Across the interviewees the views of government are remarkably narrow, reflecting the ideological campaign of the post–civil rights period to delegitimize the role of government in popular sentiment. Most of the interviewees thought of government primarily with regard to transfer payments like welfare and then claimed that they did not want or need any government help. As is true for many of the issues addressed in this analysis, those with liberal politics—and more favorable economic situations within their class positions, namely, rich white liberals and working class liberals—were more open to government providing a social safety net and also understood government to include an array of social services and benefits that are essential for civil society. It is especially in regard to the issue of the role of government that the politics in the post–civil rights period have become polarized, and it is the one issue where there has been a dramatic change in attitudes, with a divide both between whites and nonwhites and between conservative whites and liberal ones.

Would You Be Better Off If Poor People Made Fewer Demands on Government?

As reported in chapter 6, I asked the interviewees whether they thought that those who have less economically have a right to expect the government to help them. As a follow-up to that question, I also asked interviewees whether some groups make too many demands on the government and whether they themselves would be better off if some of those groups did not make so many demands. My intent in asking these questions was to get indirectly at the interviewees' views about welfare. I did not ask the question directly because the term "welfare" has such hot connotations that I did not want to trigger automatic responses.

In both New Jersey and Ohio, I was surprised that a large proportion of the interviewees said that they would not be better off if poor people made fewer demands on the government—because, they said, if the government did not use their money for responding to such demands, it would just use the money for other things. Thus, many of the respondents, even some with conservative political views, did not seem to worry as much about government services for poor people as I would have expected. The exception to this general picture emerged in the Tennessee interviews. Not long before the interviews were done, Tennessee had had a public referendum on instituting a state tax—presumably to support local public schools by reducing the size of classes and providing more state resources in order to make Tennessee more economically competitive in drawing industry from elsewhere—but the referendum had been defeated. Many of the interviewees from Tennessee were quite angry with the state for trying to pass such a bill, arguing that the government had presented the bill to the public in an underhanded way. Many of the Tennessee interviewees expressed pleasure that the government (in this case, the state government) had been put in its place by a sound defeat of such legislation. These views were especially evident among the religious conservatives from Tennessee. Among the interviewees in both New Jersey and Ohio, there was less emphasis on taxes and less antigovernment rhetoric in general.

Although taxes were frequently mentioned in the responses to the question about whether the interviewees would be better off if poor people made fewer demands on the government, most respondents said that it did not really matter much one way or the other if poor people made fewer demands. In their views on what government should or should not do, the interviewees generally did not seem to see tax reduction as a high priority. Table 7.1 provides a summary of the responses to the question about whether the respondents would be better off if poor people made fewer demands on government. The views did vary, however. Both working-class "racists" and religious conservatives were more likely than the other groups to say that they would be better off (or that the country would be better off) if poor people made fewer demands on the government. Only 41 percent of working-class "racists" and only 31 percent of religious conservatives said that it would not affect them. A majority of the middle-class conservatives (67 percent) and of the religious nonconservatives (64 percent) said that they would not be better off if poor people made fewer demands. About half (54 percent) of the apolitical majority interviewees expressed the view that poor people making fewer demands on the government would not affect them much. Rich white liberals and working-class liberals were the least likely to say that they were concerned about the demands that poor people make on the government, with 70 percent of each group saying that they would not be better off if poor people made fewer demands.

The more conservative interviewees were more likely to mention taxes and government waste or corruption. The conservatives also made occasional comments about people needing to take care of themselves. The more liberal interviewees, in contrast, were more likely to comment on the need to be concerned about the welfare of poor people. The overall message, however, was more consistent than not: that if fewer poor people made demands on the government, it would not affect the interviewees much, and it was not something that they had thought much about or were very energized about.

Working-Class "Racists"

In general, the working-class "racists" said that poor people making fewer demands on the government would lower their taxes, but most said that it would not affect them very much. For example, an Ohio self-employed trucking firm owner (E321 OH M WC) said: "If I didn't have to pay taxes, yeah, I'd be a lot better off. . . . But I could maybe be worse off too." A New Jersey woman, an unemployed retail salesperson (D021 NJ FWC), said: "I don't think that really affects me. . . . I think it's a shame to see money that could be better used toward other things continuously wasted because some people don't care and just think it's there for them." Several other interviewees turned the issue back to the poor themselves. For example, a Tennessee man who worked as a graphic designer (G520 TN M WC) said: "I guess a little bit, but I guess more than that, I think they would be better off. . . . It makes me have to pay more taxes . . . but I'm not whining. . . . It is more for their sake than my own." Similarly, another Tennessee man, the co-owner of a small company (G524 TN M WC), said: "I don't so much know I would be better off . . . but as a society, we would be better off." This point was made as well by a New Jersey man, a carpenter (D003 NJ M WC): "I think the American people in general would be better off. . . . Me personally, I think I'm okay." Thus, although several of the working-class "racists" suggested that perhaps these programs increase their tax payments, most seemed indifferent to the idea of a policy change.

Middle-Class Conservatives

Even among the middle-class conservatives, a majority said that they would not necessarily be better off if poor people made fewer demands on government. For example, an Ohio woman who worked as a development officer for a high school (B013 OH F MC) responded: "I don't think I think of it in terms of me being better off. In the long run, I think they will be better off if we don't run the welfare system the way we do." Similarly, a nurse in Ohio (E336 OH F MC) said:

> I'm not going to blame them. I'm just saying the country in general would be a little more better off. There would be more help for the schools, or

> whatever, if you weren't paying out so damn much money to these people who are too lazy to get up and work. . . . It's not necessarily blacks. It's just lazy people who want a handout.

A New Jersey small-business owner (D030 NJ M MC) said: "Hopefully [I would] pay less taxes, but I don't think I would be that much better off overall." Thus, even though as a group they were more conservative in their political views, and some alluded to welfare recipients and people trying to get a "handout," even the middle-class conservative interviewees did not seem to think that the demands of poor people on the government had a major effect on their own economic situation or quality of life.

Religious Conservatives

In contrast to the other groups, including the middle-class conservatives, a number of the religious conservative interviewees mentioned that their taxes might be lower if poor people made fewer demands on the government. For example, a very wealthy Ohio homemaker (B019 OH F MC) whose husband owned a prosperous business gave this response:

> Well, sure we'd be better off, because, you know, you wouldn't have to work so hard. Your tax dollars would be put to better use. . . . I get real frustrated . . . when I see people saying, "Well, I'm black. We've been discriminated against all these years. We should get this. We should get that." There shouldn't be any free ride for anybody. . . . Of course, I understand slavery . . . but I think you sooner or later . . . we've got to get beyond that kind of thinking.

Even when they expressed such sentiments, a number of the religious conservatives were somewhat equivocal about whether it would be better if the government did not provide services to poor people. A Tennessee music teacher (G509 TN F MC) said: "I would have less income tax and Social Security taken out of our paycheck every two weeks, so I'd be better off in that sense . . . but on the other hand, if some of those people weren't taken care of, they shouldn't be left to starve to death either."

Other interviewees among the religious conservatives did not think that having fewer demands on the government from poor people would make them better off, but their reasoning varied. An Ohio pharmaceutical sales manager (E314 OH M MC) said: "I don't think it has any impact on me at all. . . . I might pay less taxes. I would like to have more control over the money going to the government." A Tennessee woman, an editorial assistant (G502 TN F WC), thought that poor people were not the major problem with regard to government: "No, I don't think that's where our government waste goes. . . . I don't think it's the demands of people. I think it's the people in power who line their own pockets." Yet another Tennessee woman, a materials specialist whose political views were very conservative (G527 TN F MC), said: "I totally believe in the process that we have. . . . Based on the privileges that we have within this country, they can do that and that is fine." Thus, even though their responses were more conservative, more focused on the implications of paying taxes, and more disparaging about the likely characteristics of poor people, the religious conservatives were rather equivocal about government help for poor people. They felt that the demands of poor people on the government affected them, but when they considered the alternatives, they did not necessarily suggest a major change in government priorities.

Apolitical Majority

Among the interviewees I classified as the apolitical majority, some said that if poor people made fewer demands on the government, they might be able to pay less in taxes, that the money could be used for better things (than helping poor people), and that everyone would be better off, but these views were in the minority. Most said that poor people making fewer demands on the government would not affect them and that it was not a major concern to them. A male engineering manager from Ohio (B017 OH M MC) made this comment: "I can't really say that it's affected me. . . . You hope there's not as much of that abuse as is publicized. . . . I don't have a problem paying taxes." Similarly, an Ohio insurance office manager (E335 OH M MC) said: "Well, I might pay less taxes, but I don't think our tax structure is that unfair, so no." A different view, however, was expressed by another Ohio interviewee, a small-business loan officer (E349 OH M MC): "If we didn't have the welfare system, there'd be a lot more crime, which would mean that that would cost the government even more."

A Tennessee woman who worked as a librarian (G506 TN F MC) had a more philosophical view of the question about poor people making demands: "People like me are always going to be pretty much where we are because . . . we're the core. . . . We're always going to be the ones that don't stand out on the street corner with a sign. . . . I have very few soapboxes, so we are soapboxless. I guess we're existers." A New Jersey chef (D014 NJ M WC) put his views in perspective: "I personally am not against welfare. I think I'd rather have welfare than have homeless people. . . . I think the government should be responsible." Thus, overall, the apolitical majority interviewees were not especially concerned about the demands made by poor people on the government. Many felt that it did not affect them. Even though they recognized that such programs might affect the amount of taxes that they paid, they did not suggest that eliminating such programs was a high priority for them or an idea that they had thought much about.

Religious Nonconservatives

A majority of the religious nonconservative interviewees also said that the demands of poor people on the government did not affect them very much. For example, a Tennessee woman, a minister (F012 TN F MC), responded this way: "I can't really complain about anything. I pay my taxes . . . good seems to come from it." A government worker from Tennessee (F013 TN F MC) said: "I don't think there are all that many people like that out there. . . . They're hurting themselves more than anybody else." Another Tennessee woman, a travel representative (F022 TN F WC), expressed similar views: "Well, not necessarily someone like me, 'cause I don't need anything from the government. Maybe the tax rate would be lower . . . but I don't really have a problem with that." Although a few of the religious nonconservatives did express concerns about the demands being made on the government, they were in the minority among this group of interviewees.

Working-Class Liberals

A working-class building contractor from Ohio (E368 OH M WC) responded this way when asked about being better off or not if poor people made fewer demands on the government: "No, that's not fair either. I want the problems to be solved. . . . I just am absolutely convinced there are people who do need help, and that will . . . be able to turn their lives around." Several of the working-class liberal interviewees said that poor people making fewer demands on the government would not affect them; for example: a commercial artist from Tennessee (G519 TN M WC) said: "I don't think it matters one way or the other." A self-employed female construction worker from Ohio (E366 OH F WC), however, said: "Yeah, maybe the government could offer more Medicare to our elderly . . . that money might be there for the people who are really needy." A New Jersey computer technician (D008 NJ M WC) was somewhat less certain of the potential outcome if poor people made fewer demands on government: "I don't know. Sometimes I think the government sticks their nose into too much stuff. . . . As government gets involved, people start expecting the government to do a little bit more . . . and people are forgetting to be independent." Overall, however, the working-class liberals were not very concerned about the demands made by poor people, and few expressed a concern about the taxes that they paid because of such demands on the government.

Rich White Liberals

A middle-class research lab technician from Ohio (B004 OH M MC) said, when asked whether he would be better off if some people made fewer demands on the government: "No. I don't see where any of the laws that are trying to encourage or help out the other minorities or other groups . . . had that direct an effect on me." Similarly, another Ohio man, a training manager for a large company (E332 OH M MC), said: "I believe if they didn't make so many demands, it would be a more pleasant society . . . but . . . I'm doing fine, and I would hope that actually there would be a better cut for the poor primarily. . . . That's one heck of a great investment to make." A New Jersey executive (C001 NJ F MC) said it this way: "Oh, of course, but I don't need to be better off. . . . I believe that the government programs . . . it's like forced charity . . . most people don't give any money. They don't give to their church or their school or anything." Another New Jersey interviewee, a city planning director (D026 NJ M MC), said: "No, that's democracy." A New Jersey corporate attorney (C014 NJ F MC) had a different take on the issue. She said, "No, see, I never look at it from that standpoint. I blame more the government for not being as capable in dealing with the problems. . . . I don't like the money going to things that don't really get at the root of the problems." In general, the rich white liberals were not concerned about the taxes that they paid, and even if they mentioned taxes, they usually indicated that they were willing to pay them.

Summary of Views on the Poor Making Fewer Demands on the Government

Overall, even in the context of a question about whether the interviewees would be better off if fewer demands were made on the government by the poor, the interviewees seemed less concerned about taxes being used to provide services to the poor than one might have anticipated. Across all interviewees, only about one-quarter said that they would be better off if such programs were ended, fewer said that they might or might not be better off, while a majority said that they would not be better off because such programs had nothing to do with them, because the programs would not make that much of a difference in their taxes or their lives, or because they felt that the government would find other things on which to spend money if it was not spent on programs for the poor. Some suggested that the poor themselves would be better off if they were not being supported by government programs. Several said that society would be better off with fewer demands for services from the government. And some interviewees called attention to the potential waste of government funds or the undeserving nature of people who make demands on the government. But others said that it was not the poor who affected their taxes as much as the well-to-do, including perhaps corrupt or self-serving politicians, and a few said that they would prefer that such programs continue, because they did not want to see people become homeless or starving. Thus, even though the politics of the interviewees are, on average, center-right, they were not especially concerned about social service programs for the poor, even when they understood that having such programs might affect how much they would have to pay in taxes.

Given the surprisingly strong antigovernment views of so many of the respondents, I expected the question about poor people expecting help from the government to generate animated responses. I was thus somewhat surprised to find less concern about providing government services to the poor than I would have expected, and even more surprised that the respondents did not think of these government expenditures as having much of an effect on their own lives. Although there was a generally negative view of welfare and welfare recipients, the respondents did not object to welfare as a concept so much as they objected to how they believed it was provided. Several interviewees had very expansive views on what government provides. Some said that "those people" got everything paid for, including rent, food, and education. Some expressed resentment that "those people" got help when they said that they had needed help at some point along the way and could not get it.

Whenever government help is provided, the respondents generally believed, it should be temporary, it should be provided in the form of training or educational services rather than as dollars, and it should be thought of as a "hand up," not as a "hand out." In this regard, a number of the interviewees mentioned their support for welfare reform and indicated that they thought that the passage of time limits and tighter restrictions on welfare were moves in the right direction. But many of the interviewees expressed concern about those who "abused the system." To them, abuse was defined as taking help when you do not really need it, using welfare because of your failure to "try hard enough," and accepting welfare over the longer term (especially over generations). There were also some concerns expressed about those people who receive help and are not grateful for it, and even more concern that some who receive help do not use the resources or opportunities they have been given to improve life for themselves and their children.

The Problems of the Inner City

The views expressed about government services depended substantially on the social position of the interviewees, on their politics, and perhaps even more on the target of government programs. The racial subtext of

Table 7.2 Reasons Given for Problems in the Inner City

Reasons[a]	Working-Class Racists	Middle-Class Conservatives	Religious Conservatives
Percentage of the sample	12%	4.5%	19%
Poverty, low income	7	0	6
Lack of jobs, economic base	3	10	0
Lack of education, skills	10	0	22
Lack of public services	3	10	0
Poor schools	0	20	0
Flight of middle class	3	0	3
Discrimination, racism	0	0	3
Problems with families	34	50	47
Drugs, alcohol, prostitution	17	30	44
Gangs, crime, violence	0	10	31
Welfare, multigenerational	7	40	25
Lack of work ethic, motivation	24	40	11
Lack of morality, values, culture	24	30	25
Hopelessness, trapped, cycle	17	0	19
Resentment, alienation, entitlement	14	0	3
Neighborhood blight	0	30	3
Overcrowding	10	10	11
Too many children	0	20	0
Absent fathers	0	0	8
Not enough for children to do	0	0	0
Corruption	0	0	3
Teen pregnancy, permissiveness	0	0	0
Immigrants	10	0	0
Don't know	0	10	8

Source: Author's compilation.
Notes: Responses may not add up to 100 because of rounding error.
[a]Coded responses to question: "A lot of policymakers have been concerned about the deterioration of life for people living in the central cities of large urban areas. As you may know, many of these people are nonwhite. What do you think is the major reason for the problems of the inner city?"

many of the responses suggested that opposition to the government providing help was greater if the respondents conceived of the recipients of such services as black. To get at this issue more explicitly, I asked respondents what they thought were the main reasons for the problems of the inner city, and this question did bring out views that otherwise might have been masked or indirect. The divergence in the political views of

Apolitical Majority	Religious Non-Conservatives	Working-Class Liberals	Rich White Liberals	Total
37%	4.5%	6%	17%	100%
				Average
19	9	38	58	19
16	9	15	36	14
14	27	31	24	18
1	9	38	9	6
0	0	0	18	3
14	0	15	15	8
3	0	0	15	3
24	45	31	21	32
29	55	31	42	34
20	0	8	12	12
14	9	15	15	14
11	9	8	3	13
15	27	0	0	18
23	18	0	12	18
5	0	0	12	6
0	0	15	9	3
9	18	15	0	10
4	9	0	0	4
5	18	8	3	7
4	9	8	0	3
1	0	8	6	2
4	0	0	0	1
0	0	0	0	2
11	0	0	0	5

the various groups of respondents is provided in their responses as shown in table 7.2.

There are three types of responses that receive most mention. Some explanations identify structural factors, such as poverty and unemployment (first shaded area). These were more likely to be mentioned by liberal groups, such as the rich white liberals and the working-class liberals, although many interviewees mentioned the lack of education of inner-city residents as an explanation. There were also explanations such as drugs, alcohol, and problems with families that all groups mentioned (the unshaded responses following the first shaded area). These issues were discussed differently by different respondents. For example, liberal groups talked about family issues in terms of the lack of family support or the burdens on single parents, whereas conservative groups talked about parents who did not supervise or discipline their children or who did not take care of them. Similarly, more liberal groups saw drugs as derivative of the challenges for families in the inner city, whereas more conservative groups saw them as the source of problems. Finally, there were explanations (second shaded area) that emphasized the personal failings of inner-city residents. These were more likely to be mentioned by conservative groups, but both the apolitical majority and religious nonconservative interviewees mentioned these issues as well.

In general, the more liberal groups (especially rich white liberals and working-class liberals) frequently pointed to structural factors as the causes of inner-city problems, including poverty and low income, lack of jobs or the erosion of the economic base (including the flight of the middle class from the inner city), the poor support for education, or the low skills of the inner-city population. They also called attention to the lack of public services. In contrast, more conservative groups, including working-class "racists," middle-class conservatives, and religious conservatives, as well as the apolitical majority in many cases, called attention to the personal failings of inner-city residents, such as their lack of a work ethic, their lack of motivation, or their lack of morals or appropriate values. The religious conservatives and the apolitical majority also talked about the role of gangs, crime, and violence in the inner city. Conservative groups also gave more attention than liberal ones to the presumed hopelessness of inner-city residents, who were said to not know any alternatives because of the poor role models or limited exposure they had to successful people in the inner city. A number of the conservative respondents also argued that welfare dependency and government programs that foster dependency cause the problems of the inner city. Finally, almost one-third of the middle-class conservatives talked about how inner-city residents "trashed" their own neighborhoods because of their lack of respect for property and for the help that they had been given. Middle-class conservatives also faulted inner-city residents for having more children than they could afford.

Working-Class "Racists"

The working-class "racist" interviewees claimed that the problems of the inner city are due to the breakdown of families, to the lack of a work ethic and a lack of morality or values, and to hopelessness or being caught in a vicious cycle that is difficult to escape. There was some mention of drugs and alcohol, although less than from the other groups of interviewees, and surprisingly, no one in this group mentioned gangs or violence as the primary cause of inner-city problems. The working-class "racists" also mentioned issues that most other groups of interviewees did not address, including the role of immigration (they portrayed immigrants as not having American values) and the claims that inner-city residents are unable to manage money, they just are not smart enough, and blacks have problems in all countries. They also talked about the resentment and negative attitudes of blacks about slavery and discrimination, which the working-class "racists" felt were unwarranted. Thus, the working-class "racist" interviewees clearly drew a line between themselves and those who live in the inner city. They saw inner-city residents as morally "other" and as lacking the kind of work ethic and family values that they claimed for themselves. The question specified that many inner-city residents are not white, but the working-class "racist" interviewees more than others highlighted this issue.

This negative portrait of inner-city residents was outlined by an Ohio homemaker (E318 OH F WC) who contrasted her oversight of her son's schoolwork with the patterns of inner-city families: "If you have parents that are drinking, or like I said before, just don't care, those kids are going to grow up to be, nine times out of ten, those kids are going to grow up to be criminals, drug addicts, or be the role model that they saw because they don't know any better." An Ohio man, who worked as a third party hearing representative (E360 OH M WC), said: "I think it's their lack of desire to do something for themselves. . . . They're given their food stamps. They're given their housing. They're given everything that they need. They're provided food. . . . It's just a lack of them doing something for themselves on their own." A New Jersey insurance adjuster (D011 NJ M WC) was similarly explicit: "They reproduce like rabbits. . . . They feel that we owe them everything. . . . They don't work. They don't take pride in anything. . . . In the black community, it's 90 percent that are the other ones. . . . I don't think I owe them anything." Another New Jersey interviewee, a house painter (D012 NJ M WC), had a similarly negative view: "You ain't never going to change them people. They're just people that have no self-respect for themselves."

To the working-class "racists," the problems of the inner city were a reflection of people who have low morals, who are unwilling to work and to help themselves, who want others to support them, and who feel entitled to having them do so. People in the inner city, according to the working-class "racists," have children they do not take care of or properly control. Those who have the gumption and self-respect will get themselves out of the situation, and those left behind will end up with the experiences that they deserve. There is not much support from the working-class "racists" for government solutions. They see the problems of the inner city as due to personal failings, and they see the government's efforts as supporting or encouraging such misbehavior.

Middle-Class Conservatives

The middle-class conservatives were likely to mention the role of welfare, inner-city residents' lack of a work ethic and morality, neighborhood blight, overcrowding, and having too many children as reasons for problems in the inner city. Clearly, the responses of the middle-class conservatives follow a conservative framing of the lives of poor people, with emphasis on personal failings and misbehavior more than on the role of poverty or other structural factors in their environments. The most frequent response from the middle-class conservatives regarding the problems of the inner city had to do with family issues. For example, an Ohio paralegal (E364 OH F MC) said: "I think it's lack of control of the parents. I think that is a lot of it. . . . I have seen [the government] improve housing developments and . . . a lot of times when inner-city people get in them, they destroy them." Similarly, a Tennessee salesman (G505 TN M MC) said: "I think it goes back to family and home, personal responsibility. . . . Anyone who wants to get out of the inner city . . . you know, they can hop on a bus."

Predictably, a number of the middle-class conservative interviewees thought that the government was contributing to the problems of the inner city instead of resolving them. For example, an Ohio nurse (E336 OH F MC) said:

> A lot of the problem is obviously low income, the major problem, which is why everybody is robbing, stealing, killing. That's where you come into situations where generation after generation is born into welfare. . . . [The government has] made it too easy to get it, so there's people more than willing to stay on it. So they don't work.

Thus, the middle-class conservatives portrayed the problems of the inner city as stemming from the personal failings of the people who live there, dysfunctional families, dependence on welfare, lack of work ethic, lack of values, and the drug and alcohol abuse that might be associated with such lifestyles. Although there was some mention of poor schools and lack of jobs, these were not seen as obstacles that could not be overcome. As some of the interviewees suggested, if those living in the inner city did not want to live in such a negative environment, they could just "hop a bus."

Religious Conservatives

Religious conservatives called attention to the role of the family, drugs, hopelessness, and lack of morality. They also emphasized the role of crime and violence in the inner city and the influence of having multiple generations of families on welfare. For example, a high school teacher from Ohio (B001 OH M MC) said, when asked about the factors that contribute to the problems of the inner city: "United States government, federal government. They created that kind of atmosphere through its sixties programs. That pigeonholed these people. . . . It put them in a rut. . . . I think it created dependency on the government." A Tennessee editorial assistant (G502 TN F WC) also thought that welfare contributes to the problems: "They've grown up in a lifestyle. . . . Families, generations, grew up in welfare, die in welfare, have kids that grow up in welfare, die in welfare. And this shouldn't be." With regard to crime and violence, a Tennessee trim carpenter (G529 TN M WC) said: "Violence is one. I think that a lot of 'em don't have the education that is needed to make adequate wages, so they turn to drugs and whatnot to support the family. . . . Therefore, the crime rate's higher, 'cause they're getting caught doing it, which brings violence."

Of course, a number of the religious conservatives thought that the problems of the inner city are due to sin and wrong living. For example, an Ohio woman, an electrical engineering manager (B003 OH F MC), said that the problems of the inner city are, at heart, moral:

> A major problem with the inner city is that people are self-centered and unable to help themselves. They're victims of their own circumstances and are having trouble escaping it. . . . I basically think people need to be saved . . . to begin to line up their life with the principles that God has established, and blessings would follow.

A Tennessee industrial firm manager (G525 TN M MC) made the following link: "When you don't have a mother or father, it impacts both the moral and the financial stability of that family unit. . . . The government enables the breakdown by giving us support mechanisms and encouraging dysfunctional family units." Another Tennessee woman, a medical transcriptionist (F002 TN F MC), said simply: "They're not taught the values at home, and they're not taught values at school. . . . And they're not allowed to discipline kids anymore."

In summary, the religious conservatives portrayed the inner city as a place where families are troubled, morals are lacking, and people are hopeless and dependent on the government and thus as an environment that fosters drug abuse, violence, and crime. Although there was some mention of the lack of education or skills, for the most part religious conservatives' explanations for the problems of the inner city focused on personal deficiencies and not on structural conditions or the role of poverty.

Apolitical Majority

Like most of the other interviewees, the apolitical majority attributed the problems of the inner city to drugs and alcohol, crime and violence, and family issues. The apolitical majority respondents also expressed a belief that inner-city residents experience hopelessness and are trapped in a cycle of poverty. A number of the apolitical majority respondents, however, also called attention to inner-city residents' poverty and low income, as well as their lack of morality or problematic values, as factors in the problems of the inner city. A few talked about the lack of jobs or the lack of education, and they also noted the occurrence of multigenerational welfare and the effect of the middle class leaving the inner city. Thus, the interviews of the apolitical majority showed a mix of explanations suggesting that the personal failings of inner-city residents as well as structural factors might make it difficult for them to change the dynamics of their lives. Overall, however, their responses seemed to overlap more with the conservative groups than with the liberal ones. Not surprisingly, almost one in ten of the apolitical majority interviewees said that they had no idea what might cause the problems of the inner city.

A working-class factory worker from Ohio (E307 OH M WC) said that the alternative economy is too strong an attraction for kids in the inner city: "The kid that's selling crack on the corner making $1,000 a week, you're never going to get him integrated into society." The comments of a middle-class small-business loan officer from Ohio (E349 OH M MC) illustrate the mix of structural and cultural explanations characteristic of the apolitical majority interviews:

> It's economic, but it's also social. A lot of the people, like inner-city blacks, for instance, don't have the discipline within their families, and the reason for that isn't because they're black. It's because they were discriminated so poorly against in that culture to the point where it became a cultural thing. Their parents were not raised by parents who had high moral values and a lot of hard work ethics.

The theme of getting yourself out was surprisingly prevalent among the apolitical majority interviewees. For example, a middle-class woman from Ohio who worked as an educator in rehabilitation (E323 OH F MC) said: "Part of it is a sorting-out thing. . . . Those that didn't want to be poor and had some motivation left. . . . Some of it's obstacles . . . but by no means the major part of it." This issue, however, was viewed somewhat differently by a New Jersey billing clerk (D036 NJ F MC): "Maybe they don't know how to get out. I don't know why people want to live there. Like, can't they move to Florida? Maybe they don't know how to pick up and move to a nicer neighborhood or a better school district. . . .

I can't understand why people would live there." The difficult situation of the inner city with regard to jobs and the economic base was mentioned in a number of interviews. A Tennessee self-employed entertainer (G532 TN M WC) had the same explanation: "The infrastructure has deserted urban areas. With few job opportunities . . . there is not an infusion of capital and money to reinvigorate and restore these areas. If you don't have job opportunities, you can't pay for backpacks and school supplies and lunches." Another Ohio interviewee, a supervisor in a small company (B014 OH M WC), put it more succinctly: "The cities have moved out of the cities. All your shopping, dining, recreation . . . so the people don't want to live in the city that work in the city. . . . The cities themselves have moved out."

A number of the apolitical majority interviewees, however, blamed inner-city residents for the problems of the inner city. A Tennessee musician (G517 TN M MC) had a list of reasons for the problems of the inner city:

> I think the scarcity of suitable role models for young blacks I think could possibly have something to do with it. . . . I think the lack of a father figure or a father figure who is a suitable influence. . . . Drug dealers. Pimps. It goes back to the thing with flash and cash and girls and cars as opposed to somebody that can teach you the things you need to know to get along in society.

A few of the apolitical majority interviewees, however, had a somewhat more sympathetic and less negative view of the problems experienced by people who live in the inner city. A New Jersey real estate appraiser (D067 NJ M MC) called attention to the lack of marketable skills: "They don't have those suburban values, unfortunately. . . . The people you see at that soup kitchen are pretty much destitute, and they are just not hirable. . . . They are not going to get a job, most of these people." A Tennessee bookkeeper (G511 TN F MC) saw it this way: "Some people's bitterness of enslavement to their own views and lifestyle, it can't be changed."

In summary, the apolitical majority interviewees expressed views that were both structural and cultural. The comments included some explanations that were consistent with liberal views, such as the role of poverty, the lack of jobs, and the impact of the middle class moving out of the inner city, but also included some explanations that were more consistent with conservative views, such as the effects of hopelessness and being trapped in a cycle of poverty. The apolitical majority's most prevalent explanations for the problems of the inner city, however, were the ones that most other interviewees offered as well, namely, the problems in families and with parenting and the role of drugs, alcohol, and crime.

Religious Nonconservatives

More than any other group, the religious nonconservatives called attention to drug and alcohol abuse as reasons for the problems of the inner city, and they also placed a great deal of weight on family issues, including the problems of single parents or parents who do not adequately supervise their children. Religious nonconservatives also called attention to the lack of education and lack of skills of inner-city residents and the culture of poverty, and they argued that residents of the inner city experience hopelessness and feel trapped in their situation. A part-time preschool supervisor in Ohio (E330 OH F MC) characterized it this way:

> It's persons who are not getting the education enough to know that they can work hard to break the cycles that they've been raised in. . . . You do what is your way of life. Unless you have been exposed to other ways of life and been given alternatives that are obtainable, you pretty much fall into the same patterns as you grow older.

The magnitude of the problem and the challenges for making a difference were underlined by a New Jersey management consultant (D044 NJ F MC): "If we can't make this segment of our society be productive citizens, then it's a missed opportunity for us as a country, and you know, we are going to end up building more prisons." Perhaps the overall view of the religious nonconservatives is summarized in the comments of a Tennessee travel agent (F022 TN F WC):

> The family life. . . . Children being left alone, single parents having to work to provide for the children, to provide for the family, and just not being taught morals and values like generations ago. And if they don't get it at home, and they don't get it at school, and if they don't go to church, they can't get it there. I think a lot of inner-city kids are just growing up just getting whatever they can, whatever way they can.

The views of religious nonconservatives on this issue were more consistent with those of conservative interviewees than with liberal ones.

Working-Class Liberals

Many of the working-class liberals also pointed to the role of drugs and the strains on families as causes for the problems of the inner city, and they often linked these issues to the lack of jobs or resources in the community. For example, a clerical worker in Tennessee (G504 TN F WC) said: "I think a lot of it is so many of them turn to drugs and crime. . . . The fact that it is harder for them to find jobs. And a lot of them are used to not having to work. . . . They're on welfare forever and ever." A Tennessee man, a commercial artist (G519 TN M WC), made a similar point: "I mean, it is more than just schools. It's money. It's jobs. It's history. It's drug abuse." Interestingly, the working-class liberals also talked about the lack of public services in the inner city and the cost of rent. For example, a Tennessee woman, a massage therapist (G523 TN F WC), said:

> I think they could create a larger variety of lower-cost, decent housing. Instead of making these housing projects, you could encourage local developers to develop what is gonna be lower-cost houses where people could actually afford to move into a decent place. . . . We are just not designed to live like rats in a study. . . . The worst of us comes out.

An Ohio building contractor (E368 OH M WC) put it succinctly: "You know, it's economics. And if you have something that's decaying around you, and nobody has the will or the finances to do anything about it, it can't be good for anybody. It can't be good for the kids."

Thus, the working-class liberals called attention to structural factors as causes for the problems of the inner city. They were almost alone in raising the issue of the lack of public services in the inner city, and they also talked about the high cost of rents for decent housing, a topic no other group mentioned.

Rich White Liberals

Although many of the rich white liberals talked about drugs and problems in families when asked about the causes of problems in the inner city, these issues were frequently linked to the role of poverty, lack of jobs, and lack of alternatives for inner-city residents. For example, a female high school teacher from Ohio (E346 OH F MC) who had taught in the inner city said: "It's always hard to get employers to give these kids a chance. . . . And then you would have kids look at you and say, 'I can make $300 in a week dealing drugs, and you want me to go work for $4.75 an hour at McDonald's.' . . . How do you answer that?" A New Jersey woman, a corporate executive (C001 NJ F MC), also called attention to the difficulties of getting businesses to employ inner-city residents: "[My company] does a lot of good things. . . . [but it] doesn't employ the people of [the inner city]." Another New Jersey woman, a clinical psychologist (C003 NJ F MC), cited the lack of economic development and the opportunities that go with it:

> I think this is a very complicated question, including what's happened to the industrial base in our society and the fact that there aren't the kinds of factory jobs that were available. . . . There's been the erosion of our indus-

> trial base just as African Americans, who were the people who would have most likely moved into those jobs, and . . . the impact of slavery on the African American family.

Another New Jersey interviewee, a writer (C006 NJ M MC), raised a different type of issue: "It always seems to me that this argument that you can't solve problems by throwing money at them doesn't make much sense. . . . I think there should be more money put into these areas." A city planner from New Jersey (D026 NJ M MC) had a more specific explanation for the problems of the inner city:

> Highway system and mortgages. . . . Being able to put a down payment and then have a mortgage on a private house. That's what was the destruction of cities. Then after that what happened was, as your middle class moved out, you have a great disparity between the income levels. Why don't you have crime in suburbia? Because everybody's basically the same. . . . Why do you have it in inner cities? Because you have such disparity of income.

Thus, overall, the rich white liberals were likely to attribute the problems of the inner city to structural factors like poverty, inequality, and lack of jobs or a tax base in the city, and although many talked about drugs or crime, they linked these issues to the role of poverty and exclusion from jobs that would provide an alternative.

Summary of Views on the Inner City

Politics shaped the interviewees' views on the problems of the inner city. Rich white liberals and working-class liberals considered structural explanations for the problems of the inner city, but they also mentioned problems with family structure and the consequential role of drugs and alcohol. They framed their explanations as a lack of material and personal resources, not so much as personal failings. Although religious nonconservatives often shared the perspectives of the more liberal groups, on the question about the inner city, their views were less liberal. They blamed the lack of education and insufficient grounding in appropriate cultural values; drugs, alcohol, and the problems of families; and the hopelessness and the inability of inner-city residents to envision alternatives. The apolitical majority interviewees reported a mix of both structuralist and individualist explanations for the problems of the inner city, with the individualist explanations carrying more weight. More conservative groups, including religious conservatives, middle-class conservatives, and the working-class "racists," all focused on the personal failings of inner-city residents, with varying emphases on the specifics. Many of the conservative interviewees also were very critical of the role of government in creating and perpetuating the problems of the inner city, whereas the more liberal groups looked to government more positively.

Conclusions

The interviewees' views suggest some complexities in the unfavorable attitudes toward government that have been reported in political polling (Pew Research Center 2010). What is perhaps most surprising in these views is that there is such a large gap or disconnect between the interviewees' conception of "government" and what surely is a wide array of services that they receive as members of their communities. Only a small proportion of the interviewees seemed to make a connection between public services and the taxes that they paid, and a number of these interviewees did not seem to have a very clear view of what such services might cost or why they were asked to pay the taxes that they paid. Although the interviewees seemed somewhat more favorable about state or local government, they were especially unfavorable about the federal government, presumably because there was an even wider gap for them in understanding how the federal government provides them with services that are relevant to themselves and their communities.

Although some of the interviewees mentioned the role of the government in providing a defense of the country (which some defined as the sole role given the government in the Constitution), the interviewees did not seem to give much if any thought to how much defense costs in relationship to the taxes that they paid. Further, they did not think about roads, schools, parks, disaster relief services, support for research and science, regulation of commerce, and protections for labor, food, drugs, public health, and the other myriad of services that are part of the costs underwritten by the federal government. Hardly any of the interviewees thought even of benefits like Social Security and Medicare as governmental services, even though they claimed entitlement and wanted to be sure that such benefits were there when they needed them. Perhaps even more telling is that a number of interviewees felt that they should receive whatever services they were currently receiving in higher quantity and better quality. But they also wanted expanded services to cover an improvement of local schools and government-provided health care. Further, they thought that these improved or extended services should be provided for the taxes that they currently paid or perhaps even with lower taxes, if the government would just get rid of the "waste" and be more efficient.

The racial subtext in the views of the interviewees is also of interest. Many of the interviewees thought of "government" only as transfer payments, and primarily in terms of welfare "handouts." As noted, few even thought of Social Security, Medicare, unemployment insurance, or disability payments as "government," let alone the many other services that the interviewees received through the local, state, and federal governments. When many of the interviewees thought about getting things from government, they thought primarily about money rather than public services. When the interviewees did consider who was most likely to get things from the government in this context, they had in mind minorities or poor people who were "lazy" and "unwilling to work" more than about the needy in general, the infirm, the elderly, or the retired. When they put government in that context, they were much less favorable and claimed that they did not need anything, did not want anything, and did not want to pay for anything from government, and further, they said, others should not get things from government either.

The view of the interviewees about government "waste" is also noteworthy. Many of the interviewees portrayed the government as incompetent, unwise, and wasteful in the use of tax revenues. The interviewees seemed to consider government services to be a last resort that would lead only to frustration or dissatisfaction. Yet many of the interviewees wanted their Social Security payments, health care, unemployment, police and fire protection, support for the military, improvement in education, safe roads and foods, and national parks, among other things, as a right or entitlement. Very few interviewees said, like the man from Tennessee who had moved from Wisconsin where the services were much better, that "you get what you pay for."

Even with this overwhelmingly negative view of what government is and what it should do, it was surprising that so few of the interviewees thought that reducing government services to the poor would have much of an effect on them, and it was surprising that so many thought that it would not make much difference to them one way or the other. Given the constant rhetoric in the political sphere about the overreaching of the government, the dependency caused by the welfare state, and the lack of support for government programs like welfare and Medicaid or food stamps, it was surprising as well that otherwise conservative people did not consider such issues when asked if they would be better off if the government provided less to those with fewer economic resources. Indeed, the nonchalance about paying taxes in this context was especially unexpected.

For those who would like to see more favorable views of government and less antigovernment rhetoric in the political environment, these interview results should be of special interest. The depth of misunderstanding about how taxes relate to public services, about the costs of such services and how those relate to individual households, and about the range and complexity of services across government levels is clearly an issue that could use much more attention. Perhaps politicians steer clear of providing many specifics when it comes to government spending for fear that there will be new revelations that might cause embarrassment, but at the same time, it surely would be good for the political health of the country for people to have a greater understanding of how government relates to their everyday lives and well-being and what government contributes to the strength of their communities and civic life.

The racial subtext of the views of government was evident indirectly in the focus on transfer payments such as welfare when the interviewees thought about "government." But the racial attitudes of the interviewees can be seen directly in their responses to the question about the causes of problems in the inner city. All of the sociopolitical groups mentioned issues like drugs and alcohol, problems in families, and sometimes gangs and crime, but only the two more liberal groups, the rich white liberals and the working-class liberals, addressed structural issues like poverty and lack of jobs. The other groups gave more attention to individualist explanations, citing the personal failings of inner-city residents, including the "hopelessness" of their situation. These political differences were even more evident when I asked the interviewees about affirmative action and equal opportunity policies. I discuss these and the issue of immigration in the next chapter.

Chapter 8

Affirmative Action and Equal Opportunity: Changes in Access to Education and Jobs for Women, African Americans, and Immigrants

[If people actually had equal opportunity, what would that mean?]

Telecommunications executive from Tennessee (G526 TN M MC): "I don't think they should be kept from getting a job simply because of race or religion or nationality, but again, who determines whether that is what kept them from getting the job? I think that is where it goes back to the court system and not a government mandate that X number have to be in this job, and the next number has to be in that job, because if you do that you are almost getting, in my opinion, to a socialist state. . . . Because if you start getting into numbers, then do you almost get into reverse discrimination? Do you almost get to the point that you have one individual that is really more qualified but because of the color of the skin or because of their nationality or because of their gender is prohibited from getting that job? That is just as unfair."

No topic demonstrates the divergence in the political views of the various sociopolitical groups in this study more than affirmative action, which is also the program that, in general, divides black and white opinion in the United States more than any other topic (Kinder and Sanders 1996). Yet, despite the passion around the subject of affirmative action, like many Americans, very few of the interviewees actually knew how the program has worked in either theory or practice. Many of the interviewees thought of affirmative action as a program that forces employers to "hire so many of these and so many of those." The interviewees also expressed the view that whites in general and men in particular were disadvantaged by affirmative action policies. Because there is such limited public understanding of what affirmative action policies entail, I begin with a brief summary of affirmative action policies to provide a context for understanding the interviewee responses described in this chapter.

Affirmative Action Policies in Employment

There is a legislative basis for antidiscrimination policies. Most notably, Title VII of the Civil Rights Act of 1964 outlawed discrimination in employment. All employers with fifteen or more employees are covered by the law and are required to keep records of their employee population. Firms with 100 or more employees must file reports with the Equal Employment Opportunity Commission (EEOC) as part of the oversight of the legislation. Affirmative action is not based on legislation but is rather the result of presidential executive orders, case law, and regulations. As such, it is a set of policies, not a program. The blatant exclusion of racial and ethnic minorities and women from good jobs prior to the passage of the Civil Rights Act contributed both to the civil rights movement and ultimately to legal support for banning discrimination in employment. Every president as far back as Franklin Roosevelt issued executive orders to end job discrimination in federal employment and among federal contractors.[1] Although presidential executive orders have the force of law, they typically (and often by design) have had weak enforcement mechanisms. That situation continued when President John Kennedy issued executive order 10925 in 1961. His order not only outlawed discrimination—as had previous executive orders—but also required federal contractors to take "affirmative action" to ensure nondiscrimination on the basis of race, creed, color, or national origin. In 1965 President Lyndon Johnson issued executive order 11246, which reiterated Kennedy's earlier order, and then in 1967 Johnson issued executive order 11375, which added protection against sex discrimination. Affirmative action policies are primarily overseen by the Office of Federal Contract Compliance Programs (OFCCP). Antidiscrimination mandates alone did not lead to much change in employer behavior. Thus, affirmative action was seen as a necessary step toward greater equity in access to job opportunities.[2]

Affirmative action policies are applicable to employers with federal contracts and fifty or more employees or to those with federal contracts of $50,000 or more. The goals of affirmative action policies are twofold: to end existing discrimination and to expand opportunity. Because jobs are a scarce and valuable resource, from the beginning affirmative action policies have been politicized, and effective implementation of the policies has often been hampered or resisted by groups who feel that they would be adversely affected. Further, the policies have never been well understood by the public, nor perhaps by the employers who are supposed to adopt them and the agencies that are supposed to ensure compliance. Early and often, the policies have been subject to legal challenge, and as a consequence, the policies have also changed dramatically over the years in terms of their reach and requirements.

Affirmative action policies are applicable to employment, education, and federal contracting. My focus here is on affirmative action in employment. By collecting data on their employment patterns, covered employers are expected to monitor the "underutilization" of protected groups in their hiring and promotion processes; if an employer is found to have fewer employees who belong to protected categories than would be expected based on the composition of the pool of qualified applicants, there is a presumption that decisions may have been discriminatory. The company is then required to prepare an affirmative action plan that outlines its intended efforts to remedy the underutilization.

Affirmative action plans may be audited by OFCCP, with the threat that federal contracts may be canceled, terminated, or suspended and the company potentially debarred from future contracts if found not to be in compliance, but such penalties have rarely been meted out. Some highly noteworthy lawsuits have been brought against major companies, especially in the earlier days of affirmative action, but these suits have been rare. The effects of antidiscrimination laws and affirmative action policies have also varied with the political environment. In an analysis of data provided to the Equal Employment Opportunity Commission, Kevin Stainback and Don Tomaskovic-Devey (2012) found that the changes in the employment of racial and ethnic minorities and women in jobs that had previously been the purview of white men followed different patterns or trajectories depending on the group and how the impact of structural changes in the economy, institutional and organizational influences, and political uncertainty affected employer behavior. They found, for example, that most of the increase in the proportions of black men entering good jobs occurred before 1980. After taking into consideration changes in the structure of the economy and the composition of the population, Stainback and Tomaskovic-Devey also found that white men have been minimally affected in their dominance of the most desirable jobs as a result of the adoption of civil rights laws and affirmative action policies.

With the growth of a new right-wing political movement in recent decades, affirmative action has often been a target of legal challenge, so the provisions and original intent have been made stricter and more limited over the years. Following a major court ruling in *Adarand Constructors, Inc. v. Peña* in 1995, affirmative action policies became subject to "strict scrutiny" with regard to the equal protection clause of the Constitution, and program requirements in affirmative action plans were required to be "narrowly tailored" to meet a "compelling government interest" in order to be upheld. This court ruling initiated a major review of affirmation action policies by President Bill Clinton in his famous "mend it, don't end it" approach to affirmative action (Stephanopoulos and Edley 1995). The 1995 review prepared by George Stephanopoulos and Christopher Edley outlined tests of fairness that were to be used to evaluate specific affirmative action policies. They recommended that affirmative action policies first must be shown to work in ending discrimination and expanding opportunity. They further argued that affirmative action policies must be fair, which they measured by five criteria: policies must (1) avoid quotas, (2) not provide preferential treatment for unqualified individuals, (3) not create reverse discrimination, (4) be transitional or temporary, and (5) have only small or diffuse effects on nonbeneficiaries.

That affirmative action contributes to reverse discrimination has been a major claim of opponents and the subject of noted legal challenges, such as the 1978 *Bakke* ruling that the University of California–Davis could not set aside slots for minority applicants to its medical school. More recently, cases have been brought in all three realms of affirmative action—employment, education, and contracting. The evidence for reverse discrimination, however, has been very minimal. Only a small proportion of whites indicate on surveys that they believe they have lost out on jobs because of reverse discrimination (Steeh and Krysan 1996). Even fewer actually take legal action and file complaints with the Equal Employment Opportunity Commission: estimates are that only 2 to 5 percent of complaints made to the EEOC are about reverse discrimination (Bendick 1997; Burstein 1991; Pincus 2003). Further, of the small proportion of complaints that are brought on the basis of reverse discrimination, only a small number of these cases win. In one estimate, only twenty-eight of seven thousand cases were found to be credible, a proportion of only 0.004 percent (Crosby and Herzberger 1996). These estimates are consistent with the data found in this study, as will be seen shortly.

There have been many analyses of the outcomes of affirmative action policies, with some arguing that changes in the employment of minorities and women in jobs from which they had previously been excluded would have come about because of changes in the economy, even without the changes in legislation and policy. Others have argued that affirmative action, combined with antidiscrimination legislation, has made a significant difference in the opportunities available to minorities and women and that the policies are still needed because of continued inequality (Crosby, Iyer, and Sincharoen 2006; Frymer and Loury 2005; Holzer and Neumark 2000a, 2000b; Reskin 1998; Stainback and Tomaskovic-Devey 2012). Harry Holzer and David Neumark (2000a, 240) provide perhaps the most comprehensive analyses of the effects of affirmative action on employment. Based on a random sample of establishments nationally, they find that

> Affirmative Action increases the number of recruitment and screening practices used by employers, raises employers' willingness to hire stigmatized applicants, increases the number of minority or female applicants as well as employees, and increases employers' tendencies to provide training and formally evaluate employees. When Affirmative Action is used in recruiting, it generally does not lead to lower credentials or performance of women and minorities hired. When it is also used in hiring, it yields minority employees whose credentials are somewhat weaker, though performance generally is not. Overall, the more intensive search, evaluation, and training that accompany Affirmative Action appear to offset any tendencies of the policy to lead to hiring of less-qualified or less-productive women and minorities.

Given the finding of Stainback and Tomaskovic-Devey (2012) that the access of white men to desirable jobs has been minimally affected by these policies, it seems, on balance, that the effects of affirmative action meet the criteria outlined by Stephanopoulos and Edley (1995) with regard to fairness. Of course, issues about whether credentials are weaker or stronger and how credentials are related, if at all, to performance have also been hotly debated in discussions of affirmative action. The perceptions of these policies, however, continue to be highly politicized and controversial.

Public attitudes toward affirmative action continue to be very divided, with blacks far more favorable than whites. Such attitudes, however, depend on how the questions are worded and what types of policies are at issue. For both those in support and those in opposition, the reality is that few Americans know what affirmative action policies entail, to whom they are applicable, and what the law permits or limits. For example, a number of the respondents in this study could not even name the policy, let alone discuss the specifics of what it does or does not do (Alvarez and Brehm 2002; Converse 1964; Zaller 1992). Americans of all racial backgrounds have been more favorable about policies that increase recruitment efforts for minority or female applicants, but are much less favorable about policies that provide any type of preferential treatment (Holzer and Neumark 1998, 2000b).

The views of the interviewees in this study are consistent with this view and, in general, their views are consistent with the past research on affirmative action, which has found: that whites are more favorable about the policies if they are framed in terms of reaching out to women and minorities but less favorable when the policies are framed in terms of preferential hiring or admission to schools; that whites are more favorable about affirmative action for women than for blacks or other minorities; that most whites do not believe that blacks still face discrimination or that there are barriers for blacks in the job market; and that there is a discrepancy between the number who believe that whites are disadvantaged by the policies and the evidence, based on discrimination lawsuits against employers (Crosby 2004; Krysan 2000; Pincus 2003; Schuman et al. 1997). This last point was consistent with the responses from interviewees in this study as well.

Perceptions of Discrimination

After asking the interviewees about the details of their educational and job histories, I asked them whether they had ever been discriminated against in the job market. This question was asked before I made any reference to policy issues such as affirmative action, so the question was asked without any context. The responses are reported in table 8.1. Over 70 percent of the interviewees said that they had never been discriminated against. Of the approximately one-quarter who said that they had been, it is instructive to examine how they thought about what constituted discrimination. Only a small proportion of the interviewees who claimed that they had faced discrimination mentioned circumstances that might fall under the law, and even for those cases, the details of their stories were rarely clear-cut. Women were more likely than men to say that they had been discriminated against, although there were fewer women who made this claim than I would have anticipated. In most of these cases, the women interviewees talked about feeling that women are given less credit for their contributions or that they felt isolated or excluded in their jobs. Only a handful talked about being denied jobs or promotions or facing the prospect of losing a job because of being female. There were a number who claimed that they had faced sexual harassment on the job. Most of these told of flirtatious or lecherous bosses or coworkers, but few described what might fall under the quid pro quo or hostile work environment provisions of the law. A number of women interviewees, however, reported that women were being paid less than men for doing the same or similar jobs.

In addition to the mention of gender issues on the job, a small number of interviewees claimed that they had been discriminated against because of other actionable criteria. Twenty interviewees (about 8 percent of the total sample) talked about feeling that they were at a disadvantage because of being too old (that is, over forty) or too young, although several of these interviewees said that they came to their views after the fact rather than at the time such discrimination may have happened. Three

Table 8.1 Summary of Responses to Question About Being Discriminated Against

Group	No	Yes	Total	Yes Among Women	Reasons for Yes (Gender Includes Sexual Harassment)[a]
Working-class racists	76%	24%	100%	55%	Gender (women) Favoritism, not family member, wouldn't kiss up to boss Disability Age (older) No degree Not enough seniority Boss didn't like smoking and drinking Taunted as a farm boy
Middle-class conservatives	70	30	100	0	Hired instead of a minority They needed a woman Everyone interviewed was nonwhite Disability Lack of experience Not Japanese Private school background
Religious conservatives	74	26	100	6	Not black or female Token white Gender (women) Favoritism Age (two older, one younger) No degree Weight Small size Medical costs (disability) Lost sales Couldn't get in military
Apolitical majority	83	17	100	18	Gender (women) Age (six older, three younger) Gay Pregnant No degree Low grades Overqualified Favoritism Illness Poor relationship with boss Not enough whites Didn't fit in (not Southern, from New York, not Jewish, Italian, father's son)

Table 8.1 (*Continued*)

Group	No	Yes	Total	Yes Among Women	Reasons for Yes (Gender Includes Sexual Harassment)[a]
Religious nonconservatives	73	27	100	25	Gender (women) Age (one older, one younger) Resented for education
Working-class liberals	71	29	100	29	Gender (women) Age (one older, one younger) No degree Got job instead of a minority
Rich white liberals	74	26	100	32	Gender (six women, one male) Being a white male (two) Age (one older, one younger) Gay

Source: Author's compilation.
Notes: Responses may not add up to 100 because of rounding error.
[a]Coded responses to question: "Have you ever been discriminated against? If so, tell me about that."

mentioned the possibility that they had been discriminated against because of a disability (having diabetes, suffering from epilepsy, or being heavy). Two mentioned that they may have been discriminated against because of being gay.

Only a handful, however, mentioned the possibility that race had been a factor in their labor market experiences, and these cases were not straightforward either. For example, one interviewee mentioned that he had been hired instead of a minority candidate, but he felt discriminated against because the company was under pressure to hire a minority and he had almost lost out on the job. Another interviewee had gotten the job, but felt that he was the "token white." Yet another felt that he probably did not get the job he was seeking because all of the other applicants were nonwhite, so he felt that he was at a disadvantage. Only two interviewees felt certain that they had been passed over for jobs because blacks were given preference. One of these was looking for a job as a school principal in a city with a large minority population and few nonwhite principals. The other interviewee mentioned feeling that he was at a disadvantage at a job in a black-owned company. Thus, of the five interviewees (2 percent of the total sample) who mentioned race when asked about whether they had been discriminated against, two said that they ended up with the job but might have missed out because of affirmative action concerns, one did not get the job and inferred that the reason was because so many nonwhites were also applicants, while only two (fewer than 1 percent) claimed that they had applied for jobs where blacks might have been given preference. If we look at the total number of jobs held by the interviewees in this study instead of the number of people, we find that in only 0.001 percent of the jobs (two incidents across 1,463 jobs described by the respondents) did any of the interviewees face experiences that might have ended with a minority candidate hired instead of the white interviewee. Hence, just as the previous research has shown, the perceptions among the interviewees that whites and men are at a disadvantage because of policies like affirmative action are not borne out by the specific stories that the interviewees told about their own experiences with potential discrimination.

It is also instructive to consider some of the other reasons that the interviewees gave for their belief that they might have been discriminated against in the job market. In their responses, the interviewees did not seem to have affirmative action and equal opportunity policies in mind. Instead, they mentioned any type of experience where they felt that someone else may have gotten a job that they had wanted, where they felt excluded or uncomfortable in the workplace, or where they felt that others had a better relationship with the boss. Some of the reasons given in response to whether they had been discriminated against included: not being a family member or part of the in-group on the job; being of the wrong ethnicity or religion (that is, being Italian, Japanese, or Jewish); not having a degree or being resented for having one; being overqualified for a job; lacking experience or seniority; and even having a farm background or being a foster child. A few were concerned about not being a favorite of the boss, while one felt that he was targeted because he was the boss's son. Thus, "discrimination" was just as fuzzy a concept for the interviewees as "government" was. These examples suggest that the interviewees thought of discrimination as anything that interfered with their access to good jobs or to feeling comfortable and secure in their jobs. The interviewees seemed to believe that any generalized feeling of discomfort, loss, or vulnerability on the job was unfair.

Perceptions of Affirmative Action and Discrimination

Affirmative action seems to be the lens through which most whites view the issue of discrimination, and they generally see themselves as the ones at a disadvantage because of such policies. When whites think about affirmative action, they do not recognize or acknowledge that the favoritism that whites show toward each other may be thought of by minorities as a form of discrimination against them. In fact, according to Ann McGinley (1997), civil rights jurisprudence has increasingly supported the argument that favoritism is not evidence of discrimination against minorities. Employers found to show favoritism toward white workers over others have been able to defend themselves from charges of discrimination. Thus, discrimination and favoritism are thought of as legally distinct, rather than as different sides of the same coin. This leaves no legal protection for African Americans (or for other nonwhites) who may want access to the employers, clients, and jobs that whites have reserved for themselves, unless they can show in some way other than favoritism toward whites that they were the victims of discrimination. Similar reasoning was used by several interviewees who argued that "another way" besides affirmative action should be found to protect against discrimination in the workplace, because they believed that affirmative action policies are unfair and unwarranted.

For example, when asked about the possibility that employers might end up hiring only whites, a retired factory worker from Ohio (E304 OH M WC) said: "What's wrong with that?. . . Well, okay . . . if you can't get hired here, you go there, if you can't get hired there, you go to the next city. You're going to get hired somewhere." This man and others who made similar arguments said that the "real" solution to discrimination was for blacks to come to the workplace better qualified, which they said required improving education for blacks in the early years.[3] Even though arguing that those who feel aggrieved should "have their day in court," an Ohio salesman (B020 OH M WC) said: "I don't think the government should have total control over what any company hires for any reason. . . . I don't think the government should decide who gets hired. . . . That's getting too far involved." Thus, even when talking about employers who prefer to hire whites, these interviewees did not feel that there was any inherent problem that needed to be addressed.

Because affirmative action is the iconic policy in any discussion of racial inequality in the United States, I wanted to ask about it without actually using the label "affirmative action" so that I could get at more honest and less emotional responses. Thus, instead of asking specifically about affirmative action, I asked the interviewees what they thought about the "changes that have occurred in access to both education and jobs" for women, and then separately for African Americans and for Hispanic and Asian immigrants. Although many interviewees indicated that they supported civil rights, in general they opposed policies like affirmative action. There were very predictable variations in the pattern of these views. As would be expected, the conservative groups were the most negative about policies like affirmative action, the liberal groups were the most positive, and the moderate groups were somewhere in between. Across the groups, the views were most favorable about the changes for women, less so for African Americans, and for five of the seven groups least so for immigrants. I coded the interviewee responses into positive, neutral, and negative views. The results by group are shown in table 8.2.

Given the responses from the interviewees, it was clear that the word-

Table 8.2 Coded Responses of Socioeconomic Groups to Questions Regarding Affirmative Action

Dimension	Working-Class Racists	Middle-Class Conservatives	Religious Conservatives	Apolitical Majority	Religious Nonconservatives	Working-Class Liberals	Rich White Liberals	Total
Percentage of sample	12%	4.5%	19%	37%	4.5%	6%	17%	100%
								Average
Changes for women[a]								
Negative	52	45	36	25	27	0	0	26
Neutral	3	18	24	13	0	0	14	13
Positive	45	36	40	62	73	100	86	61
Total								100
Changes for African Americans[a]								
Negative	84	70	51	46	36	0	6	44
Neutral	13	10	18	16	18	7	9	14
Positive	3	20	31	38	45	93	86	42
Total								100
Changes for immigrants[a]								
Negative	68	45	60	51	36	21	11	46
Neutral	26	18	20	20	27	50	23	23
Positive	6	36	20	30	36	29	66	31
Total								100

Source: Author's compilation.
Notes: Responses may not add up to 100 because of rounding error.
[a]Coded responses to question: "There are a number of issues that policymakers in government have been considering regarding education and jobs. I would like to ask about your opinions of some of these issues. For example, over the last couple of decades there have been many changes in both education and jobs, with more women and minorities getting into schools or jobs where they weren't previously. What do you think about the changes that have occurred in the kinds of education and jobs which women have been getting in the last couple of decades?" with follow-up: "What about African Americans? And what about Hispanic and Asian immigrants?"

ing of this question captured attitudes toward affirmative action. Overall, the pattern of responses to the questions about access to education and jobs for women, African Americans, and immigrants reflected differences in political attitudes among the sociopolitical groups in this study, as was the case for other questions discussed so far. In the following section, I provide examples of the responses given by the interviewees in each sociopolitical group in regard to government policies that have improved access to education and jobs for various groups of workers. As in previous chapters, I array the responses from the most conservative groups to the most liberal ones.

Working-Class "Racists"

The working-class "racist" interviewees were the most negative among the various sociopolitical groups about changes in access to education and jobs for women, African Americans, and immigrants. On this issue, they were outspoken, sometimes angry, and generally displeased with any government efforts to address issues of inequality for women or minorities. More so than other groups, the working-class "racists" seemed to believe that gains for women and minorities were at their own expense and were likely to have come about at the cost not only of their jobs but those of their children and friends. The working-class "racists" expressed concerns about their own economic situations. For these interviewees, getting jobs that were protected from the market, that offered medical and pension benefits, and that also offered the security of seniority was what made a middle-class lifestyle possible. Most of them were not secure in their jobs, and they or their family members were not protected from the market. Many reported that they were "barely making it." Thus, the sense of competition for jobs was presumably heightened for these interviewees, and it was reflected in how they responded to the question about changes in access to education and jobs.

In response to the question about women, the working-class "racist" interviewees were either hot or cold. For example, a retired factory worker in Ohio (E304 OH M WC) was positive about the changes that have occurred for women: "I think that is excellent. . . . Back when I was growing up . . . my father passed away. Well, there my mother was, you know, and jobs didn't grow on trees for women back then. . . . [*Are you favorable?*] Oh, yes, definitely." In contrast, another Ohio interviewee, a welder (B018 OH M WC), was quite negative: "Well, why should a woman get a job that she can't do?. . . A woman goes [into a company] and they hire her because she's a woman, but she can't lift the thing up. So they have to have a man there to cover for her butt. . . . Now, that's not right. If you can't do the job, you don't need the job." The notion that there are jobs that women cannot do and that the changes in access for women have been moving them into jobs that they cannot do was a familiar theme among the working-class "racists." An Ohio woman, a custodian (E312 OH F WC), made this point as well: "I think that women are being treated more equal than they were years ago. . . . Well, there are some jobs that women just can't do that men can do. . . . If the job is not anything to do with strength and lifting, I think that a woman should be treated equal." Some of the working-class "racists" also expressed concern about the effects on family life because of women in the paid labor force. For example, a New Jersey maintenance worker (D019 NJ M WC) said: "The only thing that's a shame is that the home life for everybody has gone downhill. . . . Women [are] not being home for the children. And it would be okay if men would get more involved, but they don't." Yet another Ohio interviewee, a homemaker (E318 OH F WC), expressed the concern that women might be taking jobs that should go to men:

> I like the changes to a certain extent. I mean, equal opportunity is great. But I feel that some women are taking those opportunities away from men to support their families. I believe that if there's a man and a woman up for the same job and that woman's husband is already working and that man is not and he has a family to provide for also, I think that man should get that job. Because she can always get a part-time job somewhere if they need extra cash.

A Tennessee travel agent (F027 TN F WC) expressed opposition to the use of quotas in making hiring decisions when asked about women's access to jobs:

> That's great, but I think sometimes it can be taken too far, like they have to be qualified. I mean, if it is a job that a man does better, then that's what it should be. . . . If a woman can do a man's job as well or better, then it should go to the woman. . . . As long as it is not taken to the other extreme and they hire them just because they need to hire more women.

Thus, although there was some positive sentiment about the changes that have occurred for women, most of the working-class "racists" expressed opposition to women taking men's jobs, or taking jobs and neglecting their families, or being given preference that they do not deserve.

The working-class "racist" interviewees were especially negative in their comments about the changes for African Americans. Almost all expressed views that were unfavorable. Even seemingly favorable comments often suggested less than full support. For example, a Tennessee accountant (G508 TN F WC) said: "I grew up in the segregated South. . . . That's neither healthy nor good. But I do think that most blacks don't understand how good they've got it compared to some other countries. . . . Most black Americans have absolutely no concept of how horrible their life would be if they were back in Africa." This was a relatively favorable comment compared to most of those offered by the working-class "racists." Many raised questions about the qualifications or intelligence of blacks, about their work ethic, or about the unfairness of government policies. Although extreme, the comments of an Ohio welder (B018 OH M WC) were not that far removed from the tenor of many of the other responses from the working-class "racist" interviewees:

> It ain't right. I come from city schools, and they had the same teachers, the same books, and they scream and they cry, aw, discrimination. They use that. They been using the Civil War for years. . . . That's reverse discrimination. . . . I'm a white man over forty, but I'm at the bottom of the totem pole in this country.

Another Ohio woman, who worked in warehouse sales (E340 OH F WC), also had rather negative views: "I don't like them. . . . They just expect that they should be handed everything, because they're black, and I just don't think that's fair."

A number of the working-class "racist" interviewees mentioned their opposition to quotas and their belief that standards are often lowered for blacks. For example, a New Jersey carpenter (D003 NJ M WC) said: "If they can pass the test, okay, but if we have to lower the standards of the test for them to pass it, then send them back to Africa where they belong." After claiming that African Americans should have more access to education, a Tennessee graphic designer (G520 TN M WC) nevertheless said: "They are gonna stay in projects, 'cause . . . they weren't taught to not be in projects. . . . You can't expect someone to have a work ethic when they are third-generation welfare recipient where nobody ever had a job." Similarly, an Ohio owner of a small industrial equipment company (E350 OH M WC) said that he did not think many African Americans applied for jobs like his. As he said: "Guarantee you they haven't. Work's too hard."

The working-class "racist" interviewees were almost, but not quite, as negative in their views of immigrants as they were of African Americans. Over two-thirds made negative comments with regard to changes for immigrants in access to education and jobs, and only two made comments that could be characterized as positive. The working-class "racist" interviewees were concerned about whether immigrants are legal and whether they pay taxes. These interviewees also said that U.S. citizens should get preference over immigrants and that we should help our own first. The working-class "racists" did not have a clear conception of what might be the differences between Asians and Hispanics. They just knew that Asians seemed to be better off than Hispanics. The working-class "racists" were also very concerned about immigrants who do not speak English. They assumed that some immigrants do not speak English either because they do not want to or because they are not made to do so, and they believed that speaking English should be a requirement for immigrants who want to live in the United States.

Most comments were highly negative and often volatile. For example, an Ohio surveyor (B008 OH M WC) said: "I think everybody that's illegal in this country, if they catch them, they should export them and never let them come back. . . . And the people that hire these people should forfeit everything they own to the government. . . . They stole jobs and money from the working-class American. . . . They're a thief." Another Ohio interviewee, a welder (B018 OH M WC), was quite strongly negative about immigrants: "They ought to take that Statue of Liberty and sink it. Take that plaque and get rid of it. . . . A long time ago, we needed them to build this country, but there's too many of us now. There's not enough jobs for the Americans that are here. Close the gate. Stop it." The New Jersey carpenter (D003 NJ M WC) had similar concerns: "If they're not going to become citizens, if they're going to come to this country, if they're going to take our money and take it back to their country, I say no. . . . Spend some of the goddamn New Jersey money right here in New Jersey."

A number of the working-class "racist" interviewees expressed the view that American citizens should have priority over immigrants when it comes to jobs and education. For example, an Ohio custodian (E312 OH F WC) said: "We have a lot of people in our country that are poor, and I feel that we should help our country more before we go out and start helping all these other people." A New Jersey housepainter (D012 NJ M WC) was especially concerned about the pressure being put on him to work faster and harder because of the immigrants with whom he worked. He said:

> If they're on the job . . . the immigrants stay there. And they are kissing . . . the boss's ass. They'll do what they ain't supposed to do, which is wrong. . . . They break the rules. . . . I come to do my job. And don't make me do any more than I have to. . . . And, really, they were like . . . slaves . . . drive me as hard. I mean, I got to a point where I was afraid to go get water, which to me, I shouldn't have to be. . . . You shouldn't have to be afraid to go to the bathroom. We're grown men. . . . You know, it's kind of hard.

The fear of this interviewee was representative of that of many of the working-class "racists" when it came to immigration. Unlike many of the interviewees from other sociopolitical groups who claimed, "We were all immigrants at one time," the working-class "racists" felt that immigration poses a threat to them and their livelihoods, to their access to jobs, and to their ability to keep their jobs and feed their families.

Compared to the other groups, the working-class "racists" were clearly the most negative in their responses to the changes that have occurred in access to education and jobs for women, African Americans, and for immigrants. Although there was some positive sentiment expressed with regard to the greater opportunities available to women, even the interviewees who were positive toward women's greater access to education and jobs also raised questions about the effects on the family, the appropriateness of some types of jobs for women, and whether the gains for women might have come at the expense of men. The views expressed by the working-class "racist" interviewees with regard to African Americans and immigrants, however, were overwhelmingly negative. Given that the working-class "racist" interviewees were the group whose job situations were the most vulnerable, they were not especially positive about social changes that would create more competition for them or change their roles within their families.

Middle-Class Conservatives

The middle-class conservative interviewees, who were one of the two groups that reported being in less favorable economic circumstances compared to those with similar education, expressed very conservative views with regard to various policy issues, but were less conservative in their views about immigrants than about other groups. The middle-class conservatives were as favorable in their comments regarding immigrants as they were in their comments about women, but they were much less favorable about African Americans.

Half of the interviewees in this group were women, and all of the interviewees from this group who were favorable about the changes for women were women. They tended to see the changes for women as good for themselves and good for their daughters. An Ohio nurse (E336 OH F MC) was positive but skeptical: "I personally have always thought that everybody should be equal. . . . Women have made a lot of strides in the last fifty years, but it is still not a woman's world. . . . I think if they are capable of doing the work, they should get the same pay." This positive view of the changes for women, however, was not necessarily shared by the other middle-class conservatives. For example, another Ohio interviewee, a homemaker (B021 OH F MC), was quite negative: "I was born after my time. . . . I just believe, and it's kind of like Bible-oriented, maybe too. You know, you have your family. You raise your kids. Mom stays home. And you know . . . these women and their careers, I'd like to just tell them where to stuff half of it." A New Jersey marketing manager (D073 NJ M MC) expressed concerns about the potential effects on men of changes for women: "My philosophy has always been, I have no problem with equal job, equal pay. . . . If they can qualify for the job. . . . The only thing I object to is when it's almost reverse discrimination. Better-qualified people are not given the job because of the other person's race or gender. That is what I object to."

The middle-class conservative interviewees were even less favorable about the changes that they perceived in access to education and jobs for African Americans. For example, a New Jersey small-business owner (D030 NJ M MC) felt that blacks have certain advantages:

> A lot of times they are not qualified, and they've gotten there just because either they fill a quota or they moved up because of their color. . . . I think it causes more friction between whites and blacks, because he may not have been qualified, but he was black or African American and he's there and somebody else didn't get in because, and you knew he had better grades or you might have known both kids in school.

The response of an Ohio interviewee, a man who worked as a worldwide business manager for new products (E338 OH M MC), seemed to sum up the view of the middle-class conservative interviewees with regard to African Americans having greater access to education and jobs: "Everybody wants it to be fair. . . . Life isn't fair, and you are going to lose out on jobs because another person knows somebody in that organization. . . . You are going to lose out on lots of things in life. . . . You can't legislate everything."

The middle-class conservatives, however, were less negative in their responses with regard to immigrants than they were regarding African Americans. Although almost half expressed negative views on immigrants' access to education and jobs, more than one-third expressed positive views. For example, a New Jersey small-business owner (D030 NJ M MC) presumably hired immigrants in his company, so his response was also positive: "I don't have any problem with them. . . . Most of the time they work like maniacs. They deserve everything they get. What I like about them is that we give them the same shots as a lot of the African Americans, and they make the most out of it."

The negative views about immigrants expressed by some middle-class conservatives spanned a spectrum of concerns about language, legality, and nativism. Many of these interviewees, however, were somewhat ambivalent about immigrants. For example, an Ohio nurse (E336 OH F MC) said:

> We're like back to the slave thing almost. People get so shitty about immigrants, you know. We're letting them in. We're like the greatest country in the world. They're all here and making more money than I am. . . . My kids

> are born and raised here. Why don't they get the same opportunity as this guy from Guatemala?. . . I do think this country gives a lot to noncitizens of this country and forgets about their own.

In summary, the middle-class conservative interviewees were mixed in their views about changes in access to education and jobs for women, though more toward the conservative side. They were much less favorable in their views of these changes for African Americans, and then mixed again in their views of immigrants. These interviewees were concerned about whether these groups were getting resources for education that were not available to them or their children and whether these groups were getting jobs that they did not deserve. The middle-class conservatives also expressed their opposition to the use of "quotas" and specifically to affirmative action.

Religious Conservatives

With regard to increased access to education and jobs for women, religious conservatives were about evenly divided between positive and negative attitudes, with about two-fifths holding each view. For example, a retired Ohio teacher (B016 OH M MC) said: "I think women ought to have the same access as men and ought to be paid the same. If you do the same work, you ought to get the same pay for it. Nothing else makes sense." A Tennessee factory worker (F011 TN M WC) was equally complimentary about the contributions made by women: "I think it's great. I think women deserve it."

Other religious conservative interviewees, however, raised issues about affirmative action, and especially about quotas. For example, an Ohio woman, an electrical engineering manager (B003 OH F MC), saw personal benefits from corporate policies with regard to women: "I definitely think it's easier for us, and we're kind of lucking out, and I also believe that it's beyond the level of being fair to men. . . . [At my company] some people who are more deserving of positions did not get it, because the company needed to have a woman." An Ohio man, a pharmaceutical sales manager (E314 OH M MC) who was an executive in a major company, saw it this way: "My resentment is when they get special treatment. I think it should still be an earned thing, and we should de-neuter the decision. . . . I speak from experience. . . . [My company has] gone out of our way to promote females in certain jobs that absolutely should not be there." Another Ohio interviewee, a homemaker (E309 OH F WC), raised questions about fairness: "I don't like people hiding behind . . . well, I'm a woman, and the government says X amount of women have to be hired for this job, so therefore the woman gets the job over the man that is better qualified. That rubs me wrong."

A New Jersey heavy-industry vice president (D013 NJ M MC) was unfavorable about changes for women because he felt that women should respond to a "higher purpose":

> I would love if all women, especially if they wanted to, if they're mothers, if they can get to stay home with the children. . . . I think the design was men were supposed to work and bring home a paycheck and provide. . . . Women are designed . . . to have the opportunity for the best contribution ever, to input on their kid's life. . . . Some women give that up on purpose. I think that's a crime.

One Ohio interviewee, a practical nurse (B009 OH F WC), said rather dramatically: "Well, I think that's partly the destruction of the world. . . . If I could be home and be a mother, although my kids are grown and everything, I'd still be here. I still think a woman's place is at home."

Fewer than one-third of the religious conservative interviewees expressed positive views about the changes in education and jobs for African Americans. Among those with positive views was an Ohio owner of a small company (B010 OH M MC), who said: "I think it's tremendous. I want to see more of it." A Tennessee aircraft assembler (G535 TN M WC) similarly said:

> Well, I think they're as intelligent as I am. . . . And I know they can do the job I do. They do it every day. . . . There was a time when they were not allowed, but in my opinion, it is as level a playing ground now as you can get. 'Cause there was a time when the blacks had a little bit of an advantage, because they had to hire the blacks instead of the whites 'cause they had to have quotas. . . . I don't think they discriminate on race anymore. I think they want somebody that can do the job.

Others among the religious conservative interviewees, however, were not quite so favorable in their comments. For example, an Ohio letter carrier (E326 OH M WC) said:

> They have been given a lot of extra consideration because of lobbying groups, NCAA and things like this. Again, I think we still carry a lot of stigmatism. There's still a lot of prejudice still going on. . . . I think we're coming to the realization that a lot of them have come from backgrounds that are less educated, that they are no different than us. The ones who are willing to work and go for it, they're going to get ahead.

A New Jersey engineer (D070 NJ M MC) discussed the opportunities available to African Americans with a somewhat more differentiated view of how the black community is faring:

> I think it can either be exceptional or it can be horrible. . . . If you are an African American who has two parents and you live in the suburbs and you go to the same schools that my kids go to and you get into college, the real opportunities are as good as my kids, if not better. If, on the other hand, you are an African American who has maybe one parent, you live in Elizabeth or Newark or South Plainfield, or whatever, and you know, your mother doesn't have enough money for a college education and the area you grow up in is very poor and there are drugs in the streets and stuff like that, I would say it is almost hopeless for them to get much beyond their current socioeconomic situation. So it is kind of a double-edged sword.

Half of the religious conservative interviewees were quite negative about the increased access to education and jobs for African Americans. Many expressed displeasure with affirmative action and the use of "quotas," felt that blacks are often not qualified for the positions that they are given, or believed that standards have been lowered. Surprisingly, a number were unhappy about the existence of the United Negro College Fund, because they felt that it is unfair for blacks to have a special lobbying group that helps black kids attend college. For example, an Ohio graphic designer (E367 OH M WC) said: "It seems like there are more programs that are helping finance education for blacks. . . . I don't feel real good about specific groups supporting just one type of minority. . . . It almost . . . heightens prejudice." Given that this issue came up a number of times, it seems that there was very little recognition among these interviewees of the resource advantages in areas like education that already exist for whites. Instead, programs or services for blacks were perceived by these interviewees as African Americans getting more than their share rather than their "share" being made whole after years of discrimination. As an unemployed Ohio teacher (B007 OH F MC) said: "Whether it's women or blacks or any minorities, I think everyone should have the same access to any job. . . . Just because they belong to that group at the expense of somebody, perhaps a white male that needs a job, that's wrong too. And that's happened." Thus, the views of religious conservatives about African Americans were more negative than positive, as more of them claimed that providing African Americans with greater access to jobs and education has contributed to their getting an unfair advantage that they have not earned and do not deserve.

The religious conservative interviewees were even more negative in their responses regarding immigrants' greater access to education and jobs, with 60 percent expressing negative views and only 20 percent expressing positive views. A retired Ohio teacher (B016 OH M MC) was one interviewee who saw the issue of immigrants positively:

> I would have loved to have a room full of Asian kids if I was teaching. Gosh, talk about motivated people. I don't know what their parents put in them, but Asian kids, Jewish kids, Greek kids. . . . You could put fifty in a room and teach them with ease, because they all have this desire or a goal. I've never met a bad Asian kid.

The majority of the religious conservative interviewees, however, expressed very unfavorable views of the increased number of immigrants and their access to education and jobs. Common themes were that immigrants need to be legal and to pay taxes. There was an underlying assumption among the interviewees that illegal immigrants do not pay taxes. For example, an Ohio quality control manager (B002 OH M MC) said:

> If they're not here legally, then they have no business being here, and they should be sent back home. . . . That's one thing that drives me crazy, especially out in California. . . . They bring these people in. They haven't paid a dime into anything for their whole life. They come over here. They have a kid, and now they're going to give them Social Security and Medicaid and Medicare benefits. . . . Hit it back down to Mexico. I think you need to pay your dues.

Some of the other religious conservative interviewees expressed displeasure at the possibility that immigrants might want to change the way things are done in the United States. A Tennessee music teacher (G509 TN F MC), for example, was concerned about immigrants getting advantages over U.S. citizens:

> I think if I lived in another country that it would be the most wonderful thing in the world to come to America and have opportunities that you wouldn't have there. So my heart goes out to them . . . but I think we've gone overboard in reaching out to other countries and bringing them in when we have so many here of our own children [who cannot get] government scholarships. . . . They're getting [them] and some of our kids can't get [them].

Perhaps the views of the religious conservatives about immigration can be summarized by a New Jersey heavy-industry vice president (D013 NJ M MC) who had hired a number of immigrants in the factory that he managed: "They work hard, so I mean, God bless them. . . . This whole problem with immigration. That is a problem, I think . . . because that's a drain.... You have this system set up, and they're draining it, and they're not even legal. That's a crime."

The religious conservatives were generally favorable about the improved opportunities for women, but a number raised issues about the fairness of affirmative action or quotas, about whether women can do certain types of jobs, and especially whether families and children are adversely affected when women work outside the home. The concerns raised by religious conservatives about greater access to education and jobs for African Americans were more explicitly focused on affirmative action and the use of quotas and on whether blacks have the qualifications to be considered the "best person." The concerns about immigrants raised by religious conservatives centered on whether immigrants are legal and paying taxes or whether they are getting a "free ride." The religious conservatives felt strongly that immigrants should learn to speak English. Overall, religious conservatives appealed to norms of fairness, patriotism, and family values in their discussions about the greater access to education and jobs available to various groups since the civil rights movement.

Apolitical Majority

Most of the apolitical majority interviewees were positive about the changes that have occurred for women in access to education and jobs. For example, an unemployed Ohio cost accountant (E358 OH M WC) said: "I think that everyone should be given an opportunity to have an education.... I have no problem with that at all. I think women should have equal pay for equal jobs. If you can do what I can do, then you should make my money." A New Jersey financial analyst (D066 NJ M MC) also noted the contributions that women make: "I think it is fantastic. I mean, I think everybody should have equal opportunity. If one person can outshine another person, so be it, no matter what gender or race. I've seen all types of successful people, one of them being my mother, and she is a female. I think it's a good thing to see." An older New Jersey interviewee, a deli clerk (D020 NJ F WC), was favorable about the changes for women, but also raised a cautionary note:

> I think young girls today are just as dumb as the girls were when I was seventeen.... They're still boy-crazy and everything.... I think what happened is now ... everything is just so taken for granted. Like a girl can be anything, so it's no big deal anymore. Being the first female cop, first female fireman. It's no big deal now. So what?

A number of the apolitical majority interviewees, however, were not quite as ready to say that women entering jobs from which they had previously been excluded is not a big deal. Some were concerned about whether women can handle the jobs, and others were concerned about the likely impact on the family. The views of some interviewees were primarily shaped by their general opposition to affirmative action–type policies. For example, a self-employed Tennessee entertainer (G532 TN M WC) said:

> I'm not for affirmative action, if that's what you're looking for. . . . I think it swings the pendulum in the other way too far. It tries to overcompensate. . . . I think it swaps one problem for another . . . rather than . . . the best person wins, the best person gets the job.

This issue was raised in a somewhat different way by a New Jersey billing clerk (D037 NJ F MC): "I think sometimes it tends to hurt us, 'cause you feel like companies are hiring women just to meet some kind of quota. . . . I would rather be hired on my abilities. I don't want to think that I was hired to fill some kind of quota." A number of the apolitical majority interviewees also expressed concern about the effects of having more women in the paid labor force on family life. For example, an Ohio project engineering manager (B017 OH M MC) framed it this way:

> I'm favorable. I think they ought to have the opportunity should they so desire to do that, but I think we're paying a price. . . . When you are trying to put people to work and you are encouraging . . . a lot more people in the workforce into professional positions . . . into a market where you take away positions from single breadwinners within the family. . . . Then we got kids in day care.

Some of the apolitical majority interviewees raised other types of issues in the concerns they expressed about the improved access that women have to education and jobs. For example, an Ohio factory worker (E307 OH M WC) said: "I think women should have the same opportunities, but it's been my observation at the company I work for that women are more intimidated by supervision. . . . If they told them to move a mountain, they would try to move the mountain rather than saying, 'This is stupid. You go move the mountain.'" A New Jersey accountant (D028 NJ F MC), however, did not think that government action made much of a difference: "Maybe because I've never been confronted with any form of discrimination that it hasn't posed an issue in my mind. I've never known anybody who has ever been confronted with that, and my mother worked with a group of men. She found a job."

Overall, the apolitical majority interviewees were favorable about the changes in access to education and jobs for women, often because they could relate these changes to personal experiences or to those of people they knew. Some qualified their support by saying that women have to be able to do the jobs that men do, but the majority of the interviewees were nevertheless favorable. A sizable minority of the apolitical majority interviewees, however, expressed either negative or neutral views. Some were opposed to affirmative action or quotas, while others were concerned about the impact on the family of having more women in the paid labor force. And some claimed that these are not issues that need to be addressed by the government because it is women themselves who are making choices about how they want to live their lives. A few were favorable, but skeptical, about whether things have changed all that much. Perhaps the views of the apolitical majority are best summed up by a New Jersey customer service worker (D025 NJ F WC) who said: "I don't see why they shouldn't. Everybody has every right to do whatever they want to do."

The apolitical majority interviewees expressed views that were in between the more liberal and conservative groups on the issue of greater access to education and jobs for African Americans. They were decidedly less positive about the changes for African Americans than they were with regard to women, although their views on African Americans were slightly more positive than their views on immigrants. Almost half of the apolitical majority interviewees expressed negative views about the changes for African Americans, while not quite 40 percent expressed positive views. On the positive side, an Ohio interviewee, the owner of a small trucking company (E365 OH M WC), said: "They are people the same as you and I are, and as long as they perform, they have the same rights. . . . The only difference . . . is that they have different skin color." A Tennessee retiree (F020 TN F WC) related her views to the successes of former coworkers: "I think that changes to help them has been good. I've seen my coworkers with no more education than I had, because they worked, were able to move on, and I was very happy and proud for them. . . . And I think that is great." A Tennessee man, however, was not quite as certain that discrimination is a thing of the past. A musician (G517 TN M MC), he said:

> I think there's a huge double standard right now. . . . Oh, I just think that a lot of people, specifically white Americans, want to feel like they're doing right, and the problems of the past unfortunately have created problems now that don't create easy solutions for the multifaceted problems that we're experiencing as an integrated society. I think there's still a small amount of separate-but-equal mentality that exists.

An Ohio rehabilitation educator (E323 OH F MC) was similarly concerned that perhaps there has not been enough change with regard to African Americans when she described a local school district with two hundred teachers, only one of whom was black: "Somehow there just hasn't been another qualified minority applicant. . . . So I guess there might be a problem."

Others, however, thought that blacks bear some responsibility for their current situation, and they perceived the changes for African Americans in a negative light. For example, an Ohio high school social studies teacher (B012 OH F MC) noted:

> I feel bad for the blacks who feel that they've been left behind. And in some instances, it might be discrimination because of race, but in a lot of instances I think they have not realized that the potential was there, but it's not going to get handed to you. You really have to go out and do something to get it, besides just say that you want it and complain that you didn't get it.

Another Ohio woman, a bookkeeper in a home business (E320 OH F WC), said: "I hate to say it, but I really think they'll never be equal. . . . The stereotype, it will never go away. . . . I think there are some black people out there that ruin it for others . . . Al Sharpton. He seems crooked as the day's going to end, and I think he ruins it for a lot of black people." An Ohio woman who was an unemployed real estate agent (E334 OH F WC) raised questions about the situation for blacks: "I hate to see any ethnic group given more than others . . . because I think that anybody who finds themselves in difficult circumstances can use help. I don't know that ethnicity or race is really as much of a handicap as some people like to think it is." Skepticism was also expressed by a New Jersey special education teacher (D043 NJ F MC): "I work in a situation where sometimes they feel they are not being treated fairly, but I think that people who are not treated fairly are treated that way for a reason."

The view that African Americans are not stepping up to the opportunities given to them was a theme of a number of the apolitical majority interviewees. For example, a Tennessee woman, a librarian (G506 TN F MC), said:

> I believe that it's better, but anybody who says it's where it should be is not realistic. . . . The opportunity for loans, for aid, for getting into good schools, for God forbid that awful ratio thing that they have come up with, is there. But I believe that a lot of black Americans are held back by their heritage, that nonmarrying, raise your children on your own, no family life in a lot of cases, welfare mothers. I'm sorry, but those children will continue to grow up in a world, I don't want to say, without hope, but just not whole.

The views expressed by many of the apolitical majority interviewees, especially when they talked about African Americans, were grounded in the "dominant ideology" of individualism and self-reliance (Kluegel and Smith 1986). Although most expressed positive views about the changes for blacks in access to education and jobs, many qualified their statements by saying that the "best person" should get the job and that opportunities are there that blacks do not utilize or embrace because, as a Tennessee postal worker (F018 TN M WC) said: "There still is a lot of them that got a big chip on their shoulders." To most of these apolitical majority interviewees, even if there are barriers or difficulties, persistence and self-reliance should triumph because, they said, if you want it enough, you will be able to get it.

The apolitical majority interviewees were even less favorable in their views about access to education and jobs for immigrants. A majority expressed negative views, and another 20 percent were neutral or mixed in their responses. Fewer than one-third responded with favorable views about the opportunities available to immigrants. The respondents were asked specifically about Asian and Hispanic immigrants, and surprisingly, few had very clear understandings about the differences between these groups. Many recognized that Asians are doing better economically than Hispanics, but they tended to attribute that circumstance to the value that Asians place on education and their intelligence rather than to structural factors about each group's mode of incorporation into the country and their relative composition (Alba and Nee 2003; Massey, Durrand, and Malone 2002; Patchen 1999). Those among the apolitical majority who were favorable about opening up access to education and jobs for immigrants said such things as, "People are people," or, "Everyone deserves a chance," and they also called attention to immigrants' contributions to the country. Some claimed that immigrants take jobs that Americans do not want.

For example, an Ohio woman who worked as a door-to-door advertising manager (E302 OH F WC) said with regard to immigrants: "If they're here and they're human beings and they're doing the work . . . it shouldn't matter if they're citizens or not. They're still doing the same work. Why shouldn't they get the same pay?" A similarly tolerant view was expressed by an Ohio man, a factory worker (E307 OH M WC), who said:

> I have no problem with immigrants. I think we need to have a thoughtful immigration policy, but most of these folks are just coming here to get a better life, and having enjoyed the life I've had, how can I say that they don't have the right to want a better life? The problem is, you can't bring everybody in the world up to our lifestyle.

Half of the apolitical majority interviewees, however, were less open-minded about the presence of immigrants. Although some interviewees said that they did not know enough about them or did not have much exposure to them, others expressed concern that immigrants are taking jobs that Americans need or replacing Americans who are being pushed out of jobs because immigrants will work for less. Some were very concerned that immigrants are receiving public benefits that are not available to Americans. Many of the apolitical majority interviewees also drew a line between legal and illegal immigrants and expressed strongly negative sentiments toward the latter. A New Jersey assistant stock trader (D024 NJ M WC), for example, expressed this view: "[If illegal], I don't think they should be living here. . . . If they're illegal, they don't deserve any of these jobs." A number of the interviewees believed that if immigrants are illegal they are, by definition, not paying taxes.

The apolitical majority interviewees also were troubled by what they assumed were the social services available to immigrants. These misconceptions were evident in the comments of an Ohio licensed practical nurse (E325 OH F WC): "Any foreigner can come into the country and get help right off the bat, which is okay for short term. They shouldn't be able to stay on it. . . . The government's paying for them to set up their own business. How many times has the government helped us set up our own business? You know, Americans?" A Tennessee librarian (G506 TN F MC) also believed that social services are immediately available to immigrants: "I'm not always sure that I agree with as soon as you set foot on this soil that you should be getting welfare and food stamps and everything. . . . This is a country where we're all immigrants, but I do believe that a little bit more help could be given to some people that are already here too." In these and similar comments, the interviewees seemed to be confusing immigrants with refugees, who, by international law, are given certain protections and services if they are unable to return to their countries for fear of persecution.[4]

Concern that immigrants are taking jobs from Americans was a theme across a number of the interviews. A Tennessee vending machine route man (G522 TN M WC) claimed to have had experience with the way immigrants are affecting jobs for Americans: "When I was working in the landscaping industry, and I would go to a lot of the nurseries, they were letting go all the Caucasian people they had working for 'em and hiring Hispanics, 'cause they would work for lower wages." A New Jersey landscaper (D074 NJ M WC) was similarly concerned: "A lot of them work under the table. I see it around here. It is taking away from somebody here that could work. . . . What they'll do is that they will work here for cheap, and then they'll send the money back to their country. . . . It is taking away from the people here."

A number of the apolitical majority interviewees were also concerned about immigrants who do not speak English, and their comments reflected some nativism as well. An Ohio insurance office manager (E335

OH F WC) said with regard to immigrants: "I know that it makes me mad that English seems to be a second language in some of the schools. If you want to come to America, fine. My grandmother was an immigrant. But learn the language and live by the same rules everybody else does." An unemployed Tennessee interviewee (F014 TN M WC) believed that Americans should take care of their own first: "I don't really have a problem with it as long as they're here to apply themselves, but I think sometimes it seems like in this day and time, we can't take care of our own people. . . . I just sometimes think we need to take care of our own."

Thus, the apolitical majority interviewees raised concerns that immigrants might be getting government services that should go to Americans, that they undermine the ability of Americans to get living wages and reasonable working conditions by working for less, and that they do not learn English or assimilate to American culture. There were also concerns expressed about whether immigrants take undue advantage of American programs like Social Security and welfare and whether they send money to their home countries rather than spend it in the United States and help the U.S. economy. Although there was some expression of sympathy for the circumstances that might lead immigrants to want to come to the United States, most of the apolitical majority interviewees felt that Americans should take care of their own first.

Overall, the apolitical majority interviewees were generally favorable about improved access to education and jobs for women, much less so for African Americans, and even less so for immigrants. Most thought that it is very positive for women to have more opportunities for both education and jobs, especially with the increased demands on families to have more than one person working outside the home for pay. Those with more traditional views, however, were concerned about the impact on the family and especially on children. Some were also concerned that women are getting opportunities that should be available to men or that they are being given preference over men. The comments with regard to African Americans were dramatically less favorable. There were many concerns raised about blacks getting jobs that they do not deserve, about affirmative action or equal opportunity policies being unfair, and about blacks being "handed stuff" that they do not deserve. Concerns were also raised about whether African Americans would ever be satisfied, because some claimed that enough was never enough. A few were positive about the changes for African Americans, but sometimes qualified their statements with the condition, "if they have the qualifications." Others invoked the need to provide jobs to the "best person."

The concerns that the apolitical majority interviewees raised with regard to immigrants were partly based on a misunderstanding of the distinction between immigrants and refugees. Some apolitical majority interviewees seemed to think that immigrants have ready access to government services and programs, including welfare. Some said that the United States should take care of U.S. citizens before helping people from other countries. Although individuals with refugee status who are fleeing persecution or violence and have been admitted to the United States as refugees receive temporary services, this is not the situation for immigrants. Refugees make up a small portion of noncitizens in the United States. A few of the interviewees called attention to the contributions that immigrants make or noted that "we were all immigrants" in times past, but others felt that immigrants need to conform to U.S. culture, that they should learn to speak English, and that they should be denied access to education or jobs if they are not legal, do not pay taxes, and do not adapt themselves to U.S. culture. A number of the apolitical majority interviewees also felt that immigrants are taking jobs that should go to Americans and that they are undercutting the wage structure by working for lower wages. Some expressed concerns about the level of immigration, although many also claimed not to know much about immigration because they did not think they encountered many immigrants in their daily lives.

Religious Nonconservatives

Although religious nonconservatives expressed views similar to those of rich white liberals and working-class liberals on other policy issues, on issues like affirmative action and equal opportunity policies, religious nonconservatives were less favorable. Their views differed, however, depending on the target group. Religious nonconservatives were generally favorable about the changes for women, but much more mixed with regard to increased access to education and jobs for African Americans, and they were even less favorable with regard to immigrants.

Three-quarters of the religious nonconservatives gave favorable responses with regard to the access that women now have to education and jobs. For example, a Tennessee government worker (F013 TN F MC) said:

> I think that it has been the making of this country. When I started seeking employment, women could either be secretaries or teachers or nurses. Now my daughter can be anything she wants to be. Because of that, I think this country will be a better place . . . because she may come up with some ideas that . . . a male would never, ever think of.

Another Tennessee woman, a minister (F020 TN F MC), was also quite positive. She said: "I think it's great. . . . I think society, in general, really is accepting of women. People don't blink an eye if a woman is a police officer, fire person, doctor, lawyer."

Not all of the religious nonconservative interviewees, however, expressed favorable views about women's greater access to education and jobs. For example, an Ohio radiology technician (E329 OH F WC) expressed her concerns about quotas:

> I think that the best person should get the job, whether it's a man or a woman. I don't think the sex should have any bearing on it whatsoever. . . . I think it's taking a major flip-flop from being white male to them going, okay, we don't have enough women. . . . If we don't hire a woman, it's going to look really bad. It's not our quota. . . . The best person should get it.

Thus, religious nonconservatives were generally positive about the changes that have occurred for women in the last several decades, but a few expressed more traditional views about the roles for men and women. Some also expressed concern about equity and indicated that we should follow the principle that the "best person" gets the job.

Although religious nonconservatives were much less favorable about the changes for African Americans, some expressed positive views, such as this part-time preschool supervisor (E330 OH F MC) from Ohio:

> I know whites that have problems with affirmative action and that kind of thing. When I take a closer look at that and I compare the chances of African Americans breaking into the job cycle, if we don't do anything about it and how hard it is to break cycles and patterns that you are repeating because of your familial patterns, I think it's something that needs to be done. And I think it's working.

A Tennessee government worker (F013 TN F MC) was positive but tempered in her response: "I think it's something that was very much needed. I think that probably women have come farther than African Americans. . . . I think that people tend to think of the South as being more racist, but I think it was pervasive all over the country. . . . It's certainly not been solved yet."

Slightly more than half of religious nonconservatives expressed either neutral or negative views about the changes for African Americans. For example, a Tennessee travel representative (F022 TN F WC) said: "I don't really believe in giving the black person or the woman the job just to meet your quota if they are not qualified. It needs to be the person who is qualified for that job." A Tennessee deputy sheriff (G501 TN M MC) was especially negative about the changes that have occurred for African Americans: "What we've got is a situation where we've opened up jobs to people who are not necessarily as educated and qualified to do jobs in the workplace. . . . And I think it has been a hurt to our country. . . . I think too much has been given to these people without them earning it."

Similarly, another Tennessee man, an electronic publishing coordinator (G507 TN M WC), said: "I think there have been tremendous leaps. I don't think it's there yet. . . . I think in some cases, I think we've gone overboard to try, and it's gotten ridiculous that way."

The views expressed by religious nonconservatives with regard to changes in education and jobs for immigrants were even less favorable. For example, a Tennessee retail salesperson (F010 TN F WC) said: "I don't have a nice answer to that. I think that America is taking care of Americans very, very poorly. . . . We have a whole lot of messes right here in the United States. . . . I am ready for Americans to take care of Americans, and to come up with better solutions for ourselves before we start trying to save the world." Other interviewees said that they did not know much about the situation with immigrants. For example, a Tennessee teacher (F007 TN F MC) said: "I really don't know enough about it. . . . It seems like they tend to do more manual labor and don't get a lot of education, but I don't know whose fault that is or why. It would seem to me that blacks are much more mainstreamed now than immigrants are."

Thus, the religious nonconservatives were generally positive with regard to the changes in access to education and jobs for women, but much less so for African Americans and immigrants. A number interpreted this question in terms of affirmative action and then expressed their objection to setting quotas in the hiring process. A few outlined the importance of hiring the "best-qualified" person for the job. Some said that they did not know enough to form an opinion. Because the religious nonconservative interviewees were disproportionately from Tennessee, perhaps their views were also shaped by the general political environment of the region.

Working-Class Liberals

Working-class liberals were uniformly positive about the changes for women. For example, an Ohio interviewee who worked with her husband in a family business doing construction (E355 OH F WC) said:

> The women's rights movement was great, because they really helped women. I love seeing other women doing construction. I like seeing women doctors. I like seeing men nurses. . . . Because you know they're making just as much. . . . Why should guys be the only ones who get the high paying jobs?. . . It took forever for women to get hired, but now they're really opening up the doors and letting us in.

Among working-class liberals, the men were just as positive as the women about the improved access to education and jobs for women. For example, an Ohio man, a building contractor (E368 OH M WC), said: "Absolutely necessary and probably long overdue. . . . You can see the results from it. You know, a very good thing. I think you would have to be crazy not to think that it was necessary." A Tennessee electronics engineer (G533 TN M WC) explained his positive attitude toward the changes for women this way:

> Oh, I think it's great. . . . I grew up being raised by my mom. She was absolutely Wonder Woman. She was fierce and strong and took care of two kids on her own and earned all the money and ran the house and fed us and got us to school and loved us. And she was an extreme feminist. . . . I feel like we're all the same things inside, and I think we are all capable of the same things. . . . I'm very happy to see those kinds of things overturned and changing.

The working-class liberal interviewees were nearly as positive about the changes that have occurred for African Americans as they were about changes for women. For example, an Ohio woman who worked as a receptionist in a doctor's office (B005 OH F WC) said: "Well, they're people too. The color of their skin should not have put them in the position that they were in. . . . I don't look at the color of someone's skin and think, oh, you shouldn't have a Harvard degree. . . . It doesn't register in my mind." A Tennessee clerical worker (G504 TN F WC) said simply: "They deserve it the same as anyone else." A Tennessee small-business owner (G512 TN M WC) said: "We've got an African American working for us, and she is awesome."

Some interviewees put their support for such changes into a context. For example, a Tennessee man who worked as a commercial artist (G519 TN M WC) said: "I think it is good. . . . I understand that there are more blacks going to school and graduating. . . . I don't have a problem providing an education for black people, so long as white people, and women, and Chinese, and all that get a fair shot at it too. . . . Come on, what is the issue? I don't get it." Yet another Tennessee man, an electronics engineer (G533 TN M WC), said: "I think it is a great thing."

Given the overwhelmingly positive support from working-class liberals for increased access to education and jobs for women and African Americans, it is interesting that their views with regard to the access available to immigrants were much more mixed. Some were positive, such as this New Jersey computer technician (D008 NJ M WC), who said:

> I consider us a nation of immigrants. . . . I think that's the basis of the United States in its formative years, and I think it's still a continuation of the growth structure. . . . So I don't think it's an issue. I think we're built on

> immigrants, and I think our whole premise should be that education and workfare should be available to all of us.

But half of the working-class liberal interviewees expressed neutral views and one-fifth expressed negative views with regard to access to education and jobs for Asian and Hispanic immigrants, compared to nearly uniformly positive responses to changes for women and African Americans. The working-class liberals had concerns that immigrants might undercut wages for working-class jobs, that immigrants might expect to receive welfare, or that immigrants do not want to learn English. In some cases, the responses reflected lack of familiarity with or knowledge of immigrant populations. Unlike the views expressed by the more conservative sociopolitical groups, however, the responses of the working-class liberals with regard to immigrants, even when neutral or negative, were not necessarily angry or exclusionary. Rather, they set conditions under which immigration should be viewed more positively or as a matter of concern.

For example, an Ohio homemaker (E303 OH F WC) suggested that opportunities for immigrants should depend on conditions: "If they're living here, they're paying their taxes. . . . I mean, if they're living here and paying their dues like everybody else, they should be able to get a job just like anybody else." A Tennessee woman who worked as a massage therapist (G523 TN F WC) was similarly receptive:

> If they came from poor areas where they don't have any education, and I think it is very hard. And they are taking the lower-paying jobs here locally that no one else wants. To be honest with you, they take a lot of construction and a lot of cleaning and a lot of the McDonald's kinds of jobs. It is amazing how many are entrepreneurs. . . . I don't know if I would be that brave in their position.

Others, however, were not quite so willing to welcome immigrants. An Ohio construction worker (E366 OH F WC) made the following comment: "Well, I don't like the way they come over here. . . . If you come over here with a visa and become a U.S. citizen, learn our English, learn to read, write, and talk, fine. Become a U.S. citizen, but we should not have to support them because they're refugees." A Tennessee small-business owner (G512 TN M WC) expressed a concern that immigrants might undermine wages for U.S. citizens: "If they're not citizens . . . they could work for nothing if they wanted to, and it's going to affect people that are trying to get jobs that aren't going to make at least minimum wage."

The working-class liberal interviewees were tolerant, accepting, and supportive of increased access to education and jobs for women and African Americans, but when it came to the topic of immigrants, some were more likely to draw a line about rights and responsibilities that seemed to underscore their concerns about the quality of jobs that would be available to them and people like them. They were open to immigrants if they were legal, learned English, paid taxes, and worked at legal wages. Most working-class liberals did not think of immigrants in terms of civil rights, but rather in terms of citizenship rights. In this regard, except for the few who noted that we are a nation of immigrants, working-class liberals believed that Americans should have priority over immigrants when it came to access to jobs. They were less concerned about access to education, and those who mentioned it were favorable about immigrants having access to education if they were willing to work at it and conform to U.S. culture.

Rich White Liberals

Most rich white liberal interviewees expressed positive views about the improved access to education and jobs for women. For example, a New Jersey executive (C001 NJ F MC), a woman, said: "I think the value of it is incalculable. . . . It would be impossible for me today to tell you how significant it is today. . . . There's still so far to go." Another New Jersey interviewee, a marketing executive (D064 NJ F MC), was equally emphatic about her support for the changes for women:

> Affirmative action was and still is necessary. As again, I work in a very white, very male-dominated company right now, and they still don't get it. And so I think that there are places where you need that. I think that the Family Leave Act is the best thing. . . . I don't know that I ever could have worked if I had to go back after six weeks.

Each of these women benefited from the opportunities that opened up for women because of government policies in the post–civil rights period, and they were especially successful. Among the rich white liberals, men were also supportive of the changes that have benefited women. For example, a Tennessee musician (G530 TN M MC) said: "Women have moved way ahead, and I think it is great. . . . There's no reason for women not to be in those positions. I think they should be in those positions."

Other rich white liberal interviewees were supportive of the changes for women, but felt that there had not been enough change. For example, a New Jersey homemaker (D068 NJ F MC) expressed reservations: "I think it is good, but it is never going to be equal. . . . I still think women are underpaid compared to men. . . . I was in corporate America. I know in my own company how the men made more money." A male merchandising manager from New Jersey (D071 NJ M MC) made a similar point: "I think they've got a lot more opportunity than they had, yet it is still limited. There are still probably glass ceilings or whatever they want to call it. . . . It is good that they have got [more opportunity]. You need both of us working."

An Ohio primary school music teacher (E322 OH F MC) also expressed support, but with limitations: "I think it's fantastic, but when I'm on the third floor and there's a fire, I don't want some 120-pound firewoman coming up the ladder to carry me out. I think it's gone to the extreme in some professions. . . . No, I don't want them in those physical jobs." A New Jersey music manager (D006 NJ M MC) was supportive of the opportunities opening up for women, but he thought that there might be some jobs that women are not able to do as well as a man: "I don't know that a woman should be given equal access to a construction job." But, he also said, "I honest to God believe that women are smarter than men. . . . I think the barriers are coming down. . . . Their time is very quickly coming, becoming more broad-based, especially with all the information technology. It's about smarts. . . . It's wide open." This interviewee, however, was not especially prescient in his predictions about the future when he said: "I fully expect to see a female president within the next twenty years. I think you'll see a female president a lot faster than you'll see a black one."

Overall, however, the rich white liberal interviewees were extremely positive in their views about the improved access for women to education and jobs. They felt that the time has come, that more needs to be done, that there never should have been barriers in the first place, and that the skills women bring to the workplace are valuable and should be tapped. A number mentioned that women are still paid less and that there are still limitations to what women have the opportunity to do, but many were optimistic about continued improvement for women and did not feel that there is a way to reverse the trend.

The rich white liberal interviewees were equally supportive of the changes that have occurred for African Americans in terms of access to education and jobs. The female marketing executive from New Jersey (D064 NJ F MC) responded this way:

> Well, I think that affirmative action did amazing things. . . . Reality is, we don't have an equal education system, and if you want to have not just the highest socioeconomic African Americans going on to college and . . . since we are not investing to fix all of the school systems so they are equal, you can't have equal standards . . . you just can't. . . . Harvard would never have anything other than WASPs in it if they hadn't put in affirmative action. They would just have the husbands and the brothers and the sisters. . . . You have to consciously change that world, don't you think?

Another New Jersey interviewee, a government employee (D026 NJ M MC), made similar comments, but perhaps even more pointedly:

> Just amazing. . . . I think the general population of African Americans wasn't educated as well. . . . Even today the education isn't the same. And I find white America to be very selfish and no understanding that being born white is an automatic edge. Being born white male is an automatic edge. . . . I thought affirmative action was right. We denied basic educational rights to, and job rights to, African Americans for many, many years. . . . But I did agree that there should have been an edge given to African Americans, because the edge was given to white Americans for many, many years.

Similarly, a Tennessee school system administrator (G514 TN M MC) framed his response in terms of the positive outcomes of greater opportunities for African Americans: "Been absolutely the best and the right thing to do in the world. I think I was deprived as a child by not being in an integrated setting. Once I began to meet people who were different from me, it enriched my life."

In contrast to these very positive views of the greater access that African Americans have had to education and jobs, there were some who raised concerns. For example, a public-sector worker in New Jersey (D045 NJ M MC) spoke from the experiences that he said were occurring in his workplace when efforts were made to open opportunity to African Americans whom he felt did not have the necessary skills. As he described it:

> We take our clerks and try to promote them . . . and it is by and large a disaster. . . . They don't have the skills. . . . And these are people who graduated [from the local high school] in their honors program, which is a total farce. . . . [One clerk said,] "I don't know why you are criticizing me. I was an honors English student." And I was aghast. . . . It gives a lot of disadvantaged people the wrong idea about what their skill levels are.

Although less favorable in their responses regarding immigrants compared to women or African Americans, two-thirds of the rich white liberal interviewees gave positive responses when asked about the changes for immigrants. This represents a much more positive response than that given by any of the other sociopolitical groups of interviewees with regard to immigrants. A representative comment was made by a Tennessee record producer (G516 TN M MC), who said: "I think it's great. The more access, the better. I love diversity. That is what this country is all about, should be about. I think it's great." An Ohio engineer (E306 OH M MC) was also receptive to immigrants:

> Those groups have worked very hard, especially the Asians. . . . They have the ability, and I don't see a problem. I guess I'm a little concerned that they would come here to take jobs in the United States . . . but I look at that as more of a competitive issue in the world economy. . . . I think Americans have the same opportunities, and if they don't want to work as hard as the Asians, then they don't deserve the jobs.

A Tennessee man, a musician (G530 TN M MC), made similar comments about Hispanic immigrants: "They work their butts off. It is sort of amazing the attitude towards them is fairly good, I think. . . . They all seemed to have good families." A New Jersey man who worked as a builder (C009 NJ M MC) echoed this view: "I'm much more in favor . . . of giving people who want to achieve in any of those races or ethnicities the opportunity to do it."

Other rich white liberal interviewees were somewhat less positive in their views of the opportunities available to immigrants. For example, the Ohio primary school music teacher (E322 OH F MC) said: "I think it's important that they have some access, as long as they're not taking my job. We can't save the world. . . . We're no longer the melting pot, and we're fighting for our own now." A New Jersey man, who worked as an assistant manager in a major food company (D061 NJ M MC), suggested that Asians are experiencing more positive outcomes than Latinos: "I see an incredible dichotomy. I see the Orientals come here, and they seem to be very focused on progressing their lives and getting an education. . . . Hispanics . . . just tend not to, I guess, do as well. . . . I don't know if it is genetics or lack of interest or what." Neutral or negative views of immigrants, however, constituted only about one-third of the responses from the rich white liberals; the majority of them were positive about the opportunities available to immigrants as well as those now available to women and African Americans.

The rich white liberal interviewees again stand out as the most liberal among the interviewees. In general, they tend to be open-minded, tolerant, generous, and even, in a few cases, willing to sacrifice so that others may have the kinds of chances that they have had. Of course, they also are the most well-to-do among the interviewees, have the most education, and, based on their job positions, enjoy the most marketable skills. If any of them did lose out on job opportunities because of policies that provided greater access to groups that had been previously excluded, the rich white liberals would be best positioned to find other opportunities for themselves to secure their future. With only a few exceptions, these interviewees did not seem to be threatened by the possibility that opportunities would be opened up to women or minorities (native-born or immigrant). They affirmed the value of diversity and thought that the world is better off because of the policy changes that have moved society in the direction of broader civil rights.

Summary of Responses Regarding Access to Education and Jobs

Despite variations in the specific views across the sociopolitical groups in this study, the pattern of responses was similar in that most of the groups were more positive about the changes in access to education and jobs for women and then less so for African Americans and for immigrants. Those who were favorable about changes for women called attention to the skills that women bring to the labor force, to the need for families to have an additional earner, to the growing frequency of families in which women are the sole wage-earners, and to the hopefulness of daughters having a wider array of opportunities to pursue. Those who were unfavorable about the greater opportunities for women expressed concern about the adverse impact on families, on children, and especially on male wage-earners, who might be disadvantaged by the preferences given to women.

In contrast to the generally positive view of the changes in access to education and jobs for women, the interviewees in this study expressed widely variant views on the changes that have occurred for African Americans. The two most liberal groups, the rich white liberals and the working-class liberals, both expressed almost uniformly positive views of the greater opportunities available to African Americans, while the two most conservative groups, the working-class "racists" and the middle-class conservatives, were overwhelmingly negative about the opportunities available to African Americans. The three groups in the middle of the political spectrum expressed mixed views about the changes occurring for African Americans. The apolitical majority and religious conservatives were slightly weighted toward negative views, while the religious nonconservatives were slightly weighted toward positive views. The issues raised about the opportunities available to African Americans also varied.

Rich white liberals called attention to the importance of the changes for African Americans, to affirmative action being necessary because of continued bigotry and discrimination, and to the opening of opportunities as the right thing to do. Working-class liberals stressed the importance of fairness and noted that African Americans are "people too" and deserve a chance. The religious nonconservatives saw positive changes, but some also expressed caution about whether African Americans were doing their part and using the opportunities that were becoming available to them. Some expressed concerns about quotas and suggested that perhaps enough has been done. The apolitical majority interviewees raised concerns about the use of quotas, about giving preference to blacks, and also about the question of whether blacks are sufficiently qualified for the jobs that they are now being offered. Thus, while some were positive and supportive of the changes, almost half felt that the balance has shifted and that whites are potentially at a disadvantage. The religious conservatives were even more concerned about whether affirmative action has had an adverse effect on whites and raised concerns about standards being lowered in order to provide jobs to African Americans. The religious conservative interviewees were also more likely to add that opportunities should be available only to those who are qualified. Middle-class conservatives felt that affirmative action and equal opportunity policies have gone overboard, that they have given blacks advantages over whites, and that some blacks have gotten jobs that they do not deserve. They also said that even when performance is lacking, blacks are able to get and keep jobs that are being denied to whites. Finally, the working-class "racists" felt certain that blacks are getting jobs that they do not deserve, that this is happening at the expense of whites, and that the whole system is unfair. Some simply said that they do not like blacks and also do not like the leaders who represent them, and they were angry at the government for introducing a policy that works to their disadvantage. The working-class "racists" also expressed their displeasure, as did interviewees from some of the other groups, about special programs being available for blacks—for example, programs that provide resources for them to go to college—when they felt that their own children were denied such opportunities.

The views expressed about the increased opportunities available to immigrants were more negative still. The only group in which a majority expressed favorable views of the opportunities available to immigrants was the rich white liberals, who felt that immigrants work hard, that they deserve a break, and that we were all immigrants at one point. On this topic, the working-class liberals diverged from the rich white liberals. The working-class liberals also acknowledged that we are a nation of immigrants, but they were concerned about whether current immigrants are legal, whether they pay taxes, and, importantly, whether they are working for lower wages that might undermine their own claims to a living wage. The religious nonconservatives felt that they did not know much about immigrants, but they were concerned about whether immigrants speak English or are sending their money back to their home countries, and whether America should first take care of Americans. The apolitical majority had many of the same kinds of concerns, but expressed more emotion about the issues of whether immigrants are legal, pay taxes, and speak English and whether their entry into the United States is likely to have an adverse effect on Americans. The religious conservatives were even more concerned about whether immigrants are getting public services that are not available to citizens, whether immigrants might change the culture of the country, and whether they are paying their dues through taxes. In contrast, and surprisingly, the middle-class conservatives were more tolerant of immigrants, in some cases because they had either worked with them or hired them in the small businesses they owned. The working-class "racists," however, were quite negative about the growing numbers of immigrants in this country. They felt that immigrants should learn to speak English, that they have been able to "milk the system" to get benefits that are not available to Americans, and that their willingness to work for low wages and in poor working conditions is undermining opportunities for the American working class.

Thus, the views on affirmative action and equal opportunity, framed in terms of "changes in the access to education and jobs," were quite different between liberal groups and more conservative groups. The rich white liberals, who were not as likely to be in direct competition themselves for jobs with either African Americans or most immigrants (unless they were in an engineering or science field), were favorable about the opportunities being extended to women and to minorities alike. The working-class liberals, who were doing well for people with their level of education, were open-minded about the changes for women and for African Americans, but were more cautious about the influx of immigrants. The religious nonconservatives, the apolitical majority, and the religious conservatives expressed concerns about fairness and wondered whether those obtaining new opportunities deserved them and used them well. The middle-class conservatives and the working-class "racists" felt more vulnerable to these changes, which are creating more competition for them, and they did not necessarily see or value the growing diversity in the labor force and within society. These groups were also more concerned about whether the changes under way in the post–civil rights period might undermine traditional values and place them at an even greater disadvantage than the one at which they already perceived themselves to be.

If affirmative action and equal opportunity legislation are the hallmarks of the civil rights movement, then despite the uniform claim among all of the interviewees that they believe in "equal opportunity" and that "everyone deserves a chance," the reality of needing unequal opportunity and an inside edge to secure a middle-class lifestyle is evident in the variation across groups of interviewees in their views of the policies that have been the most iconic in the implementation of civil rights. Across the sociopolitical groups in this study, the varied responses to changes for women, African Americans, and immigrants seem to reflect not just self-interest, but also a group interest in how people like themselves might fare as various groups gain greater access to jobs like theirs. Those with educational credentials and labor market skills, especially those who were doing better economically than others with their level of education, tended to be more politically liberal. Those who were more vulnerable in the labor market compared to others with their level of education tended to be more conservative. Of course, ideology, such as is reinforced by an association with a conservative religious group, had an influence as well. Boundaries were drawn more firmly against African Americans and immigrants than against women. Women were more likely than men to support the changes for women, but some men were also supportive of new opportunities for women. Groups varied with regard to how favorably they viewed the opportunities being provided for nonwhites.

Who Benefits from Affirmative Action?

Data from the short survey filled out by the interviewees provide further insight into the respondents' views of affirmative action. The interviewees were asked whether they thought that affirmative action helps blacks, or alternatively, hurts whites. Responses to these questions are regressed on the sociopolitical groups, controlling for education, income, and gender. Results are provided in table 8.3. There were no differences among the sociopolitical groups with regard to their views on whether affirmative action helps blacks. For the most part, all felt that it does. But there were major differences with regard to whether the various groups felt that affirmative action hurts whites. Working-class "racists," middle-class conservatives, religious conservatives, and the apolitical majority were all more likely than rich white liberals (the reference category) to feel that affirmative action policies hurt whites, and the differences in perception were quite large. These are the same groups, as shown in table 4.4, that were also found to be more racially resentful, those that were less likely to feel that government policy should contribute to making things more equal, and those who felt that government policy has "gone too far" in addressing issues of inequality. The sentiments expressed in this chapter regarding the changes that have improved access to education and jobs for women, African Americans, and immigrants seem therefore to reflect underlying themes of racial resentment and inegalitarianism.

Preference for Hiring Immigrants over Blacks

Given the particular concerns among these interviewees about the opportunities available to African Americans and immigrants, I wanted to report on another question that I asked the interviewees. In the context

Table 8.3 Views on the Effects of Affirmative Action, by Sociopolitical Group

Independent Variables	Affirmative Action Helps Blacks[a]	Affirmative Action Hurts Whites[b]
Constant	5.67***	3.21***
Education	–0.07	0.08
Income	0.09	–0.07
Gender (male)	–0.25	–0.04
Working-class racists	–0.06	1.95***
Middle-class conservatives	–0.51	1.43**
Religious conservatives	–0.17	1.68***
Apolitical majority	–0.45	0.83**
Religious nonconservatives	–0.31	0.11
Working-class liberals	–0.00	0.13
R-squared	0.005	0.138

Source: Author's compilation.
Notes: Reference category: rich white liberals.
[a]Responses to question: "To what extent do you believe that affirmative action programs for blacks increased blacks' chances for jobs, promotions, and admission to schools and training programs?" Scale ranges from 1 = "not at all" to 7 = "a lot."
[b]Responses to question: "To what extent do you believe that affirmative action programs for blacks reduced whites' chances for jobs, promotions, and admission to schools and training programs?" Scale ranges from 1 = "not at all" to 7 = "a lot."
$^{+}p < 0.10$; $^{*}p < 0.05$; $^{**}p < 0.01$; $^{***}p < 0.001$.

of recent research findings that employers prefer to hire immigrants over U.S.-born blacks, I asked the interviewees if they had any explanations for this finding. Interestingly, on this question there was much less variation across groups than might be expected.

A number of recent studies have found that employers would rather hire Latino immigrants than U.S.-born blacks, although both black and Latino workers may be at a disadvantage compared to whites (Moss and Tilly 2001; Newman 1999; Waldinger 1997; Holzer 1996). The assumption from a number of these studies is that immigrants are preferred by employers because U.S.-born blacks lack what are called "soft skills," defined by Philip Moss and Chris Tilly (2001, 44) as "skills, abilities, and traits that pertain to personality, attitude, and behavior rather than to formal or technical knowledge." Based on this literature, the perception has been widespread that African Americans do less well in the low-wage labor market because they lack soft skills compared to whites. With this perception in mind, I asked the interviewees in this study to think about these research findings and to comment on why they thought employers might prefer to hire immigrants rather than U.S.-born blacks. With racial issues being such a pervasive subtext in many of the comments made by the interviewees, I had expected to hear accusations about the low motivation and poor skills of African Americans. Instead, I heard something very different. I coded the interviewee responses to the question about why employers might prefer to hire immigrants rather than U.S.-born blacks and summarized them in table 8.4, where once again I have reported the percentages of each type of explanation by sociopolitical group.

As can be seen in table 8.4, unlike the responses to other questions discussed in this chapter and the previous ones, there was no wide divergence by sociopolitical group in the explanations given for why employers might prefer to hire immigrants. Instead, there was a great deal of consistency in the responses. Across the groups of interviewees, the respondents all said that if the research findings are true about employers preferring to hire immigrants, it is because immigrants will work harder for less money and, in some cases, because they are exploitable. Explanations that centered on immigrant exploitability and low wages predominated among the white interviewees in this study across the sociopolitical groups, more so than explanations focused on blacks failing to meet the standards for hiring. Although there was some characterization of blacks as lacking a work ethic or being unreliable, especially in the responses of working-class "racists" and middle-class conservatives, even these groups were less likely to blame blacks than to highlight the willingness of immigrants to work harder for less money as the primary reason why employers might prefer to hire them over U.S.-born blacks. Further, with the exception of the working-class "racists," those groups claiming that blacks lack soft skills were as likely to say that Americans in general lack soft skills compared to immigrants, who are willing to work hard for less money. The overwhelming majority of respondents said that employers can get more for less when hiring immigrants and that is why they prefer to hire immigrants over U.S.-born blacks or other U.S.-born workers. Many fewer interviewees called attention to the characteristics of blacks (or other U.S. workers) as a possible reason why employers would prefer to hire immigrants. The following provides examples of the types of responses from the various groups, starting again with the most conservative.

Working-Class "Racists"

As might be expected, the working-class "racists" emphasized the failings of blacks more than the other interviewees did, but they too gave primary attention to the claim that immigrants are likely to be cheaper and more exploitable. For example, an Ohio salesman (E310 OH M WC) said: "I got to fault your good old American businessman. He's the one breaking the law. . . . He's getting them to work for, what, half or a third

Table 8.4 Reasons Given for Why Employers Might Want to Hire Immigrants Rather Than African Americans

Reasons[a]	Working-Class Racists	Middle-Class Conservatives	Religious Conservatives	Apolitical Majority	Religious Nonconservatives	Working-Class Liberals	Rich White Liberals	Total
Percentage of sample	12%	4.5%	19%	37%	4.5%	6%	17%	100%
								Average
Immigrants are cheaper	59	30	50	60	64	54	39	48
Immigrants work harder	38	60	44	39	73	38	33	38
Immigrants are exploitable	41	20	6	26	9	8	30	21
Immigrants are compliant	3	0	8	8	9	23	6	7
Immigrants are motivated	0	0	8	5	9	8	12	6
Immigrants are reliable	0	0	6	5	18	0	6	4
Blacks lack work ethic	31	10	17	14	18	8	15	15
Blacks are unreliable	7	20	3	1	0	0	9	4
Discrimination	0	0	3	3	0	8	21	11
Americans lack work ethic	3	30	11	14	18	0	12	5
Americans want more money	0	0	8	4	0	8	0	3
Don't know	0	0	6	3	0	0	0	2

Source: Author's compilation.
Notes: Responses may not add up to 100 because of rounding error.
[a]Coded responses to question: "Recent research has found that some employers say they would rather hire immigrants than U.S.-born minorities. Why do you think this may be the case? What do you think about this situation?"

or a fourth of what an American would work for. . . . It's a wrong practice." Another Ohio interviewee, a waitress (E317 OH F WC), said: "Because it's cheaper to hire them. They don't say anything and they don't open their mouth. They don't get opinionated because they're just happy to have a few dollars. Their employer gets off with cheap wages." Being compliant was also the issue raised by a self-employed Ohio trucking firm owner (E321 OH M WC): "Because . . . they ain't going to give you any trouble, because they're going to get exported right back out. . . . If they had equal rights and they had their passports and all that, they're not going to take that bull crap." A Tennessee accountant (G508 TN F WC) responded very similarly: "Most Americans, whatever their race, aren't willing to sweat in the Nashville heat for $5 an hour. They look at you and say you're crazy." Several of the working-class "racist" interviewees, however, were quite explicit in their negative view of blacks when asked about employer preferences. For example, an Ohio welder (B018 OH M WC) said: "Because the blacks won't work for one thing. It's a fact. They will not work. They have to force them to work. . . . The immigrants, they come and they just want a job." A New Jersey carpenter (D003 NJ M WC) said: "Because blacks feel that we owe them a freaking living, and we don't owe them shit. . . . They've got this attitude that we owe them money." Another New Jersey man, a housepainter (D012 NJ M WC), thought that whites and blacks should both be concerned about the way immigrants are undermining their position in the labor market: "Because they'll work for nothing, and they'll work them long hours. . . . The blacks better wake up. . . . The whites and the blacks are in the same boat. It's the minorities that are coming into this country. . . . They are going to take that job for five bucks an hour and put us out of work."

Middle-Class Conservatives

Although they also raised questions about the work ethic of Americans, the middle-class conservative interviewees similarly focused on the exploitability and low wages of immigrants. For example, a part-time Ohio development officer (B013 OH F MC) said: "Probably because they can get away with more as far as no benefits, lower pay, hours. . . . No overtime. They can work them to death probably." Putting a positive spin on the same issues, a New Jersey small-business owner (D030 NJ M MC) described the situation this way: "I pretty much have firsthand experience dealing with that. . . . I would rather hire immigrants. . . . They work like fiends. They have a very good work ethic. They never call in sick. They take pride in their job, and they seem like quick learners." Another New Jersey interviewee, a homemaker (D075 NJ F MC), focused more on the vulnerability of immigrants: "Let's say they have false papers or whatever. They are going to do everything not to draw attention to themselves, and they are just going to do what they are told and not answer back. And they are certainly not going [to act like] what people used to call the uppity blacks or the uppity minorities."

Religious Conservatives

The views expressed by the religious conservative interviewees were quite consistent with these other responses. For example, an Ohio pharmaceutical sales manager (E328 OH M MC) said: "Because they can pay them under the table. They don't have to pay medical benefits for them. . . . So they basically forfeit their rights in order to work." A Tennessee woman who worked as an essential materials specialist (G527 TN F MC) focused on the work ethic exhibited by immigrants as the reason they are preferred by employers: "They come to work every day on time and work hard. . . . They give me an honest day's labor for pay, instead of not knowing when they are going to show up, if they are going to work that day, or if they are going to whine and complain." Another Tennessee woman, a medical transcriptionist (F002 TN F MC), responded to this question both by calling attention to the low pay of immigrants and highlighting the concerns that employers might have about African Americans: "I would say they might be willing to work for lower pay. . . . And there's the other issue too of minorities. African Americans tend to get portrayed in the news big time as bringing lawsuits over everything . . . and they say they can't fire them, because they'll get sued." Thus, the religious conservatives also pointed primarily to the low wages and compliance of immigrants, even when making claims about the trouble that African Americans might cause for some employers.

Apolitical Majority

An Ohio factory worker (E307 OH M WC) thought that employers would rather hire immigrants because of their vulnerability: "I think immigrants probably come from more authoritarian societies and are more intimidated than American males." A Tennessee interviewee who worked as a vending machine route man (G522 TN M WC) turned the issue around, but had the same view: "Those who are already U.S.-bred, like myself, a lot of them don't want to hire us 'cause we got opinions. We want to stand up for our rights. We want to stand up for ourselves. We want more money. . . . So they are more willing to go with the immigrants, 'cause they get less flack from them." A New Jersey man, a public works superintendent (D007 NJ M WC), agreed: "Less money. The people know less as far as what their rights are. . . . And they use them." Another New Jersey interviewee, a school office assistant (D033 NJ F

WC), said: "Because they think they can get over on them. I don't think that they think of them as being as aware of the laws. . . . I think they are looking down on them. . . . They are not treating them as intelligent people." Some of the apolitical majority interviewees mentioned the attitude of blacks in their response to the question about employer preferences, but in a way that was consistent with the overall theme of these responses. A New Jersey billing clerk (D036 NJ F MC) said that employers prefer to hire immigrants "'cause I think that U.S.-born blacks have gotten to a position in their life where they don't, they are not putting up with that anymore. I think that their social scale is elevated . . . where they don't want to be low-paid scale people. They want to work on to the American dream." The words of another New Jersey woman, an IT manager (D076 NJ F MC), may have provided the best summary of the comments of the apolitical majority interviewees: "Probably because they don't know any better in terms of wages. They don't know the rights. They can be taken advantage of."

Religious Nonconservatives

A Tennessee deputy sheriff (G501 TN M MC) also thought that immigrants are basically exploitable: "Because they outwork them. They put them to shame. . . . They live in terrible conditions. . . . Maybe ten, twelve of them that will rent an apartment. . . . They send their monies home." A New Jersey management consultant (D044 NJ F MC) said: "I would assume it's because of economics. . . . They probably can pay immigrants less. . . . If they are illegal immigrants, then I am sure it's economics. . . . They are really willing to work hard." A Tennessee retail salesperson (F010 TN F WC) made this point as well: "I'll tell you a firsthand example. My brother is building this big house. A team of sixteen non-Americans showed up at his house and worked twelve- and fourteen-hour days in almost one-hundred-degree weather. . . . I don't know any Americans who would do that. You couldn't get Americans to work that way in the physical demands of outside labor." Another Tennessee woman, a minister (F012 TN F MC), said simply: "It's cheaper, and they really want to work. . . . They can also hang it over their head." Hence, again, there was consistency across the interviewee groups on this question. Immigrants are a cheap labor force, and that drives employer preferences more than the disadvantages perceived in hiring blacks.

Working-Class Liberals

The explanations provided by working-class liberal interviewees were very similar. For example, a self-employed Ohio construction worker (E366 OH F WC) said about why employers may prefer immigrants:

"They'll settle for minimum wage. . . . It's hard to make ends meet, but immigrants don't care. . . . They'll live in a one-room home with ten people. . . . I don't think [employers] will get as much grief from an immigrant." A Tennessee man, a small-business owner (G512 TN M WC), made a similar claim: "I think it's probably because they are willing to work for a lower wage and because . . . it must be worse there than it is here. They're willing to do jobs that other people won't." Thus, for the working-class liberals as well, the compromised situation of immigrants was far more salient in their responses than the characteristics of blacks.

Rich White Liberals

When asked why employers might prefer to hire immigrants, an Ohio engineer (E306 OH M MC) also pointed to exploitability and compliance: "They're probably used to working twelve-hour days, seven days a week. . . . They dare not say anything or they dare not slack off, or they'll be fired and replaced. . . . They're not going to make waves." An Ohio woman, a primary school music teacher (E322 OH F MC), made a similar point: "Because they're hungry. They're scared, and they want to get in. They will take the neglect, the abuse, and the low pay." A New Jersey man who worked as a claims administrator (D045 NJ M MC) said the same thing, but more dramatically: "Because half the time they are slaves that have been sold into indentured servitude by unscrupulous members of their own country. I know this is a major problem in the New York sweatshops in the garment industry." A Tennessee statistical analyst (F009 TN M MC) put it simply: "I think that they can exploit Hispanic workers easier than they can blacks." Some of the rich white liberals did raise questions about the work ethic of American workers. An Ohio man who worked in project management in a government laboratory (E331 OH M MC) said: "A lot of Americans simply aren't willing to do some kinds of jobs. . . . There are immigrants that will do that." The rich white liberals were much less likely, however, to mention any concern about what Americans or specifically blacks will or will not do than they were to voice the assumption that immigrants are exploitable and willing to work for less money in less desirable working conditions.

Summary of Views on Why Employers Prefer to Hire Immigrants over Blacks

Thus, across the responses of all of the sociopolitical groups, several primary explanations were given for why employers may prefer to hire immigrants: because immigrants will work for less; because they will work harder, owing to their vulnerability; because they are exploitable; and because they are more compliant. Although some of the interviewees commented on the work ethic or unreliability of black workers, most of those who did so noted that it is not just blacks but Americans in general who are not likely to work the way immigrants do. They also said that employers prefer immigrants because Americans are more likely to know their rights, to set limits on being exploited, and to expect to be paid a living wage that makes it possible for them to live a decent lifestyle. There was very little talk about deficiencies among African Americans in this regard. Instead, nearly everyone understood that the role of immigrants in the economy is to serve as low-wage laborers who can be subjected to difficult working conditions without talking back or making a fuss.

It is also worth noting that the comments of many of the interviewees cast a negative light on employers who hire immigrants and pay them low wages "under the table." Although hard work is the center of the dominant ideology in the United States about how people get ahead, many of the interviewees seemed to feel that there is a line that employers should not cross with regard to how they treat workers. Most of the interviewees seemed to assume that such conditions are not appropriate for U.S. citizens, and although some characterized Americans as a group as unwilling to work as hard or under the same conditions as immigrants, they also seemed to think that Americans should not work at such jobs. Further, in their comments, the interviewees seemed to recognize that employers may now prefer to hire immigrants rather than blacks for low-wage jobs because in the post–civil rights period blacks understand their citizenship rights and make claims to them. In other words, although the interviewees did not say it this way, they implied that blacks are less likely to be hired by employers whose intent is to exploit their workers.

Conclusions

In this chapter, I have examined the responses of the interviewees to questions about affirmative action and equal opportunity, albeit in the guise of a question about "changes in the access to education and jobs" for women, African Americans, and immigrants. The perceptions among whites that government policies such as affirmative action constitute discrimination against whites should be seen against a backdrop in which very few whites report having actually experienced discrimination on the basis of race (Pincus 2003). That is the case in this study as well. Although about one-quarter of the interviewees claimed that they had experienced some discrimination on the job, the majority of these stories were about gender discrimination, including sexual harassment, or about a variety of other criteria, such as age, disability, or sexual orientation. A very small proportion of the interviewees (fewer than 1 percent) described having actually lost out on a job, in their judgment, because of being white (at any time in their work histories). The two cases where an interviewee claimed to have lost a job because of being white constitute an infinitesimally small proportion of the jobs (0.001 percent) held by the interviewees over their lifetimes.

For the respondents in this study, the concept of discrimination was quite imprecise. Many talked about it in terms of negative experiences on the job in which they felt that they had been at a disadvantage compared to other workers, but many of these examples did not fit any situation that the law was intended to address, and they certainly were not situations that would have been affected by policies such as affirmative action and equal opportunity. Thus, even though the majority of the interviewees (including four of the seven sociopolitical groups) felt that affirmative action policies hurt whites, the evidence from their life stories did not support those perceptions.

These interviewees' views on discrimination were no more precise and informed than their views on government (as discussed in the last chapter). Most of the interviewees lived in a world focused on family and community and just getting by. For most, politics might have energized or motivated them only when they felt that the government in general or a public policy in particular was having an impact on their lives. Although their responses may have varied on many dimensions, there seemed to be patterns in their ways of thinking that were related to the structural position of their sociopolitical group. Those who lived in resource-rich family and community environments, those who had been able to get an education or valuable training, and especially those who had been able to either protect themselves from the market or develop marketable skills were more likely to see government policy in a favorable way. Those who were more vulnerable or who felt that the privileges that they had enjoyed might be threatened or undermined were much less favorable about government policies that might change the status quo. When asked about one of the major changes in the structure of the labor market in the last half-century—namely, the greater access to education and jobs for women, African Americans, and immigrants—the interviewees responded favorably if their own economic situation seemed relatively secure and they seemed to have valuable and marketable skills. For most, however, the constant challenges of maintaining a middle-class lifestyle in the context of ever-present threats to economic stability (layoffs, restructurings, technological change, environmental threats, globalization, and other employer strategies to keep wages low and workers less powerful) presumably contributed to their more mixed or negative views of the increased competition that might be introduced by policies intended to end whites' opportunity hoarding or their ability to count on privileged access to good jobs. The views of those who felt most vulnerable in the context of these changes (the working-class "racists" and the middle-class conservatives) on policies like affirmative action take on a more extreme tone. These interviewees were angry, they were frustrated, and they felt that entitlements that should be theirs were being taken away. They felt that these changes were not fair, not wise, and not deserved by the intended recipients.

As I have argued throughout this book, however, the issue is not primarily a matter of these interviewees' racism or personal values. Rather, it has to do with their socioeconomic position and the likely effect of the civil rights movement on people in their socioeconomic position. All of the sociopolitical groups equally sought unequal opportunity and an inside edge, but only some of them were able to count on these strategies to secure a middle-class lifestyle for themselves and their families. Although all of the interviewees had experienced rapid social change in their lives and in the economy, some were relatively more protected from the competition of the market than others, especially those with marketable skills or with resource-rich social and cultural capital. All of the interviewees were vulnerable to the ongoing efforts of employers to undermine labor rights and to the international competition that has reconfigured the landscape of economic opportunity, but some had more social resources to protect themselves than did others.

I divided the interviewees in this study into seven different groups that reflect the different ways in which they talked about the issues of inequality and fairness. I argue that the variation in the political views expressed by the interviewees reflects clear differences that are related to their structural positions and their means of coping with the effects of the civil rights movement on people like them. Only two groups expressed consistently liberal views on the political issues discussed in this book—the rich white liberals and the working-class liberals (a much smaller group). Even among these two groups, there was rather wide variation in their views about immigrants, presumably because the working-class liberals were more directly in competition for jobs with the influx of immigrants in the last several decades. All of the other sociopolitical groups expressed more conservative views about government policies that have improved access to education and jobs for those who had been excluded. Although the religious nonconservatives, whose politics were essentially moderate, clustered with the two more liberal groups on other issues, their views on affirmative action–type policies looked more like the views of the other groups. Similarly, the apolitical majority were "in between" (and generally disengaged), but when asked for their opinions, they were more like conservative groups than more liberal ones. Religious conservatives, the middle-class conservatives, and especially the working-class "racists" were all especially negative about affirmative action policies that had provided greater access to "good jobs."

The responses of the interviewees to the question about changes for women, African Americans, and immigrants provide insight into several themes in this book. First, their responses show the central importance to these interviewees of access to good jobs and opportunity hoarding of jobs that are protected from market competition. The strongly reactive nature of the responses of many of the interviewees to the idea that others will be given greater opportunities to compete for the same jobs they may want underlines the concern that many of them had about competition in the job market. Supporting this point is the fact that those with greater marketability and less economic vulnerability were more open to extending opportunity to others, while those who were not as certain about their economic prospects were much less welcoming of such social changes. Second, the views expressed on this question highlight as well the disconnect in the minds of these interviewees between their own active use of social capital and hoarding of opportunities and their sense that public policy that contributes to the expansion of opportunity for others is unfair and somehow provides others with advantages over them. The interviewees neither saw nor recognized their own advantages, yet they believed that those who are currently disadvantaged should not be given any additional help that might change the status quo. Third, the strong responses of the various respondents on both sides of the political spectrum show the role of policies such as affirmative action in shaping the post–civil rights political environment.

Although many of the interviewees were unclear about the specifics of affirmative action policies, the people to whom they are relevant, and how they work in practice, it seems quite likely that their political engagement would be influenced by their perceptions of party support for or opposition to such policies. In U.S. politics, the policies themselves do not have to be named or specifically addressed to have an influence on how white voters array themselves in the post–civil rights period. Democratic Party talk about fairness, inequality, and expansion of opportunity is interpreted by many white voters as support for policies that benefit blacks at whites' expense. Republican Party talk about responsibility, getting government out of our lives or off our backs, and reducing taxes so that people can "keep their own money" is translated by many white voters into opposition to policies that are thought to benefit blacks. Politicians do not have to mention race explicitly. They can frame their messages in terms of value differences or morality.

One might think that such themes as fairness, inequality, and expansion of opportunity are about class rather than race, but poverty has been racialized in the United States since the civil rights movement. The War on Poverty initially included whites in Appalachia and other rural areas, but it soon took on the image of blacks in the inner city because of the association with civil rights policies (Gilens 1999; Mendelberg 2001; Quadagno 1994). In the political dynamics that followed, and especially in the emergence of a new right-wing movement to turn the country back from liberalism, race became the subtext for any discussion of government social welfare policies. The inability of the Democratic Party to bridge the gap between class politics and racial politics is part of the same dynamic. As I have argued in this book, racial politics became religious politics in the efforts to create a renewed conservative and right-wing movement. Further, the Republican Party appeals to the white working class on the basis of implicit racial messages that have heightened the association of race with welfare state policies and benefits to African Americans. The belief among whites that these policies have been implemented at their expense has contributed to the sharp decline in perceptions of the legitimacy of government as a solution to societal problems (Pew Research Center 2010; Teixeira and Rogers 2000).

Myrdal hoped that being confronted with the reality of racial inequality in the context of the American creed of egalitarianism would lead many whites, especially in the North, to take up the cause of civil rights and racial inequality and that they would then push for dramatic social change, but the American dilemma that Myrdal anticipated did not unfold as he had expected. In the final chapter, I discuss in more detail why his predictions about the role of whites in racial politics in the United States took a different turn than he had hoped.

Chapter 9

Conclusion: Myrdal's Dilemma and the American Non-Dilemma

> The rationalism and moralism which is the driving force behind social study, whether we admit it or not, is the faith that institutions can be improved and strengthened and that people are good enough to live a happier life. With all we know today, there should be the possibility to build a nation and a world where people's great propensities for sympathy and cooperation will not be so thwarted.
>
> To find the practical formulas for this never-ending reconstruction of society is the supreme task of social science. The world catastrophe places tremendous difficulties in our way and may shake our confidence to the depths. Yet we have today in social science a greater trust in the improvability of man and society than we have ever had since the Enlightenment.
>
> —Gunnar Myrdal, *An American Dilemma* (1944, 1024)

IN his famous book *An American Dilemma,* published in 1944, Gunnar Myrdal predicted that America would eventually solve its racial problems because of the incompatibility between the commitment of Americans to what he called the American creed and the existence of racial inequality. He defined the American creed as the belief in "liberty, equality, justice, and fair opportunity for everybody" (Myrdal 1944, lxxx). Importantly, Myrdal did not argue that the American creed was simply internalized as values by American citizens. Instead, he was quite clear in his analysis that it was the embodiment of these values in the very foundation of American law and tradition—including in the most important founding documents of the country—that made the American creed so powerful as a force for change in racial inequality. Myrdal argued that the belief in equality before the law was enshrined in the Declaration of Independence, the Constitution, and the Bill of Rights, and that it was the framework out of which the courts made decisions (1944, 4). Although he acknowledged that practices in the United States, especially with regard to race, were inconsistent with the claims of these founding documents and he recognized that there was an evolution through which these principles were applied, he argued that the belief in the uniqueness of the American experience, including the belief that America was a beacon to the world as the embodiment of democracy, was so strong within the American psyche that it continually created the basis for calling Americans to account for their shortcomings. The "self-evident truths" of the Declaration of Independence and other founding documents, he argued, were continually "revolting," in the sense that whenever the practice diverged too far from the creed there was a basis for challenging the practice in law or through social movements (1944, 9).

In this regard, the analysis marshaled by the publication of his book, covering over five years of work, with approximately seventy-five people working on various aspects of it, and documenting in almost 1,500 pages every aspect of inequality by race at the end of the 1930s, Myrdal could not help but be well aware of the shortcomings in American practice. His argument was therefore certainly not that Americans believed and also practiced equality with regard to blacks, nor that their sense of guilt would be obvious, embraced, and inevitable. Instead, he argued that changes in the conditions in the country and in the world, especially at the time he was writing, were calling America to account for its failings with regard to the treatment of the Negro (the term used in the book). Because of this, he claimed, the availability of the appeal to the American creed was a strategic resource for blacks and others to push for greater equality:

> The Negro, as a minority, and a poor and suppressed minority at that, in the final analysis, has had little other strategy open to him than to play on the conflicting values held in the white majority group. In so doing, he has been able to identify his cause with broader issues in American politics and social life and with moral principles held dear by white Americans. (Myrdal 1944, lxxxiv)

Myrdal argued forcefully that the availability of the law and the foundation of the American creed, even if not practiced in the realm of race relations, was a means by which blacks could fight back. Further, he argued that they were increasingly doing so because of the dynamics brought about by the introduction of mechanization, the decline of King Cotton, increased industrialization in the South, the migration out of the South, and the ability of blacks to concentrate and organize in the North. He also predicted that black protest would grow, that there would perhaps be riots (he expected them to take place in the South), and that the international context would provide even more force for a white response to renewed black demands for equality. His argument was quite explicit:

> Caste may exist, but it cannot be recognized. Instead, the stamp of public disapproval is set upon it, and this undermines still more the caste theory by which the whites have to try to explain and justify their behavior. And *the Negroes are awarded the law as a weapon in the caste struggle.* Here we see in high relief how the Negroes in their fight for equality have their allies in the white man's own conscience. The white man can humiliate the Negro; he can thwart his ambitions; he can starve him; he can press him down into vice and crime; he can occasionally beat him and even kill him; but he does not have the moral stamina to make the Negro's subjugation legal and approved by society. Against that stands not only the Constitution and the laws which could be changed, but also the American Creed which is firmly rooted in the Americans' hearts." (Myrdal 1944, 1009–10, italics in the original)

A key dynamic in Myrdal's argument was the impact of World War II and America's likely role in the postwar period. Myrdal (1944, 997) argued that the disruption caused by previous wars had led in each instance to improved circumstances for Negroes, including following the Revolutionary War and then, of course, the Civil War. But he was especially confident that the circumstances facing the United States in the midst of World War II would require that it again be called to account and compelled to move forward toward greater equality for African Americans. He argued that the "color angle of the war" would create an unresolvable conflict for the United States if it did not address "the Negro problem" at home. Although writing in the midst of the war with the outcome uncertain, Myrdal thought that the international context and what he foresaw as the aftermath of the war were powerful forces that would bring pressure on the United States to address "the Negro problem":

> This War is an ideological war fought in defense of democracy. . . . Moreover, in this War the principle of democracy had to be applied more explicitly to race. Fascism and Nazism are based on a racial supremacy dogma—not unlike the old hackneyed American caste theory—and they came to power by means of racial persecution and oppression. In fighting fascism and Nazism, America had to stand before the whole world in favor of racial tolerance and cooperation and of racial equality. (Myrdal 1944, 1004)

Myrdal argued that the war made isolationism infeasible, and because of the need for the United States to take a leadership role in the emerging world economy, he warned, "caste is becoming an expensive luxury of white men" (1017). Although Myrdal did not give as much attention to it, there is another racial angle that strengthens his point. The influence of communism in the United States in the 1930s had a strong racial dimension. Communists endeavored to recruit adherents on the basis that racial inequality in the United States showed the failings of capitalism, but that solidarity and equality were values of the Communist movement. Further, Myrdal did mention the anticolonial movements in Africa and other places in the world—although he could not have known their full importance at the time he was writing—and the need for the United States to be on the right side of history with regard to race relations.

As Myrdal predicted, the United States did take a leadership role in the postwar global economy, and political events in the United States did lead, in fact, to an end to Jim Crow policies and to passage of civil rights laws. Thus, at least in this respect, Myrdal was quite right that the aftermath of the war would create conditions that would improve the plight of blacks in the United States.

Myrdal's book was celebrated from the time of its publication. In addition to becoming a widely read resource on racial inequality, data from the book were also used as supporting evidence for the Supreme Court's *Brown v. Board of Education* decision, which provided the basis for the desegregation of public schools. There were criticisms of the book early on, however, especially from the left, where the claim was that Myrdal had ignored issues of power and the class dynamics within capitalism (Crespi 1945, 1945 to 1946; Rose 1945 to 1946; Cox 1945). Other criticisms followed with regard to various aspects of his argument—for example, the claim that whites in the United States were not especially conflicted about racial issues (Medalia 1962; McDowell 1951; Campbell 1961; Killian and Grigg 1961; Rinder 1952; Banks 1950). With the growth of the civil rights movement, however, Myrdal's work began to fall out of favor. He was heavily criticized for failing to understand the persistence of racism, for not anticipating the rioting that would take place in the North, and again, for purportedly ignoring issues of power (see Carl N. Degler, "The Negro in America—Where Myrdal Went Wrong," *New York Times,* December 7, 1969; see also Westie 1965; Steinberg 1995 to 1996; Southern 1995). Despite the fact that Myrdal was writing long before the unfolding of the events that led to the passage of the Civil Rights Act in 1964 (which happened twenty years after the publication of *An American Dilemma*), critics argued that he was naive for thinking that education and persuasion could change the embeddedness of racism and racial inequality. For example, Stephen Steinberg (1995 to 1996) made the following charges on the fifty-year anniversary of the book's publication:

> What begs for explanation is *why* Myrdal's opus was embraced as the definitive and authoritative work on race in America. This distinction lasted for nearly two decades, but it would not endure forever. As the nation was thrust into a full-blown racial crisis in the early 1960s, it became clear not only that Myrdal had failed to anticipate black insurgency and the civil

> rights upheaval, but that his acclaimed theoretical framework was of little value in making sense of these unanticipated events. (64)

Even Jennifer Hochschild (1996), in a piece about why some "race books" lead us astray from the truth, claimed of Myrdal's book:

> Over the succeeding two decades, Myrdal's influence led well-intentioned whites (and at least some blacks) to locate the problem of race in individual psyches. If people could just learn to overcome ignorance and prejudice, everything would be fine. This belief, or hope, led to the naïve version of "contact theory": Ensure that people come to know each other personally, and racial prejudice and discrimination will melt away under the sunny influence of neighborly friendship.

Of course, Myrdal's argument was nothing of the sort. He dealt very painstakingly with the power dynamics between whites and blacks. He further predicted that one of the key pressures that would be brought to bear on whites in calling them to account would be the increased social unrest among blacks, and in discussing this issue, he predicted race riots following the war (although he expected them to occur in the South rather than the North). For example, Myrdal made note of a meeting of Southern black ministers to discuss their appeal for calm in the context of growing tensions among blacks about their denial of civil rights:

> The meeting of the Southern Negroes serves both as an attempt to prevent the racial lines from being drawn more sharply and as a disclaimer of responsibility for future violence.
>
> An important element in the situation is that the Southern Negroes, if they are attacked, are more prepared to fight this time than they have ever been before. A competent Negro social scientist, who has recently been studying conditions in the Upper South, confirms this view and, in May, 1943, confides that he expects the outbreak of serious race riots in the South within the next year. (1944, 1013–14)

This hardly sounds like an expectation that neighborly friendship and hope will be the driving force for social change.

Myrdal's argument was not that whites could be persuaded by appeal to their better selves. Instead, his was a thoroughly sophisticated political argument about the role of law, institutions, social relationships, competition for resources, and symbolic politics in the context of both domestic and international events that were changing the power relationships and the organizing capacity of various groups and creating conditions that were ripe for social change. His argument involved a series of steps, starting with the pressure of domestic and international forces creating the conditions for renewed and more vigorous Negro protest that would convince some whites to join the cause of using law and the framework of the American creed to create public oversight and regulation of behavior. He asked for "courageous" leaders in the North to take up this challenge and to bring the necessary pressure "this time" to force changes on the South and to break the hold of white Southerners over the lives of Negroes. In Myrdal's analysis, America had no choice but to solve its racial problems if it wanted to emerge out of the war as a world power, because its failure to do so would undermine its credibility in an increasingly "colored" world in which it needed to have influence and from which it needed cooperation. As Myrdal (1944, 1021) appealed in his conclusion: "In this sense the Negro problem is not only America's greatest failure but also America's incomparably great opportunity for the future."

Myrdal reconfirmed the structure of his argument in a return visit to the United States in 1948 on the occasion of an event to honor the Julius Rosenwald Fund, which had provided funding for the education of African Americans, and to share the podium again with W. E. B. DuBois. Although Myrdal claimed to no longer be up to date on U.S. race relations because of other duties after he left the United States, he reiterated once again his belief that America had to address the issue of racial inequality if it was going to fulfill a leadership role in the emerging world economy. He argued that if America failed to do so,

> We will then have the somewhat paradoxical situation of an America which is vigorously forcing fundamental economic reforms, not only on Japan and Western Germany, but on the whole of Western Europe and perhaps China . . . but leaving large groups of its own people to rot in the slums of Southern agriculture. (Myrdal 1948, 200)

He then went on to explain again that his framework assumed that a combination of social movements and the use of the legal system, drawing on the foundational principles of the American creed, would recruit leadership to force a change in the social relations that kept racial inequality in place. He did not define this as an exercise in education and persuasion. Instead, he said,

> If my assumption is right, then we should now have to look forward to a series of actions of Congress, the courts, and other agencies of Government to enforce civil rights for Negroes. We should not expect a very rapid development; it may well take a generation before the situation in the South is brought to approach even the situation in the North. But the whole psychology of the South and not the least the spirit of the Negro people, will be much different once the movement has got a definite direction and more

> of a momentum. Such a development will open opportunities for concerted action on a much broader scale for organizations like the NAACP and the labor movement. It also opens new possibilities for the humanitarian institutions, which up till now have not felt it advantageous or possible to work in the civil rights field. (Myrdal 1948, 208)

In a very curious sense, Myrdal's predictions were amazingly prescient, and the criticisms of Steinberg, Hochschild, and many others actually confirm his argument, because as whites with firm commitments to civil rights, they exemplify exactly the kind of divided consciousness among whites that he expected would emerge because of America's failure, in practice, to live up to its ideals in the area of civil rights.

Thus, I do not share the criticisms of Myrdal's work that have emerged over the almost seventy years since he wrote, while World War II was still raging, about events that he expected to occur following the end of the war. I am amazed at how much he got right: the transformation of U.S. race relations; the emergence of the civil rights movement; the joining of whites, especially from the North, with a growing social movement of blacks to press in law and the courts for a change in social practice; and the continued struggle in most institutional spheres, especially over the issue of jobs. Further, his expectation that world events would put political pressure on the United States to change was equally prescient. He foresaw the anticolonial movements in Africa and elsewhere, and he understood the significance of the juxtaposition of U.S. world leadership with racial oppression at home. Indeed, President John F. Kennedy called attention to exactly this issue in his 1963 speech, as noted in chapter 5.

The American Non-Dilemma

Despite the impressiveness of Myrdal's contributions and the solid basis of his predictions, racial inequality still exists in the United States, and most white Americans do not show evidence of experiencing a moral dilemma because of it. Furthermore, the pressures that Myrdal anticipated would force the issue seem to have dissipated. With the findings of this study in mind, I want to call attention to three factors that show the limitations of Myrdal's wisdom on the issues of race relations in the United States: (1) Myrdal's analysis was focused on discrimination instead of favoritism; (2) he had excessive faith in public institutions, unions, and progressive social change that turned out not to be warranted; and (3) he underestimated the ability of the white South to maintain its political influence and to challenge the political hegemony of the civil rights movement and the New Deal. Perhaps if he had had the same information now available to us about what emerged in the postwar period, he might have seen things differently, but he did not or could not foresee in his extensive and deep analysis the limits of the New Deal, the ambiguous role of unions in civil rights, or the continued political efficacy of the American South. Further, he placed undue emphasis on discrimination rather than on favoritism, an overemphasis that is evident among contemporary scholars as well. As might be expected, therefore, as postwar events unfolded his predictions became less relevant. Although the existence of the American creed did offer a resource to blacks in their struggle for civil rights as they mobilized a social movement and appealed to the law and the conscience of the nation, once the Civil Rights Act was passed the political pressure dissipated. Thus, racial inequality has persisted, and there does not appear to be a moral dilemma driving us toward greater racial equality.

Discrimination Instead of Favoritism

Myrdal was well aware of the depth of discrimination and racism among whites, and he noted the extent to which whites denied it, hid it, or tried to deflect it onto others. Discrimination may have been the primary mechanism for the reproduction of racial inequality at the time he was writing, prior to the passage of civil rights laws. In the post–civil rights period, however, with discrimination officially illegal, racial inequality seems to be reproduced as much through the favoritism of whites toward each other as through the active discrimination of whites toward blacks or other nonwhites. As is evident from the interviewee stories throughout this book, whites enjoy the structural advantages of social and cultural capital, which enable them to help each other get an inside edge or special access to information, influence, or opportunity. That is, whites hoard opportunities in a way that gives them unearned advantages and helps protect them from competition in the labor market.

The continued segregation in jobs and housing separates whites and nonwhites from each other and enables whites, when opportunities are available, to turn to those in their own communities and networks. Segregation further contributes to what Myrdal (1944, 40) termed the "convenience of ignorance," which enables whites to exhibit a "remarkable lack of correct information about the Negroes and their living conditions" (on "the epistemology of ignorance" in the "racial contract," see also Mills 1997). Because the structural advantages enjoyed by whites are unacknowledged and largely invisible to them, whites can believe themselves to be fully supportive of civil rights and equal opportunity even though they benefit from unequal opportunity—that is, the privileges of being white. Thus, for most whites in the United States, continuing racial inequality raises no moral dilemma. Indeed, many whites do not even acknowledge that there is continued racial inequality, and many of those who do acknowledge it believe that responsibility for it lies either with "those racists" or with blacks themselves.

My interviews suggest that the very ideology of the American creed that Myrdal believed would cause moral discomfort among Northern whites is the same ideology that now enables whites to believe that they "did it on their own," with no need to acknowledge or understand the role of the group-based preferences that helped them both get in the door and protect themselves from market competition. Despite these group-based advantages, whites attribute their life outcomes to personal effort, ability, and motivation. They believe that they succeed on their own, so they ask of blacks and other nonwhites, "Why can't those folks do it the way I did?" Such thinking also underlies the claim to "color-blindness" among my interviewees, and hence their opposition to group-specific policies that might change the structure of privilege between whites and blacks. By adhering to the notion that each individual is on his or her own and that there is no connection between their privilege and blacks' disadvantage, many—perhaps most—whites believe that blacks who have not done as well as whites did not try as hard as they did, gave up too easily, or lost hope. Indeed, because whites feel that they themselves exhibit these qualities, they feel morally justified in their opposition to government policies that they feel "create dependency." Whites speak frequently about the need to "take responsibility," to get a "hand-up, not a hand-out," and to "get over it." In other words, belief in the American creed or the American dream, rather than providing the foundation for a new social movement—a New Deal for race relations—allows whites to oppose the kinds of government intervention that were the hallmark of the civil rights movement (Hochschild 1995; Kluegel and Smith 1986).

Most of the whites in this study attributed any continued problems for blacks either to blacks themselves or to the unfortunate attitudes of "those racists," by which they meant ignorant or bigoted people who hold hostile views toward blacks and who have not accepted, as they believe themselves to have done, the enlightened values of the civil rights movement. Few of the interviewees—including those whom I labeled working-class "racists"—thought of themselves as racist, because they claimed to support the civil rights movement and to be opposed to discrimination. Further, most of the interviewees expressed a strong belief that equal opportunity is the standard of fairness that should be used as a guide to public policy. Because they did not recognize the unequal opportunity inherent in their own use of social and cultural capital to get an inside edge in the job market, most felt that government programs like affirmative action are unfair and that they violate the principles of equal opportunity. Thus, many of the interviewees seemed to think that the ability to bring lawsuits to redress discriminatory treatment is sufficient, but that positive government action on behalf of minorities is not fair.

That is, they assumed that public policy should only prevent negative things from happening to blacks and should not interfere with whites doing positive things for each other (Krieger 1995).

The interviewees often offered up a simple hiring decision as their example of discrimination (a choice between one white and one black candidate), and frequently they assumed that the choice of the black candidate in almost any circumstance would indicate discrimination against the presumably better-qualified white candidate. Hardly any of the interviewees thought of their own careers—in which they had received substantial help in the form of social and cultural capital from family and friends to obtain the majority of the jobs they had held over their lifetimes—as having violated the principle of equal opportunity. If in telling their job histories they recognized their own use of insider assistance, they would dismiss any notion that such assistance was unfair. Instead, they would claim, "That just got me in the door. Then I had to prove myself." But when pressed on the issue of whether it is ever possible to ensure that the "best person" gets the job—this being the definition that was most frequently given when equal opportunity was held up as a standard—many of the interviewees backed off of equal opportunity as a political goal. Instead, they claimed that it is not possible or even desirable for everyone to have equal opportunity, because, they said, people are not equal in either ability or motivation and so equality is not a reasonable goal. A number of interviewees finally dismissed the notion of equal opportunity with the claim, "Life's not fair." On this basis, they said that people should be satisfied with whatever they get out of life, as long as they try their best and are flexible in their goals.

Almost all of the interviewees had received help that was beyond the market throughout their work lives, but they explained their success as based in individual effort and individual achievement. As in the study by Kluegel and Smith (1986), the interviewees in my study did not feel that hardship or structural disadvantages provide sufficient justification for relying on government instead of one's own efforts. These white interviewees were absolutely certain that most of the time people are rewarded for their efforts to the extent that their talent and motivation would warrant and that while some people may experience bad luck, there is no excuse for not taking responsibility for one's own life outcomes.

When asked about what had most contributed to what they had attained in their lives, the vast majority of the interviewees cited their own talent, hard work, and persistence. Hardly any interviewee explicitly pointed to the advantages that he or she had because of the ability to live in safe and resource-rich neighborhoods, attend high-quality schools, or be supported by an extensive private network of family and friends who could pass along information, use influence on their behalf, or provide them with jobs that would protect them from having to compete in the marketplace on an equal basis with those who did not have access to the same kinds of social resources. Yet 60 to 75 percent of the time the interviewees had some type of help in obtaining a job. The only jobs that they had not obtained through the use of social capital, it seemed, were those jobs that did not pay enough to make the use of social capital worth the effort, those that were prescreened through formal recruiting mechanisms such as college placement offices (a very small proportion of the interviewees), and those obtained during times when jobs were more plentiful than applicants. In a very few cases, interviewees described circumstances when they might have used the help of family or friends but, because of their own "foolish mistakes," including addiction to drugs or alcohol or problems with the law, they were unwilling or unable to do so. Most of these interviewees regretted their failure to draw on the social capital that would have been available to them at an earlier stage of their lives, and they all recognized that had they done so, their lives would have been better and they would have gotten further ahead than they had done with jobs that they obtained only through "equal opportunity" (that is, through the market). In many of these cases, family and neighborhood connections helped them get back on track by their midtwenties, so that, despite having been "young and foolish," as some suggested, limits were put on their downward mobility or they were given a second chance to find a job that was protected from the market and that could support a middle-class lifestyle.

Hence, all of the interviewees, no matter what their political views or social class position, were about equally likely to draw on social and cultural capital to the extent that it was available to them in their family and neighborhood environments. Despite the importance of such inside assistance to the opportunities available to them throughout their lives, most did not recognize that in using social and cultural capital in this way they were not subjecting themselves to equal opportunity but in fact were hoarding opportunities in a way that protected them from the downsides of the marketplace. The variability in the life experiences of the interviewees seemed to provide fairly clear evidence of what the absence of social and cultural capital would have meant in their lives. Those who could draw on such social resources were usually able to find jobs that paid at least a family wage, often with insurance benefits and a pension of some sort, while those who were left to their own devices in the marketplace, in contrast, had often lived at the edge of poverty. Social resources had provided some of these white interviewees with much more lucrative opportunities than had been available to others, but in almost all cases, the jobs that they were able to obtain through the use of social resources were better jobs than the ones they would have obtained without them.[1] Of course, as the economy continues to change, both domestically and globally, and as employers keep up the pressure to undermine the protections of workers in the labor market, all jobs are vulnerable, and their children, especially those from the working class, may not be so fortunate in their own careers.

Myrdal understood that whites benefit from discrimination against blacks, but in his analysis he framed racial inequality in terms of negative things happening to blacks rather than as positive things happening to whites. That framework is evident from the outset of *An American Dilemma:* as he notes in the preface, Myrdal was quite clear that the problems of racial inequality were about whites rather than blacks. Although he claimed that "we shall in this book have to give *primary* attention to what goes on in the minds of white Americans" (italics in the original), Myrdal and his collaborators went on for 1,500 pages, despite this claim, to give primary attention, not to what whites were doing, but on the contrary, to an examination of the lives and circumstances of Negroes.

Of course, in the pre–civil rights period, when the exclusion of blacks from jobs, housing, and schools was legal and expected, discrimination was open and explicit. In the post–civil rights period, with discrimination made formally illegal, the assistance that whites give to each other through acts of favoritism presumably took on a larger role. Importantly, these two processes are not just different sides of the same coin, because discrimination is illegal, but favoritism is not (McGinley 1997). Further, because whites think of racism in terms of discrimination but not in terms of favoritism, they perceive their own behavior quite differently as a result of the focus on discrimination and not favoritism. By not doing bad things to blacks, whites are able to maintain their sense of self as fair people with good values. In this sense, they can be the decent and good people that Myrdal said most Americans want to be. In other words, the reproduction of racial inequality through processes by which whites do not have to be racists is the ultimate white privilege. Whites can gain structural advantage without a sense of personal guilt, and hence, also without invoking a moral dilemma.

Faith in Public Institutions and Progressive Unions

A second area in which there are limitations to Myrdal's analysis is his perhaps overly strong faith in the power of institutions and law to protect workers in general, and blacks in particular, from either discrimination or favoritism. Writing in the late 1930s and in the context of his own contributions to the development of Swedish social democracy, Myrdal placed a great deal of weight on the ability of "public regulation" to rebalance power inequities, especially in the area of race relations (Myrdal 1948). He seemed to see the New Deal as an initial step in providing a framework for progress toward racial equality, although he acknowledged that it did not provide full benefits to blacks. Further, given the struggles in the 1930s leading up to the New Deal and to passage of the National Labor Relations Act (known as the Wagner Act), which provided the rights to bargain collectively, Myrdal understandably also seemed to have faith that unions would act in progressive ways and could become allies in the fight for racial equality. His faith in public institutions and labor unions certainly made sense at the time that he was writing, since it was a period of active organizing that, supported by new legislation, only strengthened as the Depression ended and World War II got under way. Further, the unions of the Congress of Industrial Organizations (CIO) included both whites and blacks in their efforts to organize across occupational categories within industries. And the purported Communist influence on CIO unions underscored the ideological campaign over race that was adding to the pressure on the U.S. government to address racial issues. Thus, for some time after Myrdal finished his book, there were movements in the directions that he had predicted. Of course, he could not foresee the continued tensions that would unfold within industrial unions over the issue of race, nor presumably would he have fully understood the implications of blacks' widespread exclusion from the benefits of either the New Deal or the postwar growth in organized labor (Katznelson 2005; Quadagno 1994).

Even so, if one looks at the immediate effects of the New Deal in the postwar period, Myrdal's inclinations were correct. The policies of the New Deal and their implementation strengthened the role of government in providing public benefits, including to blacks, despite the limitations placed on their eligibility for the most important programs (Massey 2007). About these issues Myrdal (1944, 1000–1001) wrote, for example:

> In the enjoyment of *public services* the Negro was discriminated against severely in the South in blunt repudiation of the Constitution and the state laws. But even in this sphere we saw a slow improvement of his status as a result of the rising legal culture of the region; the pressures from the Negroes, from public opinion in the North, from the federal courts, and administration as well as from the white Southerners' own better conscience. . . . Without question the New Deal was of tremendous importance for the Negro in respect to the share he received of public services. It is true that the Washington administration did not dare and, in any case, did not succeed in stamping out discrimination in relief, agricultural policies, or anything else in the South, but it definitely decreased it.

Similarly, the influence of unions in the immediate postwar period contributed to rising wages and progressive reform on some issues. Although unions did not necessarily serve the interests of blacks, the distribution between capital and labor was more moderated in the postwar period when the New Deal and labor unions were both at their strongest (Massey 2007). Even though he was criticized for not recognizing the barriers to civil rights created by some labor leaders and the limitations of the New Deal as applied to blacks, Myrdal was not naive about the politics of resistance to social change. He did not and undoubtedly could not have foreseen some of these developments.

In the broader framework, unions were, of course, often used to enact and then to enforce opportunity hoarding among whites, with sharp boundaries drawn against blacks and other nonwhites. Prior to the 1930s, most blacks were excluded from white unions. In fact, as an available labor supply, blacks were often thrust into the role of strikebreakers in the hard-fought and often violent conflict between workers and employers. Thus, there was direct tension between labor rights, represented by solidarity with the union, and civil rights, as reflected in the efforts of blacks to gain access to the jobs that had been hoarded by white union members. Even in CIO unions that included blacks, exclusionary policies persisted such that most blacks were given access only to the dirtiest and most dangerous jobs. Blacks were also denied training—for example, they were often excluded from the apprenticeships for the best and highest-paid jobs among unionized workers. In addition to this constant tension between blacks and whites throughout the period of unionization, there was a presumption among many white union members that blacks took jobs that undermined the seniority rights, labor rules, and pay rates of white workers. Many white workers also often thought of blacks as "scabs" and as tools of employers who were collaborating on efforts to undermine or destroy union power.

By the time the 1964 Civil Rights Act was passed, labor leaders from the craft unions were seen as obstacles to progress for blacks. Throughout the development of the civil rights movement, and especially after passage of the Civil Rights Act, a conflict arose within the labor movement between the craft and industrial unions over the efforts of civil rights groups and ultimately the government to force the integration of the building trades unions. Jill Quadagno (1992, 620–21) argues that unionized workers in the skilled trades competed with civil rights activists to define the meaning of economic justice. She contrasts the two groups as follows:

> For unionized workers in the skilled trades, economic justice meant the right to protect wages and to seek fair treatment in the workplace. For the civil rights movement, economic justice meant access to jobs. These competing claims, which challenged the Democratic party's basis of authority, became the focus of a political struggle between organized labor and the civil rights movement.

The conflict between workers' rights (represented by the craft unions in the building trades) and civil rights (represented by activists in the civil rights movement and government officials who supported the challenge to the craft unions) led to contention within the labor movement between the industrial unions, such as the United Auto Workers, that actively supported the civil rights movement and the building trades unions of the AFL-CIO. It also raised race-versus-class issues within the Democratic Party that made it difficult for the party to maintain its New Deal coalition by suppressing attention to racial issues. Finally, the conflict also served the interests of the Republican Party: by playing up the conflict between white working-class union members and civil rights activists, the Republicans made progress in their efforts to split the Democratic coalition. Indeed, by 1968 the fortunes of the Democratic Party had been reversed from the high point of its coalition support represented by Johnson's election in 1964. With the vote split in the three-way race between Democratic nominee Hubert Humphrey, third-party candidate George Wallace, and Republican nominee Richard Nixon, the Republicans were able to take back the White House in the 1968 election.

There is some evidence that groups like the National Alliance of Businessmen (NAB)—which arose during the civil rights movement in response to the 1960s riots and would promote opening up apprenticeship training for blacks in a program called NAB-JOBS—were also using this conflict within unions over civil rights to undermine union control of apprenticeship training (DiTomaso 1977). The purpose of NAB was to enlist the support of businesses to improve job opportunities for poor and minority youth, but the programs undertaken by NAB were also intended to help companies gain access to skilled labor during the labor shortages of the Vietnam War. By trying to force the Bureau of Apprenticeship and Training (BAT) to provide shortened training programs for blacks, the program served several purposes (MacLaury 2010). It met the immediate goal of improving the jobs picture for black youth at a time when race riots were taking place across the country. It provided a means for companies to hire skilled machinists during the labor shortage of the war, when the demand for their products was accelerating both because of the war effort and because of the heated-up economy. The program also, however, took the control over the apprenticeship training out of the hands of the unions that worked with BAT to set the conditions for training (DiTomaso 1977). The conflict that arose between BAT and the NAB-JOBS program, as an example, highlights the race-versus-class tensions that arose during the civil rights movement. President Lyndon Johnson's secretary of labor, Willard Wirtz, was personally committed to the cause of civil rights. After jawboning BAT to either open up apprenticeship training to more blacks or lose union control of the training altogether, Wirtz and the unions reached a compromise: the unions could continue to engage in the kind of nepotism among white union members that had been standard in the apprenticeship training programs, as long as they added apprenticeship slots for blacks (MacLaury 2010).

Thus, the race-versus-class tension, especially between organized labor and civil rights leaders, was not an illusion. Control over the content and availability of training had been a constant source of negotiation and politics ever since BAT was established in 1937, but craft unions had gained effective control over apprenticeship training, despite oversight by the U.S. Department of Labor as part of its workforce development policy. The unions worked in coordination with employers, under the auspices of BAT, to match job-seekers with training opportunities in companies in the skilled trades. The unions watched carefully to try to keep the number of slots at a minimal level so that the demand for labor and wages would remain high. Importantly, however, apprenticeship slots were treated like property that could be passed down from one generation to another by those already in the skilled trades in various unions. It was the usual practice for access to apprenticeship training to be limited to the sons and nephews, and sometimes even the daughters, of current (white) union members. If unions had less influence on the availability of training, then they would also have less opportunity to pass along apprenticeship slots to their children, other relatives, or friends, and they would not be able to draw as firm a boundary against black intrusion into "their" jobs. Thus, in the midst of the Vietnam War, with the war-induced labor shortage in the skilled trades, upper-middle-class white government bureaucrats and employer groups formed a coalition to solve the racial problems facing the country in a way that took the form of undermining union control of apprenticeship training, both by expanding the number of slots available and by reducing the years of training from what the union had claimed was necessary to a much shorter period (DiTomaso 1977).

Another important aspect to this overall story is also, of course, that blacks would undoubtedly have been perceived by the white union members as undeserving. The blacks who entered these programs might have had less formal education and would have presented a different kind of demeanor and attitude toward the white union members than their own sons and other relatives. Further, some might have thought that blacks were being rewarded for rioting. On all counts, union members were angry about the encroachment on their "property" (that is, their jobs). Taking away control of their access to jobs through apprenticeship training was a direct threat to white union members, and it was perceived as such. Similar reactions probably greeted blacks' attempts to gain access to semiskilled jobs as well in unionized factories, as evidenced by some of the comments of the interviewees in this study.

The conflict over access to apprenticeships is just one example of the larger conflict between labor rights and civil rights that was heightened during the civil rights movement and the subsequent implementation of civil rights policies. There are other examples as well, including some that are much more visible. When Lyndon Johnson tried to force local governments to open up job opportunities to blacks through the various antipoverty programs (such as the Manpower Development and Training Act of 1962, which was originally introduced by President John Kennedy to combat unemployment due to automation but was later incorporated into the antipoverty programs), he faced recalcitrance from local political leaders, many of whom had close relations with union leaders who had helped them get elected (DiTomaso 1977; Quadagno 1992). To force a change in behavior, and specifically to open up the opportunities that unions were hoarding, Johnson began to circumvent local leaders and provide antipoverty program funds directly to newly created community action agencies (CAAs) at the local level. The political volatility of this effort stemmed from the conflict over who would gain access to which jobs.

Although it was the Republican Nixon administration that introduced the "Philadelphia Plan" to explicitly force greater minority hiring in the building trades unions, the political costs were primarily paid by the Democratic Party, which had become more closely identified with support for the civil rights policies that were conflicting with the ability of labor unions to maintain access to jobs for members' family and friends and to protect their wages from market competition. An additional goal of the integration of the building trades was to reduce the wages being paid in these types of jobs (Quadagno 1992).

The politics of the interviewees in this study reflected some of these dynamics as they emerged during the civil rights movement and then in reaction to the legislation that followed it. Critical to understanding how these dynamics continue to be expressed today is the fact that, although most of the interviewees had drawn on social and cultural capital to help protect themselves from market competition, they were not secure in their job situation for life. Rather, in the job histories of the interviewees can be seen the processes that constantly put employees at risk of changes in the nature of their jobs, their companies, and the economy. Employers are constantly introducing new technologies. Companies come and go. Mergers and acquisitions take place and change the nature of the employment contract. Globalization leads to jobs being outsourced or offshored or otherwise moved away from where workers live. And sometimes workers get themselves into jobs that they cannot handle or into work situations where they are not one of the favored few, and other times their jobs become vulnerable because an employer wants to make way for a family member or friend.

Hence, there is a constant need for vigilance and investment in the social capital ties that workers count on to maintain a decent lifestyle for themselves and their families. Moreover, it is often precisely because of the uncertainties of life itself over time—the unpredictable complications that arise such as divorce, serious illnesses, disability, death in the family, stress, or mental health challenges—that workers are always looking for ways to protect themselves from the market (Parks-Yancy, DiTomaso, and Post 2005). When such challenges or setbacks emerged for the interviewees in this study, they looked for someone who could help them with information, influence, or opportunity. In such circumstances, they tried their best not to have to actually fend for themselves in the labor market. Thus, civil rights policies, many of which were intended to open up access to the kinds of good jobs that provide decent lives for workers, have presented many white Americans with a dilemma—perhaps the real moral dilemma. Although white Americans affirm the need to eliminate discrimination and feel that "everyone deserves a chance," they do not want civil rights to interfere with their ability to protect themselves from the market by gaining an inside edge to good jobs.

The ongoing conflict between civil rights and labor rights that has drawn people to different sides of the political battles of the post–civil rights period is reflected in the lives of the interviewees in this study. Their political views on issues of inequality and opportunity appear to depend on their structural position in the economy, on their ability to gain marketable skills should they need them, and sometimes on the psychological factors that have an important impact on whether members of their community persist and have confidence in their abilities. For example, the anger and explicitly antiblack sentiments of the working-class "racists" seemed to exemplify the reactions of union members to the perceived threat that blacks were taking their jobs. These interviewees were more likely to be working in factory jobs or in the skilled trades, or to have held a unionized job to which blacks were either trying to get access or had actually gotten access because of various government policies. These interviewees were angry because they perceived that blacks were taking jobs that should have been available to their own children, such as the interviewee from Ohio who claimed that he had friends who could not help their children get apprenticeship positions. Further, they thought that blacks were undeserving. They attributed a poor work ethic, weak skills, or a bad attitude to the black workers they encountered in jobs like the ones they held themselves. They said that blacks did not "want to work" and that they were insufficiently deferential to management or to other workers. They also claimed that employers were "afraid" of black workers, who supposedly could not be fired for fear of lawsuits.

The working-class "racists" among the interviewees seemed to feel a specific sense of vulnerability and anger about government policies that were intended to provide access to jobs for racial minorities (and sometimes for women). They believed that it was their jobs or those of their children or other family members that were being given to blacks through the mechanisms of affirmative action. Although one may argue that the jobs at stake were not "theirs" in any legal sense, that is not how they saw it. These interviewees claimed to believe in equal opportunity and said that fairness dictates that the best people should get the jobs, but they did not necessarily apply these standards in their own lives. Instead, from their view, what was fair was for them to get jobs for which they were capable, whether or not they had formal educational credentials. They also thought that it was fair to use connections to family members or friends to get jobs that provided decent income with benefits. Although many expressed strong confidence in their abilities and motivation, they also recognized that their relative lack of education created a disadvantage for them in the labor market and that living a middle-class lifestyle depended on their ability to get—and keep—a "good job" with benefits and decent wages. While these interviewees were certain that they had done it "on their own," that no one had helped them, and specifically that the government had done nothing for them, they felt that the government, with the support of liberals with much better educations than they had, had interfered with their ability to use their social ties (their social capital) to get good jobs. They were angry at the prospect of losing their current jobs to plant closings or layoffs and being left on the outside if they could not draw on family and friends to get another job.

The political attitudes of the small group of middle-class conservatives were similar to those of the working-class "racists." Even though the middle-class conservatives had college degrees, they felt vulnerable about their economic situations. These interviewees were comfortable with hierarchy, did not feel that inequality is a problem that needs to be solved, and did not think that it is the responsibility of government to provide services to the poor. The middle-class conservatives did not think that they got what they deserved from the government, but they also said that they did not want anything. They attributed poverty to welfare dependency, laziness, and lack of effort.

Although the religious conservative interviewees expressed similar anti-government and anti–welfare state views, the underlying reasons for their views were not necessarily the same as the reasons underlying the views of the working-class "racists" and the middle-class conservatives. The majority of the religious conservatives had developed their political views in interaction with members of their churches or with friends who shared their religious views. They argued that God mandates that everyone take responsibility for their own lives and not become dependent on the rest of the community. There are some hints in the interview material about the grounding of religious politics in racial politics. For example, Southern interviewees had been strongly affected by the school desegregation orders imposed on their communities by the legal challenges of the civil rights movement. It was at this time, according to many of the interviewees from Tennessee, that either they themselves or their children moved out of public schools into privately funded "Christian academies." While some acknowledged the role of desegregation in their decision to attend or send their children to a private "Christian" school, most of the interviewees disclaimed that these decisions had anything to do with racial antagonism. Instead, they stressed the positive goals of wanting their children to "learn about Jesus" and to remove them from what they described as the lack of discipline and adverse social environment that they associated with public schools. Private "Christian" schools did arise, however, in concert with efforts to desegregate public schools in the South, and they played an important role in the rise of the Religious Right. Although the original organizations of the Religious Right did not continue, the social movement that they sparked through conservative Protestant churches did endure, and it apparently spread beyond the South to conservative Protestant churches throughout the country, as evidenced by the fact that all of the interviewees in both Ohio and even New Jersey who identified themselves as religious conservatives expressed the same conservative political views.

To be fair, it is worth noting that the responses to the civil rights movement and to the pressures to desegregate schools looked quite different in the South and the North, for reasons that went beyond racism. Blacks and whites in the South were more likely to live near each other than was the case in the North. In the South, neighborhoods were less likely to be segregated before the civil rights movement, but there were separate school systems for whites and blacks. To maintain the segregation of schools after the civil rights movement required the creation of a parallel school system that could exclude blacks when public schools were forced to integrate (Orfield and Lee 2007). In the North, in contrast, blacks and whites lived in separate neighborhoods, presumably because the formal rights available to blacks earlier in the North had contributed to other ways of keeping blacks and whites physically separate in segregated housing and neighborhoods—and thus segregated schools.

Compared to the other groups, the apolitical majority interviewees did not have well-formed political views, and most of them did not seem to feel that their lives had been substantially affected by the policies that arose out of the civil rights movement. Even so, they still expressed general opposition to affirmative action (in the form of quotas), and they felt that welfare should be limited to those who are willing to help themselves. While not mobilized into any specific political group, the apolitical majority expressed views, once asked, that were generally consistent with an individualist ideology and belief that the American dream is available to anyone who puts forth enough effort. Also when asked, they expressed political views that were more conservative than liberal. In this regard, they were similar to the profile of the growing group of political independents in the country.

The religious nonconservatives, a small proportion of the religiously identified interviewees, were more moderate than liberal in their political views. Accordingly, on most policy questions on which religious conservatives had very conservative views, the views of the religious nonconservatives were mixed, but often leaned toward more positive or tolerant views. There was no readily apparent structural difference that would have differentiated the religious nonconservatives from the religious conservatives. They seemed to be different only in terms of their politics.

Although structurally the working-class liberals may have seemed to be like other members of the working class, they had a more positive outlook on life and on the government, and they were more tolerant and inclusive on issues of racial inequality. They viewed their own economic situations more favorably than the working-class "racists" viewed theirs. They were also more likely to be concerned about inequality and more likely to believe that the government should provide assistance to people who are poor. They felt that they got what they deserved from the government and that it would not make much difference in their lives if poor people made fewer demands on the government. The working-class liberals in this study included building contractors, small-business owners, clerical workers, and service workers. They did not mention a desire to pass along to their children the opportunity to get into jobs like theirs. Indeed, an Ohio building contractor characterized as a working-class liberal had three children who had all gone to college. He was very pleased that his sons were not going to follow in his footsteps and that they would not want a job like his. For him, the issue of civil rights was more distant from his everyday work, although he mentioned some negative encounters with blacks he had had at various times in his life. But he wanted to protect his children from the market by providing them with marketable skills rather than by helping them get into unionized jobs, as many of the working-class "racists" wanted to do for their children.

The rich white liberals expressed support for government programs that provide services and opportunities to those who are disadvantaged by class or race. It seemed that the policies that they supported would not have much material or substantive effect on their own life outcomes, because they and their children already had good educations, lived in segregated communities, had rich social resources from which to draw, and for the most part were in jobs or life situations that would not be affected very much by the implementation of affirmative action programs or an increase in welfare spending. In other words, these interviewees were not as personally affected in a material way by the policies of the civil rights movement and could "afford to be generous" (Sachdev and Bourhis 1991) in the form of support for public policies that they perceived to benefit the least advantaged and the most vulnerable in society.

The rich white liberals seemed to believe that their own lives and the lives of their children would be better off if there were not so much inequality, but they did not necessarily see any interdependence between the choices and opportunities in their own lives and the lives of the disadvantaged and vulnerable. That connection had not crossed the minds of most of these interviewees. The rich white liberals supported government redistributive programs, were concerned about issues like poverty and inequality, and seemed more personally influenced by the ideas of the civil rights movement than other interviewees, but with their higher income and education levels, perhaps they also were likely to be the least affected substantively by the implementation of civil rights policies. The rich white liberals who expressed a strong commitment to the civil rights movement and government efforts to help minorities and the poor probably had people like the working-class "racists" in mind when they thought about "those racists" who are still blocking access to civil rights.

In today's political landscape, those with liberal views, like those in this study, are clearly in the minority and no longer command at a policy level the support and enthusiasm that were evident during and after the initial passage of civil rights legislation. Instead, the country seems to have drifted toward greater skepticism about the efforts of government, especially the federal government, to redistribute opportunity or income or take other steps toward greater equality (Kohut 2009; Teixeira and Rogers 2000). Because these white interviewees had experienced no moral dilemma with regard to racial inequality, few of them were likely to be candidates to lead the social movement that Myrdal hoped would emerge. On the one hand, the interviewees already believed themselves to be supporters of civil rights and equal opportunity. On the other hand, it seems to be precisely the efforts to implement civil rights policies that would create greater racial equality that have not only invoked political opposition to government policies but also led to the new conservative politics that threatens the gains of both the civil rights movement and even the New Deal. In this political environment, both labor rights and civil rights are threatened. In the competition between labor groups and civil rights activists to define economic justice, support for both has eroded and the institutional supports for both have been threatened and weakened. The progressive acts of unions and New Deal politics on which Myrdal pinned his hopes for furthering the goals of racial equality did indeed contribute to important changes, but they also invoked continued and substantial resistance that has stalled progress and threatens further movement toward greater racial equality.

The Persistent Political Influence of the South

Myrdal was especially concerned in *An American Dilemma* about the political environment of the American South and the tenant farming organization of Southern agriculture. Although he was aware that there were problems in the North as well, he hoped that the pressures being brought to bear for change would transform the North and that the North would then force changes on the South. For example, in the 1948 paper in which he revisited some of his argument, albeit this time after the war was over and America's international role had become clear, he said:

> The discouraging fact is, that the deep-seated defects of the Southern agricultural system—let me just cite some of the traditional slogans: tenancy, credit, cotton, one-crop system, soil erosion, and let me add: poverty, insecurity, ignorance, low health standards, lack of an enterprising spirit, high birth rates, and large families—have been recognized and accepted by a unanimous expert opinion, and remedial plans worked out, for at least two generations without much being done about it. Fundamentally, Southern agriculture is suffering from not having had a land reform when slavery was abolished after the Civil War. . . . In all likelihood Southern agriculture will remain a strategic problem area for Negro welfare and policy after the war. (Myrdal 1948, 199–200)

Further arguing that the "great national compromise . . . by which the North had left the Negroes in the South to the mercy of the Southern whites, was drawing to a close" (Myrdal 1948, 207), he went on to remind his 1948 audience of his predictions about the postwar transformation of the South and the North's role in the process. As he said in *An American Dilemma*:

> We have become convinced in the course of this inquiry that the North is getting prepared for a fundamental redefinition of the Negro's status in America. The North will accept it if the change is pushed by courageous leadership. And the North has much more power than the South. The white South is itself a minority and a national problem. (Myrdal 1944, 1010)

Myrdal reiterated his explanation in the 1948 paper by citing claims he had made in *An American Dilemma:* "The outside observer feels convinced that an increasing number of white Northerners mean business this time. . . . The North cannot well afford any longer to let the white Southerners have their own way with the Negroes as completely as they have had" (Myrdal 1944, 1014). Myrdal's belief that the "color angle of the war" and the influence of the postwar international situation—both in terms of the international leadership role that the United States had to play and the fallout from the anticolonial movements in Africa, which were being watched around the world—would keep the pressure on the U.S. North. He therefore believed that change would come about through social movements, political action, the courts, and the growing visibility of Negro inequality, especially as blacks moved out of the South and gained voting rights in the North. As he argued in *An American Dilemma:* "The Negro vote and the labor vote in the North also have considerable weight in checking Southern conservatism and have increasing power to do so" (1015).

In the midst of the war and in the immediate aftermath, following the passage of the New Deal legislation and with unions' growing success in organizing and expanding labor rights, it is understandable that Myrdal might have placed confidence in the power of institutions and social movements to effect change. In that context, he did not foresee that the South could maintain its political influence on the country. Nor could he have known, nor probably imagined, the successes of a renewed right-wing movement to secure Southern influence through a takeover of the Republican Party in the post–civil rights period. Although there was a long gap between the publication of Myrdal's book and subsequent events in the Republican Party, the seeds were being planted at the time he was writing, especially in the postwar period. That is, the threat of change to the South was so imminent, and looked to be so consequential, that efforts to resist or redirect the inevitable changes were already under way in the aftermath of the war.

Myrdal was correct to assume that the postwar dynamics would lead to a renewed struggle for political power between the North and South, but he was incorrect to believe that the South was too weak to prevail. Events during World War II (such as the 1943 Detroit race riot and the "Zoot Suit" riots in Los Angeles and elsewhere) and in its aftermath (black soldiers returning to the United States received a less than enthusiastic welcome) created substantial pressure on Northern politicians to support civil rights. Not only did President Truman face substantial unrest domestically both during and following the war, but as Myrdal had predicted, he had to respond to the international context as well as the domestic one. Although not known as a strong proponent of civil rights, Truman appointed the Presidential Commission on Civil Rights in 1946. The commission report, *To Secure These Rights,* made far-reaching recommendations, including the desegregation of the Army, the creation of a permanent Fair Employment Practices Commission, the elimination of poll taxes, and antilynching legislation (Presidential Commission on Civil Rights 1947). Truman endorsed the commission's recommendations in his 1947 and 1948 State of the Union addresses. The recommendations provided a backdrop for two subsequent executive orders, including those issued by Truman in 1948 to desegregate the military and outlaw discrimination in the federal civil service.

Truman's efforts angered Southern politicians, and as discussed in chapter 5, Strom Thurmond, then governor of South Carolina, reacted by forming the States' Rights Democratic Party (the "Dixiecrats") to run against Truman in the 1948 election. Truman was also challenged from the left by Henry Wallace, Roosevelt's vice president from 1941 to 1945, who ran as a nominee of the Progressive Party. Wallace was a strong supporter of civil rights whose presidential bid included campaigning for full voting rights for African Americans. Although Truman won, the heightened focus on civil rights in the 1948 campaign and Truman's actions in response to the pressures on him at home and abroad contributed to subsequent events that transformed the two parties and solidified the influence of the South on national politics. As discussed at length in chapter 5, Thurmond became one of the first Southern politicians to leave the Democratic Party for the Republican Party, and then he played a significant role in the rise of the New Right. Both he and fellow Southerner Jesse Helms, a senator from North Carolina, were instrumental in the rise of the New Right and in linking the New Right to what became the Religious Right. Both worked behind the scenes with various right-wing groups in their efforts to take over the Republican Party and turn the country back from the liberalism of the New Deal and especially to undermine the movement for civil rights. Their efforts also had a significant impact on the challenges mounted from the right to the emergence of welfare state policies, from the New Deal to the War on Poverty and ultimately to policies of both the Clinton and Obama administrations.

Thus, Myrdal was correct in his prediction that the battle between the North and the South would be renewed, but contrary to his prediction, the South has continued to have substantial influence on national politics. The reshaping of post–civil rights politics began immediately after World War II, and Myrdal did anticipate many of the factors that would contribute to the success of the civil rights movement and then to the transformation of U.S. politics: the social movements, the institutional responses to those movements, and the use of the courts and the law in the political struggle for equality, all unfolded as he had foretold. But he underestimated the tenacity of the South and the resource base that supported its continued influence—and he specifically underestimated racial politics in the South. I have argued in this book that post–civil rights party politics was transformed from racial politics into religious politics, and that religious politics has been practiced by the same people who previously espoused racial politics and whose explicit and/or implicit motivations have remained the same. The Religious Right (supported by the New Right) has provided both the organization and the mechanisms for the South to continue in its role as a major player on the national stage. Largely through the workings of a myriad of organizations supported by a small group of right-wing billionaires, the Republican Party has now been taken over, as most observers would agree, by an increasingly conservative right-wing movement (Kohut et al. 2011). Even though support for civil rights became normative within the country as a whole, including in the South, the policy changes that interpreted and supported civil rights were and continue to be highly contested.

The various sociopolitical groups identified in this study reflect the dynamics that have been reshaping post–civil rights politics. Of course, the interviewees included only U.S.-born whites in their prime working years, so they did not represent the whole of U.S. politics in the post–civil rights era. But many of them did represent the sociopolitical groups that have been most hotly contested in the intense struggle of the two major parties to put together winning and continuing electoral majorities. The religious conservatives, working-class "racists," and rich white liberals in this study belonged to groups of voters who have been the targets of each party, and the apolitical majority interviewees similarly reflected the growing number of white independents who do not affiliate with either party and are quite mixed and uncertain in their politics.

The Republican Party has fostered its relationship with conservative churches to the point that white Protestant evangelicals have now become the base of the party. Both parties have been trying to capture the support of working-class "racists" ever since the presidential campaigns of George Wallace, the segregationist governor of Alabama in the late 1960s and 1970s. Although blue-collar workers were a reliable part of the New Deal coalition, the explicit support of the Democratic Party for black civil rights created major tension between the politics of class and the politics of race that has not been resolved to this day. Thus, blue-collar workers, especially those like the working-class "racists" in this study, are an important constituency who could tip the balance in swing states, especially in the Midwest, in presidential elections.

The rich white liberals seem to be reliably liberal in their politics (and in this study were primarily located among the New Jersey interviewees). People like the rich white liberals in this study have gradually left the Republican Party to become a major part of the Democratic coalition, especially because of their support for civil rights and social liberalism. The fact that their class is not especially consistent with their politics, however, raises a problem for the Democratic Party: they are as likely to vote for a third-party candidate as for a Democrat, or to sit out an election in which the Democratic candidate is someone who they feel does not properly represent their values or who may have made too many compromises with other politicians who violate their liberal sensibilities.

The smaller groups that showed up among the interviewees did not necessarily match the larger constituencies of contemporary politics, and members of each of these smaller groups had their own political hot buttons that could shift their support one direction or another. Especially because of the close divide in the electoral college, regional politics is critical to party coalitions and to each party's success at both the national and state levels. Recent political events have underlined how important control of governorships and state legislatures is for mounting campaigns and counting the votes. Further, the policy agenda for the country starts at the state and local levels.

In summary, the South has continued, contrary to Myrdal's expectations, to have substantial political influence in the country, and it sparked the new right-wing social movements that have influenced politics across the country. Instead of the North forcing the South to leave its conservative politics behind, the South has extended its conservative politics, albeit in new guises, to the rest of the country.

Conclusion

Despite his prescience about the direction of changes in the postwar period and the transformation that would be wrought by the civil rights movement, Gunnar Myrdal did not foresee the mechanisms that would allow racial inequality to continue and enable white Americans to avoid being troubled by a moral dilemma. His analysis was not, as some subsequent critics have claimed, either naive or disconnected from the reality of racism on the ground. But Myrdal thought of the reproduction of racial inequality as a process of discrimination and gave insufficient attention to the ways in which whites help each other through favoritism, opportunity hoarding, and exchanges of social and cultural capital. Myrdal also strongly believed in the power not only of social movements but of the institutional support that he felt certain would solidify the gains of social movements in law and practice. He seemed to have great confidence in the promise of the New Deal and the progressive role of unions. Unfortunately, the New Deal, however profound its impact on the country, has now become a constant target of equally strong right-wing social movements trying to erode its provisions and undermine the political coalition built around it, and labor unions, though they have often played a progressive role, have also been a primary mechanism by which the white working class in particular hoards job opportunities and protects itself from the vagaries of market competition. With the Democratic Party proving unable to resolve the class-versus-race tensions, unions have not been able to play the role that Myrdal seemed to expect of them. Myrdal also miscalculated the political strength of the South in U.S. politics and the continued influence of the South on post–civil rights politics.

Despite his contributions and insight into racial inequality in the United States, Myrdal misunderstood the contradictory and paradoxical nature of the reproduction of racial inequality and the ability of those who benefit from privilege to convince themselves that they have earned their good fortune because it is the result of their own hard work and effort. The domestic and international pressures that forced civil rights onto the political agenda in the postwar United States did lead to social movements, institutional and legal reforms, new legislation, and unprecedented transformations of long-standing policies and practices that had contributed to the reproduction of racial inequality. But despite the continued existence of racial inequality, whites in the United States still do not experience a moral dilemma over their role in racial politics that would lead them to support greater racial equality.

Even though discrimination against blacks was outlawed and support for civil rights became normative throughout the country, whites were able to maintain their privileges in the post–civil rights era through the accumulation of social and cultural capital and the use of opportunity hoarding—that is, through favoritism and cronyism—as they had done before. It seems that the major changes in the lives of blacks in the aftermath of the civil rights movement came about because of changes in the economy and as a result of government policies that forced employers and other institutions to take account of their actions more than their attitudes (Smith and Welch 1984; Wilson 1987). Although the New Deal made a major difference in the lives of most Americans, that was much less the case for blacks than for whites (Katznelson 2005; Quadagno 1994). Unions have played a contradictory role in civil rights: some have fostered racial progressivism, but others have resisted the inclusion of blacks when civil rights have been used to challenge labor rights (DiTomaso 1977). And a right-wing movement that has funded, encouraged, and fostered a new racial politics in the guise of religious politics has had an impact on the reproduction of racial inequality as well (DiTomaso 1977; Lienesch 1982; Massey 2005). The South, the largest region in the United States, has continued to play a major political role in the opposition to the implementation of civil rights, and it has led the effort to reshape post–civil rights politics into the current competition between the Democratic and Republican Parties.

In this context, most whites do not view racial inequality as a problem to be solved. Seeing themselves as supporters of civil rights, as being in opposition to discrimination, as supporters of equal opportunity, and as upholders of American values (in the form of the dominant ideology), most whites believe themselves to be good and decent people, as Myrdal characterized what most Americans believe about themselves. Racial inequality does not present them with a moral dilemma because they often are not aware of its extent and do not see that they have anything to do with its continued existence. Most believe that blacks now have the same legal rights as whites, that they have the same opportunities, and that if blacks feel aggrieved, they have the courts and the law to support them. Most whites believe that they have been on the right side of history when it comes to civil rights, that they have upheld key American values, and that they have been both good citizens and good neighbors by helping themselves and helping their friends. Continued racial inequality in the United States has less to do with racism and discrimination than academic scholarship and the popular press would lead us to believe. The ultimate white privilege in the United States is that most whites do not have to be racists to gain the advantages of racial privilege. Because they do not have to do bad things to black people in order to secure their own futures, they do not feel guilt or condemnation when racial issues are raised in the media. From a position of structural advantage, they need only engage in helping each other (DiTomaso et al. 2007) through the mechanisms of opportunity hoarding and exploitation, and as they do so they remember only the uncertainty they experienced, the efforts that they made, and the persistence with which they pursued their goals. Both at a psychological level in which in-group favoritism is not necessarily combined with out-group derogation (Fiske et al. 2002) and at a structural level in which privileged positions and access to resource-rich communities and families provide the means to merit and achievement (Coleman 1988; Putnam 2000), white Americans feel anxiety about their futures, but not about their role in the reproduction of racial inequality. About racial issues, there is no American dilemma among white Americans.

Perhaps we could revisit some of Myrdal's insights to understand how a moral dilemma regarding racial inequality might be created. It would need to start with a social movement to support opportunity, inclusion, and justice for those who are disadvantaged (that is, those who lack the advantages of being able to draw on social resources). Such a social movement would have to draw on the foundations of the American creed about the promise of civil rights and the pursuit of happiness for all. Such a movement would have to make visible the mechanisms by which inequality is reproduced across race-ethnic and gender groups, and it would undoubtedly have to call attention to and name the injustice of hoarding opportunities for family and friends. To be successful, a social movement of the disadvantaged would have to gain allies among the advantaged who become convinced, perhaps like the rich white liberals, that a more egalitarian society would be good for them and their children. Thus, a successful social movement would have to be based on a coalition that crosses race-ethnic and class lines and brings their interests together. Importantly, for a social movement for justice to gain widespread support in the country, it would have to show how change would improve the lives of everyone, not of one group at the expense of another. In other words, civil rights cannot be fostered at the expense of labor rights or vice versa, so a new and successful social movement has to encourage economic growth, access to education and a social safety net, and a politics based on merit and not just on advantage and the ability to get ahead. Undoubtedly, such a social movement, if successful, would move the United States in the direction of social democracy, perhaps drawing from the kind of vision that Myrdal brought to his native Sweden before he was called to undertake the project of *An American Dilemma.* Contemporary politics is very far removed from this agenda. As Myrdal noted long ago, it will take courageous and persistent leaders to create a social movement that brings whites and nonwhites together for the purposes of reducing inequality and creating a more just society for all. In the ever more volatile global context, there continue to be great challenges to racial equality, but perhaps we also have greater opportunity and new means for constructing visions that allow us to dream new dreams.

Appendix A Case Information for American Non-Dilemma Study, by Sociopolitical Group

Sociopolitical Group[a]	Batch	Group Number	Survey/ Interview Number	Age	Occupation	File Name[b]
AM	B	2	6	25	Delivers dry wall (construction)	B006 OH M WC Delivers dry wall (construction)
AM	B	2	11	55	Factory worker, tool grinder	B011 OH M WC Factory worker, tool grinder
AM	B	2	12	60	High school social studies teacher	B012 OH F MC HS social studies teacher
AM	B	2	14	45	Supervisor at small company	B014 OH M WC Supervisor small company
AM	B	2	15	43	Part-time postal worker	B015 OH F WC Part time postal worker
AM	B	2	17	42	Project engineering manager	B017 OH M MC Project engineering manager
AM	B	2	20	29	Wireless phone salesman	B020 OH M WC Wireless phone salesman
AM	B	2	22	47	Heavy equipment operator in steel mill	B022 OH M WC Heavy equipment operator in steel mill
AM	C	3	107	58	Accounting clerk	C007 NJ F WC Accting clerk
AM	C	3	111	25	Clerical worker in creative arts	C011 NJ F WC Clerical
AM	C	3	112	38	Crossing guard	C012 NJ F WC Crossing guard
AM	D	4	201	40	Unemployed engineer	D001 NJ M MC Unemployed engineer
AM	D	4	204	27	Hairdresser	D004 NJ F WC Beautician
AM	D	4	205	46	Unskilled worker	D005 NJ M WC Unskilled worker
AM	D	4	207	43	Assistant superintendent, public works	D007 NJ M WC Superint-pubworks
AM	D	4	210	25	Merchandiser in retail sales	D010 NJ F MC Retail sales

Appendix A (*Continued*)

Sociopolitical Group[a]	Batch	Group Number	Survey/ Interview Number	Age	Occupation	File Name[b]
AM	D	4	214	41	Chef in food service	D014 NJ M WC Chef-foodservice
AM	D	4	215	37	PC support technician	D015 NJ M MC PC support tech
AM	D	4	216	44	Broadcast engineer	D016 NJ M WC Broadcast engineer
AM	D	4	217	42	Executive chef	D017 NJ M WC Exec chef
AM	D	4	218	50	Purchasing agent	D018 NJ M MC Purchasing agent
AM	D	4	220	52	Deli clerk	D020 NJ F WC Deli clerk
AM	D	4	222	38	Insurance administrative assistant	D022 NJ F WC Insurance admin asst
AM	D	4	223	30	Nurse	D023 NJ F MC Nurse
AM	D	4	224	35	Assistant stock trader	D024 NJ M WC Asst stock trader
AM	D	4	225	37	Customer service worker	D025 NJ F WC Customer Service Worker
AM	D	4	227	51	Primary school teacher at private school	D027 NJ M MC Private school teacher
AM	D	4	228	29	Accountant	D028 F MC Accountant
AM	D	4	229	40	Laboratory technician in large company	D029 M WC Lab tech
AM	D	4	231	28	Senior trade analyst at large company	D031 F WC Senior trade analyst
AM	D	4	233	50	Development office assistant for private school	D033 NJ F WC Office asst for school
AM	D	4	234	31	Toxicologist in research lab of large company	D034 NJ M MC Toxicologist

AM	D	4	235	44	Facilities manager at golf course	D035 NJ M WC Facilities mgr
AM	D	4	236	57	Billing clerk in medical office	D036 NJ F MC Billing clerk
AM	D	4	237	26	Billing clerk in large company	D037 NJ F MC Billing clerk
AM	D	4	239	35	Part-time high school drama teacher	D039 NJ F MC High School drama teacher
AM	D	4	243	33	Special education teacher	D043 NJ F MC Special ed teacher
AM	D	4	249	45	Special education teacher	D049 NJ F MC Special ed teacher
AM	D	4	250	46	Manager of doctor's office	D050 NJ F WC Mgr-doctor's office
AM	D	4	254	44	Actuary	D054 NJ M MC Actuary
AM	D	4	255	40	Unemployed (degree in art history)	D055 NJ F MC Unemployed (art degree)
AM	D	4	257	33	Head frontline clerk on Wall Street	D057 NJ M MC Clerk on Wall St
AM	D	4	260	40	Part-time football coach	D060 NJ M MC Part-time football coach
AM	D	4	262	47	Patent attorney	D062 NJ M MC Patent attorney
AM	D	4	263	37	Regional manager for party sales	D063 NJ F WC Part sales mgr
AM	D	4	265	51	Actress	D065 NJ F MC Actress
AM	D	4	266	30	Financial analyst for real estate company	D066 NJ M MC Financial analyst
AM	D	4	267	42	Real estate appraiser	D067 NJ M MC Realestate appraiser
AM	D	4	274	35	Self-employed landscaper	D074 NJ M WC Landscaper
AM	D	4	276	36	IT manager at major company	D076 NJ F MC IT Mgr
AM	E	5	302	55	Door-to-door advertising manager	E302 OH F WC Door to door advertising manager
AM	E	5	305	29	Owner of small gift shop	E305 OH F WC Owner small gift shop
AM	E	5	307	53	Factory worker, tool checker	E307 OH M WC Factory worker, tool checker

Appendix A (*Continued*)

Sociopolitical Group[a]	Batch	Group Number	Survey/ Interview Number	Age	Occupation	File Name[b]
AM	E	5	315	50	Supervisor for cleaning business	E315 OH M MC Supervisor cleaning business
AM	E	5	316	29	Teacher	E316 OH F MC Teacher
AM	E	5	320	33	Bookkeeper in home business	E320 OH F WC Bookkeeper in home business
AM	E	5	323	44	Educator in rehabilitation	E323 OH F MC Educator in rehabilitation
AM	E	5	324	45	Self-employed programmer	E324 OH M WC Self employed programmer
AM	E	5	325	37	Licensed practical nurse	E325 OH F WC LPN
AM	E	5	333	39	Preschool teacher	E333 OH F WC Preschool teacher
AM	E	5	334	55	Unemployed real estate agent	E334 OH F WC Unemployed real estate agent
AM	E	5	335	50	Insurance office manager	E335 OH F WC Insurance office manager
AM	E	5	337	43	Clinical therapist, mental health	E337 OH F MC Clinical therapist, mental health
AM	E	5	341	47	Government accountant	E341 OH F MC Government accountant
AM	E	5	342	31	Student in optician program	E342 OH M WC Student in optician program
AM	E	5	343	34	Auto mechanic	E343 OH M WC Auto mechanic
AM	E	5	344	52	Disabled industrial arts teacher	E344 OH M MC Disabled industrial arts teacher
AM	E	5	345	50	Telephone company billing clerk	E345 OH F WC Telephone company billing clerk
AM	E	5	347	59	Beautician	E347 OH F WC Beautician

AM	E	5	349	52	Small-business loan officer	E349 OH M MC Small business loan officer
AM	E	5	352	50	Order entry in large company	E352 OH M WC Order entry in large company
AM	E	5	356	33	Attorney	E356 OH M MC Attorney
AM	E	5	357	43	Dentist	E357 OH M MC Dentist
AM	E	5	358	50	Unemployed cost accountant	E358 OH M WC Unemployed cost accountant
AM	E	5	362	46	Unemployed/disabled attorney	E362 OH F MC Unemployed/disabled attorney
AM	E	5	363	33	Remodeling in small firm	E363 OH M WC Remodeling in small firm
AM	E	5	365	45	Owner of small trucking company	E365 OH M WC Owner small trucking company
AM	F	6	404	41	Hairstylist	F004 TN F WC Hairstylist
AM	F	6	414	45	Unemployed	F014 TN M WC Unemployed
AM	F	6	418	45	Postal worker	F018 TN M WC Postal worker
AM	F	6	419	45	Office assistant	F019 TN F WC Office asst
AM	F	6	420	55	Retired	F020 TN F WC Retired
AM	F	6	423	37	Homemaker	F023 TN F MC Homemaker
AM	F	6	425	51	Commercial art instructor	F025 TN M MC Art instructor
AM	G	7	506	47	Librarian	G506 TN F MC Librarian
AM	G	7	510	27	Self-employed	G510 TN F MC Self employed
AM	G	7	511	39	Bookkeeper	G511 TN F MC Bookkeeper
AM	G	7	515	42	Chef	G515 TN M WC Chef
AM	G	7	517	31	Musician	G517 TN M MC Musician
AM	G	7	522	36	Vending machine route man	G522 TN M WC Vending machine route man
AM	G	7	532	31	Self-employed entertainer	G532 TN M WC Self employed entertainer
AM	G	7	536	33	Self-employed photographer	G536 TN F WC Self employed photography

Appendix A *(Continued)*

Sociopolitical Group[a]	Batch	Group Number	Survey/ Interview Number	Age	Occupation	File Name[b]
MCC	B	2	13	48	Part-time development officer in high school	B013 OH F MC Part time development officer in HS
MCC	B	2	21	42	Homemaker (was dental assistant)	B021 OH F WC Homemaker (was dental assistant)
MCC	D	4	230	30	Small business owner, family company	D030 M MC Small business owner
MCC	D	4	240	29	Insurance claims adjuster for large company	D040 NJ M MC Insurance adjuster
MCC	D	4	273	49	General manager of marketing for major foreign firm	D073 NJ M MC Mkting mgr
MCC	D	4	275	55	Unemployed homemaker	D075 NJ F MC Homemaker
MCC	E	5	327	34	Part-time college instructor, doctoral student	E327 OH F MC Part-time college instructor, doctoral student
MCC	E	5	336	44	Registered nurse	E336 OH F MC Nurse, RN
MCC	E	5	338	48	Worldwide business manager for new products	E338 OH M MC Worldwide business manager for new products
MCC	E	5	364	53	Paralegal	E364 OH F MC Paralegal
MCC	G	7	505	42	Sales	G505 TN M MC Sales
RC	B	2	1	49	High school teacher	B001 OH M MC High school teacher
RC	B	2	2	41	Quality control manager	B002 OH M MC Quality control manager
RC	B	2	3	37	Electrical engineer manager	B003 OH F MC Electrical engineer manager
RC	B	2	7	48	Unemployed teacher, housewife	B007 OH F MC Unemployed teacher housewife
RC	B	2	9	47	Practical nurse	B009 OH F WC Practical nurse

RC	B	2	10	45	Executive CEO of small company	B010 OH M MC Executive CEO of small company
RC	B	2	16	60	Retired teacher	B016 OH M MC Retired teacher
RC	B	2	19	50	Homemaker	B019 OH F MC Homemaker
RC	C	3	102	41	Homemaker, dentist	C002 NJ F MC Homemaker
RC	C	3	115	26	Firefighter, landscaper	C015 NJ M WC Firefighter
RC	D	4	213	38	Vice president of heavy-industry small firm	D013 NJ M MC VP-heavy industry
RC	D	4	241	44	Billing clerk for hospital	D041 NJ F WC Billing clerk
RC	D	4	246	54	Primary school music teacher in inner city	D046 NJ F MC Primary school music teacher
RC	D	4	269	47	Self-employed paper hanger	D069 NJ M WC Paper hanger
RC	D	4	270	46	Staff engineer at major company	D070 NJ M MC Staff engineer
RC	E	5	309	38	Homemaker	E309 OH F WC Homemaker
RC	E	5	311	43	Manager of insurance office	E311 OH M MC Manager insurance office
RC	E	5	313	39	Lawn and garden equipment sales and service	E313 OH M WC Law and garden equipment sales and service
RC	E	5	314	61	Pharmaceutical sales manager	E314 OH M MC Pharmaceutical sales manager
RC	E	5	326	48	Letter carrier	E326 OH M WC Letter carrier
RC	E	5	328	37	Pharmaceutical sales manager	E328 OH M MC Pharmaceutical sales manager
RC	E	5	348	40	Unemployed customer service representative	E348 OH M MC Unemployed customer service representative
RC	E	5	355	48	Nurse BSN	E355 OH F MC Nurse BSN
RC	E	5	361	31	Graphic designer	E361 OH M WC Graphic designer
RC	E	5	367	35	Graphic designer	E367 OH M WC Graphics designer
RC	F	6	401	53	Teacher	F001 TN F MC Teacher

Appendix A *(Continued)*

Sociopolitical Group[a]	Batch	Group Number	Survey/ Interview Number	Age	Occupation	File Name[b]
RC	F	6	402	25	Medical transcription	F002 TN F MC Medical transcription
RC	F	6	403	56	Account clerk	F003 TN F WC Account clerk
RC	F	6	405	40	Manager	F005 TN M MC Manager
RC	F	6	408	53	School headmaster	F008 TN M MC School headmaster
RC	F	6	411	45	Factory worker	F011 TN M WC Factory worker
RC	F	6	416	54	Homemaker	F016 TN F MC Homemaker
RC	F	6	424	38	Purchasing manager	F024 TN M MC Purchasing mgr
RC	G	7	502	55	Editorial assistant	G502 TN F WC Editorial assistant
RC	G	7	503	49	Administration	G503 TN M MC Administration
RC	G	7	509	53	Music teacher	G509 TN F MC Music teacher
RC	G	7	518	48	Construction manager	G518 TN M MC Construction manager
RC	G	7	525	46	Manager at industrial firm	G525 TN M MC Manager industrial firm
RC	G	7	526	43	Telecommunications executive	G526 TN M MC Telecommunications executive
RC	G	7	527	28	Essential materials specialist	G527 TN F MC Essential materials specialist
RC	G	7	528	25	Office manager	G528 TN F MC Office manager
RC	G	7	529	23	Trim carpenter	G529 TN M WC Trim carpenter
RC	G	7	531	37	Accounting	G531 TN F WC Accounting
RC	G	7	534	48	Sales	G534 TN M MC Sales
RC	G	7	535	36	Aircraft assembler	G535 TN M WC Aircraft assembler
RC	G	7	537	44	Homemaker	G537 TN F WC Homemaker
RNC	D	4	244	41	Management consultant in own firm	D044 NJ F MC Mgmt consultant

RNC	E	5	329	35	Radiology technician	E329 OH F WC Radiology technician
RNC	E	5	330	25	Part-time preschool supervisor	E330 OH F MC Part-time preschool supervisor
RNC	F	6	407	41	Teacher	F007 TN F MC Teacher
RNC	F	6	410	33	Retail sales	F010 TN F WC Retail sales
RNC	F	6	412	30	Minister	F012 TN F MC Minister
RNC	F	6	413	50	Government service	F013 TN F MC Govt service
RNC	F	6	415	41	Electronics technician	F015 TN M WC Electronic tech
RNC	F	6	422	54	Travel consultant	F022 TN F WC Travel rep
RNC	G	7	501	56	Deputy sheriff	G501 TN M MC Deputy sheriff
RNC	G	7	507	49	Electronic publishing coordinator	G507 TN M WC Electronic publishing coordinator
RWL	B	2	4	45	Technician in research laboratory	B004 OH M MC Technician in research laboratory
RWL	B	2	23	45	High school drama teacher	B023 OH F MC High school drama teacher
RWL	C	3	101	42	Executive	C001 NJ F MC Executive
RWL	C	3	103	45	Clinical psychologist	C003 NJ F MC Clinical psych
RWL	C	3	104	46	Executive director of law firm	C004 NJ M MC Law firm director
RWL	C	3	105	48	Physician	C005 NJ F MC Physician
RWL	C	3	106	55	Unemployed writer	C006 NJ M MC Writer
RWL	C	3	108	45	Television writer	C008 NJ F MC TV Writer
RWL	C	3	109	39	Builder	C009 NJ M MC Builder
RWL	C	3	114	46	Corporate attorney	C014 NJ F MC Corp. attorney
RWL	D	4	206	36	Manager of music business	D006 NJ M MC Music mgr
RWL	D	4	226	41	Director of city planning department	D026 NJ M MC Direct city planning
RWL	D	4	232	47	Special education teacher and coordinator	D032 NJ F MC Special ed teacher
RWL	D	4	238	48	Unemployed salesman	D038 NJ M MC Unemploy salesman

Appendix A (*Continued*)

Sociopolitical Group[a]	Batch	Group Number	Survey/ Interview Number	Age	Occupation	File Name[b]
RWL	D	4	242	38	Social work manager in housing for homeless	D042 NJ F MC Social worker for homeless
RWL	D	4	245	53	Claims administrator in government office	D045 NJ M MC Claims admin
RWL	D	4	247	52	Insurance company executive	D047 NJ M MC Insurance exec
RWL	D	4	248	34	Attorney	D048 NJ M MC Attorney
RWL	D	4	251	37	Technical sales manager (EE)	D051 NJ M MC Tech sales mgr
RWL	D	4	253	48	Vice president of human resources in high-tech firm	D053 NJ F MC VP-HR
RWL	D	4	258	37	Freelance computer-based training expert	D058 NJ F MC Computer expert free lancer
RWL	D	4	259	59	Bond trader	D059 NJ M MC Bond trader
RWL	D	4	261	51	Assistant general manager of major food company	D061 NJ M MC Asst. mgr major food company
RWL	D	4	264	37	Senior brand manager for major company	D064 NJ F MC Sr brand mgr
RWL	D	4	268	36	Homemaker (unemployed meeting planner)	D068 NJ F MC Homemaker
RWL	D	4	271	48	Merchandising manager in food company	D071 NJ M MC Merchandising mgr
RWL	D	4	272	36	Unemployed nursing home administrator	D072 NJ F MC Unemploy nursing home admin
RWL	D	4	277	56	Customer service team leader in major company	D077 NJ F MC Customer service leader

RWL	E	5	306	47	Engineer	E306 OH M MC Engineer
RWL	E	5	308	54	Retired attorney	E308 OH M MC Retired attorney
RWL	E	5	319	49	Registered nurse	E319 OH F MC Nurse, RN
RWL	E	5	322	52	Primary school music teacher	E322 OH F MC Primary school music teacher
RWL	E	5	331	43	Project manager in government laboratory	E331 OH M MC Project manager government laboratory
RWL	E	5	332	45	Training manager for large company	E332 OH M MC Training manager for large company
RWL	E	5	346	31	High school business teacher	E346 OH F MC High school business teacher
RWL	E	5	353	54	Homemaker (trophy wife)	E353 OH F MC Homemaker (trophy wife)
RWL	F	6	409	54	Statistical analyst supervisor	F009 TN M MC Stat analyst supervisor
RWL	F	6	421	52	Christian denomination professional	F021 TN F MC Religious profession
RWL	G	7	514	56	School system administrator	G514 TN M MC School system administrator
RWL	G	7	516	40	Record producer musician	G516 TN M MC Record producer musician
RWL	G	7	521	53	Health care executive	G521 TN F MC Healthcare executive
RWL	G	7	530	25	Musician	G530 TN M MC Musician
WCL	B	2	5	33	Receptionist in doctor's office	B005 OH F WC Receptionist in doctor's office
WCL	D	4	202	49	Recreation assistant, substitute teacher	D002 NJ F WC Rec asst
WCL	D	4	208	50	Computer technician	D008 NJ M WC Computer tech
WCL	E	5	301	47	Custodian	E301 OH F WC Custodian
WCL	E	5	303	41	Homemaker	E303 OH F WC Homemaker

Appendix A (*Continued*)

Sociopolitical Group[a]	Batch	Group Number	Survey/ Interview Number	Age	Occupation	File Name[b]
WCL	E	5	359	38	Front-desk clerk at medical center	E359 OH F WC Front desk clerk at medical center
WCL	E	5	366	41	Self-employed construction worker	E366 OH F WC Self employed construction worker
WCL	E	5	368	52	Building contractor	E368 OH M WC Building contractor
WCL	G	7	504	38	Clerical worker	G504 TN F WC Clerical
WCL	G	7	512	40	Small-business owner	G512 TN M WC Small business owner
WCL	G	7	513	26	Web designer	G513 TN M WC Web designer
WCL	G	7	519	43	Commercial artist	G519 TN M WC Commercial artist
WCL	G	7	523	33	Massage therapist	G523 TN F WC Massage therapist
WCL	G	7	533	40	Electronics engineer	G533 TN M WC Electronics engineer
WCR	B	2	8	50	Surveyor	B008 OH M WC Surveyor
WCR	B	2	18	42	Welder	B018 OH M WC Welder
WCR	C	3	110	42	Police officer	C010 NJ M WC Policeman
WCR	C	3	113	38	Gas station owner	C013 NJ M WC Gas station owner
WCR	D	4	203	48	Carpenter	D003 NJ M WC Carpenter
WCR	D	4	209	46	Disabled railroad worker	D009 NJ M WC Disabled RR worker
WCR	D	4	211	30	Insurance adjuster	D011 NJ M WC Insurance adjuster
WCR	D	4	212	47	Housepainter	D012 NJ M WC House painter
WCR	D	4	219	48	Maintenance worker in large company	D019 NJ M WC Maintenance worker
WCR	D	4	221	41	Unemployed, retail sales	D021 NJ F WC Unemployed retail sales
WCR	D	4	252	57	Truck driver for flower shop	D052 NJ M WC Truck driver-florist shop
WCR	D	4	256	54	Self-employed real estate owner	D056 NJ F WC Real estate owner

WCR	D	4	278	39	Waitress and house cleaner	D078 NJ F WC Waitress-cleaner
WCR	E	5	304	52	Retired factory worker in meat plant	E304 OH M WC Retired factory worker in meat plant
WCR	E	5	310	53	Salesman	E310 OH M WC Salesman
WCR	E	5	312	38	Custodian	E312 OH F WC Custodian
WCR	E	5	317	42	Waitress at fast-food restaurant	E317 OH F WC Waitress at fast food restaurant
WCR	E	5	318	34	Homemaker	E318 OH F WC Homemaker
WCR	E	5	321	33	Self-employed trucking firm owner	E321 OH M WC Self employed trucking firm owner
WCR	E	5	339	31	Self-employed truck driver	E339 OH M WC Self employed truck driver
WCR	E	5	340	37	Warehouse sales	E340 OH F WC Warehouse sales
WCR	E	5	350	40	Owner of small industrial equipment company	E350 OH M WC Owner small industrial equipment company
WCR	E	5	351	52	Mortgage loan originator	E351 OH F WC Mortgage loan originator
WCR	E	5	354	51	Self-employed landscape business	E354 OH M WC Self-employed landscape business
WCR	E	5	360	45	Third party hearing representative for workman's compensation	E360 OH M WC 3rd party hearing rep for workmen's comp
WCR	F	6	426	41	Route sales and service	F026 TN F WC Route sales
WCR	F	6	427	31	Travel agent	F027 TN F WC Travel agent
WCR	G	7	508	44	Accounting	G508 TN F WC Accounting
WCR	G	7	520	27	Graphic designer	G520 TN M WC Graphic designer
WCR	G	7	524	36	Co-owner of small company	G524 TN M WC Co-owner of small company

Source: Author's compilation.

Notes: [a]Sociopolitical Groups: AM = Apolitical Majority; MCC = Middle-Class Conservative; RC = Religious Conservative; RNC = Religious Nonconservative; RWL = Rich White Liberal; WCL = Working-Class Liberal; WCR = Working-Class "Racist."

[b]File Names: OH = Ohio; NJ = New Jersey; TN = Tennessee; M = Male; F = Female; MC = Middle-Class; WC = Working-Class.

Appendix B **Case Information for American Non-Dilemma Study, by Case Number**

Sociopolitical Group[a]	Batch	Group Number	Survey/ Interview Number	Age	Occupation	File Name[b]
RC	B	2	1	49	High school teacher	B001 OH M MC High school teacher
RC	B	2	2	41	Quality control manager	B002 OH M MC Quality control manager
RC	B	2	3	37	Electrical engineer manager	B003 OH F MC Electrical engineer manager
RWL	B	2	4	45	Technician in research laboratory	B004 OH M MC Technician in research laboratory
WCL	B	2	5	33	Receptionist in doctor's office	B005 OH F WC Receptionist in doctor's office
AM	B	2	6	25	Delivers drywall (construction)	B006 OH M WC Delivers dry wall (construction)
RC	B	2	7	48	Unemployed teacher, housewife	B007 OH F MC Unemployed teacher housewife
WCR	B	2	8	50	Surveyor	B008 OH M WC Surveyor
RC	B	2	9	47	Practical nurse	B009 OH F WC Practical nurse
RC	B	2	10	45	Executive CEO of small company	B010 OH M MC Executive CEO of small company
AM	B	2	11	55	Factory worker, tool grinder	B011 OH M WC Factory worker, tool grinder
AM	B	2	12	60	High school social studies teacher	B012 OH F MC HS social studies teacher
MCC	B	2	13	48	Part-time development office in high school	B013 OH F MC Part time development office in HS
AM	B	2	14	45	Supervisor at small company	B014 OH M WC Supervisor small company
AM	B	2	15	43	Part-time postal worker	B015 OH F WC Part time postal worker
RC	B	2	16	60	Retired teacher	B016 OH M MC Retired teacher

AM	B	2	17	42	Project engineering manager	B017 OH M MC Project engineering manager
WCR	B	2	18	42	Welder	B018 OH M WC Welder
RC	B	2	19	50	Homemaker	B019 OH F MC Homemaker
AM	B	2	20	29	Wireless phone salesman	B020 OH M WC Wireless phone salesman
MCC	B	2	21	42	Homemaker (was dental assistant)	B021 OH F WC Homemaker (was dental assistant)
AM	B	2	22	47	Heavy equipment operator in steel mill	B022 OH M WC Heavy equipment operator in steel mill
RWL	B	2	23	45	High school drama teacher	B023 OH F MC High school drama teacher
RWL	C	3	101	42	Executive	C001 NJ F MC Executive
RC	C	3	102	41	Homemaker, dentist	C002 NJ F MC Homemaker
RWL	C	3	103	45	Clinical psychologist	C003 NJ F MC Clinical psych
RWL	C	3	104	46	Executive director of law firm	C004 NJ M MC Law firm director
RWL	C	3	105	48	Physician	C005 NJ F MC Physician
RWL	C	3	106	55	Unemployed writer	C006 NJ M MC Writer
AM	C	3	107	58	Accounting clerk	C007 NJ F WC Accting clerk
RWL	C	3	108	45	Television writer	C008 NJ F MC TV writer
RWL	C	3	109	39	Builder	C009 NJ M MC Builder
WCR	C	3	110	42	Police officer	C010 NJ M WC Policeman
AM	C	3	111	25	Clerical worker in creative arts	C011 NJ F WC Clerical
AM	C	3	112	38	Crossing guard	C012 NJ F WC Crossing guard
WCR	C	3	113	38	Gas station owner	C013 NJ M WC Gas station owner
RWL	C	3	114	46	Corporate attorney	C014 NJ F MC Corp. attorney
RC	C	3	115	26	Firefighter/landscaper	C015 NJ M WC Firefighter
AM	D	4	201	40	Unemployed engineer	D001 NJ M MC Unemployed engineer
WCL	D	4	202	49	Recreation assistant, substitute teacher	D002 NJ F WC Rec asst

Appendix B **(*Continued*)**

Sociopolitical Group[a]	Batch	Group Number	Survey/ Interview Number	Age	Occupation	File Name[b]
WCR	D	4	203	48	Carpenter	D003 NJ M WC Carpenter
AM	D	4	204	27	Hairdresser	D004 NJ F WC Beautician
AM	D	4	205	46	Unskilled worker	D005 NJ M WC Unskilled worker
RWL	D	4	206	36	Manager of music business	D006 NJ M MC Music mgr
AM	D	4	207	43	Assistant superintendent, public works	D007 NJ M WC Superint-pub works
WCL	D	4	208	50	Computer technician	D008 NJ M WC Computer tech
WCR	D	4	209	46	Disabled railroad worker	D009 NJ M WC Disabled RR worker
AM	D	4	210	25	Merchandiser in retail sales	D010 NJ F MC Retail sales
WCR	D	4	211	30	Insurance adjuster	D011 NJ M WC Insurance adjuster
WCR	D	4	212	47	Housepainter	D012 NJ M WC House painter
RC	D	4	213	38	Vice president of heavy-industry small firm	D013 NJ M MC VP-heavy industry
AM	D	4	214	41	Chef in food service	D014 NJ M WC Chef-food service
AM	D	4	215	37	PC support technician	D015 NJ M MC PC support tech
AM	D	4	216	44	Broadcast engineer	D016 NJ M WC Broadcast engineer
AM	D	4	217	42	Executive chef	D017 NJ M WC Exec chef
AM	D	4	218	50	Purchasing agent	D018 NJ M MC Purchasing agent
WCR	D	4	219	48	Maintenance worker in large company	D019 NJ M WC Maintenance worker
AM	D	4	220	52	Deli clerk	D020 NJ F WC Deli clerk
WCR	D	4	221	41	Unemployed, retail sales	D021 NJ F WC Unemployed retail sales

AM	D	4	222	38	Insurance administrative assistant	D022 NJ F WC Insurance admin asst
AM	D	4	223	30	Nurse	D023 NJ F MC Nurse
AM	D	4	224	35	Assistant stock trader	D024 NJ M WC Asst stock trader
AM	D	4	225	37	Customer service worker	D025 NJ F WC Customer Service Worker
RWL	D	4	226	41	Director of city planning department	D026 NJ M MC Direct city planning
AM	D	4	227	51	Primary school teacher at private school	D027 NJ M MC Private school teacher
AM	D	4	228	29	Accountant	D028 F MC Accountant
AM	D	4	229	40	Laboratory technician in large company	D029 M WC Lab tech
MCC	D	4	230	30	Small-business owner, family company	D030 M MC Small business owner
AM	D	4	231	28	Senior trade analyst at large company	D031 F WC Senior trade analyst
RWL	D	4	232	47	Special education teacher and coordinator	D032 NJ F MC Special ed teacher
AM	D	4	233	50	Development office assistant for private school	D033 NJ F WC Office asst for school
AM	D	4	234	31	Toxicologist in research lab of large company	D034 NJ M MC Toxicologist
AM	D	4	235	44	Facilities manager at golf course	D035 NJ M WC Facilities mgr
AM	D	4	236	57	Billing clerk in medical office	D036 NJ F MC Billing clerk
AM	D	4	237	26	Billing clerk in large company	D037 NJ F MC Billing clerk
RWL	D	4	238	48	Unemployed salesman	D038 NJ M MC Unemploy salesman
AM	D	4	239	35	Part-time high school drama teacher	D039 NJ F MC HS drama teacher

Appendix B ***(Continued)***

Sociopolitical Group[a]	Batch	Group Number	Survey/ Interview Number	Age	Occupation	File Name[b]
MCC	D	4	240	29	Insurance claims adjuster for large company	D040 NJ M MC Insurance adjuster
RC	D	4	241	44	Billing clerk for hospital	D041 NJ F WC Billing clerk
RWL	D	4	242	38	Social work manager in housing for homeless	D042 NJ F MC Social worker for homeless
AM	D	4	243	33	Special education teacher	D043 NJ F MC Special ed teacher
RNC	D	4	244	41	Management consultant in own firm	D044 NJ F MC Mgmt consultant
RWL	D	4	245	53	Claims administrator in government office	D045 NJ M MC Claims admin
RC	D	4	246	54	Primary school music teacher in inner city	D046 NJ F MC Primary school music teacher
RWL	D	4	247	52	Insurance company executive	D047 NJ M MC Insurance exec
RWL	D	4	248	34	Attorney	D048 NJ M MC Attorney
AM	D	4	249	45	Special education teacher	D049 NJ F MC Special ed teacher
AM	D	4	250	46	Manager of doctor's office	D050 NJ F WC Mgr-doctor's office
RWL	D	4	251	37	Technical sales manager (EE)	D051 NJ M MC Tech sales mgr
WCR	D	4	252	57	Truck driver for flower shop	D052 NJ M WC Truck driver-florist shop
RWL	D	4	253	48	Vice president of human resources in high-tech firm	D053 NJ F MC VP-hr
AM	D	4	254	44	Actuary	D054 NJ M MC Actuary
AM	D	4	255	40	Unemployed (degree in art history)	D055 NJ F MC Unemployed (art degree)

WCR	D	4	256	54	Self-employed real estate owner	D056 NJ F WC Real estate owner
AM	D	4	257	33	Head frontline clerk on Wall Street	D057 NJ M MC Clerk on Wall St
RWL	D	4	258	37	Freelance computer-based training	D058 NJ F MC Computer expert free
RWL	D	4	259	59	Bond trader	D059 NJ M MC Bond trader
AM	D	4	260	40	Part-time football coach	D060 NJ M MC PT football coach
RWL	D	4	261	51	Assistant general manager of major food company	D061 NJ M MC Asst. mgr major food company
AM	D	4	262	47	Patent attorney	D062 NJ M MC Patent attorney
AM	D	4	263	37	Regional manager for party sales	D063 NJ F WC Part sales mgr
RWL	D	4	264	37	Senior brand manager for major company	D064 NJ F MC Sr brand mgr
AM	D	4	265	51	Actress	D065 NJ F MC Actress
AM	D	4	266	30	Financial analyst for real estate company	D066 NJ M MC Financial analyst
AM	D	4	267	42	Real estate appraiser	D067 NJ M MC Realestate appraiser
RWL	D	4	268	36	Homemaker (unemployed meeting planner)	D068 NJ F MC Homemaker
RC	D	4	269	47	Self-employed paper hanger	D069 NJ M WC Paper hanger
RC	D	4	270	46	Staff engineer at major company	D070 NJ M MC Staff engineer
RWL	D	4	271	48	Merchandising manager in food company	D071 NJ M MC Merchandising mgr
RWL	D	4	272	36	Unemployed nursing home administrator	D072 NJ F MC Unemploy nursing home admin

Appendix B ***(Continued)***

Sociopolitical Group[a]	Batch	Group Number	Survey/ Interview Number	Age	Occupation	File Name[b]
MCC	D	4	273	49	General manager of marketing for major foreign firm	D073 NJ M MC Mkting mgr
AM	D	4	274	35	Self-employed landscaper	D074 NJ M WC Landscaper
MCC	D	4	275	55	Unemployed homemaker	D075 NJ F MC Homemaker
AM	D	4	276	36	IT manager at major company	D076 NJ F MC IT mgr
RWL	D	4	277	56	Customer service team leader in major company	D077 NJ F MC Customer service leader
WCR	D	4	278	39	Waitress and house cleaner	D078 NJ F WC Waitress-cleaner
WCL	E	5	301	47	Custodian	E301 OH F WC Custodian
AM	E	5	302	55	Door-to-door advertising manager	E302 OH F WC Door to door advertising manager
WCL	E	5	303	41	Homemaker	E303 OH F WC Homemaker
WCR	E	5	304	52	Retired factory worker in meat plant	E304 OH M WC Retired factory worker in meat plant
AM	E	5	305	29	Owner of small gift shop	E305 OH F WC Owner small gift shop
RWL	E	5	306	47	Engineer	E306 OH M MC Engineer
AM	E	5	307	53	Factory worker, tool checker	E307 OH M WC Factory worker, tool checker
RWL	E	5	308	54	Retired attorney	E308 OH M MC Retired attorney
RC	E	5	309	38	Homemaker	E309 OH F WC Homemaker
WCR	E	5	310	53	Salesman	E310 OH M WC Salesman
RC	E	5	311	43	Manager of insurance office	E311 OH M MC Manager insurance office
WCR	E	5	312	38	Custodian	E312 OH F WC Custodian

RC	E	5	313	39	Lawn and garden equipment sales and service	E313 OH M WC Lawn and garden equipment sales and service
RC	E	5	314	61	Pharmaceutical sales manager	E314 OH M MC Pharmaceutical sales manager
AM	E	5	315	50	Supervisor for cleaning business	E315 OH M MC Supervisor cleaning business
AM	E	5	316	29	Teacher	E316 OH F MC Teacher
WCR	E	5	317	42	Waitress at fast-food restaurant	E317 OH F WC Waitress at fast food restaurant
WCR	E	5	318	34	Homemaker	E318 OH F WC Homemaker
RWL	E	5	319	49	Registered nurse	E319 OH F MC Nurse, RN
AM	E	5	320	33	Bookkeeper in home business	E320 OH F WC Bookkeeper in home business
WCR	E	5	321	33	Self-employed trucking firm owner	E321 OH M WC Self employed trucking firm owner
RWL	E	5	322	52	Primary school music teacher	E322 OH F MC Primary school music teacher
AM	E	5	323	44	Educator in rehabilitation	E323 OH F MC Educator in rehabilitation
AM	E	5	324	45	Self-employed programmer	E324 OH M WC Self employed programmer
AM	E	5	325	37	Licensed practical nurse	E325 OH F WC LPN
RC	E	5	326	48	Letter carrier	E326 OH M WC Letter carrier
MCC	E	5	327	34	Part-time college instructor, doctoral student	E327 OH F MC Part-time college instructor, doctoral student
RC	E	5	328	37	Pharmaceutical sales manager	E328 OH M MC Pharmaceutical sales manager
RNC	E	5	329	35	Radiology technician	E329 OH F WC Radiology technician
RNC	E	5	330	25	Part-time preschool supervisor	E330 OH F MC Part-time preschool supervisor

Appendix B ***(Continued)***

Sociopolitical Group[a]	Batch	Group Number	Survey/ Interview Number	Age	Occupation	File Name[b]
RWL	E	5	331	43	Project manager in government laboratory	E331 OH M MC Project manager government laboratory
RWL	E	5	332	45	Training manager for large company	E332 OH M MC Training manager for large company
AM	E	5	333	39	Preschool teacher	E333 OH F WC Preschool teacher
AM	E	5	334	55	Unemployed real estate agent	E334 OH F WC Unemployed real estate agent
AM	E	5	335	50	Insurance office manager	E335 OH F WC Insurance office manager
MCC	E	5	336	44	Registered nurse	E336 OH F MC Nurse, RN
AM	E	5	337	43	Clinical therapist, mental health	E337 OH F MC Clinical therapist, mental health
MCC	E	5	338	48	Worldwide business manager for new products	E338 OH M MC Worldwide business manager for new products
WCR	E	5	339	31	Self-employed truck driver	E339 OH M WC Self employed truck driver
WCR	E	5	340	37	Warehouse sales	E340 OH F WC Warehouse sales
AM	E	5	341	47	Government accountant	E341 OH F MC Government accountant
AM	E	5	342	31	Student in optician program	E342 OH M WC Student in optician program
AM	E	5	343	34	Auto mechanic	E343 OH M WC Auto mechanic
AM	E	5	344	52	Disabled industrial arts teacher	E344 OH M MC Disabled industrial arts teacher
AM	E	5	345	50	Telephone company billing clerk	E345 OH F WC Telephone company billing clerk

RWL	E	5	346	31	High school business teacher	E346 OH F MC High school business teacher
AM	E	5	347	59	Beautician	E347 OH F WC Beautician
RC	E	5	348	40	Unemployed customer service representative	E348 OH M MC Unemployed customer service representative
AM	E	5	349	52	Small-business loan officer	E349 OH M MC Small business loan officer
WCR	E	5	350	40	Owner of small industrial equipment company	E350 OH M WC Owner small industrial equipment company
WCR	E	5	351	52	Mortgage loan originator	E351 OH F WC Mortgage loan originator
AM	E	5	352	50	Order entry in large company	E352 OH M WC Order entry in large company
RWL	E	5	353	54	Homemaker (trophy wife)	E353 OH F MC Homemaker (trophy wife)
WCR	E	5	354	51	Self-employed landscape business	E354 OH M WC Self-employed landscape business
RC	E	5	355	48	Nurse BSN	E355 OH F MC Nurse BSN
AM	E	5	356	33	Attorney	E356 OH M MC Attorney
AM	E	5	357	43	Dentist	E357 OH M MC Dentist
AM	E	5	358	50	Unemployed cost accountant	E358 OH M WC Unemployed cost accountant
WCL	E	5	359	38	Front-desk clerk at medical center	E359 OH F WC Front desk clerk at medical center
WCR	E	5	360	45	Third-party hearing representative for workman's compensation	E360 OH M WC 3rd party hearing rep for workmen's comp
RC	E	5	361	31	Graphic designer	E361 OH M WC Graphic designer
AM	E	5	362	46	Unemployed/disabled attorney	E362 OH F MC Unemployed/disabled attorney
AM	E	5	363	33	Remodeling in small firm	E363 OH M WC Remodeling in small firm

Appendix B **(*Continued*)**

Sociopolitical Group[a]	Batch	Group Number	Survey/ Interview Number	Age	Occupation	File Name[b]
MCC	E	5	364	53	Paralegal	E364 OH F MC Paralegal
AM	E	5	365	45	Owner of small trucking company	E365 OH M WC Owner small trucking company
WCL	E	5	366	41	Self-employed construction worker	E366 OH F WC Self employed construction worker
RC	E	5	367	35	Graphic designer	E367 OH M WC Graphics designer
WCL	E	5	368	52	Building contractor	E368 OH M WC Building contractor
RC	F	6	401	53	Teacher	F001 TN F MC Teacher
RC	F	6	402	25	Medical transcription	F002 TN F MC Medical transcription
RC	F	6	403	56	Account clerk	F003 TN F WC Account clerk
AM	F	6	404	41	Hairstylist	F004 TN F WC Hairstylist
RC	F	6	405	40	Manager	F005 TN M MC Manager
RNC	F	6	407	41	Teacher	F007 TN F MC Teacher
RC	F	6	408	53	School headmaster	F008 TN M MC School headmaster
RWL	F	6	409	54	Statistical analyst supervisor	F009 TN M MC Stat analyst supervisor
RNC	F	6	410	33	Retail sales	F010 TN F WC Retail sales
RC	F	6	411	45	Factory worker	F011 TN M WC Factory worker
RNC	F	6	412	30	Minister	F012 TN F MC Minister
RNC	F	6	413	50	Government service	F013 TN F MC Govt service
AM	F	6	414	45	Unemployed	F014 TN M WC Unemployed
RNC	F	6	415	41	Electronics technician	F015 TN M WC Electronic tech
RC	F	6	416	54	Homemaker	F016 TN F MC Homemaker
AM	F	6	418	45	Postal worker	F018 TN M WC Postal worker

AM	F	6	419	45	Office assistant	F019 TN F WC Office asst
AM	F	6	420	55	Retired	F020 TN F WC Retired
RWL	F	6	421	52	Christian denomination professional	F021 TN F MC Religious profession
RNC	F	6	422	54	Travel consultant	F022 TN F WC Travel rep
AM	F	6	423	37	Homemaker	F023 TN F MC Homemaker
RC	F	6	424	38	Purchasing manager	F024 TN M MC Purchasing mgr
AM	F	6	425	51	Commercial art instructor	F025 TN M MC Art instructor
WCR	F	6	426	41	Route sales and service	F026 TN F WC Route sales
WCR	F	6	427	31	Travel agent	F027 TN F WC Travel agent
RNC	G	7	501	56	Deputy sheriff	G501 TN M MC Deputy sheriff
RC	G	7	502	55	Editorial assistant	G502 TN F WC Editorial assistant
RC	G	7	503	49	Administration	G503 TN M MC Administration
WCL	G	7	504	38	Clerical	G504 TN F WC Clerical
MCC	G	7	505	42	Sales	G505 TN M MC Sales
AM	G	7	506	47	Librarian	G506 TN F MC Librarian
RNC	G	7	507	49	Electronic publishing coordinator	G507 TN M WC Electronic publishing coordinator
WCR	G	7	508	44	Accounting	G508 TN F WC Accounting
RC	G	7	509	53	Music teacher	G509 TN F MC Music teacher
AM	G	7	510	27	Self-employed	G510 TN F MC Self employed
AM	G	7	511	39	Bookkeeper	G511 TN F MC Bookkeeper
WCL	G	7	512	40	Small-business owner	G512 TN M WC Small business owner
WCL	G	7	513	26	Web designer	G513 TN M WC Web designer
RWL	G	7	514	56	School system administrator	G514 TN M MC School system administrator
AM	G	7	515	42	Chef	G515 TN M WC Chef
RWL	G	7	516	40	Record producer musician	G516 TN M MC Record producer musician
AM	G	7	517	31	Musician	G517 TN M MC Musician
RC	G	7	518	48	Construction manager	G518 TN M MC Construction manager

Appendix B ***(Continued)***

Sociopolitical Group[a]	Batch	Group Number	Survey/ Interview Number	Age	Occupation	File Name[b]
WCL	G	7	519	43	Commercial artist	G519 TN M WC Commercial artist
WCR	G	7	520	27	Graphic designer	G520 TN M WC Graphic designer
RWL	G	7	521	53	Health care executive	G521 TN F MC Healthcare executive
AM	G	7	522	36	Vending machine route man	G522 TN M WC Vending machine route man
WCL	G	7	523	33	Massage therapist	G523 TN F WC Massage therapist
WCR	G	7	524	36	Co-owner of small company	G524 TN M WC Co-owner of small company
RC	G	7	525	46	Manager at industrial firm	G525 TN M MC Manager industrial firm
RC	G	7	526	43	Telecommunications executive	G526 TN M MC Telecommunications executive
RC	G	7	527	28	Essential materials specialist	G527 TN F MC Essential materials specialist
RC	G	7	528	25	Office manager	G528 TN F MC Office manager
RC	G	7	529	23	Trim carpenter	G529 TN M WC Trim carpenter
RWL	G	7	530	25	Musician	G530 TN M MC Musician
RC	G	7	531	37	Accounting	G531 TN F WC Accounting
AM	G	7	532	31	Self-employed entertainer	G532 TN M WC Self employed entertainer
WCL	G	7	533	40	Electronics engineer	G533 TN M WC Electronics engineer
RC	G	7	534	48	Sales	G534 TN M MC Sales
RC	G	7	535	36	Aircraft assembler	G535 TN M WC Aircraft assembler
AM	G	7	536	33	Self-employed photographer	G536 TN F WC Self employed photography
RC	G	7	537	44	Homemaker	G537 TN F WC Homemaker

Source: Author's compilation.
[a]Sociopolitical Groups: AM = Apolitical Majority; MCC = Middle-Class Conservative; RC = Religious Conservative; RNC = Religious Nonconservative; RWL = Rich White Liberal; WCL = Working-Class Liberal; WCR = Working-Class "Racist."
[b]File Names: OH = Ohio; NJ = New Jersey; TN = Tennessee; M = Male; F = Female; MC = Middle-Class; WC = Working-Class.

Notes

Acknowledgments

1. See Lamont (1992, 2000) and Lamont and Fournier (1992). Lamont's methodology involves taking random samples of selected zip codes, sending letters, and then following up with phone calls to invite those who fit relevant criteria to be interviewed for the study. In this study, zip codes in middle-class areas and in working-class areas were chosen in New Jersey, Ohio, and Tennessee. About one-third of those who were reached by phone and eligible to participate agreed to be interviewed.

Prologue

1. Both Ogbu (1978) and Fordham (1996) have been widely cited, and the claims about oppositional culture among black youth have been largely taken as given. After having had children of my own in this same age group and having the opportunity to observe them and many of their friends, I have a new appreciation for the meaning of oppositional culture, and I do not think that it is exclusive to black youth; see, for example, Milner (2004). Its consequences, however, affect blacks far more than whites because of whites' access to social and cultural capital.

Chapter 1

1. Myrdal (1944, 997, 1018–19, 20, 21, 1003).
2. Myrdal's book has often been subject to caricature about his central argument regarding the American dilemma, which he identified as the contradiction between the ideal in the American creed of egalitarianism and the existence of racial inequality. I believe that this characterization of Myrdal is unfair. His discussion of this argument is sophisticated, grounded in substantive analysis, and he recognizes the distance between the claims of the American creed and practice in the United States. He believed, however, that the tension between the ideal and the reality presented the opportunity for change, especially in the context of World War II and its aftermath.
3. See the summary of this literature in Sidanius and Pratto (1999) and Sidanius, Pratto, and Bobo (1996). David Sears's work on symbolic racism is rep-

resentative of the view that whites are really racists (Sears 1988a), but in a way that differs from what has been called "old-fashioned racism"; see also Sniderman and Carmines (1997), Sniderman and Piazza (1993), Bobo, Kluegel, and Smith (1997), Bonilla-Silva (2003), Dovidio and Gaertner (1986), Gaertner and Dovidio (1986), and Essed (1991). The work of both Sidanius and Bobo is representative of the perspective that white attitudes on policy issues reflect their efforts to maintain group dominance (Blauner 1972). The work of Sniderman and his colleagues represents the position that white attitudes reflect American values and are not necessarily indicators of racism (Banaji and Prentice 1994).

4. Two other forms of racism are related but not of the same nature as these concepts. "Institutional racism" is a label given to rules or procedures that are built into institutional practices or social relationships and may be neutral on their face but have the effect of reinforcing white advantage and black disadvantage (see, for example, Pratto et al. 1994; Sidanius and Pratto 1999). "Implicit racism" is a label given to nonconscious associations that link evaluative meaning to categorizations of different types of people. For example, one might associate black with bad and white with good. To overcome such associations requires active mindfulness and often a process of relearning (see Greenwald and Krieger 2006).
5. I borrowed the title of this section from Edsall and Edsall (1992), a book that details the ways in which support for civil rights undermined the Democratic coalition and contributed to the rise of a Republican majority.
6. Although I selected the majority of the respondents randomly, I also conducted thirty-one preliminary interviews (fifteen in New Jersey and sixteen in Ohio) to use them to test the study materials. Because these interviews were themselves exceedingly rich and did not differ significantly from the randomly selected interviews, I included them in the study. In addition, several interviewees strongly suggested that I talk with a friend of theirs. I scheduled an interview if that person seemed to have characteristics that were underrepresented in the random sample; such referrals led to seven additional interviews in Ohio. In Tennessee it was initially difficult to get respondents to agree to be interviewed, perhaps because they were not familiar with Rutgers University; I was also told by at least one respondent that my Italian name clearly marked me as someone not from the area. Because the time in which I could be in Tennessee was limited, I endeavored to contact people in several churches (one Baptist and one Methodist). I obtained about 40 percent of the Tennessee interviews from these sources. There were no major differences between the interviewees I contacted through these churches and those who emerged from the random sample, with the possible exception that more of the church-based interviewees were born and raised in Tennessee, whereas more of the randomly selected interviewees had moved to Tennessee from other parts of the country. So, in general, I feel that the sample was enhanced by the inclusion of those interviewees who came from nonrandom sources, especially because they were not part of my own personal social networks and I would most likely not have had contact with them otherwise.
7. For the reasons discussed in the prologue, I did not try to interview non-

whites or to expand the scope of the study. My interest in the contrast with Myrdal contributed to the emphasis in my analysis on the black-white divide, but I believe that the issues I raise here have broader implications for understanding inequality.

8. For example, one interviewee was six credits short of finishing her bachelor's degree, she had married an attorney, and both of them had inherited substantial amounts of money, so they lived in one of the most exclusive areas of the city. This interviewee obviously had a lot of financial resources, and it did not seem reasonable to call her working-class just because she had not finished her four-year degree. There were only a few of these types of cases; in each case, I took into account the education of the spouse, the level of income, and the characteristics of the neighborhood in which the respondent lived in deciding on a class categorization. The majority of interviews took place in the respondent's home, but a few respondents felt more comfortable meeting at a university office or restaurant, and so it was not possible to see the kind of neighborhood or house where these respondents lived. Interestingly, there were more interviewees in Tennessee who wanted to be interviewed at the university than was the case in either New Jersey or Ohio.
9. Sears, Henry, and Kosterman (2000) divided egalitarianism into two components, which they labeled "equal chance" (more purely egalitarian) and "gone too far" (explicitly inegalitarian).
10. The term "racial resentment" comes from Kinder and Sanders (1996). "Racial resentment" is another name given to what others have called "symbolic racism" (for example, McConahay and Hough 1976; Sears 1988a).
11. I used Atlas.ti for this study.
12. See appendix B for a listing of all interviewees by case number. Throughout the book I identify each interviewee by a code number assigned when each was interviewed and by state, gender, and class, abbreviated as follows: NJ = New Jersey, OH = Ohio, TN = Tennessee, M = male, F = female, MC = middle class, and WC = working class.
13. CNN.com, "Election Center 2008." Available at: http://www.cnn.com/ELECTION/2008/results/polls/#USP00p1 (accessed September 25, 2012). See "Vote by Ideology."

Chapter 2

1. Since this company was one of the "best" employers in the city, I came across a number of interviewees in Ohio who told a similar story of having had to repeatedly apply for a job at this company before succeeding in getting a job. One interviewee proudly reported that he had gotten a job at the company after "only" three months of persistent effort to show the company that he really wanted a job there. Most of the others who reported that they had applied to the company but had not been offered a job did not describe going back multiple times to demonstrate their interest.
2. See Mark Granovetter's (1995) appendix to the second edition of his book for a summary of the job search literature. Waldinger (1997) also discusses the potential tensions between employers and employees when employees recommend their friends for jobs. See also Bearman (2005).

3. Of course, not all middle-class people who lose their jobs are able to find jobs of comparable quality in terms of salary and benefits. In her study of downward mobility among members of the middle class, Katherine Newman (1988) found that a significant proportion had to change their lifestyle after losing their job. My point, however, is that those in this situation are still better positioned to find another job with a salary that will enable them to live a "decent" life compared to people like my working-class interviewees, who would have ended up in the job market without a college education and might have had a harder time finding a job that was protected from the market.
4. Of course, because I defined the groups and placed interviewees in various categories based on the political views they expressed, my analyses are intended not so much to test the differences between groups as to display them in a way showing that the qualitative data are consistent with the quantitative data. Further, I want to show the specific relationship between the political views expressed on various topics and the views expressed about racial issues.
5. As already noted, although African Americans may make the same effort to pass along opportunities to their family members and friends, especially in the enclaves in which they hold senior positions, the overall inequality between blacks and whites means that fewer valuable social resources are available within the black community than are available to whites. Further, the relative structural vulnerability of the economic positions of African Americans makes them both less effective in hoarding opportunities for others like themselves and often more reluctant to help their friends for fear that doing so might have an adverse effect on their own jobs. See Falcon and Melendez (2001), Granovetter (1995), Kirschenman and Neckerman (1991b), Korenman and Turner (1996), Newman (1999), Parks-Yancy (2010), Smith (2007), and Waldinger (1996).
6. My reference is primarily to the U.S. context. There are, of course, different solutions to market competition in other countries. In Europe, for example, citizenship rights may include access to education, health care, and income support at a minimal level, but even in Europe there are variations in the treatment of immigrants and in eligibility to claim citizenship rights.
7. Thomas Friedman (2005) argues that the opening up of the labor markets in China, India, and the former Soviet Union has had the consequence of doubling the size of the relevant labor force that can compete for the jobs of U.S. workers.

Chapter 3

1. Unfortunately, the issue of job injuries, often leading to disability, was raised several times among the working-class interviewees. Many of the interviewees were pushing the limits of their health and safety by going without sleep in order to work the shifts required by their jobs. Also, a number of the interviewees, like the New Jersey painter described in chapter 2, worked around dangerous chemicals or machinery and often without safety equipment. Even when equipment was provided by the company, workers would some-

times avoid using it because it was inconvenient or uncomfortable, or perhaps because it sometimes reduced the productivity on which their wages were based. Ironically, some of the working-class interviewees who were injured or otherwise disabled were able to avail themselves of financial support from state agencies for vocational rehabilitation and in this way pay for at least two years of college and an associate's degree, which they would not have been able to afford otherwise.

2. Some labor market studies find that workers can incur costs because of job changes, but the findings here show that networks expand with age and that job changes often involve help from family or friends. Granovetter (1995, 18) finds the same thing: in his study, fewer than half of younger workers found jobs through personal contacts, whereas almost two-thirds of the older workers in his sample did.
3. These averages are calculated on the first ten jobs, because the numbers of cases in the eleventh and subsequent jobs are uneven and contribute to distortions in the calculation of the averages.
4. Melvin Oliver and Thomas Shapiro (1995) found that whites have accumulated about ten times as much wealth as blacks. The economic downturn in the late 2000s led to an even greater disparity (see also Shapiro 2004).
5. See Fiske and Taylor (1991). The chapters on attribution theory are especially relevant to these dynamics.
6. Granovetter (1995, 141–46) argues that job search outcomes have to be seen in the context of the neighborhoods or social groups of which people are a part and not in terms of individual characteristics. He further notes that about one-third of those who end up with jobs did not seek them out.
7. "Jobs and freedom" was the theme of the 1963 March on Washington, which was sponsored by a coalition of civil rights groups. This event marked a key turning point in the growing support for the civil rights movement and for civil rights legislation.
8. That the research tends to underestimate the number of personal connections used in getting jobs is a key point made by Granovetter (1995), who claims, among other things, that about one-third of people who get jobs did not have to search for them. See also Mouw (2003) and Waldinger (1997).

Chapter 4

1. In my discussion here, I identify only rich white liberals and working-class liberals as having liberal politics. Although the religious nonconservatives often had views that were similar to those of the more liberal groups, most of them identified their politics as moderate. Only one of the religious nonconservatives indicated being liberal, whereas the majority of the rich white liberals (60 percent) and the working-class liberals (64 percent) identified their political orientation as liberal.
2. The individualism scale is measured with different types of questions than the composite measure of individualist explanations for inequality. The first uses items from the American National Election Studies, such as, "If people work hard, they almost always get what they want." The individualist explanations for inequality used in the Kluegel and Smith (1986) study include

such items as that the rich are rich because of "personal drive and willingness to take risks," that the poor are poor because of "lack of thrift and proper money-management skills." See the appendix for the list of items.

3. For example, such courses are available at Northwestern University, the University of Michigan, and Rutgers University.

Chapter 5

1. As I do throughout the book, in this chapter I focus on the white-black divide rather than attempt to deal with dynamics across all racial-ethnic groups. Limiting the discussion to the effects of race on politics rather than consider group differences more broadly was both a practical and a theoretical decision. Trying to include all aspects of U.S. racial-ethnic history would be unwieldy for my purposes here, but even more importantly, I argue that the white-black divide is the one that has been most problematic in shaping post–civil rights politics. Although other groups mobilized as a result of the black civil rights movement, blacks still hold an especially salient position in U.S. politics and one that is distinct from that of other minority groups.
2. Paul Frymer and John David Skrentny (1998) argue, however, that through the first Nixon administration, the Republican Party still considered trying to court black votes, but especially after the Wallace campaigns, it turned more toward efforts to capture white, working-class Democrats.
3. Even in the 2008 election, Obama was able to gain only 43 percent of the white vote, which represented an increase of the white vote compared to Democratic candidates in recent previous elections, but clearly not the landslide in white votes that some commentators imagined and claimed. Obama received only 39 percent of the white vote in the 2012 election.
4. The two major parties were also challenged by Henry Wallace of the Progressive Party.
5. A small portion of the popular vote went to a number of candidates, especially in the South. Kennedy was also denied fifteen electoral votes when electors in Alabama, Mississippi, and Oklahoma cast ballots for Harry Byrd of Virginia as president and for Strom Thurmond as vice president (with one electoral vote for vice president going to Barry Goldwater).
6. President John F. Kennedy, "Radio and Television Report to the American People on Civil Rights, June 11, 1963," in "Selected Speeches of John F. Kennedy." Available at: http://www.jfklibrary.org/Research/Ready-Reference/JFK-Speeches/Radio-and-Television-Report-to-the-American-People-on-Civil-Rights-June-11-1963.aspx (accessed November 21, 2012).
7. The Republican primary was hotly contested between conservatives and moderates. Gov. Nelson Rockefeller of New York had led the moderate wing of the party, but he ultimately lost the nomination to Barry Goldwater. Many moderate Republicans then gave limited support to Goldwater in the general election.
8. The "Southern strategy" is the term given to the efforts of the Republican Party to make up for its minority status by trying to capture the electoral votes of Southern states with appeals, usually in coded language, to white Southerners who opposed the implementation of civil rights legislation, es-

pecially federal enforcement of school desegregation. Although often attributed to Kevin Phillips in his 1969 book *The Emerging Republican Majority,* it was already part of the campaign strategy taken in 1964 by Barry Goldwater, who was advised by Strom Thurmond about how to win the South. Indeed, Thurmond himself used a type of Southern strategy in his own bid for the presidency in 1948 when he attempted to throw the election into the House of Representatives and deny Harry Truman the White House. Thurmond won five states of the Deep South, and Goldwater similarly won only five Southern states, plus his home state of Arizona. All Republican presidential candidates since have adopted some form of appeal to the South (Carmines and Stimson 1989).

One of Strom Thurmond's staff members, Harry Dent, is credited with developing the Southern strategy. Dent later became an adviser to President Nixon. Later in his life, Harry Dent expressed regret for his participation in the anti–civil rights campaign.

9. The protests reached a climax in 1970 when National Guard members shot and killed four student protesters at Kent State University in Ohio and two at Jackson State College in Mississippi.
10. The organizations created during this period have been impressive not only for their impact but also for their diversity, in that they have successfully influenced public policy, the media, education, law, and civil rights, as well as the political process and the realignment of the political parties. As a whole, the creation of these various organizations clearly had an impact on redirecting the political landscape in the post–civil rights period, but whether they constitute a conspiracy or an exception to normal politics is in dispute. Jenkins and Shumate (1985) have argued that, contrary to the assumption that a new wealthy elite entered the political arena in an unprecedented manner, it was the national corporate elite who funded the New Right just as they had previously funded the "Old Right." Further, Chip Berlet and Matthew Lyons (2000) and Sara Diamond (1995) argue that wealthy individuals and corporations have funded right-wing movements throughout American history, and that any acceleration of those efforts in the last several decades may have more to do with their success in mobilizing popular support than with a secret conspiracy. Indeed, what is new is the response to these groups and their ability to successfully take over government power, not so much their efforts at doing so. See People for the American Way Foundation, "Buying a Movement: Right-Wing Foundations and American Politics" (n.d.), available at: http://www.pfaw.org/media-center/publications/buying-movement; People for the American Way Foundation, "The Federalist Society: From Obscurity to Power" (n.d.), available at: http://www.pfaw.org/media-center/publications/the-federalist-society-from-obscurity-to-power (accessed November 21, 2012); and Viguerie (1979).
11. Adam Bernstein, "Evangelist Billy James Hargis Dies: Spread Anti-Communist Message," *Washington Post,* November 30, 2004.
12. Hargis was also one of the prominent televangelists accused of sexual misconduct and forced from office.
13. The deal arranged by Nixon, according to Dan Carter (1996), was part of a "dirty trick" in that Nixon, assuming that the votes Wallace was taking were

coming from potential Republican voters, had threatened to bring indictments for various charges of corruption against members of Wallace's family; in exchange for dropping the investigations, Wallace agreed not to run again as a third-party candidate.

14. Howard Phillips ran for president as the nominee of the U.S. Taxpayers Party in 1992 and 1996 and of the Constitution Party in 2000. Both of these parties are successors to or offshoots of the American Independent Party.
15. Gordon MacInnes (1996), for example, argues that the Democratic Party has been ill advised to focus on a constituency that is 10 percent of the population at the risk of losing support from the other 90 percent.
16. Teixeira and Rogers (2000) similarly argue that racism is not the reason why the white working class has left the Democratic Party.
17. There are several differences between the analyses of Teixeira and Rogers (2000) and Bartels (2006) that might account for these different claims. First, Bartels uses a definition of the South that conforms to the U.S. Census Bureau's regional classification: the eleven former Confederate states plus Delaware, Kentucky, Maryland, Oklahoma, West Virginia, and the District of Columbia. Teixeira and Rogers do not mention how they distinguish between the South and the non-South in their analyses. Second, Bartels uses the elections from 1952 through 2004 and apparently compares end points, whereas Teixeira and Rogers examine election "eras" by combining 1960 and 1964 (Kennedy-Johnson), 1968 and 1972 (Nixon), 1980 and 1984 (Reagan), and 1992 and 1996 (Clinton). Teixeira and Rogers also weight their sample to equalize case counts within eras. Third, the Teixeira and Rogers analyses were done earlier than Bartels's, so differences may reflect some fluctuations in the vote across elections (or eras). Finally, Teixeria and Rogers do not provide any details to their claim (which is made only in a parenthetical statement), whereas Bartels provides detailed tables on a series of measures, including income, education, and policy attitudes.
18. There are important differences between religious groups defined as fundamentalists and those defined as evangelicals, although these terms have tended to be conflated in the popular media. In fact, historically there was active conflict between these groups in the United States. Fundamentalists tended to be theologically more conservative, with an emphasis on the literal interpretation of the Bible and also separation from the "world." They were called "fundamentalists" because of the effort of such groups in the early part of the twentieth century to call Christians back to the "fundamentals" of the faith. Evangelicals share many of the same beliefs, but they distinguish themselves from fundamentalists in having a more outward orientation toward nonbelievers as a means to evangelize or proselytize for the faith. See, for example, Pew Research Center for the People and the Press (1996) and Massey (2005).
19. Reynolds was part of the "vast right-wing conspiracy" of which Hillary Clinton spoke. He was instrumental in the development of the Federalist Society and served on its board. He was evidently so hostile to civil rights while serving as assistant attorney general for civil rights that he was not confirmed when nominated to the position of assistant attorney general, even though Republicans controlled the Senate (Carter 1996, 57).

20. In late 2007, a series of editorials in the *New York Times* presented the case both for and against Reagan's campaign having been motivated to mobilize racist white Southerners as part of a Southern strategy to create a winning coalition for a new conservative Republican Party. The occasion for the series of editorials may very likely have been the publication of Paul Krugman's book *The Conscience of a Liberal* (2007)—written as a challenge to Goldwater's book *The Conscience of a Conservative* (1960), which helped launch his 1964 presidential campaign. The case for Reagan having opened his campaign with the speech near Philadelphia, Mississippi, to solicit support from former Wallace voters was made by Krugman (November 19, 2007) and by Bob Herbert (November 12, 2007). The argument that this is a misinterpretation of Reagan's motivations was made by David Brooks (November 9, 2007) and Lou Cannon (November 18, 2007).
21. In their analyses, Valentino and Sears (2005) use a measure of symbolic racism that does not include specific policy preferences (Guth et al. 2001).
22. Members included Evan Bayh, John Breaux, Russ Carnahan, John Edwards, Rahm Emanuel, Dianne Feinstein, Dick Gephardt, Al Gore, Bob Graham, John Kerry, Mary Landrieu, Joseph Lieberman, Bill Nelson, Sam Nunn, Chuck Robb, and, perhaps most notedly, Bill and Hillary Clinton.
23. The DLC argued in what was called the "Hyde Park Declaration" for social policies (based on its own list) grounded in free enterprise, public activism, the role of government to equip workers for the new economy, expanding trade and investment, global rules and institutions, fiscal discipline, a progressive tax system, expanded opportunity, education as the great equalizer, access to health insurance, crime prevention and punishment of criminals, both responsibilities and rewards for work, strong families, the creation of wealth as a solution to poverty, flexible public institutions, choice and competition within government, enhancing civil entrepreneurs, environmental protection, progressive internationalism, a technologically superior defense, common civic ideals, and ultimately a balance between rights and responsibilities. In addition, the DLC argued that government must combat discrimination and protect the legality of abortion at the same time that it encourages policies that would make abortion less necessary (Democratic Leadership Council 2000).
24. Although there are still references to the Progressive Policy Institute (PPI) on the web, the links to its website are no longer active. The agenda for a "third way" in politics seems to have been taken up instead by the Third Way Foundation, which like PPI, has received funding from a number of corporate groups, including the conservative Bradley Foundation, whose support has raised red flags for liberal Democrats about the purpose of the DLC, PPI, and now the Third Way Foundation as well.
25. These issues also contributed to the volatile reaction of Obama supporters to Hillary Clinton's candidacy for the Democratic nomination in 2008.
26. During the 2008 election, the left-wing supporters of Barack Obama continually dismissed the achievements of the Clinton presidency.
27. Of course, by the time of the 2004 primary, the Iraq War had already become a heated issue: party activists on the left were strongly opposed to the war,

while Democratic elected officials and staff represented by the DLC were more moderate in their views of the war.

28. Until the 2008 election, however, these conflicts within the Democratic Party were not explicit or salient in party rhetoric, because being open about these controversies would have highlighted the seemingly incompatible interests across these three groups. Instead, the controversies have often been fought on issues regarding party structure and campaign strategy—such as represented in the conflict between Howard Dean and Rahm Emanuel regarding whether to campaign in the South or to concentrate campaign efforts on the areas where Democrats had more of a chance to win elections.
29. By the time of the 2006 election, even the Clintons were no longer willing to align themselves with the DLC. In the 2008 election, the DLC as a formal organization did not play a major role, but the issues that it was trying to address in terms of divisions within the Democratic Party have continued to be problematic in the party's ability to hold together a coalition that can win elections in both the primaries and the general election.
30. Alexander Keyssar, "The Strange Career of Voter Suppression, " *New York Times,* February 12, 2012.
31. Alexander Keyssar, "The Strange Career of Voter Suppression, " *New York Times,* February 12, 2012.

Chapter 6

1. The relationship of income and education to voting patterns has become somewhat more ambiguous in recent years as increasing numbers of highly educated professionals have moved to the Democratic Party. There is some evidence that this shift is a negative reaction to the growing identification of the Republican Party with religious conservatives and to its public anti-intellectual persona. At the same time, the white working class has become less tied to the Democratic Party, thus also blurring the lines between income and party identification (Bartels 2008a; Bolce and De Maio 1999a; Teixeira and Halpin 2011).
2. The rise of neoliberalism and the celebration of the market have contributed to the erosion of institutional protections from the market. Few workers can really count on removing themselves from market competition, but to the extent that whites still maintain a structural advantage by holding a much greater proportion of the best jobs and the positions in which decisions are made about hiring, promotions, and job rewards, they still have the opportunity to hoard opportunities and help each other to "get ahead."

Chapter 8

1. In response to a threatened March on Washington headed by A. Philip Randolph, President Franklin Roosevelt issued executive order 8802 in 1941 to outlaw racial discrimination in the federal government and war industries. In 1948 President Harry Truman moved to desegregate the military through executive order 9981. In 1953 President Dwight Eisenhower issued executive order 10479 outlawing discrimination by government contractors and then,

in 1955, executive order 10590 to outlaw racial discrimination in the federal civil service. The Kennedy and Johnson executive orders, which specifically called for affirmative action, then followed.

2. This history is readily available from many sources, including: Bergmann (1996); Holzer and Neumark (2000a, 2000b); Kravitz et al. (1997); Reskin (1998); Skrentny (1996, 2001); Stainback and Tomaskovic-Devey (2012); Stephanopoulos and Edley (1995).
3. Several interviewees argued that the "real" problem of inequality is that blacks need better-quality education, but did not combine this suggestion with support for the desegregation of schools and housing or with acknowledgment that segregation in these spheres might be one reason why blacks come to the labor market less well prepared. Similarly, some interviewees preferred lawsuits and court protection as ways to remedy inequality over changing employer policies or opening up access to jobs that are passed from one white person to another. Even when acknowledging both the costs and the small chance of winning associated with lawsuits, the interviewees still thought that there "must be another way" besides affirmative action and mandates to employers regarding hiring processes.
4. Immigrants do not have rights to governmental support, whereas refugees or asylum seekers, who are deemed to be displaced because of fear of persecution or violence, are given temporary shelter and services, in conjunction with international law. The primary goal of refugee policy is to return the individuals to their home countries, but when that is not possible because of conflict or disruptions in the home country, the refugees can apply to stay in the country that has accepted them. Not all of those claiming persecution or fear of violence are accepted into refugee status. Their claims must be adjudicated, and many who seek such status are denied. Those fleeing their home countries for economic reasons to seek employment or a better life are not considered refugees under the law. Refugee policy has become more challenged since 9/11, especially with the growing number of conflicts around the world that have displaced people from their home countries (Kerwin 2011).

Chapter 9

1. Luis Falcon and Edwin Melendez (2001, 366–68) found, in contrast, that African Americans and Latinos tend to find worse jobs when they use social networks because segregation often limits their connections to people who work in organizations with larger percentages of minority workers, at lower pay, and in worse jobs.

References

Abramowitz, Alan I. 1994. "Issue Evolution Reconsidered: Racial Attitudes and Partisanship in the U.S. Electorate." *American Journal of Political Science* 38(1): 1–24.

———. 1995. "It's Abortion, Stupid: Policy Voting in the 1992 Presidential Election." *Journal of Politics* 57(1): 176–86.

Abramowitz, Alan I., and K. L. Saunders. 1998. "Ideological Realignment in the U.S. Electorate." *Journal of Politics* 60(3): 634–52.

Achen, Chrisopher H., and Larry M. Bartels. 2004. "Musical Chairs: Pocketbook Voting and the Limits of Democratic Accountability." Presented to the annual meeting of the American Political Science Association. Chicago, September 1–5.

Alba, Richard, and Victor Nee. 2003. *Remaking the American Mainstream: Assimilation and Contemporary Immigration.* Cambridge, Mass.: Harvard University Press.

Alvarez, R. Michael, and John Brehm. 2002. *Hard Choices, Easy Answers: Values, Information, and American Public Opinion.* Princeton, N.J.: Princeton University Press.

Andrews, Kenneth T. 2002. "Movement-Countermovement Dynamics and the Emergence of New Institutions: The Case of 'White Flight' Schools in Mississippi." *Social Forces* 80(3): 911–36.

Banaji, Mahzarin, and Deborah A. Prentice. 1994. "The Self in Social Context." *Annual Review of Psychology* 45: 297–332.

Banks, W. S. M., II. 1950. "The Rank Order of Sensitivity to Discriminations of Negroes in Columbus, Ohio." *American Sociological Review* 15(4): 529–34.

Bartels, Larry M. 2006. "What's the Matter with *What's the Matter with Kansas?*" *Quarterly Journal of Political Science* 1(2): 201–6.

———. 2008a. *Unequal Democracy: The Political Economy of the New Gilded Age.* New York and Princeton, N.J.: Russell Sage Foundation and Princeton University Press.

———. 2008b. "The Study of Electoral Behavior." August. Available at: http://www.princeton.edu/~bartels/electoralbehavior.pdf (accessed October 15, 2011).

Bearman, Peter. 2005. *Doormen.* Chicago: University of Chicago Press.

Benabou, Roland, and Jean Tirole. 2002. "Self-Confidence and Personal Motivation." *Quarterly Journal of Economics* 117(3): 871–915.

———. 2003. "Intrinsic and Extrinsic Motivation." *Review of Economic Studies* 70(3): 489–520.

———. 2006. "Belief in a Just World and Redistributive Politics." *Quarterly Journal of Economics* 121(2): 699–746.

Bendick, M., Jr. 1997. *Declaration: Statement Submitted to the Supreme Court of California in Response to Proposition 209.* September 26.

Berger, Joseph, Bernard P. Cohen, and Morris Zelditch Jr. 1972. "Status Characteristics and Social Interaction." *American Sociological Review* 37(3): 241–55.

Bergmann, Barbara R. 1996. *In Defense of Affirmative Action.* New York: Basic Books.

Berlet, Chip, and Matthew N. Lyons. 2000. *Right-Wing Populism in America: Too Close for Comfort.* New York: Guilford Press.

Black, Earle. 1971. "Southern Governors and Political Change: Campaign Stances on Racial Segregation and Economic Development, 1950–1969." *Journal of Politics* 33(3): 703–34.

Black, Earle, and Merle Black. 2002. *The Rise of Southern Republicans.* Cambridge, Mass.: Harvard University Press.

———. 2007. *Divided America: The Ferocious Power Struggle in American Politics.* New York: Simon & Schuster.

Blauner, Robert. 1972. *Racial Oppression in America.* New York: Harper & Row.

Blumer, Herbert. 1958. "Race Prejudice as a Sense of Group Position." *Pacific Sociological Review* 1(1): 3–7.

Bobo, Lawrence D. 1999. "Prejudice as Group Position: Microfoundations of a Sociological Approach to Racism and Race Relations." *Journal of Social Issues* 55(3): 445–72.

Bobo, Lawrence, James R. Kluegel, and Ryan A. Smith. 1997. "Laissez-Faire Racism: The Crystallization of a Kinder, Gentler, Anti-Black Ideology. " In *Racial Attitudes in the 1990s: Continuity and Change,* edited by Steven A. Tuch and Jack K. Martin. Westport, Conn.: Praeger.

Bobo, Lawrence D., Camille Z. Charles, Maria Krysan, and Alicia D. Simmons. 2012. "The *Real* Record on Racial Attitudes." In *Social Trends in American Life: Findings from the General Social Survey since 1972,* edited by Peter V. Marsden. Princeton: Princeton University Press.

Bolce, Louis, and Gerald De Maio. 1999a. "Religious Outlook, Culture War Politics, and Antipathy Toward Christian Fundamentalists." *Public Opinion Quarterly* 63(1): 29–61.

———. 1999b. "The Anti-Christian Fundamentalist Factor in Contemporary Politics." *Public Opinion Quarterly* 63(4): 508–42.

Bonilla-Silva, Eduardo. 2003. *Racism Without Racists: Color-Blind Racism and the Persistence of Racial Inequality in the United States.* Lanham, Md.: Rowman & Littlefield.

Bourdieu, Pierre. 1985. "The Forms of Capital." In *Handbook of Theory and Research for the Sociology of Education,* edited by John Richardson. New York: Greenwood Press.

Braddock, Jomills Henry, and James M. McPartland. 1987. "How Minorities Continue to Be Excluded from Equal Employment Opportunities: Research on Labor Market and Institutional Barriers." *Journal of Social Issues* 43(1): 5–39.

Brewer, Marilynn B. 1998. "In-Group Favoritism: The Subtle Side of Intergroup Discrimination." In *Codes of Conduct: Behavioral Research into Business Ethics,* edited by David Messick and Ann Tenbrunsel. New York: Russell Sage Foundation.

Brewer, Marilynn B., and Norman Miller. 1984. "Beyond the Contact Hypothesis: Theoretical Perspectives on Desegregation." In *Groups in Contact: The Psychology of Desegregation,* edited by Norman Miller and Marilynn B. Brewer. New York: Academic Press.

Brooks, Clem, and Jeff Manza. 1997. "The Social and Ideological Bases of Middle-Class Political Realignment in the United States, 1972 to 1992." *American Sociological Review* 62(2): 191–208.

Burstein, Paul. 1991. "Reverse Discrimination: Cases in the Federal Courts: Mobilization by a Countermovement." *Sociological Quarterly* 32(4): 511–28.

Campbell, Ernest Q. 1961. "Moral Discomfort and Racial Segregation: An Examination of the Myrdal Hypothesis." *Social Forces* 39(3): 228–34.

Carmines, Edward G., and James A. Stimson. 1989. *Issue Evolution: Race and the Transformation of American Politics.* Princeton, N.J.: Princeton University Press.

Carter, Dan T. 1996. *From George Wallace to Newt Gingrich: Race in the Conservative Counter-Revolution, 1963–1994.* Baton Rouge: Louisiana State University Press.

Coleman, James S. 1988. "Social Capital in the Creation of Human Capital." (Supplement) *American Journal of Sociology* 94: 95–120.

Collins, Sharon M. 1989. "The Marginalization of Black Executives." *Social Problems* 36(4): 317–31.

Congressional Budget Office (CBO). 2011. "Trends in the Distribution of Household Income Between 1979 and 2007." Washington: CBO.

Conley, Dalton. 1999. *Being Black: Living in the Red.* Berkeley: University of California Press.

Converse, Philip. 1964. "The Nature of Belief Systems in Mass Publics." In *Ideology and Discontent,* edited by David E. Apter. New York: Free Press.

Cose, Eliot. 1993. *The Rage of a Privileged Class.* New York: HarperCollins.

Cotton, Jeremiah. 1988. "Discrimination and Favoritism in the U.S. Labor Market: The Cost to a Wage Earner of Being Female and Black and the Benefit of Being Male and White." *American Journal of Economics and Sociology* 47(1): 15–28.

Cox, Oliver C. 1945. "An American Dilemma: A Mystical Approach to the Study of Race Relations." *Journal of Negro Education* 14(2): 132–48.

Crespi, Leo P. 1945. "Is Gunnar Myrdal on the Right Track?" *Public Opinion Quarterly* 9(2): 201–12.

———. 1945–1946. "Mr. Crespi Replies." *Public Opinion Quarterly* 9(4): 540–42.

Crosby, Faye J. 2004. *Affirmative Action Is Dead: Long Live Affirmative Action.* New Haven, Conn.: Yale University Press.

Crosby, Faye J., and Sharon D. Herzberger. 1996. "For Affirmative Action." In *Affirmative Action: Pros and Cons of Policy and Practice,* edited by Rita J. Simon. Washington, D.C.: American University Press.

Crosby, Faye J., Aarti Iyer, and Sirinda Sincharoen. 2006. "Understanding Affirmative Action." *Annual Review of Psychology* 57: 585–611.

Democratic Leadership Council (DLC). 2000. "The Hyde Park Declaration: A

Statement of Principles and a Policy Agenda for the Twenty-First Century." Available at: http://www.dlc.org/contentid=1926print37a3.html (accessed November 18, 2008).

———. 2001. "The New Democrat Credo." January 1. Available at: http://www.dlc.org/ndol_ciae29.html?kaid=86&subid=194&contentid=3775 (accessed November 18, 2008).

Diamond, Sara. 1995. *Roads to Dominion: Right-Wing Movements and Political Power in the United States.* New York: Guilford Press.

———. 1998. *Not by Politics Alone: The Enduring Influence of the Christian Right.* New York: Guilford Press.

DiMaggio, Paul. 2003. "The Myth of Culture War: The Disparity Between Private Opinion and Public Politics." In *Fractious Nation? Unity and Division in Contemporary American Life,* edited by Jonathan Rieder and Steven Steinlight. Berkeley: University of California Press.

DiMaggio, Paul, John Evans, and Bethany Bryson. 1996. "Have America's Social Attitudes Become More Polarized?" *American Journal of Sociology* 102(3): 690–755.

DiTomaso, Nancy. 1977. "The Department of Labor: Class Politics and Public Bureaucracy." Ph.D. diss., University of Wisconsin.

———. 2001. "The Loose Coupling of Jobs: The Subcontracting of Everyone?" In *Sourcebook on Labor Markets: Evolving Structures and Processes,* edited by Ivar Berg and Arne L. Kalleberg. New York: Plenum Press.

DiTomaso, Nancy, Corinne Post, D. Randall Smith, George F. Farris, and Rene Cordero. 2007. "Effects of Structural Position on Allocation and Evaluation Decisions for Scientists and Engineers." *Administrative Science Quarterly* 52(2): 175–207.

DiTomaso, Nancy, and Steven A. Smith. 1996. "Race and Ethnic Minorities and White Women in Management: Changes and Challenges." In *Women and Minorities in American Professions,* edited by Joyce Tang and Earl Smith. Albany, N.Y.: State University of New York Press.

Dovidio, John F., and Samuel L. Gaertner, eds. 1986. *Prejudice, Discrimination, and Racism.* New York: Academic Press.

D'Souza, Dinesh. 1995. *The End of Racism.* New York: Free Press.

Edsall, Thomas B., and Mary D. Edsall. 1992. *Chain Reaction: The Impact of Race, Rights, and Taxes on American Politics.* New York: W. W. Norton.

Essed, Philomena. 1991. *Understanding Everyday Racism: An Interdisciplinary Theory.* Newbury Park, Calif.: Sage Publications.

Falcon, Luis M., and Edwin Melendez. 2001. "Racial and Ethnic Differences in Job Searching in Urban Centers." In *Urban Inequality: Evidence from Four Cities,* edited by Alice O. O'Connor, Chris Tilly, and Lawrence D. Bobo. New York: Russell Sage Foundation.

Farley, Reynolds. 1984. *Blacks and Whites: Narrowing the Gap?* Cambridge, Mass.: Harvard University Press.

———. 1999. "Racial Issues: Recent Trends in Residential Patterns and Intermarriage." In *Diversity and Its Discontents: Cultural Conflict and Common Ground in Contemporary American Society,* edited by Neil J. Smelser and Jeffrey C. Alexander. Princeton, N.J.: Princeton University Press.

Fiorina, Morris, Samuel Abrams, and Jeremy Pope. 2006. *Culture War? The Myth of a Polarized America,* 2d ed. New York: Longman.

Fiske, Susan T., Amy J. C. Cuddy, Peter Glick, and Jun Xu. 2002. "A Model of (Often Mixed) Stereotype Content: Competence and Warmth Respectively Follow from Perceived Status and Competition." *Journal of Personality and Social Psychology* 82(6): 878–902.

Fiske, Susan T., and Shelley E. Taylor. 1991. *Social Cognition,* 2d ed. Reading, Mass.: Addison-Wesley.

Fiske, Susan T., Jun Xu, and Amy C. Cuddy. 1999. "(Dis)Respecting Versus (Dis) Liking: Status and Interdependence Predict Ambivalent Stereotypes of Competence and Warmth." *Journal of Social Issues* 55(3): 473–89.

Fordham, Signithia. 1996. *Blacked Out: Dilemmas of Race, Identity, and Success at Capital High.* Chicago: University of Chicago Press.

Frank, Thomas. 2004. *What's the Matter with Kansas? How Conservatives Won the Heart of America.* New York: Metropolitan Books.

Freeman, Richard B. 2007. *America Works: Critical Thoughts on the Exceptional U.S. Labor Market.* New York: Russell Sage Foundation.

Friedman, Thomas. 2005. *The World Is Flat: A Brief History of the Twenty-First Century.* New York: Farrar, Straus and Giroux.

Frymer, Paul. 1999. *Uneasy Alliances: Race and Party Competition in America.* Princeton, N.J.: Princeton University Press.

Frymer, Paul, and John David Skrentny. 1998. "Coalition-Building and the Politics of Electoral Capture During the Nixon Administration: African Americans, Labor, Latinos." *Studies in American Political Development* 12(spring): 131–61.

Frymer, Roland G., and Glenn C. Loury. 2005. "Affirmative Action and Its Mythology." *Journal of Economic Perspectives* 19(3): 147–62.

Gaertner, Samuel L., and John F. Dovidio. 1986. "The Aversive Form of Racism." In *Prejudice, Discrimination, and Racism,* edited by John F. Dovidio and Samuel L. Gaertner. Orlando, Fla.: Academic Press.

Gilens, Martin. 1995. "Racial Attitudes and Opposition to Welfare." *Journal of Politics* 57(4): 994–1014.

———. 1999. *Why Americans Hate Welfare: Race, Media, and the Political of Antipoverty Policy.* Chicago: University of Chicago Press.

Glenn, Evelyn Nakano. 2002. *Unequal Freedom: How Race and Gender Shaped American Citizenship and Labor.* Cambridge, Mass.: Harvard University Press.

Goldwater, Barry. 1960. *The Conscience of a Conservative.* New York: Hillman Books.

Granovetter, Mark. 1995. *Getting a Job: A Study of Contacts and Careers,* 2d ed. Chicago: University of Chicago Press.

Green, John C. 2000. "Religion and Politics in the 1990s: Confrontations and Coalitions." In *Religion and American Politics: The 2000 Election in Context,* edited by Mark Silk. Hartford, Conn.: Pew Program on Religion and the News Media, Center for the Study of Religion in Public Life, Trinity College.

Greenberg, Stanley B. 2004. *The Two Americas: Our Current Political Deadlock and How to Break It.* New York: Thomas Dunne Books/St. Martin's Press.

———. 2008. "Goodbye, Reagan Democrats." *New York Times,* November 10.

Greenwald, Anthony G., and Linda Hamilton Krieger. 2006. "Implicit Bias: Scientific Foundations." *California Law Review* 94(4): 945–67.

Guth, James L., John C. Green, Lyman A. Kellstedt, and Corwin E. Smidt. 1996. "Onward Christian Soldiers: Religious Activist Groups in American Politics." In *Religion and the Culture Wars: Dispatches from the Front,* edited by John C. Green, James L. Guth, Corwin E. Smidt, and Lyman A. Kellstedt. Lanham, Md.: Rowman & Littlefield.

Guth, James L., Lyman A. Kellstedt, John C. Green, and Corwin E. Smidt. 2001. "America Fifty/Fifty." *First Things* 116(October): 19–26.

Hacker, Andrew. 1992. *Two Nations: Black and White, Separate, Hostile, Unequal.* New York: Ballantine Books.

Hochschild, Jennifer L. 1981. *What's Fair: American Beliefs About Distributive Justice.* Cambridge, Mass.: Harvard University Press.

———. 1995. *Facing Up to the American Dream: Race, Class, and the Soul of the Nation.* Princeton, N.J.: Princeton University Press.

———. 1996. "When Books on Race Don't Help Us Know the Truth." *Journal of Blacks in Higher Education* 12(summer): 69–73.

Hogg, Michael A. 2001. "A Social Identity Theory of Leadership." *Personality and Social Psychology Review* 5(3): 184–200.

Holzer, Harry J. 1994. "Black Employment Problems: New Evidence, Old Questions." *Journal of Policy Analysis and Management* 13(4): 699–722.

———. 1996. *What Employers Want: Job Prospects for Less-Educated Workers.* New York: Russell Sage Foundation.

Holzer, Harry J., and David Neumark. 1998. "What Does Affirmative Action Do?" Working paper 6605. Cambridge, Mass.: National Bureau of Economic Research (June).

———. 2000a. "What Does Affirmative Action Do?" *Industrial and Labor Relations Review* 53(2): 240–71.

———. 2000b. "Assessing Affirmative Action." *Journal of Economic Literature* 38(3): 483–568.

Hout, Michael, and Claude S. Fischer. 2002. "Why More Americans Have No Religious Preference: Politics and Generations." *American Sociological Review* 67(2): 165–90.

Jackman, Mary R. 1994. *The Velvet Glove: Paternalism and Conflict in Gender, Class, and Race Relations.* Berkeley: University of California Press.

Jackman, Mary R., and Michael J. Muha. 1984. "Education and Intergroup Attitudes: Moral Enlightenment, Superficial Democratic Commitment, or Ideological Refinement?" *American Sociological Review* 49(6): 751–69.

Jaynes, Gerald David, and Robin M. Williams Jr., eds. 1989. *A Common Destiny: Blacks and American Society.* Washington, D.C.: National Academies Press.

Jencks, Christopher. 1992. *Rethinking Social Policy: Race, Poverty, and the Underclass.* Cambridge, Mass.: Harvard University Press.

Jenkins, J. Craig, and Teri Shumate. 1985. "Cowboy Capitalists and the Rise of the 'New Right': An Analysis of Contributors to Conservative Policy Formation Organizations." *Social Problems* 33(2): 130–45.

Jorstad, Erling. 1971. "The Politics of Doomsday: Fundamentalists of the Far Right." *Theology Today* 28(1): 129–31.

———. 1981. "The New Christian Right." *Theology Today* 38(2): 193–200.

Jost, John T., and Kimberly D. Elsbach. 2001. "How Status and Power Differences Erode Personal and Social Identities at Work: A System Justification Critique of Organizational Applications of Social Identity Theory." In *Social Identity Processes in Organizational Contexts,* edited by Michael A. Hogg and Deborah J. Terry. Philadelphia: Psychology Press.

Judis, John B. 2008. "America the Liberal: The Democratic Majority: It Emerged!" *The New Republic,* November 19. Available at: http://www.tnr.com/article/america-the-liberal (accessed November 18, 2008).

Judis, John B., and Ruy Teixeira. 2002. *The Emerging Democratic Majority.* New York: Scribner.

Kahneman, Daniel, and Amos Tversky. 1979. "Prospect Theory: An Analysis of Decision Under Risk." *Econometrica* 47(2): 263–91.

Kalleberg, Arne L. 2011. *Good Jobs, Bad Jobs: The Rise of Polarized and Precarious Employment.* New York: Russell Sage Foundation.

Katz, Michael B. 1989. *The Undeserving Poor: From the War on Poverty to the War on Welfare.* New York: Pantheon Books.

Katznelson, Ira. 2005. *When Affirmative Action Was White: An Untold History of Racial Inequality in Twentieth-Century America.* New York: W. W. Norton.

Kefalas, Maria. 2003. *Working-Class Heroes: Protecting Home, Community, and Nation in a Chicago Neighborhood.* Berkeley: University of California Press.

Keister, Lisa A., and Stephanie Moller. 2000. "Weath Inequality in the United States." *Annual Review of Sociology* 26: 63–81.

Kerwin, Donald M. 2011. "The Faltering U.S. Refugee Protection System: Legal and Policy Responses to Refugees, Asylum Seekers, and Others in Need of Protection." Florence, Italy: European University Institute, Robert Schuman Centre for Advanced Studies.

Killian, Lewis M., and Charles M. Grigg. 1961. "Rank Orders of Discrimination of Negroes and Whites in a Southern City." *Social Forces* 39(3): 235–39.

Kinder, Donald R., and Lynn M. Sanders. 1996. *Divided by Color: Racial Politics and Democratic Ideals.* Chicago: University of Chicago Press.

Kirschenman, Joleen, and Kathryn M. Neckerman. 1991a. "'We'd Love to Hire Them, But . . .': The Meaning of Race for Employers." In *The Urban Underclass,* edited by Christopher Jencks and Paul E. Peterson. Washington, D.C.: Brookings Institution.

———. 1991b. "Hiring Strategies, Racial Bias, and Inner-City Workers." *Social Problems* 38(4): 433–47.

Kluegel, James. R. 1985. "'If There Isn't a Problem, You Don't Need a Solution': The Bases of Contemporary Affirmative Action Attitudes." *American Behavioral Scientist* 28(6): 761.

Kluegel, James R., and Elliot R. Smith. 1986. *Beliefs About Inequality: Americans' Views of What Is and What Ought to Be.* New York: Aldine de Gruyter.

Kohut, Andrew. 2007. "Trends in Political Values and Core Attitudes: 1987–2007." Washington, D.C.: Pew Research Center for the People and the Press.

———. 2009. "Trends in Political Values and Core Attitudes: 1987–2009." Washington, D.C.: Pew Research Center for the People and the Press.

———, ed. 2010. "The People and Their Government: Distrust, Discontent, Anger, and Partisan Rancor." Washington, D.C.: Pew Research Center for the People and the Press.

Kohut, Andrew, Carroll Doherty, Michael Dimock, and Scott Keeter. 2011. "Beyond Red vs. Blue: Political Typology." Washington, D.C.: Pew Research Center for the People and the Press.

Korenman, Sanders, and Susan C. Turner. 1996. "Employment Contacts and Minority-White Wage Differences." *Industrial Relations* 35(1): 106–22.

Kozol, Jonathan. 1991. *Savage Inequalities: Children in America's Schools.* New York: HarperCollins.

Kravitz, David A., David A. Harrison, Marlene E. Turner, Edward L. Levine, Wanda Chaves, Michael T. Brannick, Donna L. Denning, Craig J. Russell, and Maureen A. Conrad. 1997. *Affirmative Action: A Review of Psychological and Behavioral Research.* Bowling Green, Ohio: Society for Industrial and Organizational Psychology.

Krieger, Linda Hamilton. 1995. "The Content of Our Categories: A Cognitive Bias Approach to Discrimination and Equal Employment Opportunity." *Stanford Law Review* 47(July): 1161–1248.

———. 1998. "Civil Rights Perestroika: Intergroup Relations After Affirmative Action." *California Law Review* 86(December): 1254–1334.

Krugman, Paul. 2007. *The Conscience of a Liberal.* New York: W. W. Norton.

———. 2009. "Why Americans Hate Single-Payer Insurance." *New York Times,* July 28.

Krysan, Maria. 2000. "Prejudice, Politics, and Public Opinion: Understanding the Sources of Racial Policy Attitudes." *Annual Review of Sociology* 26: 135–68.

Ladd, Everett Carll, and Karlyn Bowman. 1998. *What's Wrong? A Survey of American Satisfaction and Complaint.* Washington, D.C.: AEI Press.

Lamont, Michele. 1992. *Money, Morals, and Manners.* Chicago: University of Chicago Press.

———. 2000. *The Dignity of Working Men: Morality and the Boundaries of Race, Class, and Immigration.* Cambridge, Mass., and New York: Harvard University Press and Russell Sage Foundation.

Lamont, Michele, and Marcel Fournier, eds. 1992. *Cultivating Differences: Symbolic Boundaries and the Making of Inequality.* Chicago: University of Chicago Press.

Layman, Geoffrey. 2001. *The Great Divide: Religious and Cultural Conflict in American Party Politics.* New York: Columbia University Press.

Levison, Andrew. 2012. "The Surprising Size of White Working Class America—Half of All White Men and 40 Percent of White Women Still Work in Basically Blue-Collar Jobs." *The Democratic Strategist.* Strategy memo (June 29). Available at: http://www.thedemocraticstrategist.org/_memos/tds_SM_Levison_Working_Class_American.pdf (accessed September 9, 2006).

Lienesch, Michael. 1982. "Right-Wing Religion: Christian Conservatism as a Political Movement." *Political Science Quarterly* 97(3): 403–25.

Louria, Donald. 2005. "National Study: Americans Optimistic About Their Futures." Newark: University of Medicine and Dentistry of New Jersey, Department of Preventive Medicine. Available at: http://www.prnewswire.com/cgi-bin/stories.pl?ACCT=104&STORY=/www/story/05-17-2005/0003633280&EDATE= (accessed February 9, 2006).

Lublin, David. 2004. *The Republican South: Democratization and Partisan Change.* Princeton, N.J.: Princeton University Press.

MacInnes, Gordon. 1996. *Wrong for All the Right Reasons: How White Liberals Have Been Undone by Race.* New York: New York University Press.

MacLaury, Judson. 2010. "President Kennedy's E.O. 10925: Seedbed of Affirmative Action." *Federal History* (online): 42–57. Available at: http://shfg.org/shfg/wp-content/uploads/2011/01/4-MacLaury-design4-new_Layout-1.pdf (accessed July 2, 2012).

Martin, William. 1996. *With God on Our Side: The Rise of the Religious Right in America.* New York: Broadway Books.

Massey, Douglas S. 2005. *Return of the L-Word: A Liberal Vision for the New Century.* Princeton, N.J.: Princeton University Press.

———. 2007. *Categorically Unequal: The American Stratification System.* New York: Russell Sage Foundation.

Massey, Douglas S., Jorge Durand, and Nolan Malone. 2002. *Beyond Smoke and Mirrors: Mexican Immigration in an Era of Economic Integration.* New York: Russell Sage Foundation.

McCall, Leslie. 2001. *Complex Inequality: Gender, Class, and Race in the New Economy.* New York: Routledge.

McConahay, John B., and Joseph C. Hough. 1976. "Symbolic Racism." *Journal of Social Issues* 32(2): 23–46.

McDowell, Sophia Fagin. 1951. "Teaching Note on the Use of the Myrdal Concept of 'An American Dilemma' with Regard to the Race Problem in the United States." *Social Forces* 30(1): 87–91.

McGinley, Ann C. 1997. "The Emerging Cronyism Defense and Affirmative Action: A Critical Perspective on the Distinction Between Colorblind and Race-Conscious Decision Making Under Title VII." *Arizona Law Review* 39(3): 1004–59.

McIntosh, Peggy. 1988. "White Privilege: Unpacking the Invisible Knapsack." Wellesley, Mass.: Wellesley College, Center for Research on Women. Available at: http://www.nymbp.org/reference/WhitePrivilege.pdf (accessed January 3, 2010).

Mead, Lawrence M. 1992. *The New Politics of Povery: The Nonworking Poor in America.* New York: Basic Books.

Medalia, Nahum Z. 1962. "Myrdal's Assumptions on Race Relations: A Conceptual Commentary." *Social Forces* 40(3): 223–27.

Mendelberg, Tali. 2001. *The Race Card: Campaign Strategy, Implicit Messages, and the Norm of Equality.* Princeton, N.J.: Princeton University Press.

Mills, Charles W. 1997. *The Racial Contract.* Ithaca, N.Y.: Cornell University Press.

Milner, Murray, Jr. 2004. *Freaks, Geeks, and Coolkids: American Teenagers, Schools, and the Culture of Consumption.* New York: Routledge.

Morris, Aldon D. 1993. "Birmingham Confrontation Reconsidered: An Analysis of the Dynamics and Tactics of Mobilization." *American Sociological Review* 58(5): 621–36.

Moss, Philip, and Chris Tilly. 2001. *Stories Employers Tell: Race, Skill, and Hiring in America.* New York: Russell Sage Foundation.

Mouw, Ted. 2003. "Social Capital and Finding a Job: Do Contacts Matter?" *American Sociological Review* 68(6): 868–98.

Murray, Charles. 1984. *Losing Ground: American Social Policy, 1950–1980.* New York: Basic Books.

Myrdal, Gunnar. 1944. *An American Dilemma.* New York: Harper & Row.

———. 1948. "Social Trends in America and Strategic Approaches to the Negro Problem." *Phylon* 9(3): 196–214.

Newman, Katherine S. 1988. *Falling from Grace: Downward Mobility in an Age of Affluence.* Berkeley: University of California Press.

———. 1999. *No Shame in My Game: The Working Poor in the Inner City.* New York: Alfred A. Knopf.

Ogbu, John U. 1978. *Minority Education and Caste: The American System in Cross-Cultural Perspective.* New York: Academic Press.

Oliver, Melvin L., and Thomas M. Shapiro. 1995. *Black Wealth/White Wealth: A New Perspective on Racial Inequality.* New York: Routledge.

Orfield, Gary, and Chungmei Lee. 2007. "Historical Reversals, Accelerating Resegregation, and the Need for New Integration Strategies." Report of the UCLA Civil Rights Project/Proyecto Derechos Civiles. Los Angeles: University of California (August).

Parks-Yancy, Rochelle. 2010. *Equal Work, Unequal Careers: African Americans in the Workforce.* Boulder, Colo.: Lynne Rienner Publishers.

Parks-Yancy, Rochelle, Nancy DiTomaso, and Corinne Post. 2005. "The Cumulative Effects of Social Capital Resources on Disadvantages." *Sociological Imagination* 41(1): 47–70.

Patchen, Martin. 1999. *Diversity and Unity: Relations Between Racial and Ethnic Groups.* Chicago: Nelson-Hall Publishers.

Payne, Charles M. 1995. *I've Got the Light of Freedom: The Organizing Tradition and the Mississippi Freedom Struggle.* Berkeley: University of California Press.

Pettigrew, Thomas F. 1979. "The Ultimate Attribution Error: Extending Allport's Cognitive Analysis of Prejudice." *Personality and Social Psychology Bulletin* 5(4): 461–76.

Pew Research Center for the People and the Press. 1996. "The Diminishing Divide . . . American Churches, American Politics." June 25. Available at: http://www.people-press.org/1996/06/25/the-diminishing-divide-american-churches-american-politics (accessed November 18, 2008).

———. 2010. "Distrust, Discontent, Anger, and Partisan Rancor: The People and Their Government," April 18, p. 5.

Phillips, Kevin P. 1969. *The Emerging Republican Majority.* New Rochelle, N.Y.: Arlington House.

Pincus, Fred L. 2003. *Reverse Discrimination: Dismantling the Myth.* Boulder, Colo.: Lynne Reinner Publishers.

Piven, Frances Fox. 1977. *Poor People's Movements: Why They Succeed, How They Fail.* New York: Pantheon.

Portes, Alejandro. 1998. "Social Capital: Its Origins and Applications in Modern Sociology." *Annual Review of Sociology* 24(1): 1–24.

Portes, Alejandro, and Patricia Landolt. 1996. "The Downside of Social Capital." *American Prospect* 26(May-June): 18–22.

Portes, Alejandro, and Rubén G. Rumbaut. 1996. *Immigrant America: A Portrait.* Berkeley: University of California Press.

Pratto, Felicia, Jim Sidanius, Lisa M. Stallworth, and Bertram F. Malle. 1994. "Social Dominance Orientations: A Personality Variable Predicting Social and Political Attitudes." *Journal of Personality and Social Psychology* 67(4): 741–63.

Presidential Commission on Civil Rights. 1947. *To Secure These Rights: The Report of the President's Committee on Civil Rights.* Washington: U.S. Government Printing Office (October).

Putnam, Robert. 2000. *Bowling Alone: The Collapse and Revival of American Community.* New York: Simon & Schuster.

Quadagno, Jill. 1992. "Social Movements and State Transformation: Labor Unions and Racial Conflict in the War on Poverty." *American Sociological Review* 57(5): 616–34.

———. 1994. *The Color of Welfare: How Racism Undermined the War on Poverty.* New York: Oxford University Press.

Reich, Robert. 1991. *The Work of Nations: Preparing Ourselves for Twenty-First-Century Capitalism.* New York: Vintage Books.

Reskin, Barbara F. 1998. *The Realities of Affirmative Action in Employment.* Washington, D.C.: American Sociological Association.

Ridgeway, Cecilia L. 1986. "Expectations, Legitimation, and Dominance Behavior in Task Groups." *American Sociological Review* 51(5): 603–17.

———. 2001. "The Emergence of Status Beliefs: From Structural Inequality to Legitimizing Ideology." In *The Psychology of Legitimacy,* edited by John T. Jost and Brenda Major. Cambridge: Cambridge University Press.

Rinder, Irwin D. 1952. "Some Observations on the 'Rank Order of Discrimination' Hypothesis." *Journal of Negro Education* 21(4): 541–45.

Rose, Arnold. 1945–1946. "Myrdal: Pro and Con." *Public Opinion Quarterly* 9(4): 539–40.

Royster, Deirdre A. 2003. *Race and the Invisible Hand: How White Networks Exclude Black Men from Blue-Collar Jobs.* Los Angeles: University of California Press.

Sachdev, Itesh, and Richard Y. Bourhis. 1991. "Power and Status Differentials in Minority and Majority Group Relations." *European Journal of Social Psychology* 21(1): 1–24.

Sager, Ryan. 2006. *The Elephant in the Room: Evangelicals, Libertarians, and the Battle to Control the Republican Party.* Hoboken, N.J.: John Wiley & Sons.

Said, Carolyn. 2004. "In Critical Condition: Health Care in America: Retiree Benefits Dwindling." *San Francisco Chronicle,* October 12.

Schaller, Thomas F. 2006. *Whistling Past Dixie: How Democrats Can Win Without the South.* New York: Simon & Schuster.

Schuman, Howard, Charlotte Steeh, Lawrence Bobo, and Maria Krysan. 1997. *Racial Attitudes in America: Trends and Interpretations,* rev. ed. Cambridge, Mass.: Harvard University Press.

Sears, David O. "Symbolic Racism." 1988a. In *Eliminating Racism: Profiles in Controversy,* edited by Phyllis Katz and Dalmas A. Taylor. New York: Plenum.

———. 1988b. "Racism and Politics in the United States." In *Confronting Racism: The Problem and the Response,* edited by Jennifer Eberhardt and Susan T. Fiske. Thousand Oaks, Calif.: Sage Publications.

Sears, David O., P. J. Henry, and Rick Kosterman. 2000. "Egalitarian Values and Contemporary Racial Politics." In *Racialized Politics: The Debate About Racism in America,* edited by David O. Sears, Jim Sidanius, and Lawrence Bobo. Chicago: University of Chicago Press, 2000.

Sears, David O., Jim Sidanius, and Lawrence Bobo. 2000. *Racialized Politics: The Debate About Racism in America.* Chicago: University of Chicago Press.

Shapiro, Thomas M. 2004. *The Hidden Cost of Being African American: How Wealth Perpetuates Inequality.* New York: Oxford University Press.

Sidanius, Jim, and Felicia Pratto. 1999. *Social Dominance: An Intergroup Theory of Social Hierarchy and Oppression.* Cambridge: Cambridge University Press.

Sidanius, Jim, Felicia Pratto, and Lawrence Bobo. 1996. "Racism, Conservatism, Affirmative Action, and Intellectual Sophistication: A Matter of Principled Conservatism or Group Dominance?" *Journal of Personality and Social Psychology* 70(3): 476–90.

Simon, Herbert A. 1947. *Administrative Behavior.* New York: Macmillan.

Skrentny, John David. 1996. *The Ironies of Affirmative Action.* Chicago: University of Chicago Press.

———, ed. 2001. *Color Lines: Affirmative Action, Immigration, and Civil Rights Options for America.* Chicago: University of Chicago Press.

Smith, James P., and Finis Welch. 1984. "Affirmative Action and the Labor Market." *Journal of Labor Economics* 2(2): 269–301.

Smith, Sandra. 2007. *Lone Pursuit: Distrust and Defensive Individualism Among the Black Poor.* New York: Russell Sage Foundation.

Sniderman, Paul M., and Edward G. Carmines. 1996. "Beyond Race: Social Justice as a Race-Neutral Ideal." *American Journal of Political Science* 40(1): 33–55.

———. 1997. *Reaching Beyond Race.* Cambridge, Mass.: Harvard University Press.

Sniderman, Paul M., and Thomas Piazza. 1993. *The Scar of Race.* Cambridge, Mass.: Harvard University Press.

Sørensen, Aage B. 2000. "Toward a Sounder Basis for Class Analysis." *American Journal of Sociology* 105(6): 1523–58.

Southern, David W. 1995. "An American Dilemma After Fifty Years: Putting the Myrdal Study and Black-White Relations in Perspective." *The History Teacher* 28(2): 227–53.

Stainback, Kevin, and Donald Tomaskovic-Devey. 2012. *Documenting Desegregation: Private-Sector Employment Segregation Since the Civil Rights Act.* New York: Russell Sage Foundation.

Steeh, Charlotte, and Maria Krysan. 1996. "The Polls—Trends: Affirmative Action and the Public, 1970–1995." *Public Opinion Quarterly* 60(1): 128–58.

Steinberg, Stephen. 1995. *Turning Back: The Retreat from Racial Justice in American Thought and Policy.* Boston: Beacon Press.

———. 1995–1996. "An American Dilemma: The Collapse of the Racial Orthodoxy of Gunnar Myrdal." *Journal of Blacks in Higher Education* 10(winter): 64–70.

Stephanopoulos, George, and Christopher Edley Jr. 1995. "Review of Federal Affirmative Action Programs." Washington: The White House.

Teixeira, Ruy. 2010. "Demographic Change and the Future of the Parties." Washington, D.C.: Center for American Progress Action Fund.

Teixeira, Ruy, and John Halpin. 2011. "The Path to 270: Demographics Versus Economics in the 2012 Presidential Election." Washington, D.C.: Center for American Progress.

Teixeira, Ruy, and Joel Rogers. 2000. *America's Forgotten Majority: Why the White Working Class Still Matters.* New York: Basic Books.

Thernstrom, Stephan, and Abigail Thernstrom. 1997. *America in Black and White: One Nation Indivisible.* New York: Simon & Schuster.

Tilly, Charles. 1998. *Durable Inequality.* Berkeley: University of California Press.

Valentino, Nicholas A., and David O. Sears. 2005. "Old Times There Are Not Forgotten: Race and Partisan Realignment in the Contemporary South." *American Journal of Political Science* 49(3): 672–88.

Viguerie, Richard A. 1979. "Mobilizing the Moral Majority." *Conservative Digest* 5(8): 14–17.

Waldinger, Roger. 1996. *Still the Promised City? African-Americans and New Immigrants in Postindustrial New York City.* Cambridge, Mass.: Harvard University Press.

———. 1997. "Social Capital or Social Closure? Immigrant Networks in the Labor Market." Working paper. Los Angeles: University of California, School of Public Affairs, Ralph and Goldy Lewis Center for Regional Policy Studies.

Weber, Max. 1968. *Economy and Society,* translated by Guenther Roth and Claus Wittich. New York: Bedminister Press.

Weeden, Kim A. 2000. "Why Do Some Occupations Pay More Than Others? Social Closure and Earnings Inequality in the United States." *American Journal of Sociology* 108(1): 55–101.

Wellman, David T. 1993. *Portraits of White Racism,* 2nd ed. Cambridge: Cambridge University Press.

Westie, Frank R. 1965. "The American Dilemma: An Empirical Test." *American Sociological Review* 30(4): 527–38.

Weyrich, Paul M. 2003. "The Most Important Legacy of Joe Coors." March 24. Available at: http://www.enterstageright.com/archive/articles/0303/0303coors.txt (accessed January 3, 2010).

Wilson, Douglas. 2003. *The Case for Classical Christian Education.* Wheaton, Ill.: Crossway Books.

Wilson, William J. 1987. *The Truly Disadvantaged: The Inner City, the Underclass, and Public Policy.* Chicago: University of Chicago Press.

———. 1996. *When Work Disappears: The World of the New Urban Poor.* New York: Alfred A. Knopf.

Zaller, John. 1992. *The Nature and Origins of Mass Opinion.* Cambridge: Cambridge University Press.

Index

Boldface numbers refer to figures and tables.